MW01688054

dreamwork for the Soul

A Spiritual Guide to Dream Interpretation

ROSEMARY ELLEN GUILEY

BERKLEY BOOKS, NEW YORK

This book is an original publication of The Berkley Publishing Group.

DREAMWORK FOR THE SOUL

A Berkley Book / published by arrangement with the author

All rights reserved.
Copyright © 1998 by Rosemary Ellen Guiley.
This book may not be reproduced in whole or in part,
by mimeograph or any other means, without permission.
For information address: The Berkley Publishing Group, a member of
Penguin Putnam Inc.,
200 Madison Avenue, New York, New York 10016.

The Penguin Putnam Inc. World Wide Web site address is
http://www. penguinputnam.com

ISBN: 0-7394-0030-4

BERKLEY®
Berkley Books are published by The Berkley Publishing Group, a member of
Penguin Putnam Inc.,
200 Madison Avenue, New York, New York 10016.
BERKLEY and the "B" design
are trademarks belonging to Berkley Publishing Corporation.

PRINTED IN THE UNITED STATES OF AMERICA

For Rita Dwyer

CONTENTS

Part II: Navigating the Dreamscape

Part III: High Dreamwork

PREFACE

THIS BOOK IS A GUIDE TO WHAT I CALL *HIGH DREAMWORK*—WORKING WITH DREAMS AS PART OF A SPIRITUAL PATH TO WHOLENESS AND ENLIGHTENMENT. THE MATERIAL CAN BE USED by both beginning and experienced dreamworkers.

I have kept the focus on dreams primarily but not exclusively within the Western tradition. Our modern beliefs about dreams—and our very dreams themselves—have been shaped by a heritage of deeply held collective views about spirituality, the nature of reality, science, mind-body interaction, and so on. There are Eastern influences, to be sure, that go way back in history, and these are reflected in the contents. But an encyclopedic treatment of all dream traditions would have been prohibitively long.

The book is divided into seven sections. Part I is an overview of how our dream history has developed. It is important to see how our dream heritage has been shaped. This section also introduces the reader to dreams as exceptional human experiences and their place in new physics, and to concepts of alchemy that play a role in dreams.

Part II covers extraordinary elements in dreams such as psi, lucidity, out-of-body travel, and having dreams with others. These elements occur in many dreams, and are essential to understand in order to do high dreamwork.

Part III lays out the basics of dream interpretation, incubation, improved recall, and understanding symbols. In addition, the special roles of numbers, colors, and the messages of animals are given. The dream is treated as having multiple facets that relate to this and other worlds.

Part IV demonstrates how dreams help us with healing, creativity, decision-making, and surviving—and triumphing from—disastrous turns in life.

In Part V, we see how dreams bring us into contact with otherworldly beings such as angels and spiritual masters, and how dreams are part of spiritual awakening.

Part VI looks at dreams of contact with the dead, dreams of facing death, and dreams of visits to the other side.

Part VII features dreams of past lives and visionary dreaming of the future. We consider how dreams are part of our evolving consciousness and are related to other experiences, such as near-death experiences, visions of religious figures, doomsday prophecy, and more.

Throughout the book, I have included numerous dreams to illustrate the topics. Some of these dreams come from my own journals; others come from scores of individuals who contributed them. With some exceptions, I have identified dreamers with their first name and last initial or first name only; a few persons requested pseudonyms.

In my book *The Miracle of Prayer,* I stated that prayer is one of the most important tools for transformation of consciousness. Dreams belong in that category, too. Both connect us to the divine. We know that about prayer, but we've forgotten that about dreams. High dreamwork can restore that connection.

introduction

POWER DREAMING

MY INTRODUCTION TO POWER DREAMING CAME EARLY IN LIFE, WHILE I WAS IN MY TEENS. PERHAPS THIS WAS DUE TO THE PSYCHIC THREAD IN MY FAMILY, WHICH INCLUDED EXTRA-sensory perception, or psi, in dreams. Early on, I saw dreams as a wonderful, extraordinary experience that held great mystery and untapped potential.

I didn't call it power dreaming back then. It was a term I applied much later as my dreams unfolded from the symbolic to the paranormal to the otherworldly and mystical. I have devoted myself to the study of dreams throughout my life. I have kept dream journals and done dreamwork in a variety of settings. In addition, I have studied the paranormal, alchemy, and the mystical, and have developed my own spiritual path that bridges Western and Eastern philosophies. This study and dreamwork led me to the conclusion that we in the West have lost an important part of the art of dreamwork. We have become disconnected from the dream's Truth. It is essential to regain this connection if we are to become whole and if we are to further the evolution of our consciousness.

Conventional wisdom treats the dream as a symbolic mirror of ourselves: Everything in a dream represents something about us or inside of us. That is true, but it is only one facet of the dream. What we overlook is the heart of the dream: the dream is a real experience that takes place in another reality. When we enter this reality, this dreamscape, we are able to transcend limitations of the physical world. Our dreams are teaching tools, showing us how to grow and improve. If we dismiss the dream as a fantasy, we miss out on much that it has to teach us. Dreams are the original language of the spiritual path.

The ancients understood this, and many cultures around the world preserve this wisdom about the dream. But we in the modern West need to restore it. Without it, we will not be able to fully benefit from the riches dreams have to offer.

We need to recognize that dreams move us from beyond the symbolic to experiences of Truth. Dreams are a straight connection to the divine heart of the cosmos. In dreams, we can receive high spiritual guidance, meet otherworldly beings, visit other dimensions, have contact with the dead, and explore new frontiers of consciousness. The wisdom and insight we gain from such experiences can be brought back into the material world to apply to life, now.

This is what power dreaming is about: mastery of the dreaming consciousness in order to fulfill our great potential as human beings and as souls. By mastery, I do not necessarily mean control, although it is possible to learn how to direct one's dreams. Mastery is wisdom and understanding, and the knowledge of how to apply them. Our dreams are teaching tools not only for this world but for other realms we have begun to experience.

We are hungry for spiritual experience and nourishment, yet one of the greatest spiritual experiences is laid at our doorstep every night when we dream. We keep looking for ways to connect with the Source, yet every night, we have a hot line to God.

One night I asked my husband to set the clock radio alarm for the next morning. We are early risers and only use an alarm when we have to get up extra early. When the alarm went off, the very first thing that came over the radio were these words: "Thanks for listening, and may the Lord bless you and keep you." It was a wonderful synchronicity underscoring the divine guidance that comes through dreams. God speaks to us through dreams, and here I was, being thanked for listening.

Not every dream is a big dream. Our dreams are busy creatures with a big agenda. Over the years, I began to see three essential levels to dreams: a personal level that relates to everyday life, an archetypal level that uses mythical symbols and carries a bigger message, and a transpersonal level that deals with other realms. As I explain in this book, a dream may involve all three levels, but primarily focus upon one level. We can go through phases in life where one level will be more prominent than others.

Dreaming for Love and Enlightenment

Dreams do more than help us understand ourselves better. They help to awaken us to our full identity and potential—that we are souls, not egos. When we are awakened, we walk the Path of Truth and Beauty. We are true to the divine laws that govern creation, and we are true to ourselves. We spend our time and our gifts wisely, upon pursuits that further Truth. We know what we are capable of and what we are not. We know what we are willing to do and what we are not. We say yes with pleasure and no with grace. We hear the song of the soul, we craft a vision for our life, and we hold fast to our vision through sun and storm. When we are awakened, we are constantly guided by our dreams and intuition.

When we walk the Path of Truth, we walk the Path of Beauty. The Truth within us radiates forth as the beautiful, divine light of Love. The soul that shines resplendent as a diamond light of Truth, Beauty, and Love attracts to it the infinite good from the inexhaustible Source.

Do you wish to know love? Your dreams will show you first how to love yourself. Until you have mastered the lessons of self-esteem, self-love, and self-empowerment, how can you attract your ideals, accomplish your goals, or love anyone else? Self-love is not the same as egotism, though the two are often confused. Self-love is knowing your own worth, your own divinity within, your part in the greater whole. Yes, you are important. Yes, you have a valuable role to play. When you recognize your own worth, your innate and unique gifts are released. The currents of divine love flow freely through you. True self-love is humble. When we express our Truth for the sheer beauty of it, we need no superficial reward. The Truth is its own reward.

When you have mastered self-love, your dreams will guide you in loving others. They put relationships under an honest microscope. Too often we fool the ego into thinking things are all right when they are not, but we cannot fool the soul, which speaks through dreams. Do you wish to strengthen your relationships with friends and loved ones? Ask your dreams, and they will tell you.

Do you wish to know enlightenment? Dreams can help you touch the greatest expression of love, the unconditional love that emanates from God. In guiding you through the lessons of love, dreams expand the heart lotus. You can have mystical experiences of this ineffable love in your dreams—unforgettable dreams that will leave you transformed forever.

Do you wish to know prosperity? Is your life a desert rather than an oasis? Do you lack rather than have? If so, you are not following your Truth. Pay attention to your dreams.

In any situation, your dreams will give you what you need to heal, to grow, to improve, to prosper, and to love. They will offer to you a wealth of information from the depths of your being, show you the dark pieces of yourself that need to be loved into light, and show you the ways you are ready to soar. Dreams are wonderfully responsive. If we seek help from them, they oblige. If you think your dreams make no sense, they do. It's a matter of understanding their language. If you have trouble remembering your dreams, you can improve that as well.

Dreams do not themselves solve problems or create magic—they provide the information, insight, and inspiration that we need to do the work. They are messengers, conduits of energy.

A treasure chest lies waiting to be opened each night. Do not delay. Look inside.

PART I

Our Dream Heritage

c h a p t e r o n e

THE DIVINE GIFT OF DREAMS

THE DIRECT CONNECTION TO GOD THROUGH DREAMS WAS SEEN BY THE ANCIENTS AS A DIVINE GIFT. PEOPLE DID NOT HAVE DREAMS; THEY WERE GIVEN DREAMS. THE GODS SENT THEM IN answer to human need and pleas for help. Dreams occupied a bridge world—the *mundus imaginalis,* or world of imagination—that spans the world of matter and the world of spirit. The appearance of a god in dreams was taken as the actual appearance of a god. The same was true for the appearance of the dead.

Our Western tradition of dreamwork dates to the Sumerians, Assyrians, and Babylonians, who studied dreams for omens of state and political importance and for solutions to community disputes and problems. Dream incubation was practiced, and correct interpretation—in order to ensure good fortune—was an art.

The early peoples of Assyria and Mesopotamia paid particular attention to the dreams of rulers and eminent men, and they distinguished between divine dreams and ordinary dreams. Divine dreams were visits of the gods to kings and priests and concerned revelation and messages about state destiny. The decisions of the gods were arbitrary, but through dreams, humans could obtain information about what the gods decided and why. Ordinary dreams, on the other hand, occurred to the masses. These were subdivided into two categories: good dreams sent by the gods, and bad dreams sent by demons. Bad dreams could cause illness and misfortune. Ritual cleansings and exorcisms frequently were undertaken to dispel the effects of dreams deemed to be bad.

Records of divine dreams contain numerous descriptions of interactions with gigantic supernatural beings like the *karibu*, winged half-man, half-beast guardian figures placed around buildings. There are also numerous descriptions of giant, glorious human figures, often identified as gods and resembling later descriptions of angels.

The oldest dream book in existence comes from Assyria: a collection of clay cylinders found at Ninevah in the library of the famous Assyrian king, Assurbanipal, who ruled from 669 to 626 B.C.E. The tablets show that Assyrian dream interpretation relied heavily upon contraries, or opposites. For example, to dream of being blessed by a god actually meant one would be punished by a god.

Dreams in Egypt

The Egyptians absorbed some of the Assyrian and Mesopotamian dream practices into their own culture. They, too, divined dreams, practiced dream incubation, and were visited by the gods in dreams. In sleep, humans had access to another realm not ordinarily available to them in waking life. They considered dreams to be a revelation of truth and thus attached great divinatory significance to dreams, looking to dreams alone for omens. The Mesopotamians, on the other hand, included dreams among many other methods of divination.

Instructions given in a dream were to be acted upon; otherwise, misfortune could occur. Thus, it was of great importance to be accurate in interpreting a dream lest the gods be angered.

During the eighteenth dynasty (c. 1400 B.C.E.), a young prince was hunting in the Giza plateau near the Sphinx. He rested there and fell asleep in the statue's giant shadow. The Sphinx sent the prince a dream in which it promised him the throne of Egypt if he would clear away all the sand that had accumulated over the Sphinx's body. The prince did as instructed. In time, he became pharaoh—Thutmose IV. He recorded the story on a stele and planted it between the paws of the Sphinx. The Dream Stele, as it is called, remains there today, its story an example of the rewards of paying attention to one's dreams.

The primary interpreters of dreams and guardians of official dreamwork practices were called *lector priests*. The lector priests were attached to the House of Life, an institution at most cult and some mortuary temples throughout the land. They were learned men who kept the sacred books containing the religious lore and laws and magical rites. They were renowned dream interpreters.

The lector priests were not part of the main temple hierarchy and did not participate in the daily services but instead performed occasional magical rites. The House of Life was a building or a small group of buildings where the temple library was kept and where lay people could come for consultation, such as dream interpretation and spells to solve problems. The dream and magical books were carefully guarded in order to protect the magical status of the priests. Besides the priests, there were scribes and literate wealthy and noble persons who were likely to possess private books of dream spells and interpretations.

Temple and private dream books were written on scrolls of papyrus and stored in boxes or jars. Fragments have survived, giving us a look at how Egyptians viewed their dreams. The earliest known fragment, called the Chester Beatty Papyrus 3, dates to the twelfth dynasty (2050–1790 B.C.E.), and now is owned by the British Museum. The author of the fragment is unknown. The document gives instructions for interpreting dreams. A table lists the theme of a dream, states whether it is good or bad, and provides a brief meaning. There are 143 good and 91 bad dreams. Since only a fragment of this document survives, we can assume that the list actually was much longer.

The interpretations show that Egyptians, like the Assyrians, relied heavily upon contraries, or dreams meaning the opposite of what they showed. They also relied upon puns and plays on words. Some of the themes reflect the belief in sympathetic magic. All of the interpretations begin with the phrase "If a man sees himself in a dream . . ." Some examples follow:

If a man sees himself in a dream . . .

Slaying a hippopotamus: Good. It means a large meal from the palace.
Plunging into the river: Good. It means purification from all evil.
Making love to a woman: Bad. It means mourning.
Making love to his mother: Good. It means his fellow citizens will support him.
Looking at an ostrich: Bad. It means harm will befall him.

Drinking blood: Good. It means putting an end to his enemies.
Copulating with a pig: Bad. It means being deprived of possessions.
Uncovering his backside: Bad. It means the dreamer will be an orphan later.
Seeing himself dead: Good. It means a long life before him.

It is difficult for us to gauge how much the context of a dream might have altered these interpretations or if these were applied to all dreams containing such imagery, regardless of context. Contradictions do exist, and it is possible that more than one writer contributed to the document.

Dreams figured prominently in magical practices. Spells and rituals provided for sending dreams to other people to influence their thinking and actions. Even the dead could send dreams to the living. Bad dreams were thought to be sent by persons (living or dead) of evil intent. Such dreams could cause illness or even death.

The dead played an important role in Egyptian dream magic. By virtue of their existence in another realm, the dead were believed to have great power, which could be controlled through magic. The dead were summoned to enforce curses and spells via dreams and also to appear in dreams in order to answer questions about the future. People who had drowned in the Nile were especially believed to have a divine gift of prophecy and were commanded to come to the dreams of a priest or magician.

Dreams among the Early Hebrews

The early Hebrews placed a high value on dreams as real experiences of the direct voice of God. The Old Testament, or Torah, is replete with examples of dreams and waking visions, affirming these as primary ways that a concerned God speaks to human beings to provide direction and guidance. It is often difficult to distinguish between dreams and visions, however. Christian scholar Morton T. Kelsey observed that "there is no clear-cut distinction between the dream and the vision in the Hebrew language; where moderns see a great gulf of separation, the Hebrews did not. Although the two experiences were sometimes distinguished, more often they were seen as aspects of the same basic perception of reality, different sides of the same encounter from beyond the world of sense experience."[1] Thus we find references to a "vision of the night" (as in 1 Samuel 3:15, Job 20:8, Isaiah 29:7, and Daniel 2:19 and 7:2), or "in the night I saw" (as in Zechariah 1:8), or "in the visions of my head as I lay in bed" (Daniel 4:13) as descriptions probably referring to dreams.

These biblical dreams/visions are characterized by the voice of God (direct audition), the appearance of angels as messengers, angels and the Lord appearing as bright lights and fire, and otherworldly images, all elements that still appear in transpersonal dreams today.

The first biblical reference to a dream is found in Genesis 15:12–16. While the prophet Abram (later renamed Abraham) is in a deep sleep, God gives him the prophecy that Abram's descendants will be enslaved in a foreign land (Egypt) for four hundred years, but that they will be liberated with great possessions and return to their own land.

Abraham's grandson, Jacob, had significant dreams, the most famous of which is his vision of a ladder to heaven filled with angels moving up and down it (Genesis 28:11–22). He was so awestruck by the dream that he declared the spot as "the house of God . . . the gate of heaven."

Jacob's son Joseph, sold into slavery in Egypt by his brothers, excelled in dream interpretation and thus gained the pharaoh's favor.

The tradition for God to address prophets through dreams is established in Numbers 12:6, when God tells Moses, Miriam, and Aaron, "Hear now my words: If there be a prophet among you, I the Lord will make myself known unto him in a vision, and will speak unto him in a dream." God goes on to say that Moses is different from other prophets, for God speaks directly ("mouth to mouth") to him.

Many other biblical prophets, patriarchs, and rulers were inspired and directed by dreams or visions, among them Samuel, Saul, Solomon, Elijah, Jeremiah, Job, Isaiah, Ezekiel, and Daniel. Their experiences include the voice of God, the appearances of angels, and visions of heaven. These dreams were not experienced for personal entertainment or enrichment but were the instruments by which God spoke to the people; prophets were duty bound to report their dreams.

Losing contact with God through dreams was a crisis—a serious loss of power. Saul, the first king of Israel, suddenly finds that God no longer speaks to him in dreams. Desperate for guidance, he breaks his own law and hires a medium to perform necromancy, the summoning of the dead for divination. Saul seeks out the spirit of the prophet and judge, Samuel.

By about the eighth century B.C.E., the Hebrew prophets became concerned about false prophets using false dreams to sway people. The Israelites were admonished to beware of false prophets and not to consult the soothsayers of other peoples or practice their dream incubations. Deuteronomy gives such warnings (18:9–22); as we shall see in the next chapter, apparent mistranslations of these admonitions prejudiced Christians against paying attention to dreams in general.

Ecclesiastes warns, "For a dream comes with much business, and a fool's voice with many words," and "For when dreams increase, empty words grow many: but do you fear God." (Ecclesiastes 5:3, 7) The apocryphal book of Ecclesiasticus, or Sirach, comments that "dreams give wings to fools" and cautions against any divinations and omens that do not come from the Most High as a visitation. "For dreams have deceived many, and those who put their hope in them have failed. Without such deceptions the law will be fulfilled, and wisdom is made perfect in truthful lips" (Sirach 34:6–7).

These warnings probably refer to the dreams of false prophets; nonetheless, as Kelsey noted, these passages have been cited for centuries by church officials who wish to discourage attention to dreams.

The importance of dreams is emphasized in other Jewish sacred texts as well. The Talmud, a body of rabbinical teachings based on the Torah and put in written form between 200 and 500 C.E., discusses dream interpretation. Professional dream interpreters were respected and paid for their work. The Talmud distinguishes between good dreams and bad and says that although bad dreams can be avoided by fasting, we might not want to avoid them because they are better teachers. Numerous dream interpretations of the sages are offered, especially in the tractate *Berakhot*. There is no systematic analysis and interpretation. Even the Pentateuch, the first five books of the Torah, which lays down rules, laws, and regulations for society, has no rules for dreams, despite their importance.

Talmudic interpreters relied upon scripture but did understand the personal and subjective nature of dreams. Meanings often depended on slight shifts in the way that scripture was read aloud. For example, Proverbs 2:3, "Yea, if those call for understanding," was read as "Yea, you will call understanding mother," which involved a mere change of a vowel point. Thus a dream of a man making love to his mother means that he will acquire understanding. (Recall earlier that an Egyptian interpretation of the same imagery means "Good . . . his fellow citizens will support him.") Interpreters also used plays on words and anagrams to decipher dreams. They considered the dreamer's age, occupation, social position and personal life, a technique probably borrowed from Graeco-Roman dream interpretation. The associations and opinions of the dreamer about the dream were not taken into consideration, however.

Many of the interpretations offered in the Talmud are positive, because it was the job of the dream interpreter to help the client release anxieties—much the same approach we take today. Interpreting a dream meant dissolving it in terms of its effect on the dreamer.

The reverence for dreams continued on through the Middle Ages, as seen especially in the works of the great philosopher, Maimonides (1135–1204), called the "second Moses," and in the body of secret mystical teachings called the Kabbalah.

Two kabbalistic works recorded in the thirteenth century, the *Sefer ha-Zohar* (Book of Splendor) and the *Sefer Hasidim* (Book of the Devout), concern the interior life, of which dreams are a part. The *Zohar* was written down by Spanish kabbalist Moses de Leon. It declares that everything that happens is made known first through a dream or proclamation: "Nothing takes place in the world but what has previously been made known, either by means of a dream, or by means of a proclamation, for it has been affirmed that before any event comes to pass in the world, it is first announced in heaven, whence it is proclaimed to the world."[2]

The *Zohar* takes issue with the disparaging statement about dreams in Ecclesiastes 5:3 ("a dream comes with much business, and a fool's voice with many words"). The existence of false dreams are acknowledged, but if some dreams were not true, they would not have been included in Scripture. Thus, dreams do have value for humanity.

The *Sefer Hasidim,* written by German pietists, distinguishes between dreams (occurring during sleep) and visions (occurring during waking consciousness), though both are primarily channels of communication between the living and the dead. When we sleep, our thoughts mingle with those of an angel or a demon; hence it is essential to know true from false dreams. The existence of dream demons and of a ruler over the demons has its roots in the Babylonian Talmud. When the Jews were in captivity in Babylonia, they were exposed to the supernatural beliefs of that culture and absorbed some of those beliefs.

Dream incubation was not encouraged but was practiced, according to the *Sefer Hasidim.* Dreams were held to be very private and told only to close friends, never to the public.

In the sixteenth century, an important text on dream interpretation was published by the philosopher Solomon Almoli. It was first titled *Chelmin* (Dream Mediator) and then retitled *Pitron Chalomot* (The Interpretations of Dreams). In it, Almoli lays out eight "gates" as a systematic way of understanding dreams. He said that most dreams represent the dreamer's thoughts and mundane concerns. These do not come from the "Master of Dreams" (God) but from one's own imagination, woven by the "Spinner of Dreams." Freud cited this work in his own *Interpretation of Dreams,* in which he puts forth the concept of "day residues" as the grist of most dreams.

Almoli believed that the dreamer's emotions were important to the interpretation. He also integrated ideas from the ancient Greeks, as we shall see below, such as considering context and the dreamer's daily life as part of the interpretation.

Dreams in Greece and Rome

The ancient Greeks were influenced by the dream beliefs and practices of the Egyptians, Mesopotamians, and Hebrews. Dreams were events that were witnessed: The Greeks did not *have* dreams but *saw* them. In the earliest beliefs, the gods made real visits to the dreamer, entering a bedroom through the keyhole and standing at the head of the bed while they delivered their message. The importance given dreams is evidenced by their roles in Greek literature: the epic Homeric poems and various tragedies tell of gods and the dead appearing in dreams to give direct instructions and impart warnings. Such dreams were considered to be objective events that happened independently of the dreamer and did not arise from within the dreamer.

Like the Hebrews, the Greeks drew little or no distinction between dreams and other kinds of visionary experiences that happened during both day and night, in sleep, trance, and waking consciousness. Christian scholar Morton T. Kelsey pointed out twelve different Greek terms for such experiences. The emphasis was on the content of the experience and on the ability of humans to perceive and communicate with another reality.

Around the seventh century B.C.E., a shamanic and Eastern idea about dreams was introduced to Greek culture: Rather than be visited by gods, the dreamer traveled out-of-body at night to visit the gods and receive important information, either of a direct or symbolic nature. This concept was embraced by the Greek religious movement called Orphism, which influenced many of Greece's later great thinkers, including Pythagoras and Plato.

Following the thread of Orphic thought, Plato (427?–347 B.C.E.) called dreams "the between state," a real place where the human soul went during sleep to meet the gods and demigods who are otherwise inaccessible. He said that dreams are another way to know the world besides sense and experience; we can receive "the inspired word" of the divine in our sleep. His "between state" can be seen as part of the *mundus imaginalis,* the bridge between the worlds of matter and spirit.

Plato keenly observed that dreams embody the heights and the depths of human consciousness. The heights are the revelations of the gods, and the depths are dreams emanating from our dark, instinctual side. Dreams provide an outlet for instinct, "the lawless wild-beast nature" that exists in all of us, said Plato centuries before Freud would make the same observations. Furthermore, Plato believed that dreams could be controlled in order to see truth. If we go to sleep with the "appetites" under control, and if our lives are in harmony and balance, then the rational side of the soul would be free to experience the divine, know truth, and see past, present, and future.

Plato recorded the dream experiences of his teacher, Socrates (469–399 B.C.E.), the great Athenian philosopher, who left behind no writings of his own. Socrates paid attention to his inner guidance, which came in the form of daimonic voices (a daimon is a type of guiding spirit that can be either good or bad), and to his dreams.

Aristotle (384–322 B.C.E.), one of Plato's pupils, took a radical departure from the conventional dream wisdom of the times. Aristotle rejected Plato's idea of dreams as one way to know the world. He said that all we can know about the world comes only through our senses. Since dreams do not, they are illusory and of virtually no significance. They are entirely natural, he said, arising from the random reexperiencing of the day's events. We do not have the capability in sleep to know that the images are not reality. Dreams considered prophetic are simply due to the infinite variety and quantity of dreams. Some are eventually bound to resemble later events. But because the mind relaxes in sleep and becomes more aware, a few dreams are genuinely prophetic and clairvoyant, Aristotle acknowledged. However, prophetic dreams might merely be suggestions that the dreamer is predisposed to anyway, and thus would bring about his or her own self-fulfilling prophecy. This latter thought is especially significant, presaging recognition of the dream's power to guide life that would arise centuries later.

To Aristotle, it was quite obvious that dreams were not of divine origin, for if the gods were so intelligent, why would they send dreams to simple people? Rather, divine dreams would be sent only to those who possessed the faculties for understanding them and would not be sent to the masses. Aristotle further argued that animals seem to dream, and God would not present himself to such lowly creatures.

Aristotle did allow for prodromic dreams, that is, dreams that forecast physical illness. Dream incubation for healing was raised to a high art among the Greeks and in turn the Romans, and numerous famous physicians of the day placed great faith in dreams (see Chapter 15).

Aristotle's views about dreams were not popular during his day. Later, the Roman philosopher and senator Cicero was one who echoed them, but centuries had to pass before they generally caught on, such as in the works of Saint Thomas Aquinas, one of the greatest theologians and thinkers of the Middle Ages.

Aristotle's contemporaries and those who followed later adhered to mainstream philosophy about dreams as divine experiences. The Greeks had much to say about the divinatory role of dreams. The Stoic philosopher Posidonius (c. 135–150 B.C.E.) said that dreams are a natural form of divination. They can foretell the future because in sleep the soul communicates directly with the gods or with an "immortal soul," one of the many divine beings who exist in the air beneath the moon and who know the future. They can impart their knowledge to humans only when the soul is free of the body in sleep.

Cicero (106 B.C.E.–43 C.E.) was skeptical about dreams, arguing that if the gods truly want to warn us of impending events, they should do so during the day and under clear circumstances, not during the confusion of dreams at night. Unfortunately, neither dreams nor waking visions warned Cicero of his own impending death. He was executed by Mark Antony over politics.

Augustus Caesar (63 B.C.E.–14 C.E.) took dreams so seriously that he proclaimed a new law: Anyone who dreamed about the commonwealth was required to proclaim it in the marketplace. Perhaps he hoped to avoid the fate of his grand-uncle Julius Caesar by the public airing of potentially prophetic dreams concerning matters of state—and assassination plots.

Plutarch (c. 46–120 C.E.) reasserted the divinatory power of dreams, calling them the "oldest oracle." He argued that everybody—not just selected priests and oracles—could experience prophecy in dreams.

Plutarch recorded the dreams of persons of historical note, many of them Romans, in the classical world. Most of these dreams related to death, war, and conflict. For example, the Roman general Pompey, who waged civil war against Augustus Caesar, dreamed on the eve of their decisive battle that he made a formal entrance to the public theater to the shouts of many people. He joined a retinue and carried spoils of war to offer at a temple of Venus the Victorious. At first blush, the dream seemed to foretell his victory. But on deeper analysis, Pompey was seized with fear that it foretold Caesar's victory. Why? Because Caesar's family name was derived from Venus. That subtle symbolism proved to be correct, and the following day, Pompey's army was routed by Caesar's forces. Pompey escaped to Egypt, where he was killed.

Plutarch credited Calpurnia, the wife of Julius Caesar, with a prophetic dream of his death the night before he was assassinated. The Roman emperors Tiberius, Caligula, and Domitian also dreamed of their deaths.

The first recorded dream book in Greek dates to the fifth century B.C.E. and is credited to Antiphon, an Athenian statesman. The oldest surviving dream book in Greek, *Oneirocritica* (The Study of Dreams), dates from the second century C.E. It was written by Artemidorus of Daldi, a Greek professional dream interpreter who spent part of his career in Rome and who collected an astounding three thousand dreams from his clients. He believed strongly in the benefit of understanding dreams, writing in his book that "dreams and visions are infused into men for their advantage and instruction." He devoted himself fully to his profession, recording that he spent day and night meditating "in the judgment and interpretation of dreams."

Artemidorus considered the context of a dream relevant to its meaning. In addition, he took into account the life of the dreamer—his profession, social position, personality, daily habits, and such—as well as whether or not a dream was part of a recurring pattern. Without context, he said, the full meaning of a dream would not reveal itself; meanings that were too simple and arbitrary would be misleading. Dream interpretation was an intuitive art, involving associations by the learned interpreter.

In anticipation of Freud, Artemidorus saw certain dreams as wish fulfillment and wish substitution. For example, a man in love with a woman might not dream of her but instead see a substitute object, such as a ship, the sea, or a horse.

Some of Artemidorus's symbolisms are straightforward: a blossoming tree means happiness and prosperity, an abyss means impending danger. Others are less so, perhaps because they reflect more of the daily life of the times. Artemidorus also borrowed dream interpretations from Assyrian and Egyptian sources. Like the Egyptians, he used puns.

Artemidorus distinguished dreams from visions, oracles, fantasies, and apparitions—differences not always drawn by other ancient peoples. He also made distinctions between types of dreams: those dealing with the present (*insomnium*) and those forecasting the future (*somnium*). He noted that the *insomnium* were full of rich, symbolic material and much more difficult for the average person to understand. Centuries later, Carl Jung would make similar observations about "great" dreams full of archetypal images and numinous effects.

Artemidorus's *Oneirocritica* has survived into modern times and has found its way into many popular dream dictionaries over the centuries. Some of the meanings, relating to puns of language and to a time and culture long past, no longer make sense. Nonetheless, many of his interpretations and observations have parallels in modern psychotherapy, demonstrating that in many ways, human beings have dreamed the same dreams with the same essential meanings for thousands of years.

The Greeks profoundly influenced the Christian view of dreams. As Christianity struggled to gain a foothold after the death of Jesus, it survived on a merger of Greek and Hebrew cultures. Well into the Middle Ages, Greek philosophy continued to have a profound impact upon the church's most important theologians.

But something happened during the development of Christianity: The dream began to decline in importance.

Dreams in Early Christianity

Initially, Christianity continued to honor dreams and visions as a primary way that God communicates with humans. Dreams and visions literally shaped the birthing and early development of Christianity. Angels are the chief messengers of God; descriptions of them coming and standing before people are reminiscent of the Greek Homeric dreams in which gods came and stood by the head of the bed while they delivered a message in a dream. As in the Old Testament, distinctions are not always made between dreams and other kinds of visionary experiences.

Christianity begins with a visionary experience in which Zechariah is visited by the angel Gabriel and told that his elderly wife will have a son, to be named John, who will become John the Baptist (Luke 1:1–11). Later, Gabriel is sent by God to inform the virgin Mary that she will conceive a child through the Holy Spirit (Luke 1:26–38). Her betrothed, Joseph, decides to leave her when he discovers she is pregnant. But an angel appears to him specifically in a dream and tells him to marry her, that she has conceived with the Holy Spirit, and will bear a son to be named Jesus who will "save his people from their sins" (Matthew 1:18–25). Joseph, in keeping with time-honored tradition to follow divine directives given in dreams, acted accordingly when he awoke.

Angels proclaim the birth of Jesus and direct people to where he can be found (Luke 2:9, 13). Joseph is given another dream warning him to take his family and flee to Egypt in order to save the baby Jesus from death at the hand of the jealous Herod (Matthew 2:13–14), and is told in yet another dream to return to Israel when Herod has died and it is safe (Matthew 2:19–23).

Jesus had numerous visionary experiences during his life, some of which involved the audition of the voice of God and that were shared by others. He encounters angels and Satan, hears the direct voice of God speaking from the heavens, and becomes filled with radiant light in a transfiguration involving the presences of Elijah and Moses. After the arrest of Jesus, Pontius Pilate's wife is warned in a dream that her husband should have nothing to do with him (Matthew 27:19).

Acts is full of dream/visionary experiences. In fact, all major events are marked by them. When the apostles are filled with the Holy Spirit at Pentecost (2:3–11), it is seen as a fulfillment of a prophecy in the Old Testament book of Joel (2:28): "And it shall come to pass afterward, that I will pour out my spirit on all flesh;

your sons and your daughters shall prophesy, your old men shall dream dreams, and your young men shall see visions." Saul's conversion into the evangelist Paul is a visionary experience. Throughout his ministry, Paul is guided by nighttime visions that may have been dreams. Paul's epistles and John's book of Revelation, are instructions and prophecy based upon direct visionary experience.

Clearly, the intervention of nonordinary reality into the affairs of humans via dreams and visions was accepted by the early Christians. There also was concern about true and false dreams and visions. Rather than blame false ones on false prophets, the Christians tended to see them as the product of demonic, evil interference. Thus, one had to be careful about the voices one listened to.

With such a rich documentation of powerful and transcendent experiences involving the key figures of Christianity, it would be natural to think that the theologians who shaped the church, would have given a firm endorsement to dreams as a way to know God. Many of them did write positively about dreams. In the early centuries, the church fathers, many of whom were Platonic philosophers and Greek converts, reaffirmed the tradition of God speaking through dreams and visions. Justin Martyr, Irenaeus, Clement of Alexandria, Origen, Tertullian, Athanasius, Augustine, John Chrysostom, Anthony, Basil the Great, Gregory of Nazianzen, Gregory of Nyssa, Ambrose, Gregory the Great, and John Cassian are among those who upheld dreams as a proper way to maintain contact with God. But after a few centuries, the subject just withered away. Kelsey, in his search of the literature, found that dreams have been ignored in most biblical criticism. What happened?

The Negative Influence of Jerome

Attitudes toward dreams began to change significantly in the fourth century with Saint Jerome, who translated the Bible from Greek and Hebrew into the Latin Vulgate. Jerome was raised in an affluent Christian family but devoted himself to an intense study of the pagan classics. Calling himself a Christian while studying the pagans may have created a conflict deep within himself that he repressed. During a severe illness, he had a dream that changed the course of his life:

Suddenly I was caught up in the spirit and dragged before the judgment seat of the Judge; and here the light was so bright, and those who stood around were so radiant, that I cast myself upon the ground and did not dare to look up. Asked who and what I was I replied: "I am a Christian." But he who presided said: "Thou liest, thou art a follower of Cicero and not of Christ. For 'where thy treasure is, there will thy heart be also.'" Instantly I became dumb, and amid the strokes of the lash—for He had ordered me to be scourged—I was tortured more severely still by the fire of conscience, considering with myself that verse, "In the grave who shall give thee thanks?" Yet for all that I began to cry and to bewail myself, saying: "Have mercy upon me, O Lord: have mercy upon me." Amid the sound of the scourges this cry still made itself heard. At last the bystanders, falling down before the knees of Him who presided, prayed that He would have pity on my youth, and that He would give me space to repent of my error. He might still, they urged, inflict torture on me, should I ever again read the works of the Gentiles. . . .

Accordingly I made an oath and called upon His name, saying "Lord, if ever again I possess worldly books, or if ever again I read such, I have denied Thee." Dismissed, then, on taking this oath, I returned to the upper world, and, to the surprise of all, I opened upon them eyes so drenched with tears that my distress served to convince even the credulous. And that this was no sleep nor idle dream, such as those by which we are often mocked, I call to witness the tribunal before which I lay, and the terrible judgment which I feared. . . . I profess that my shoulders were black and blue, that I felt the bruises long after I awoke from my sleep, and that thenceforth I read the books of God with a zeal greater than I had previously given to the books of men.[3]

After this event, Jerome retired to the desert as a hermit for several years. He then resumed his career as scholar and biblical consultant and headed a monastic community in Bethlehem.

Despite his own dream experience, Jerome sided with the Old Testament prophet Jeremiah in skepticism about dreams. He agreed that dreams can be a vehicle of revelation to a soul, but also held that the impure and unrighteous could twist dreams for their own self-serving ends. He declared that the word of God could not be sought through pagan practices of dream incubation, such as offered in the Aesculapian temples.

Jerome's greatest accomplishment was the Latin Vulgate Bible. Kelsey has shown that Jerome seems to have deliberately mistranslated a Hebrew word so as to condemn dreams as witchcraft or soothsaying. According to Kelsey, Jerome's mistranslation was of the Hebrew term *anan,* which means witchcraft or soothsaying. *Anan* appears ten times in the Old Testament. Seven times Jerome translated it as "witchcraft." Three times he translated it as "observing dreams." For example, Leviticus 19:26 was changed from "You shall not practice augury or witchcraft" (soothsaying) into "You shall not practice augury nor observe dreams." Another reference against soothsaying that he changed is found in Deuteronomy 18:10–11: "There shall not be found among you . . . any one who practices divination, a soothsayer, or an augur, or a sorcerer, or a charmer, or a medium, or a wizard, or a necromancer." These passages are part of the body of rules, regulations, and laws laid down to govern Hebrew society. The mistranslation is curious, said Kelsey, in light of the fact that Jerome was an excellent scholar and correctly translated the term seven other times. Kelsey concluded that the mistranslation may have been deliberate, perhaps because of Jerome's frightening dream.

Jerome's translation of the Bible remained the authoritative version in Western Christianity up until the mid–twentieth century. Recently the New Oxford, New Jerusalem, and other modern editions of the Bible have restored the original meaning of *anan*.

Aquinas Questions the Validity of Dreams

In the thirteenth century, Saint Thomas Aquinas, one of the greatest scholars of the Christian church (some would say *the* greatest scholar), contributed to the decline of the dream by supporting the Aristotlean view that our knowledge of the world must come only through sense experience and rational thought. Aquinas wanted to modernize the church and felt Aristotle's philosophy would do so. Aquinas said that dreams in general have no significance because we have no direct contact with spiritual reality. Thus he denied the reality of the *mundus imaginalis.*

Because of biblical tradition, however, Aquinas had to acknowledge that some dreams could come from God and could be prophetic in nature. For the most part, he said, dreams came from demons, false opinions, and natural causes such as conditions of the body. It was not unlawful to divine from dreams as long as you were certain that the dreams were from a divine source and not from demons. Such ambivalence would not have been encouraging to anyone of the day stepping forward to announce a revelation or prophecy from a dream. Indeed, the argument of demon-based deception proved to be a convenient tool of persecution for the church during the Inquisition.

Aquinas had a profound impact on the subsequent development of Western thought. The *mundus imaginalis* receded from religion and philosophy, replaced by dualism, skepticism, behavioralism, and rationality—but fortunately remained a part of the Western mystery tradition, kept alive by alchemy and other esoteric streams of thought.

Like Jerome, Aquinas had life-changing dreams or visionary experiences that altered the course of his work. During his composition of his great work, *Summa Theologica,* he struggled with completing a theological passage. One morning he suddenly dictated it with ease. He told his scribe that he had had a dream in which he conversed with the apostles Peter and Paul, and they told him what to say.

In December 1273, Aquinas suddenly quit work on *Summa Theologica* and also abandoned other writings and even his daily routine. He reportedly said to his scribe, "I can do no more. Such things have been revealed to me that all I have written seems like straw, and I now await the end of my life."[4] Perhaps Aquinas had a shattering revelation in a dream. Some historians say this remark is blown out of proportion, and that most probably Aquinas suffered a stroke or breakdown from nervous exhaustion caused by overwork. He became ill a few months later and died on March 7, 1274.

Although dreams fell by the wayside as a direct communication with God—except for certain saints and sages—they continued to serve a purpose for the church in its efforts to spread the doctrine of purgatory. Dreams of the unhappy dead in purgatory were used as teaching examples for adhering to church doctrine (see Chapter 23).

The Reformation of the sixteenth century brought the end of widespread belief in miracles and supernatural events. By the eighteenth century, the dream was nearly finished as a spiritual experience. At the popular level, dream interpretation was sought from wizards and astrologers and was the subject of magical formulas and various divination handbooks. Many of the handbooks were translations and variations of the work of Artemidorus.

Influential philosophers also contributed to the spiritual demise of the dream. For example, René Descartes supported the Aristotelian view. Like Aquinas, he thought dreams to be merely the products of food eaten. And, like Jerome and Aquinas, he disparaged dreams yet was influenced by them himself. One of Descartes's most important philosophical works, *Discourse on Method* (1637) was inspired by a dream.

Dreams would not return to importance in the West until the twentieth century.

c h a p t e r t w o

THE RENAISSANCE OF THE DREAM

NEW LIFE WAS BREATHED INTO THE DREAM AROUND THE TURN OF THE TWENTIETH CENTURY IN THE EMERGENCE OF PSYCHOLOGY. IN HIS PIONEERING WORK, *THE INTERPRETATION OF Dreams* (1900), Sigmund Freud (1856–1939) said dreams were the "royal road" to the unconscious. He considered them wish fulfillments of repressed infantile desires. Freud was adamant that most symbols in dreams were sexual in nature. Events during the day, or "day residues," triggered nocturnal releases of these repressed elements in the form of dreams. The imagery and content of dreams essentially was a mask for repressed material. If a dream didn't seem to disguise anything, then it was a mere fantasy. Freud said dreams have little practical importance; they are part of pathology. His pupil Carl G. Jung (1875–1961) disagreed and restored dreams to their ancient importance.

Jung considered dreams to be the expression of the contents of two types of unconscious: the personal unconscious, which relates to personal experience, and the collective unconscious, which is the repository of human beliefs and experiences collected throughout history, shared by all people. The purpose of dreams is compensatory: to provide information about the self, achieve psychic equilibrium, or offer guidance. Jung believed that dream symbols from the collective unconscious have universal, or archetypal, meanings, but those from the personal unconscious do not, and they take on meaning from the individual's experiences, beliefs, and cultural, racial, ethnic, and religious heritage.

Archetypes

Jung developed, but did not originate, the concept of archetypes, which are central to modern dreamwork. The Greek philosopher Heraclitus was the first to view the psyche as the archetypal first principle. Plato articulated the idea of archetypes in his theory of forms, which holds that the essence of a thing or concept is its underlying form or idea. The term *archetype* occurs in the writing of Philo Judaeus, Irenaeus, and Dionysius the Areopagite. The concept, but not the term, is found in the writings of Augustine.

Archetypes appear in myth, legend, and folktales. They are primordial images of unknown origin that have been passed down from an ancestral past that includes not only early man but man's prehuman and animal ancestors. Archetypes are not part of conscious thought but are predispositions toward certain behaviors—patterns of psychological performance linked to instinct—such as fear of the dark or the maternal instinct, which become filled out and modified through individual experience.

Archetypes are endless, said Jung, created by the repetition of situations and experiences engraved upon the psychic constitution. God, birth, death, rebirth, power, magic, the sun, the moon, the wind, animals, and the elements are archetypes, as are traits embodied in the hero, the sage, the judge, the child, the trickster, the earth mother, and so on. Associations, symbols, situations, and processes are archetypes. Archetypes are present at birth and can become activated at any time. Their role in the personality changes as an individual grows and encounters new situations. Archetypes communicate with the conscious, and one may achieve insight into the self by attempting to identify and pay attention to archetypal forces in one's life. Engagement with archetypal energy is usually numinous, that is, charged with a mysterious, transcendent quality. Archetypes, said Jung, are psychic forces that demand to be taken seriously, and if they are neglected, they cause neurotic and even psychotic disorders.

Jung said the existences of archetypes can be proved through dreams, their primary source, and also through active imagination—fantasies produced by deliberate concentration. He said other sources of archetypal material are found in the delusions of paranoids, the fantasies of trance states, and the dreams of children from ages three to five.

For his insights into dreams, Jung drew from the well of his own rich, visionary dream experiences. From early in life until the end, he had many dreams that were full of alchemical, mythical, and transcendent symbols; he recorded forty-two of these in his autobiographical *Memories, Dreams, Reflections.*

The earliest dream that he could recall occurred when he was between three and four years old, and it was filled with archetypal symbols. In the dream, Jung was in a meadow, where he suddenly discovered a dark, rectangular, stone-lined hole in the ground. Peering into it, he saw a stairway leading down. Frightened but curious, he descended. At the bottom was a doorway with a round arch, closed by a heavy, sumptuous, green brocade curtain. He pushed the curtain back.

I saw before me in the dim light a rectangular chamber about thirty feet long. The ceiling was arched and of hewn stone. The floor was laid with flagstones, and in the center a red carpet ran from the entrance to a low platform. On this platform stood a wonderfully rich golden throne. I am not certain, but perhaps a red cushion lay on the seat. . . . Something was standing on it which I thought at first was a tree trunk twelve to fifteen feet high and about one and a half to two feet thick. It was a huge thing, reaching almost to the ceiling. But it was of a curious composition: it was made of skin and naked flesh, and on top there was something like a rounded head with no face and no hair. On the very top of the head was a single eye, gazing motionlessly upward.[1]

The eye was topped with an aura of brightness. The thing did not move, yet Jung had the terrible feeling that at any moment it would creep off the throne toward him. He stood paralyzed, and then heard his mother's voice from up and outside call, "Yes, just look at him. That is the man-eater!" Jung awoke in a sweat of terror. For many nights, he was afraid to go to sleep, lest he have the same dream again.

Years later, Jung realized that the trunklike object in his dream was a huge, ritual phallus. The hole in the meadow was a grave, which in turn was an underground temple symbolizing the mystery of Earth (the green). The red of the carpet symbolized blood. The light around the tip of the phallus pointed to the etymology of the term phallus, which means "shining, bright." Said Jung:

Through this childhood dream I was initiated into the secrets of the earth. What happened then was a kind of burial in the earth, and many years were to pass before I came out again. Today I know that it happened in order to bring the greatest possible amount of light into the darkness. It was an initiation into the realm of darkness. My intellectual life had its unconscious beginnings at that time.[2]

Jung was unable to speak about this dream until he was sixty-five. He considered it evidence of the collective unconscious.

Thus Jung experienced a profound breakthrough of the archetypal realm into waking consciousness. As a boy, Jung began to feel that he had two separate personalities: one who was his normal self and a second, archetypal personality who was much older, lived outside of time, and personified all the experiences of human life. As he grew older, the second personality, who he named Philemon, increased in dominance and was in conflict with his first personality.

Jung's dreams were a constant source of creativity and inspiration to him. Dreams inspired his study of archaeology and mythology, and later alchemy. Throughout his life, as he developed his ideas, Jung was aided and guided by dreams. When he searched for answers to questions, dreams often led him in the right direction.

The Break with Freud

Jung became increasingly unsettled about what he perceived as Freud's inability to recognize the deep, symbolic contents in Jung's own dreams. One particular dream, very important to Jung, involved him finding himself in a multistoried house that seems to be his. As he descends stairs, he discovers that the house becomes older the lower he goes—the ground floor seems to date from medieval times. He discovers a heavy door opening to a stone stairway leading down into a cellar that dates from Roman times. There he discovers a stone slab with a ring in it on the floor. He lifts it and sees another stone stairway leading down to a cave cut from rock. Everything is very old there, even ancient, like the remains of a primitive culture. Thick dust covers the floor. There are shards of pottery and scattered bones. Jung finds two human skulls, partially disintegrated. The dream ends.

This dream resembles the dream of his boyhood, in which Jung discovered the stone stairway leading to the chamber with the ritual phallus. It speaks of going into the depths—one's own inner depths—to connect with something primal. In fact, Jung later credited this dream with leading him to the concept of the collective unconscious.

Freud, however, could not get past his own obsession with wish fulfillment as the driving force for all dreams. He focused on the skulls, repeatedly asking Jung what wish he had in connection with them. Jung guessed that Freud wanted the dream to be about Jung's secret death wishes. He had "violent resistance to any such interpretation," but played along with it. He told Freud that perhaps he had secret death wishes against his wife and sister-in-law, although he was newly married and quite happy. Freud was satisfied and relieved by the answer, which did not challenge his own position on dreams. Jung said that Freud was "completely helpless" in dealing with certain kinds of dreams and had to "retreat to his doctrine."[3]

In interpreting his own dream, Jung equated the ground floor of the house with the first level of consciousness. The deeper he went, the more alien and primitive became his surroundings, until he reached a layer scarcely illumined by consciousness and very difficult to reach. "The primitive psyche of man borders on the life of the animal soul, just as the caves of prehistoric times were usually inhabited by animals before men laid claim to them," he said.[4] It is from this deep level, the collective unconscious, that archetypal images arise and break through, such as in dreams.

Archetypes in dreams put us in touch with a mythical realm that transcends space and time. How real are archetypes? As real as each of us chooses. The person who believes in them or places a measure of credence in them "is just as right or just as wrong as someone who does not believe in them," Jung said. "But while the man who despairs marches toward nothingness, the one who has placed his faith in the archetype follows the tracks of life and lives right into his death. Both, to be sure, remain in uncertainty, but one lives against his instincts, the other with them."[5]

Jung felt that Freud, with his rigid ideas about sexual repressions and wish fulfillments lurking behind every dream image, was marching toward nothingness. Jung cut himself loose.

Descent into the Archetypal Realm

After the break with Freud, Jung went through a tumultuous six-year period, often described as a breakdown, characterized by psychotic fantasies. Actually, it was more of a break*through* to a new understanding of consciousness. He was way beyond his time, and was labeled a mystic for his unusual ideas and was shunned by his peers. But this phase was a productive one for him, incubating many of the ideas that he would spend the rest of his life developing. Jung experienced numerous paranormal phenomena and vivid dreams and visions. The distinction between his dreams and visions faded, and he later recorded episodes of both in detail. He became immersed in the world of the dead, which led to his inspired writing of *Seven Sermons to the Dead,* penned under the name of the second-century Gnostic writer, Basilides, and published in 1916. Jung described the spirits of the dead as "the voices of the Unanswered, Unresolved and Unredeemed."

The Psychoid Unconscious

Another of Jung's concepts important to modern dreamwork is that of the psychoid unconscious, which gave rise to the psychoid archetype. The psychoid unconscious refers to a most fundamental level of the unconscious that cannot be accessed by the conscious, and that has properties in common with the organic world. It is formed of, and bridges, two worlds; it is both psychological and physiological, material and nonmaterial. Thus a psychoid archetype expresses a psychic/organic link: the psychic that is in the process of becoming material. This is also the *mundus imaginalis,* the bridge between the physical and spiritual realms. Dreams play an important role in helping material move from the spiritual realm into manifestation in the physical.

A Dream of Life's Completion

Three days before he died, Jung had the last of his visionary dreams and a portent of his own impending death. In the dream, he had become whole. A significant symbol was tree roots interlaced with gold, the alchemical symbol of completion. When he died at his home in Zurich on June 6, 1961, a great storm arose on Lake Geneva and lightning struck a favorite tree of his.

The story of Jung's life can be properly understood only from his inner experiences. The experiences of the outer world were pale and thin by comparison for him. He said he could understand himself only in the light of his inner happenings.[6]

Jung's contributions to our understanding of consciousness, dreams, and the striving for psychic integration and wholeness continue to provide the foundation for most modern dreamwork. Some of his other ideas and techniques are discussed in subsequent chapters of this book.

The Liberation of Dreamwork

Since Freud and Jung, other theories adding to their work have been put forward on the nature, function, and meaning of dreams. Astonishingly, the examination of dreams still was discouraged from lay participation as late as the 1970s. It was considered dangerous to look too deeply into one's own dreams; dreamwork was best handled by a trained analyst, who became the substitute for the ancient dream priest or interpreter.

Since about the 1970s, dreamwork has entered the public domain. Rather than being dangerous, individual dreamwork has proved fruitful in many areas. Researchers have explored the diagnostic and healing content of dreams, the psi content of dreams, and the nature of lucid dreams and shared dreams. But as much as dreamwork has flourished in the twentieth century, there is still a tendency to view the dream analytically. We see dream images primarily as pieces of ourselves. We look primarily for personal meaning in relation to our daily lives. Certainly dreams address daily life. But they also address our spiritual life: our relationship to the whole, whether it be the whole of humanity, the whole of the planet, or the whole of creation. If we focus only on the personal meaning of dreams, we miss much of wisdom that dreams have to offer.

Not every dream is a big dream, full of crackling power and archetypal images, but every dream has some nuance of the spiritual in it. The time has come for us to once again appreciate the *whole* of the dream, in all of its personal, spiritual, and transcendent glory.

The Dreamscape and New Physics

The land of dreams, or dreamscape, is not an imaginary place concocted from our fantasies. It does incorporate the world we know, our memories, anxieties, and activities. But the dreamscape extends far beyond into reaches we may not even comprehend. It exists beyond the limits of time and space, incorporates past, present, and future simultaneously, and is populated with both persons familiar to us and its own denizens.

The land of dreams is part of the *mundus imaginalis,* or imaginal world, a real place recognized by cultures around the world since ancient times. This place—perhaps state of being would be a better description—is also called the *imaginal realm,* a term coined by scholar Henri Corbin. *Imaginal* is not the same as *imaginary,* the stuff of fantasy. The imaginal world or realm corresponds to the Dreamtime of the Australian Aborigines: a timeless reality from which continually arises the material world, like a dream of the universe.

In the terms of quantum physics, the dreamscape emerges from the implicate order. According to physicist David Bohm, the implicate ("enfolded") order is the seamless whole of the universe, the unbroken continuum of all things. Like the Dreamtime, it is a deep level of reality that contains all time and yet is timeless. It holds all potentiality. It is fluid. From the implicate order comes the explicate ("unfolded") order, which is what we know as material reality. There is a constant flow of energy between the two orders. There is no cause and effect, but rather influences that give rise to the acausal connections we know as synchronicity.

The implicate order is the realm of the mystics: a state of being that is eternal. We can gain direct knowledge of this realm through spiritual discipline, such as meditation and prayer. We also gain knowledge of it through our dreams. Our dreams take us into the implicate order, where we have access to potentiality, and thus can bring it into manifestation.

Dreams As Exceptional Human Experiences

Many of the dreams we experience are more than dreams—they are exceptional human experiences (EHE). The term *exceptional human experience* was coined in 1990 by researcher Rhea A. White to describe a wide range of anomalous, nonordinary, and (at present) inexplicable experiences reported by people. White has defined 150 types of exceptional experiences in five broad categories. Taken together, these experiences may form a new paradigm of consciousness and a new approach to what we consider psychical, mystical, and paranormal experience.

White's ground-breaking research in this area has its origins in her own near-death experience (NDE), which occurred in 1952 in an automobile accident that killed the friend she was riding with.[7] Motivated by the NDE, she became a research fellow at J.B. Rhine's parapsychology lab at Duke University in North Carolina, which was setting the pace for parapsychology research. After four years, she went to the American Society for Psychical Research, doing research and editing their journal.

White then launched a dual career by becoming a trained reference librarian, and set up the library at the Department of Psychiatry at Maimonides Medical Center in Brooklyn, New York. There, White assisted with the research in ESP in dreams conducted by Montague Ullman and Stanley Krippner.

White's interest in transformative experiences led to a book, *The Psychic Side of Sports,* coauthored in 1978 with Michael Murphy, cofounder of the Esalen Institute in Big Sur, California. The book documents the exceptional experiences of athletes and sports men and women, such as ecstasy, timelessness, out-of-body experience, supernormal perception and strength, weightlessness, and awareness of "the Other," an unknown and often helpful presence. A much-expanded edition under the title *In the Zone* was published in 1995.

Within parapsychology, White found herself increasingly frustrated by a behaviorist methodology that ignored subjective and psychological factors concerning EHEs. Parapsychology by and large has focused on trying to fit the paranormal into the scientific paradigm by measuring it, quantifying it, and replicating it under controlled laboratory conditions. Although psi has been demonstrated in the laboratory, it resists fitting into the scientific paradigm, since it operates outside the bounds of time and space. Furthermore, science ignores anecdotal evidence, which is precisely the core of an EHE: a personal experience meaningful in a subjective way to the individual.

White recognized that many of these experiences have a powerful, transformative impact upon people. Worldviews can shift dramatically after an OBE or NDE, for example. A new approach needed to be taken if we are to fully understand the significance of these experiences and derive the fullest benefit from them.

In 1994–95, White founded the Exceptional Human Experience Network, a nonprofit organization that collects and studies life-transforming experiences. Interestingly, White was guided—unknowingly—by dreams she had in the 1950s to move in this direction: to make a break with parapsychology and push out a new frontier of consciousness research, which she accomplished thirty-two years later. She did not realize this until 1992, when she remembered one dream and checked back to her dream journal of the '50s.

"The dreams were about parapsychology's need (and obviously my own) to take in a wider frame of reference," White said. "They indicated that an entirely new approach was needed, one that was the opposite of the one in use in the 1950s and that is still privileged today. The dreams indicated that simply looking at the field in a new way would reveal new understandings of psychic phenomena and new ways of conceptualizing research approaches. That which had been baffling would become clear."[8]

Public opinion polls show that, depending on the type of experience surveyed, 25 to 85 percent of respondents report having an experience with "anomalous" phenomena. About 59 percent report transcendent experiences.

Dreams fit all five categories of EHEs:

Psychical: Forms of psi (clairvoyance, telepathy, precognition, psychokinesis). Many dreams involve these elements.

Death-related: Experiences of sensing a separation of the physical and nonphysical self, especially related to one's own NDE or another person's death; also memories of between lives and the time prior to a new birth. We dream of visiting the afterworld, of having contact with the dead, and sometimes of the souls who are about to be born to us.

Mystical: Experiences of a sense of greater connection, sometimes amounting to union with the divine, other people, life-forms, objects, or one's surroundings, up to and including the universe itself. We have transcendent dreams of all of these types of experiences.

Encounter: Experiences of sensing, perceiving, or "knowing" the presence of an "unusual or unexpected being." In dreams, we often encounter angels, aliens, spiritual guides and masters, and other nonhuman entities.

Enhanced experiences: Experiences that are at the limit of what the Euro-American culture considers normal. These involve peak experiences of emotion and transcendence, bursts of unusual mental and physical abilities, etc. Dreams that fit here are lucid, out-of-body, miraculous healing, creative genius, and so on.[9]

Three Levels to the Dream

Sometimes in order to understand the essence of a dream, we must simply accept it for what it is—an experience in another reality. We must become dream shamans and enter the dreamscape with the knowledge that our experiences in it are real and have their own validity and integrity.

How should we view the dream? A dream is like a diamond; it has many facets, each with its own beauty, yet part of a whole. Dreams are metaphors reflecting our inner state of being. They show dramas of life, using the residues of the day and symbols to provide information. On another level, dreams take us to other realities that have their own ontological integrity. Dreams do not have one meaning, but often have three, simultaneous meanings:

1. *Personal level.* Everything in a dream expresses a part of ourselves. We find meaning in day residues and symbols expressing mundane events and emotions.
2. *Archetypal level.* Some elements in a dream express archetypal energy from the collective unconscious. These images exist in their own right in the dream and must be experienced as such.
3. *Transpersonal level.* Dreams are experiences of cosmic consciousness in which the fabric of the universe is revealed to us. The boundaries of time and space disappear. We see the past and the future and realize the ever-present now. We see into other realms, such as the kingdom of angels, the dimensions of the ascended masters, and the land of the dead. We hear the voice of God. We are linked to the consciousness of all sentient beings.

Dreamwork can teach us much about the nature of consciousness and how our consciousness is evolving. EHEs certainly are life-enhancing; on a collective level, they are instructive about our consciousness as a species. Our consciousness is evolving, and its frontiers are spiritual/mystical. Michael Murphy notes in his book *The Future of the Body* that experiences that we now consider extraordinary will be considered ordinary in the future. I believe that among them will be dreams that help us reunite the realms of matter and spirit.

chapter three

INNER ALCHEMY

IN ORDER TO PERCEIVE THE FULL DEPTH OF THE ARCHETYPAL AND SPIRITUAL CONTENT OF DREAMS, IT IS IMPORTANT TO UNDERSTAND THE FUNDAMENTALS OF ALCHEMY. THE REVIVAL OF ALCHEMY, ESPEcially as it pertains to dreamwork, was another of Jung's great accomplishments.

Alchemy is the ancient art of transformation by refining the impure into the pure. It is thousands of years old in both the East and the West, and is generally considered to be the precursor of chemistry. It is a mystery teaching and thus is both an inner and outer art. The outer art of alchemy is the transmutation of base metals, such as lead, into silver or gold. The inner art of alchemy is the attainment of immortality, or a deathless state—the gold of enlightenment.

Life itself is alchemical. We go through life striving to improve ourselves, to refine away our impurities. The goal we seek is the gold of wholeness or enlightenment—Jung called it individuation—that illuminates our understanding of our eternal essence. Our dreams are an important part of this process, revealing information about the alchemical stages we pass through in life.

The Hermetica

The foundation of Western alchemy rests upon the Hermetic tradition, a body of esoteric teachings said to have been created by the legendary Hermes Trismegistus (thrice greatest Hermes), a composite of the Egyptian god of magic and wisdom, Thoth, and his Greek counterpart, Hermes. The composite was created by the Greeks who settled in Egypt and who identified Thoth and Hermes with one another. Thoth ruled mystical wisdom, magic, writing, and other disciplines, and was associated with healing. Hermes was the personification of universal wisdom and the patron of magic; a swift, wing-footed messenger, he carried a magic wand, the caduceus. Both were associated with the spirits of the dead: Thoth weighed their souls in the Judgment Hall of Osiris; Hermes escorted shades to Hades. Both were credited with writing the sacred books of science, healing, philosophy, magic, and law, and revealing the wisdom to mankind.

Thrice greatest refers to Hermes Trismegistus as the greatest of all philosophers, the greatest of all kings, and the greatest of all priests. According to legend, he was a mythical king who reigned for 3,226 years. He carried an emerald, upon which was recorded all of philosophy, and the caduceus, a staff entwined by two snakes, that was the symbol of mystical illumination.

Hermes Trismegistus wrote forty-two sacred books (by some accounts many more) conveying the teachings of the gods. Most likely the books were authored between the third century B.C.E. and first century C.E.—or even later, well into the Middle Ages—by anonymous persons in succession who signed them Thoth to give them weight and the appearance of antiquity.

This corpus, collectively known as the Hermetica, was housed in the great library in Alexandria. Most of them were lost when the library was burned by Christians. Surviving books were protected by a succession of initiates.

The most important Hermetic work is *The Divine Pymander*, consisting of seventeen collected fragments of the original Hermetic concepts, including the way divine wisdom and the secrets of the universe were revealed to Hermes, and how Hermes established his ministry to spread the wisdom throughout the world. Another work, *The Vision*, tells of Hermes's mystical vision, cosmogony, and the Egyptians' secret sciences of culture and the spiritual development of the soul. Some passages are similar to the Gospel of Saint John, Plato's *Timaeus*, and the writings of Philo.

Hermes Trismegistus's Emerald Tablet (or Emerald Table) is said to be inscribed with the whole of the Egyptians' philosophy, including the magical secrets of the universe. According to legend, it was found clutched in the hand of the body of Hermes Trismegistus in his cave tomb. (Another version has it that Hermes Trismegistus's mummy was interred in the Great Pyramid of Giza.)

The Emerald Tablet is cited as the credo of adepts, particularly the alchemists, who believed that mystical secrets were hidden in Hermetic allegories. The Emerald Tablet holds that "as above, so below," meaning that the physical world, the microcosm, mirrors the universe, or macrocosm. It also holds that everything emanates from the One. The sun represents the masculine principle and the moon represents the feminine principle. The goal of alchemy can be attained through the purified unification of opposites.

The Essence of Alchemy

Alchemy is complex. For our purposes with dreamwork, we can focus on its key elements and see how they apply to dreams.

The process of alchemy is called the Great Work, or Work. The alchemist strives to create a philosopher's stone, a mysterious substance never precisely defined, and created with equally mysterious chemical procedures. The philosopher's stone enables the transformation of base metals into silver or gold to take place. It is also called the lapis (not to be confused with the semiprecious stone lapis lazuli), the jewel, and the elixir, among other names. The Emerald Tablet represents the stone as a teaching of Truth that facilitates spiritual transformation.

To begin the Work, the alchemist starts with *prima materia,* or first matter, a substance from chaos that is the living essence of any thing. The *prima materia* cannot be seen or weighed, yet from it the elements and everything is made. It is rather like the living soul, or *anima mundi,* of the world.

To get the *prima materia,* the alchemist subjects his ingredients (such as metals, minerals, and chemicals) to heat and cold, so that they are cooked, evaporated, liquefied, distilled, condensed, separated, and recombined. The idea is to extract the *prima materia,* kill it, and revive it in a purified and perfected form. *Solve et coagula* (dissolve and coagulate) was the motto of the alchemists.

There are three key ingredients in the Work: salt, sulfur, and mercury.

The Work is divided into three principal stages, though some alchemists described more. The first stage, called the *nigredo* (blackness) begins the Work with a disintegration or putrefaction that breaks the ingredients down into their essential components. Through laboratory procedures, components are recombined in different ways. Especially, the alchemists sought to transmute by working with opposites. The second stage, the *albedo* (whiteness) is the process of refining and purification by washings in various solutions. The third stage, the *rubedo* (redness) occurs as the Work comes to fruition with the philosopher's stone.

The Work cannot be hurried or done impatiently. Medieval alchemists who tried to hurry their work were called "puffers" because they overused their bellows in the fires of their laboratories. The procedure of going from *nigredo* to *rubedo* would have to be repeated many times in order for the *anima mundi* to be released and the philosopher's stone to be created.

The alchemists knew that the ability to create silver and gold from base metals was only the outer part of the Work. They could not be successful unless they created gold in the inner world. A spiritual philosopher's stone would enable them to transform physically and achieve immortality, thus escaping death. Alchemists did inner work. To help the alchemical uniting of opposites, they had working partners of the opposite sex. Since the alchemists of old invariably were male, their partners were female, usually a wife or sister, who was called the *soror mystica,* or mystical sister.

The work of alchemy traditionally was done in great secrecy, for each alchemist wanted to discover the formula for the philosopher's stone and keep it to himself. Most of the medieval alchemists truly were looking for the secret recipe for making gold so that they could become both wealthy *and* immortal. Consequently, the language of alchemy was deliberately veiled in order to protect the Work. Symbols were used to describe entire procedures and the goals of procedures. For example, opposites were often represented by masculine-feminine correspondences: the sun and moon, red and white, sulfur and mercury, or king and queen. The hermaphrodite was the unification of opposites. Salt represented the body. Animals represented various characteristics of the Work. The rose represented the perfection of the Work.

Only persons initiated into the secrets of the Work could interpret and understand its pictorial language. One famous alchemical text has not a single word of text: the *Mutus Liber,* or Silent Book, composed in the sixteenth century. Bits of high magic and angel magic were woven into alchemy, along with astrology and numbers mysticism.

Alchemists also relied heavily upon their dreams, visions, and inspirations for guidance in their work. It was not uncommon for alchemical works to contradict each other or even themselves.

Flamel's Alchemical Dream

One of the most famous stories involving dreams and alchemy concerns Nicholas Flamel (1330–1416), a French scribe turned alchemist. Flamel and his wealthy wife, Pernelle, lived comfortably. He worked as a scribe copying manuscripts. Some likely were alchemical in nature. Flamel wasn't interested in alchemy, however, until he experienced a dream one night. An angel appeared to him and held out a beautiful book of obvious antiquity. The angel said, "Flamel, look at this book. You will not in the least understand it, neither will anyone else; but a day will come when you will see in it something that no one else will see." In the dream, Flamel reached out to take the book, but both it and the angel vanished in a golden cloud.

In 1357, Flamel purchased from a vendor a mysterious, gilded book that was large, very old, and not made of paper or parchment, but from the thin bark of tender shrubs. Its cover was made of copper and was engraved with strange symbols. Inside, it contained equally strange drawings and a claim that it was authored by Abraham Eleazar, or Abraham the Jew, a prince, astrologer, and philosopher. It also delivered curses against anyone who should set his eyes on the book, lest he be a sacrificer or scribe.

Feeling exempt from the curses, Flamel examined the book and determined that it was an alchemical text that told how to transmute metals into gold, so that Jews could pay levies due to the Roman empire. The secret remained hidden in the drawings, some of which were not accompanied by explanatory text. On every seventh leaf, there was an illustration of one of three icons: a caduceus (staff) with intertwined serpents; a serpent crucified on a cross; or a snake-infested desert with beautiful mountains. Among other drawings was one of a winged Mercury (Hermes) with Saturn holding an hourglass and scythe, and a mountain with a rose (with a blue stalk and red and white flowers) blown in the north wind.

Flamel and his wife tried in vain for years to decipher the book. In 1378, Flamel made a pilgrimage to Spain, where he met a converted Jew who conveniently revealed enough secrets to Flamel prior to dying so that Flamel could decipher his book.

According to Flamel, by 1382, he and Pernelle had created the philosopher's stone and began creating silver and gold. Legend has it that they founded and endowed fourteen hospitals, built three chapels, made generous gifts to seven churches, and paid for the repair of numerous church buildings.

Flamel kept his secrets. He did commission paintings of some of the drawings from the book as frescoes in an archway he had built in the Cemetery of the Holy Innocents in Paris. The paintings symbolize the Great Secret and were the object of many pilgrimages by alchemists into the seventeenth and eighteenth centuries.

Pernelle died in 1397. Flamel died on November 22, 1416 (he is also said to have died in 1417 or 1418). His house was futilely ransacked by fortune hunters seeking the secrets to transmutation. It was widely believed by other alchemists that Flamel did achieve the philosopher's stone, but his secrets apparently died with him and his success was not achieved by others.

Sightings of the Flamels circulated around Europe well into the eighteenth century. By then, alchemy was in decline in the face of the rise of the age of science and reason. It was discredited as a pseudoscience and remained in obscurity until Jung rediscovered it.

The Revival of Alchemy

Jung had alchemical dreams and visions long before he knew what alchemy was about. Once he became immersed in it, he was able to understand dreams and visions from a new perspective, and he also was able to develop his theories on the personality. In fact, it was alchemy that led to one of his most important concepts, individuation, which is the process of becoming whole. Through our experiences in life, we are challenged to integrate pieces of ourselves. Each one of us has a feminine side, called the anima, and a masculine side, called the animus, which must be brought into harmony with each other. In addition, we have the shadow, parts of us that are repressed. Individuation enables us to become conscious of both our smallness and our great uniqueness in the grand scheme of things.

Jung's Wake-up Calls

Like many of his contemporaries, Jung considered alchemy as "something off the beaten track and rather silly."[1] But between 1926 and 1928, he had a series of dreams that changed his mind and his life.

In the first dream, in 1926, he finds himself in South Tyrol during wartime. He is on the Italian front, driving back from the front lines in a horse-drawn carriage with a little peasant man.

Shells explode all around them; the journey is very dangerous. They cross a bridge and then go through a tunnel whose vaulting has been partially destroyed by the shelling. At the other end is a sunny landscape and the radiant city of Verona. The landscape looks lush and green. Jung notices a large manor house with many annexes and outbuildings. The road leads through a large courtyard and past the house. They drive through a gate and into the courtyard. Another gate at the far end opens onto the sunny landscape. Just as they are in the middle of the courtyard, the gates at both ends clang shut. The little peasant leaps down from his seat and announces, "Now we are caught in the seventeenth century." Jung thinks to himself, "Well, that's that! But what is there to do about it? Now we shall be caught for years." He is then consoled by another thought: "Someday, years from now, I shall get out again."[2]

The dream was prophetic: Jung would spend much of the rest of his life looking into alchemy, which peaked in Europe in the seventeenth century.

Jung began searching through works on history, religion, and philosophy to try to illuminate this puzzling dream, but to no avail.

Other dreams occurred with the same theme. In them, he sees a previously unknown annex to his own house. He wonders how he could not have known about it. Finally, he enters the annex and finds that it contains a wonderful library, full of large sixteenth- and seventeenth-century books, hand-bound with pigskin and illustrated with strange symbolic copper engravings. He has never before seen such symbols.

In 1928, Richard Wilhelm gave Jung a copy of the *Golden Flower,* a Chinese alchemical text. He was so intrigued by it that he asked a bookseller to send him anything he obtained on the subject of alchemy. Soon he received a copy of a collection of classic sixteenth-century alchemical texts, *Artis Auriferae Volumina Duo.*

But the book and its strange symbols still looked like nonsense to him, and Jung left it largely untouched for two years. Finally, he realized that the language of alchemy *is* symbols, and he set about to decipher them. He then understood his dreams.

In the house dreams, the house represented his own consciousness, and the annex represented something that belonged to him but that was just emerging into his conscious mind. The library with its old books represented alchemy itself. Within fifteen years, Jung had assembled a library similar to the one in his dream.

Jung had long sought to find a way to bridge the present and the past, to relate analytical psychology to myth through a historical context, and now he found that bridge in alchemy. The intellectual thread of Western alchemy extended back to the Gnostics, whom Jung had studied. He saw that the Gnostics and the alchemists were concerned with the same inner landscape as he.

Jung also recognized the archetypal nature of alchemical symbols and observed them in the dreams of his patients, who knew nothing about alchemy. He was able to understand certain dream motifs that had previously puzzled him. For example, one of his patients had a dream of an eagle flying into the sky. In this dream, the eagle begins to eat his own wings, then drops back to earth. Jung interpreted the dream on a personal level as a reversal of a psychic situation. He then discovered an alchemical engraving of an eagle eating its own wings and thus saw the image in the dream as archetypal as well.

Christ As Lapis

Much of Jung's efforts concerned relating analytical psychology to Christianity. Alchemy provided a bridge. Jung saw the Christ figure as the lapis or philosopher's stone, the agent that transforms the impure into the pure, the base metal into gold. One night, Jung awakened from sleep to see a startling vision at the foot of his bed: a brightly lit figure of Christ on the cross, not quite life size, and breathtakingly beautiful. Christ's body was greenish gold. Jung was no stranger to powerful dreams or visions, but he was shaken by this one.

In interpreting the vision, Jung saw that Christ represented the *aurum non vulgi* (not the common gold) of the alchemists. This referred to the more serious, esoteric purpose of alchemy, to produce not just ordinary gold, but *aurum philosophicum,* or philosophical gold—a transmutation of a spiritual nature.

The greenish gold of Christ's body represented the living essence in all matter: the *anima mundi* or World Soul or World Spirit, which fills everything in existence. Thus, the alchemical Christ is a union between the spiritual and the physical.

Alchemy in Dreams

All of our dreams are alchemical in nature because they are part of life itself. From birth to death, life is the Great Work. Initially, we try to make our gold—our successes—in the outer world. At some point, perhaps through spiritual or philosophical study or a crisis or trauma in life, we realize that we can't truly make outer gold until we learn to make inner gold. The outer person is a reflection of the inner person. This is the core of the Hermetic axiom, "as above, so below"—as inside, so outside; as spiritual, so material.

Life is a series of alchemical operations. A loss, for example, is the process of separation. A lot of intellectual or mental activity is the process of evaporation. Going within to contemplate and reassess is coagulation. Being overwhelmed with emotion is dissolution. The *prima materia* is the unconscious, which, when we first begin to examine it, seems chaotic. The alchemical king and queen are the animus and anima, and their union represents the integration of the ego with the unconscious. The three basic ingredients of alchemy have their symbolic counterparts: salt represents the body, sulfur represents the spirit, and mercury represents the mind. The philosopher's stone is transformation in life.

Nigredo dreams can be characterized by severe actions such as turmoil, death, endings, violence and upheaval, darkness, and going down into the earth. When we have a serious turning point or a crisis that leaves us feeling as though we have to start over, we begin *nigredo.* When something in life comes to an end or needs to come to an end, we face *nigredo.*

Albedo dreams often feature baptisms and immersions in water, initiation-like imagery comparable to the level of the neophyte, and quests and journeys.

Rubedo dreams are characterized by high-level initiations (comparable to the level of adept), accomplishment, achievement, union, and acquisition. We find the treasure for which we have searched. In life, we go through these processes again and again, often lingering in one phase longer than another. Death and rebirth, which we symbolically experience many times in life, is the alchemists' ultimate *solve et coagula* (dissolve and coagulate).

Sometimes our dreams are dramatically alchemical, as Jung noticed in those dreams containing strong archetypal images. They can tell us where we are, alchemically, in life or where we have imbalances. Perhaps we have too much mental activity and not enough contemplation. Perhaps we are struggling with a *nigredo,* wondering when the light of dawn will appear. Perhaps we intuitively know we need to engage or disengage in something, but we put off dealing with it. Dreams with a major alchemical theme are likely not to be clear-cut in terms of one particular alchemical stage or another but may involve elements of two or all three. So it is as we move through life. Alchemical dreams, like all dreams, also address more than one level and more than one issue.

Examples of Alchemical Elements in Dreams

Alchemical Treatments for Spiritual Healing

Roberta B., a student of alchemy, had this dream during a painful period that followed two broken relationships. The first was her marriage and the second was a tumultuous transition relationship. She knew the second relationship was wrong for her but was having a hard time breaking free of it and finally facing her aloneness.

I am undergoing some kind of treatments that are alchemical in nature. I go to a clinic and a male doctor and female nurse treat me. I seem to have been doing this awhile . . . This is one of a series of treatments.

I receive an injection in my right arm. I don't like these injections, which are powerful and hurt, but I want the treatment. The shot makes me a little woozy, putting me into a twilight state. This state deepens, and I faint. I talk gibberish, which amuses the doctor, who mimics me.

They prepare the second shot, which will go directly into the chest where the heart is. I resist, rallying, but they prevail. This one floods my being, and I go into another altered state. Some sort of healing or transformation takes place while I am in this state. I can see an outline of my body and how the medicine is coursing through it.

The first shot is gold and forms an outline around my body. The second shot is antimony and goes through the core of myself.

In alchemy, antimony has the power to strip gold of its impurities. Thus, metaphorically, it strips my soul of its imperfections so that it can obtain a higher state. But antimony is both medicine and a poison. Metaphorically, it will become poison to me if I slip backward.

The doctor and nurse (the alchemist and the soror mystica*) are angels of healing, looking on me in the dream state, treating me in order to raise my vibrations for the new phase of work and life I have begun. The process has been under way for awhile; in the dream, these treatments have been going on. They are painful because they require leaving a lot of things behind—a lot of letting go.*[3]

Awakening Higher Consciousness

A man who is pursuing spiritual work has this dream.

I was with a group of people going to a meeting place, or house. We were passing through rolling hills. On our left, a rounded hill had a hole in its center, surrounded by brushwood. I understood that a great fish or creature lived in the hole, and it was dangerous. On getting to the house, we gathered together and we were there to call up the great fish. It appeared slowly and gracefully through a trap door in the floor. It was very beautiful and symmetrical in every line, silver in color; but as it appeared, I saw that it was not so much a fish as a great creature, a mixture between a black panther and seal, with a smooth, legless body. It reared its head, and I saw it had an emerald at its brow, just above its eyes. Our reason for calling it up was to get the jewel. Then somebody—the man who had called it up—said that the next thing was the most difficult. The beast then came out of the hole and changed into an enormous eight-foot-tall woman who was tremendously obese and cruel. She had huge water-filled breasts hanging to her waist. Everybody scattered in fear.[4]

The dream relates to the struggle to integrate the unconscious with the higher consciousness. The rounded hill with the hole in the center symbolizes a cosmic mandala of creation. The emerald jewel evokes the Emerald Tablet of Hermes Trismegistus, as well as the philosopher's stone. It is positioned at the third-eye chakra (spiritual vision) of the creature. The creature, coming up out of the earth and water, represents the untamed primitive instincts. The jewel of enlightenment cannot be obtained without dealing with the creature. Initially, it seems to be a fish (a messenger from the deep; also the Christ, or higher, consciousness) of silver color (perfection), but it transforms into an animal-fish and then a devouring mother with exaggerated sexual characteristics. Note that it is a man who summons the creature up. There is still work to be done integrating the animus and anima.

Kundalini

Eastern traditions of alchemy influenced the development of the Western alchemical tradition. In the East, the process of the Great Work involves the activation of a powerful psychospiritual energy called kundalini. Since Eastern alchemical concepts have become part of the modern Western spiritual lexicon, it is helpful to understand a few basics in order to see how symbols representing them function in dreams.

Kundalini is the very energy of life and consciousness. It resides sleeping within the chakra system, which is part of the subtle envelope of energy around and interpenetrating the body. Chakras (a Sanskrit term for wheels) are interfaces of energy: they enable the universal life force, a substance that permeates the universe (also known as *prana, chi, ki, mana,* and other terms), to be absorbed by the aura and the body. The chakras have spokes and rotate like wheels. If they become sluggish or blocked, our emotional, mental, or physical health can be affected.

There are seven primary chakras aligned approximately along the spine from the base to the top of the head. In addition to having its own color, each one governs certain physical and psychological functions and spiritual development. The higher the chakra, the greater the number of its spokes and more refined its energy and functions.

The term *kundalini* also means "she who is coiled," so-named because in Tantra Yoga, it is an aspect of Shakti, the divine female energy and consort of Shiva, and because it lies coiled like a serpent in the root chakra at the base of the spine. Kundalini is dormant as long as we are spiritually asleep, but as soon as we put our energy and intention into spiritual matters, it begins to activate. Sometimes it is activated spontaneously by an intense emotional experience (childbirth has been known to awaken it) or severe trauma, such as an accident or injury. When awakened, kundalini rises up the chakra system. If it reaches the crown, it brings illumination and mystical experience.

Kundalini actually is a universal phenomenon in esoteric teachings and has been known by various names for perhaps three thousand years. Kundalini-type descriptions or experiences are found in the esoteric teachings of the Egyptians, Tibetans, Chinese, some Native Americans, and the !Kung bushmen of Africa. Kundalini has been interpreted from the Bible as "the solar principle in man." It is referenced in the Koran, the works of Plato and other Greek philosophers, alchemical tracts (it is the philosopher's stone), and in Hermetic, Kabbalistic, Rosicrucian, and Masonic writings.

The path that kundalini takes up the chakra system follows two psychic channels called the *ida* and *pingala,* which twist along the spine like a double helix from the base of the spine to the top of the head. In the Hermetic tradition, this is symbolized by the snake-entwined caduceus staff of Hermes and Hermes Trismegistus.

Phenomena associated with kundalini activation include sensations of heat, electricity, fire racing through the body, brilliant light, rocking motions, spontaneous bursts of physical movements, auditory sounds (bells, buzzing, roaring, the music of the spheres, or the primordial sound of creation), visual impressions (balls or forms of light, spiritual beings, brilliant colors), and so on.

Following a significant experience of kundalini energy, people often become very clear-headed and have an increase in creativity. They frequently need less sleep or may be unable to sleep and may be hypersensitive to noise. Psychic experiences often increase.

Gopi Krishna, a modern Indian mystic who experienced some intense awakenings of kundalini after prolonged meditation, called the energy "the most jealously guarded secret in history" and "the guardian of human evolution." He believed it to be the driving force behind genius and inspiration. He also believed that the brain has within it the blueprint for mankind to evolve into a higher level of consciousness, one that will make use of kundalini. In educating others about it, Krishna told how it regenerates and restores the body and thus could be useful in discovering ways to improve health and lengthen life. He also suggested it could be useful in eradicating such conditions as mental retardation.

Transpersonal dreams accompany kundalini awakenings. Jung saw images associated with kundalini in the dreams of his patients. In the following chapters in this book, we will see many examples of kundalini in different types of dreams, especially psi dreams, lucid dreams, dreams of spiritual guides, and mystical dreams of merger with Christ, cosmic consciousness, a unified whole, or a transcendent reality. Kundalini also figures in many dreams of snakes, especially involving bodily contact with snakes (a symbol of the serpent power coursing through the body), and in ecstatic flying dreams and dreams of visiting beautiful temples, libraries, and schools in the astral plane.

Looking at dreams from an alchemical perspective adds a rich dimension to dreamwork. Alchemy reaches down into the archetypal realm and expands our vision. Through alchemy, we see dreams more as processes than as events.

PART II

Navigating the Dreamscape

chapter four

PSI IN DREAMS

THE DREAMSCAPE IS A CROSSROADS OF DIMENSIONS. IT SERVES AS A MEDIUM FOR PSYCHIC AWARENESS—FOR THE OBTAINING OF INFORMATION THROUGH MEANS OTHER THAN THE FIVE SENSES. Many dreams contain elements of psi such as telepathy, precognition, and clairvoyance, which have a bearing upon events in waking life. In earlier times, dreams were relied upon heavily for foretelling the future. Dream prediction is no longer an official activity of state, but our dreams nonetheless continue to see into the future, picturing events of both individual and collective importance. How do we know when a dream is psychic? And how reliable are psychic dreams in their accuracy?

Science has attempted to give us some answers. Some light has been shed on the occurrence of psi in dreams, but much of it remains a mystery. However, there are ways that you can learn about the psychic nature of your own dreams.

Psi Content in Dreams

Most psi in dreams involves premonition, precognition, and prophecy. All three terms relate to an awareness of future events; prophecy is generally applied to matters of collective or state importance. According to studies, most such glimpses of the future occur within one, sometimes two, days of the actual event. However, it is not unusual to see a future event months or even a year in advance. Of course, some of the most famous prophets of history, who drew from their dreams and visions, forecast centuries ahead: Nostradamus and the biblical prophets are among these great seers.

In modern times, ordinary people are experiencing what seem to be prophetic dreams of an apocalyptic nature; these are discussed later in the book.

A smaller percentage of dreams involve telepathy, in which information is communicated. Telepathy also appears to be a factor in shared dreams, where two or more people have the same or a similar dream on the same night (see chapter 7).

Clairvoyance dreams involve the obtaining of information about distant objects or people or the obtaining of information not readily available to the dreamer. Still less common are dreams involving psychokinesis, in which the dreamer finds changes in the physical environment as a result of a dream. Psychokinesis (also called mind over matter) is the movement of objects or changes to the environment through mental effort or projection of will. In dream psychokinesis, objects in waking life may be rearranged as a result of activity in a dream. Examples of both of these types of psi dreams can be found in chapter 23, which discusses contact with the dead.

Psi is not always direct, and so we don't always know we've experienced psi until after an event has taken place. For example, the wife of King Henry IV of England (1367–1413) dreamed before his assassination that the gems of her crown were changed into pearls. Pearls were a symbol of mourning, but this prophetic content was not recognized until after the king was murdered.

Other times, psi in dreams is quite specific. In 1865, President Abraham Lincoln had a dream in which he discovered that someone was lying in state in the White House. He asked a soldier who was dead and was told, "The president. He was killed by an assassin." Two weeks later, Lincoln was murdered at Ford's Theatre. On the morning of June 28, 1914, Bishop Joseph Lanyi of Grosswardein in Hungary, former tutor to the Archduke Franz Ferdinand of Austria, had a dream in which he was shown and told that the archduke and his wife would be assassinated on that day in Sarajevo. They were, and World War I was started.

Who Has Psi Dreams and Why

Anyone can experience a psi dream. For most of us, it is an infrequent or rare experience; for others, psi dreams occur quite regularly. Children can have psi dreams as well as adults, as in this dream reported by Laure R.

My four-year-old daughter woke up one morning before I took her to day care and said she had a bad dream in which there was a small fire in the house but we somehow put it out and everything turned out okay and no one was hurt.

The next night, my husband was working on our squeaky drier, which sits in a closet in my kitchen area, and while the drier was on, he was trapped behind it against the wall, penned in, and sprayed lubricant in the back of it, hoping to grease the squeak while it was on and the gear was turning. It started a fire, and flames were coming up out of the drier with my husband behind it, trapped. I grabbed my Dutch oven, filled it with water, and dumped it onto the back of the drier. It extinguished it, he got out, and all was okay.[1]

Most cases of reported precognition, either in dreams or in waking consciousness, involve traumatic events, especially to people known to the dreamer. We are linked by cords of psychic energy that extend out from the heart. These cords are strongest to the people, animals, and places to which we feel the closest. In the unbounded dreamscape, information can travel more freely along these psychic lines. The intensity and shock of trauma or dying sends stronger waves of energy along the lines, which are more likely to penetrate into the dreamscape and thus into waking consciousness. It is less common to have a psi dream about someone when nothing in particular is happening in their lives.

Jeri B. has experienced several psi dreams/visions foretelling the deaths of family members.

All my life I have had dreams that connect me with relatives that have passed away and sometimes tell me of a death to come in the family. When I was fourteen, I had a dream that I was taking a math test. My teacher came to me and tapped my shoulder, telling me that someone was there to pick me up and I had to go home. I turned around to see my father at the door, and I immediately started to cry because I knew he must have bad news. Then I woke up before I could find out what it was.

A few days later, I was taking a math test, and my teacher came up and tapped me on my shoulder. I started sobbing before I even turned around and then saw that my father was there. Apparently, my great aunt and uncle had been robbed and killed at their store and my father had come to take me home.

In 1991, my favorite aunt had been suffering with kidney failure and was on dialysis. She was also having problems with congestive heart failure, and there had been a couple of times that we had to rush to the emergency room when the doctors didn't think she was going to make it.

I had a dream where I was in a big, round room with windows all around it. I couldn't see anything out the windows but clouds. My mother came in the room and said there was someone else there to see me, and then she left. My grandmother came in and waved at me, and then she also left the room. My grandfather came in next. He was smiling and saying how great it was to be in heaven with his family, and he was especially happy now because he said my aunt would soon be joining them. I told him no, that I didn't want her to go, but he said it was her time. I woke up crying and couldn't forget about the dream.

A couple of weeks later, I received a call saying I had to get to the hospital quickly. When I arrived, it was too late. My aunt had already passed away.[2]

Sometimes, however, we just seem to pick up things on the psychic telegraph lines, even though we have no personal connection to the people involved, such as in the following dream that occurred to a woman.

I dreamed I was walking across a bridge with two other people. It was wide enough for a car and seemed to be made out of cement. I was walking on the right side, and water started to seep up on the left very rapidly. Too rapidly, for I could not get away in time. Then the bridge started to break apart in huge pieces. I went sliding down on a piece of bridge. This was the end of the dream.

The next day on the news, they showed a California flood, where a man was stuck on a bridge in his vehicle and was rescued by a chopper. They said he thought he could make it across, but the water came up too fast. They showed a piece of land breaking up in the fashion that the bridge broke up in my dream.[3]

Parapsychological Studies

Study of the psychic nature of dreams has been an interest in parapsychology since psychical research became organized in the late nineteenth century. Frederic W. H. Myers, one of the founders of the Society for Psychical Research (SPR) in London, included dreams in his concept of the subliminal, the realm that is beneath the threshold of ordinary consciousness. Dreams, he said, have an "unexplained potency" of their own that goes beyond the experiences of the waking self.

Parapsychological studies show that of psi experiences in general, dreams are involved in up to 70 percent of all cases. In the 1960s, researcher Louisa B. Rhine said that dreams may be the most efficient carriers of psi messages, because in sleep, the barriers to the conscious mind seem to be lower. In other words, it is easier for information from the implicate order to penetrate our time-and-space oriented explicate order.

Psi has been demonstrated in the laboratory in numerous studies, but what confounds researchers is that it defies the so-called laws of science: it cannot be quantified, qualified, or replicated with any reliability. Psi seems to function according to its own rules, varying by individual and fluctuating according to mood, emotions, and even the expectations of the researchers themselves.

Telepathy in Dreams

Some dreams are spontaneously telepathic. The ancients often did rituals for sending dreams in order to influence the thoughts and actions of others in such a way as to seem to be instructions from the gods. Sigmund Freud observed that "sleep creates favorable conditions for telepathy," and he referred often to dream telepathy in his clinical work with patients. The founders of the SPR in London collected 149 dream telepathy cases in their study of spontaneous paranormal experiences, published in *Phantasms of the Living* by Edmund Gurney in 1886. More than half of the dream cases involved death, followed by crises or distress. In these cases, the overwhelming majority of the percipients were emotionally close to the person who died or was in serious trouble.

The first known effort to induce telepathic dreams in an experiment was conducted in the nineteenth century by an Italian psychical researcher, G. B. Ermacora. Interestingly, Ermacora involved the spirit world in his experiment. He used a medium whose control or primary spirit, allegedly sent telepathic dreams to the medium's four-year-old cousin.

Of all types of psi in dreams, telepathy has proved the easiest to study in the laboratory. The most famous dream psi research was conducted in the 1960s by Montague Ullman and Stanley Krippner at the Dream Laboratory of the Maimonides Medical Center in Brooklyn, New York. When subjects were in REM (rapid eye movement) stages—when much dreaming occurs throughout the night—a person in another room attempted to telepathically transmit a target art image, usually depicting people and archetypal in character. The subjects were then awakened and asked to describe their dreams. The next day, they were shown several possible targets and asked to rank them in terms of matching the content and emotions of their dreams. In some cases, the dream correspondences would occur one to two days after the target had been transmitted. Overall, the correlation of dream images to target images was significantly above chance. The rapport between the sender and percipient was an important factor in success (thereby demonstrating the esoteric factor of energy cords between people). Characteristics that accompanied psi in dreams included unusual vividness, colors, and detail.

Parapsychological interest in dreams has lessened but continues with small studies.

Identifying Psi in Dreams

Most of us will experience at least one psi dream in life, and some of us will experience them frequently. Psi dreams that come few and far between can be harder to identify than those that occur frequently. So, if we dream of a car accident, for example, how do we determine whether it's a psi dream about a future event or a dream that is symbolic of our life?

Psi dreamers find that their psi dreams have certain signals in them that distinguish them from other dreams. These signals can be the appearances of certain persons, especially deceased; certain emotional tones during and after the dream; certain vivid details, such as colors or unusual objects; and so on. The signals are unique to the dreamer.

Emotional Impact

Intense emotions during and after a dream are one of the commonest and strongest clues to psi dreams. The dreamer awakens *knowing* with deep conviction that the dream is a portent.

Debbie had such a dream prior to the death of a close friend in a distant state.

The following is a story I have told to only a few people mainly because of the emotions *[author's emphasis] it brings to the surface. In 1980, my daughter, who was only thirteen months old, became ill with a serious childhood disorder. She almost died, but she survived with minimal problems. Trying to find help for her led me to a foundation for this disorder. The man there urged me to start a chapter where I was living at the time.*

As the years passed by, he and I became very close friends. He had lost his son several years prior. J. always supported me and tried to make me realize that I deserved to be happy. In exchange, I made him laugh and took some of the pain away. Because we lived in different states, we only saw each other occasionally. But we always kept in touch through cards, letters, and phone calls.

One Tuesday very early in the morning, I had a dream that was so real and disturbing that it woke me up and stayed with me for several days. I was in a church, someplace where it was cold and there was snow on the ground. My family, including my sisters, were there; my husband; and several friends, some of whom I met through the foundation; and J.'s wife. People were talking of an accident and more than one asked, "How's Debbie holding up?" It was obvious by the casket that it was a funeral. I was overcome by a horrible sadness to the point I felt numb. I couldn't look in the casket.

When I woke from this dream, I can't explain the way I felt. I knew something horrible was going to happen. The first thing I assumed was that it was my son. The next day, my husband and son had to drive to New York. I begged them not to go. My husband thought I had truly lost it and laughed at me. The next couple of days, life got really busy and I tried to forget the dream. On Sunday, my sister called and said that she heard on the radio that J. was missing—he had left on Tuesday afternoon for a three-hour trip and could not be found. On Monday afternoon, they found his car at the bottom of a ravine. He was dead.

When I attended the funeral in the state where he lived the following week, the church was exactly as it appeared in my dream. People were even dressed as I had dreamed. I had never been to that state before that funeral. I learned that J. apparently had died on Tuesday night or possibly Wednesday morning.

I wanted to believe it was only a coincidence that I dreamed this, but there is truly no way to explain it.

Since that experience, I have had several other similar dreams. When my mother passed away two years ago, she came to me in a dream the night she died. Although she had been ill with lung cancer for a long period of time, we all hoped she would survive. She died on a Saturday morning around five A.M. While I knew she was sick, no one expected her to leave so fast. All that I remember of the dream is that I woke around four or four-thirty and vividly remember my mother telling me good-bye and that she loved me. It was so real that for a few minutes I thought I was actually talking to her. Because of the incident that I had experienced in 1984, it really shook me up. So I called my sister at seven o'clock and she told me she had just gotten the call from the hospital that our mother had died in her sleep.

I believe these dreams are a way that the people we love try to help us cope with changes in our lives.[4]

Emotional intensity also was a tip-off to author Frank Tribbe to pay attention to a dream concerning his son.

In 1964, when my son, Alan, was fifteen, I was living in Washington, D.C., and he was living with my parents in nearby Fairfax County, Virginia. At about four A.M. one night, I dreamed that Alan held up one of his hands to show me that the ends of his four fingers had been cut off and the stumps were bleeding. No word was spoken. I sat up, wide awake, shaking with fright, and could not go back to sleep that night.

I had studied dream research and had attended dream evaluation groups, so I knew that dreams were of several categories, had different origins, were often couched in symbolisms, and were only rarely predictive of future events for most people. Nevertheless, I had a deep conviction that this dream was significant and important and should not be ignored, but the question was, What could and should I do about it? I regularly spent every Saturday with him in Virginia, but I determined that I would not tell him of the dream.

In considering how it might be possible for him to have his fingers mutilated as I had seen in my dream, I decided that two real possibilities did exist. Nearly every week he did a fair amount of lawn-mowing for his grandfather and some of the area was fairly rough; every summer there were stories of injuries from gasoline-powered rotary mowers, often because something such as a stick would stall the mower; but if the mower was not shut off before the obstruction was removed, it would sometimes start cutting again and injure the operator, whose hands were near the blade.

Accordingly, I took the opportunity that Saturday to give him safety instructions on mower operation. Also, I knew that one of his high school courses was in shop, which included the operation of carpentry equipment.

In my own high school days, my closest friend lost the first joint of his forefinger while operating the carpentry electrical table saw in an unsafe manner.

So, on the next Saturday, I asked Alan about the various pieces of equipment used in his shop course at school, and I proceeded to explain to him the safe and unsafe ways to operate the equipment, especially the potentially dangerous items such as the electric saw.

Alan is now forty-eight; I have never told him of that dream. He went through the Vietnam War unscathed; he has held pilot licenses for several grades of civilian aircraft, and jobs as pilot, without accident or injury. He still has all ten fingers. Did my dream and my action to protect him from injury save him from such an injury? I have no idea, but I'm glad I handled the matter as I did.[5]

Note that in both cases, the dreamer had a close relationship to the person featured in the dream. As Tribbe notes, it is difficult to prove that his dream was precognitive, since the dreamed-of event did not take place. It can be argued that surely one of the purposes of having psi dreams is to be able to take appropriate remedial action. Many times, however, psi dreams warn of events that seem inevitable—perhaps to cushion the shock.

For psi dreams that do not involve trauma but feature clairvoyance, telepathy, or shared dreams, emotions may be at the other end of the spectrum: joy, ecstasy, or a feeling of transcendence.

Unique Symbols

For a period in her life, my mother experienced psi dreams involving death. The identity of the soon-to-die person was not always clear. Like Debbie's dream, images, scenes, and such would bear out after the fact. Sometimes her dreams related to the collective. For example, she dreamed of President John F. Kennedy's death shortly before it happened in 1963. She dreamed that she was watching his funeral cortege as it passed along Pennsylvania Avenue. With her was her deceased mother.

The presence of her mother, coupled with a bad feeling in a dream, were a psi signature in my mother's dreams. Dreaming of the dead does not automatically denote psi (see chapter 23) or forecast death; it happened to be the case for my mother, but *only* if the dream also featured a death or accident and a black emotional tone, which often manifested as a bad feeling in her stomach, both in and out of the dream.

Lucidity, brilliant colors, and a supercharged atmosphere to a dream also can be psi signatures.

Repeating Dreams

Dreaming the same dream of an incident over and over again, especially an accident or traumatic event, can indicate psi. It should be noted that many dreams repeat, such as nightmares related to past traumas and dreams that are trying to get our attention about unresolved issues.

For about a year, Marlene experienced a recurring dream in which she was riding along in a car. Sometimes she was the driver and sometimes the passenger. Suddenly, everything would go black. The dream created a great deal of anxiety, but Marlene could not solve the mystery of it. She worried about having an accident and took precautions to be careful. She even sold her car.

One Christmas, she traveled to another state by plane to visit her family. Prior to leaving, she was filled with foreboding. On the return trip, as she was getting ready to disembark the plane, a celestial voice told her, "You will be all right. You have yet to complete your mission here." A friend picked her up at the airport. En route home, they were in a serious accident. Everything suddenly went black, and Marlene later awoke in a hospital. She was critically injured, suffering a split head, broken collarbone, neck and ribs, and internal injuries. She was not expected to survive. She credits prayer with her miraculous survival and recovery.

Marlene spent many hours reassessing the events, wondering if there was anything she could have done to prevent the accident. Why would her dreams forewarn her of it if there was nothing she could do? She considered her experience a wake-up call to reprioritize her life. In fact, she saw that prior to the accident, she had experienced other events that were wake-up calls—the accident was the most urgent. She put a plan into action.

Marlene's questions are hard to answer. Perhaps there might have been preventive action possible, as in Frank Tribbe's dream. If Marlene had made changes in her life earlier, would the accident have been necessary as an urgent wake-up call? Or was it part of her destiny? The answers may never be known.

Evaluating Dreams for Psi

Despite the fact that psi does occur in dreams, in waking consciousness, and in laboratory tests, creating a system of reliability around it has proved to be another matter. Efforts to collect psi data in order to prevent disasters have failed.

On October 21, 1966, 28 adults and 116 children were killed when a landslide of coal waste tumbled down a mountain in Aberfan, Wales, and buried a school. Up to two weeks beforehand, at least 200 persons experienced premonitions about the disaster, according to three surveys taken afterward. Premonitions included depression, a feeling that something bad was about to happen (some persons accurately pinpointed the day), sensations of choking and gasping for breath, uneasiness, and impressions of coal dust, billowing black clouds, and children running and screaming.

London psychiatrist J. A. Barker, who studied precognition, then established the British Premonitions Bureau to collect precognitive data in an attempt to avert disasters. Barker succeeded in finding a number of "human seismographs" who tuned in regularly to forthcoming disasters, but the entire effort was plagued from the beginning by problems of pinpointing correct times and locations, as well as other details.

In 1968, the Central Premonitions Bureau was established in New York City for the same purpose. Both bureaus struggled along for years on low budgets and with public relations obstacles. Most of the tips they received did not come to pass; those that did often were inaccurate in terms of time, rendering them equally useless. The bureaus eventually ceased operation.

What does this tell us about psi? Since psi operates outside of time and space, we may never be able to fit it into a time-space consciousness. Psi seems to deal with probabilities, not certainties. I have always cautioned people about psychic readings to view a predicted outcome as a probability based upon present forces in motion. Other probabilities exist, and forces in motion (thought, belief, action) constantly change.

So how should we look at psi in dreams?

We should certainly recognize that psi can and does happen in dreams, but we should exercise the utmost caution in assessing potential psi and in drawing conclusions from it. If you do not like to fly and you dream the night before a plane trip that a plane crashes, does this mean your plane will crash, or does it reflect your fear of flying? In all likelihood, the latter.

Always look for the simplest explanation in a dream first. Most dreams are *not* psi dreams. Analyze a dream for its symbolic content. If that doesn't seem satisfactory, consider psi possibilities. Is the emotional tone of the dream unusually intense? Do you have a "knowing" about the dream? Does the dream foretell something plausible to you?

Telepathy in dreams and shared dreams are often easier to verify, simply by comparing notes with someone.

I believe that the incidence of psi dreaming in Western society is on the increase. As more people develop their spiritual consciousness through prayer, meditation, devotion, and such, they will experience more psychic phenomena as they expand their awareness beyond the third dimension. This is part of the evolutionary track of human consciousness. In other chapters, we will explore how this can develop and the benefits to us.

chapter five

OUT-OF-BODY DREAM TRAVEL

SOMETIMES WE ARE AWARE IN A DREAM THAT WE EXIT OUR BODIES AND TRAVEL ABOUT IN A SECOND BODY. WE MAY FIND OURSELVES VISITING DISTANT PLACES ON EARTH, ENTERING THE DREAM-scapes of others, or visiting places in the astral and high spiritual planes where we meet guide figures or receive spiritual instruction.

Out-of-body experience (OBE) dreams usually happen spontaneously, though some individuals learn how to induce them. It is not necessary to sleep first to travel OB, though the sleep state seems conducive to the experience.

The second body of the OBE has been called various names: the astral body, the etheric body, the soul body, the second body, the dream body. It acts as a nonphysical, subtle vehicle for consciousness. This subtle body is a ghostly, semitransparent double of the physical body that can be naked, clothed in duplicate clothing, or clothed in other apparel. It may have attached to it a silver cord like an umbilical cord, which seems to be connected to the physical body. To other individuals, the second body is usually invisible, though its presence may be sensed. If seen, it appears to be an apparition. Some individuals report having no form at all or being points of light or presences of energy. In this body, we are able to move with the speed of thought, appearing wherever we think we wish to be.

Historical Perspectives on the OBE

Knowledge that the consciousness can separate from the body is ancient and universal. The ancient Egyptians described a *ba,* or soul-like essence that manifested during sleep and after death. It was often portrayed as a bird with a human head. The *ka* was the vital essence, more of a collective energy but part of every individual, which could be projected outward. In the Eastern mystical traditions, existence of the second body is acknowledged, and techniques for mastering it are taught in the various forms of Yoga. In the West, Plato held that the soul could leave the body and travel. Socrates, Pliny, and Plotinus gave descriptions of experiences that resemble OBEs; Plotinus wrote of being "lifted out of the body into myself" on many occasions. Plutarch described an OBE that occurred to Aridanaeus in 79 C.E. Saints and mystics recorded out-of-body experiences.

Sages, gurus, and healers put OBE dreams to use to enter the dreams of others to convey information or perform healing. Sai Baba of India is renowned for his appearance in the dreams of others, in answer to their needs, when no verbal or written communication has taken place. The shaman learns how to navigate OBE at will through otherworldly dimensions to perform healing and divine the future.

In the West, modern attention to the OBE began around the turn of the twentieth century. The American researcher Sylvan Muldoon began having spontaneous OBEs beginning at age twelve. Muldoon was a sickly youth who spent a good deal of time in bed. As his health improved, his OBEs became less frequent. Muldoon traveled about in an exact duplicate of his physical body. He believed that dreams of falling and flying corresponded to movements during astral travel. He wrote of his research in *The Projection of the Astral Body,* coauthored with the eminent psychical researcher Hereward Carrington.

Like Muldoon, Englishman Oliver Fox, born Hugh G. Calloway in 1885, was a sickly child. However, he did not experience OBEs until adulthood, when he succeeded in inducing them in dreams. He conducted numerous experiments, some solo and some with friends, between 1902 and 1938. Fox's "Dream of Knowledge" was an effort to remain awake mentally while sleeping physically. His experiences are published in his book, *Astral Projection.* Fox viewed his lucid dreamworld as comparable to the astral plane described in Theosophy. He experienced false awakenings, or waking up in the dream thinking he was really awake; telepathy with others; religious visions, such as the figure of Christ (which he decided was a thought form); and precognition (he viewed a test prior to his taking it and correctly saw two questions that would be asked). Fox initially believed that the dream state was essential to have his astral experiences. Eventually, he discovered that he could project himself out-of-body without going to sleep, but by staying in just a drowsy state. This drowsy state is called the hypnagogic state, and it marks our descent into sleep. It is often filled with fleeting imagery and voices. We're often in a hypnagogic state when we take a short nap. We can remain aware of our surroundings. Similar to Fox, the occultist P. D. Ouspensky taught himself how to enter lucid dreams from a waking state that he called the "half-dream" state.

In 1958, an American radio and television executive named Robert A. Monroe began traveling spontaneously out-of-body while relaxed and near sleep. Monroe had incredible experiences not limited to the earth plane but also to realms in which he visited the afterlife transition plane and had contact with discarnate humans and a variety of nonhuman beings. Like Fox, he conducted his own research, which eventually led to several books and the establishment of The Monroe Institute in Faber, Virginia. Monroe began working with inducement techniques using guided meditation and sound. His work has inspired thousands of people to experience travel out-of-body.

During the same time period that Monroe was making his discoveries, the modern religion of Eckankar was founded by Paul Twitchell in 1965. Eckankar, a blend of Western and Eastern mystical traditions, has attracted a worldwide following. Central to Eckankar is the mastery of the ancient art of soul travel, which is the expansion of inner consciousness through the physical, astral, causal, mental, and etheric planes. Soul travel provides the direct path to realization of SUGMAD (a sacred name of God, neither masculine nor feminine), and enables one to break the chain of karma and reincarnation. The dream state is the medium for some, but not necessarily all, soul travel. The travel is done in the *Atma Sarup,* the soul body. Soul travel may be done alone, but it is preferable to be accompanied by a spiritual master who has attained the soul plane and is living. Accordingly, Eckists are guided by the Dream Master, who is the head of Eckankar, called the Mahanta or Living Eck Master. This position has been held by Sri Harold Klemp since 1981.

Although most OBE dreams are spontaneous, we can learn how to enter them more at will. We become lucid, or conscious, in our dreaming.

Monroe's Experiences

Monroe called the OBE body the second body, preferring it to the more conventional astral body, which he felt had an occult connotation that many people would misunderstand. He said that the second body begins as a duplicate of the physical body, but as the OBE goes on, it begins to deteriorate in form (probably to its essence as energy), but could be rehabilitated into a physical duplicate by thought. His own second body appeared as a bright, glowing outline duplicating the physical, and it recorded the sensation of touch and moved according to his thought.

Monroe's initial experiences began when he would lie down to go to sleep. Before he reached sleep—when he was in the hypnagogic stage—he would experience a buzzing and vibrating and feel himself lift out of his body. Like an explorer touching the shores of an unknown land, Monroe explored and mapped this state of being. He first experienced what he called Locale I, which involved people and places in the physical world. He could instantly go to distant locations and see what people there were doing. Then he pushed into Locale II, or the astral plane, where most OBEs and dreams take place. Locale II is vast, he said, and incorporates our ideas of heaven and hell. Here he met the dead as well as nonhuman entities, many of whom were intelligent and could communicate with him. The lower reaches of Locale II are closest to earth, he said, and are populated by unpleasant entities obsessed with emotional and sexual gratification—what many people would call demonic energies.

Locale III is located on the other side of a hole in the space-time continuum, and it appears to be a near-identical physical world to ours—perhaps a parallel universe.

Monroe observed what many others have before him: that the relaxed state of presleep, the hypnagogic state, is an ideal medium for traveling out-of-body. The key is developing the ability to hold onto lucidity, or awareness, instead of falling asleep. He called this "mind awake body asleep." Monroe later patented a soundwave system called Hemi-Sync (for hemispheric synchronization), which balances the right and left hemispheres of the brain and which is used in the Monroe training systems. While a bodily vibration seemed to be intrinsic to Monroe's own experiences, it does not occur to everyone.

Monroe also found another piece of ancient knowledge about the OBE: that it is closely related to sexual energy and arousal. Heightened sexual energy often facilitated the experience, and sexual arousal and a kind of astral intercourse (a sort of merging of energies) could be experienced with the OBE. Sexual energy is part of the kundalini force, which is related to the attainment of enlightenment. Many spiritual experiences are charged with sexual energy.

Monroe noted that fear is the biggest barrier to being able to have an OBE: fear of what might happen, fear of death, fear of not being able to reenter the body. Although Monroe did have some experiences with unpleasant entities and a few episodes of difficulty getting back into his body, he believed that overall, the OBE posed no real hazards. Beyond Locale III are many levels remaining to be explored, some of which are simply beyond our ability to comprehend, he said.

Monroe found that many of the places that he visited in Locale II, the astral plane, had a familiar feel to them. They are the creations of consciousness, he said, and have been mapped and visited by countless souls.

OBE Dreams

As Monroe observed, many OBE dreams take us into the realm we call the astral plane. Here is where the Swedish mystic Emanuel Swedenborg (1688–1772) encountered heaven and hell. The astral plane also probably was the destination of many biblical-era prophets who had dream/visionary experiences of being swept up into heaven, such as Isaiah and Enoch. Saint John Bosco (1815–1888) of Italy, founder of the Salesian Order of Don Bosco, visited both heaven and hell in the dream state, accompanied by a guide figure. These dreams involved religious instruction for Bosco, lessons in how others fell into sin and how they could be redeemed. (More about these experiences can be found in chapters 6 and 24.)

Going to Astral School

Dreams of going to school are common, but sometimes the classroom or teaching institution is clearly otherworldly. During sleep we may go out-of-body to the astral plane where we attend class for spiritual instruction. Sometimes we remember these visits and other times we don't. I frequently have such dreams, as do others I know, especially those whose psychic senses have been opened through spiritual discipline. Sometimes I remember the content of the dreams; other times, I remember only being at astral school. I may just simply be there, or I may travel there, out-of-body, going through planes of realities that pass like the strata on sheets of rock. The teachers are always spiritual masters or beings, and the instruction focuses on esoteric topics.

Michael Talbot, author of *The Holographic Universe* and other books on mysticism, reincarnation and the new physics (see chapter 25), had astral school dreams often.

Throughout my high school and college years I had vivid and frequent dreams that I was attending classes on spiritual subjects at a strangely beautiful university in some sublime and other worldly place. These were not anxiety dreams about going to school, but incredibly pleasant flying dreams in which I floated weightlessly to lectures on the human energy field and reincarnation. During these dreams I sometimes encountered people I had known in this life but who had died, and even people who identified themselves as souls about to be reborn. Intriguingly, I have met several other individuals, usually people with more than normal psychic ability, who had also had these dreams (one, a talented Texas clairvoyant named Jim Gordon, was so baffled by the experience that he often asked his nonplussed mother why he had to go to school twice, *once during the day with all the other children, and once at night while he slept).*[1]

When Anne Beckley decided in 1994 to undergo a rigorous, four-year graduate-level training program in alternative healing, she began to experience lucid, out-of-body dreams to the astral plane. After studying all day, she found herself studying at night with fellow students who were also OB. Sometimes they were tutored by teachers from the earth plane and other times by other-worldly guide figures. Sometimes Anne would wake up feeling mentally worn out.

In some of the dreams, Anne became lucid as she was arriving at the astral campus. Other times, she suddenly found herself in class.

The instructors always give the same message: "Trust yourself." A lot of these dreams involve instructions for healing techniques. I'm always in a group, learning about the energy anatomy of the body and how to be guided by my intuition. The lessons deal with being more aligned with my

Guided Self and thus able to work better with the energy bodies. We also are taught how to telepathically communicate with people. We learn about the structure of the universe, what is the fundamental nature of reality. Sometimes we have to demonstrate what we have learned. One night, we were given specific instructions on trusting ourselves to see auras. I mostly feel auras.

In one dream, there were extraterrestrials participating. I was scared. I was feeding off the fear of a lot of others around me. That dream had to deal with the structure of the universe.

Nothing negative happened involving the extraterrestrials, however.

In some dreams, I've been practicing a lot of flying. At first I could only get three or four feet off the ground. Then later, I got eleven to twelve feet off, and then up to the treetops.

In one dream I saw the silver cord. I saw myself lying on the couch while I was flying around. I was in a third awareness.

I control where I go. You just have to think about where you want to be. You don't actually need flying, you just use your mind.

Anne said that she is usually wearing the color indigo in the healing teaching dreams. Indigo, as noted in chapter 11 on the meaning of colors, is the color of the third-eye chakra, the seat of spiritual awareness. In general, the colors in these dreams are quite vivid: "The colors are not of this earth. They are lighted from within the objects, radiating out." These descriptions correspond to reports of near-death experiences (see chapter 25).

Anne's OB dreams are filled with the emotion of love.

There is always a lot of love in these dreams. Nobody is there to correct you, but to guide you. It's a supportive environment.

There is a male person who often shows up. His appearance is sometimes different, but his eyes are always the same—they are an otherworldly blue that I've never seen here on earth. They are deep and compassionate and see right through you with unconditional love. His presence is love. I have a problem with that, that there is no such thing as unconditional love. He's like the nudge. He says, "Do you love me?" I always have a problem answering that. One time I could say, "Yes, I love you." It was universal love. Then I received a nice embrace.

He has a sense of humor. A lot of his messages are, "Don't take yourself too seriously. Be in love with the funny games."[2]

Anne awakens with an inner knowing from these dreams. She finds it hard to articulate precisely what she learns but has an understanding of it on a deeper level.

Helping the Newly Dead

Once Anne felt a need for a spiritual assignment and asked her higher self for one. Several weeks later, Anne was given her assignment in a dream trip to the astral plane.

I awoke to a landscape where I knew I was dreaming of sorts, but it was not the usual dreamscape I am familiar with. There was an ocean with haze, but the ground was not the usual solid consistency. I realized that I was on the astral plane, where people cross over when they have died. It was the blue island. I knew that I had not died, but at first I did not realize my purpose there, until I had ascertained that I was on the astral plane.

Seeing people emerge from various parts of the landscape, I knew that they had just crossed over. Some did know where they were, but others, alas, had no idea where they were. One man had drowned. I asked him if he knew where he was. He replied that he had been drowning but was now saved and was just fine. I had to gently let him know that he was dead and had crossed over, but he was in total disbelief. I asked him what was the last thing he remembered before coming here. He said he was drowning, but it was now obvious that he had been saved and was okay. I said that was just the point, he had drowned, and since he was just fine he now found himself in a new land, the astral plane. He was angry. I wanted to shout, "You're dead, get a grip, you cannot go back," but I acted with diplomacy in greeting the new folks arriving.

I was given a lit blue candle (an unreal blue not found on Earth) that had an inscription along the top wax that I could not decipher, by a gentleman who obviously was a teacher or guide. I knew I was supposed to give the welcome ritual, but I felt so unprepared—or rather, unworthy of this assignment. I took with courage this assignment and greeted the new arrivals to the astral plane to explain where they were. Again, some others accepted this, and others were in shock and disbelief. I explained that there are new rules that govern existence, and over time everyone would be learning about the new environment, how to navigate in it, and what lessons each person would learn. The island held an ocean, a bay, a marsh, and a cornfield, with a small town with more of a populace.

I felt I was given my first assignment as a neophyte soul. My first lesson was to recognize where I am in the dreamscape; in this case, it was the astral plane. My second lesson was to have compassion.[3]

We still have much to learn about the dreamscape: what it is, what exists in it, how we can travel consciously in it, and what we can learn from our adventures.

Summoned for Healing

Sometimes when Monroe was out-of-body, he was called or drawn by a signal or energy that pulled him to another location, usually where he found another person in need of help. For example, he met newly deceased souls who had arrived in the astral plane but were not aware that they were dead.

As mentioned earlier, Sai Baba and other adepts travel in the dream state to perform healing, summoned by a call that goes out not consciously in the physical realm but silently in the dreamscape, the astral realm.

In England, healer Kai Kermani has had spontaneous out-of-body summonings by patients. Kai, as he prefers to be called, is a licensed medical doctor, stress-management consultant, counselor, healer, author, and poet who is well-known in England's alternative health care field. His credentials are long and impressive. I met Kai in the early 1990s during my research for *The Miracle of Prayer*. Kai is remarkable not just for his work with his patients, especially those who are HIV-positive, but for his own story as well. Using meditative prayer and autogenics, a technique of deep relaxation and meditation, Kai healed himself of retinitis pigmentosa, saving himself from a fate the medical community said was certain and irreversible: total blindness. Truly a miracle.

A session with Kai usually lasts about one and a half hours. The initial portion is devoted to counseling, followed by about an hour of energy healing. Kai works on the chakras front and back, as well as on any areas of damage, disease, or distress, or areas he is drawn to intuitively through his hands or third eye. Sometimes Kai uses crystals and holds or passes them over the body. He and often his patients are aware of the presence of spirit guides during the sessions. Patients, who receive the treatment while lying on a body work table, often fall into the hypnagogic state of sleep, and some even into a deeper sleep.

Kai believes strongly in teaching his patients self-empowerment and self-healing, and gives them homework exercises to do between sessions, in which they use autogenics. Kai also does a form of psychic surgery when called for, as he describes below.

I sometimes perform psychic or what I prefer to call "active thought surgery" if it feels appropriate or I am guided to do so. Often there is quite a bit of confusion and misunderstanding about this subject. I do not go into a trance or use instruments and such like. I hold my hands very still over the affected area during the depth of the standard healing and in my mind's eye go through the relevant surgical procedure that I would have done if I were performing conventional surgery. The only additional thing that I sometimes use is my favorite large double terminator clear quartz crystal, when I want to concentrate the energy to a fine point, like laser. However, I usually do not allow the point of the crystal to actually touch the individual. I have seen many lumps and bumps and even an ovarian cyst disappear after use of this technique. It is interesting that the technique does not seem to work on everyone. I do not know the reason why that should be.

One of Kai's clients was a woman, who we will call Rebecca, who had been diagnosed with a benign but fast-growing tumor on the nerve to one ear that was putting pressure on the brain stem. She also suffered from a severe bleeding disorder similar to hemophilia. Despite the blood disorder, her doctors had advised surgery. They warned her that without surgery, she risked severe disability when the tumor eventually invaded the brain stem. Possible complications included inability to eat or breathe unaided, painful paralysis of part of the face, mental confusion, progressive deafness, loss of balance, and total incontinence.

Reluctantly, she agreed to have a risky operation rather than face those consequences. However, the surgeon canceled the operation the day before it was scheduled because tests showed that Rebecca's blood disorder was worse than originally thought. She was now left with the prospect of a gruesome and inexorable deterioration.

When she came to see Kai, she was already suffering from a range of physical problems due to the tumor, including headaches, tinnitus, moderate deafness, dizziness and loss of balance, and muscular pains. These were complicated by the effects of rheumatic arthritis and severe anxiety and depression.

After a few months of treatment, most of her symptoms were improved and she was in a better emotional and mental state. Rebecca opted to have radiation treatment of the tumor, with disastrous results. Her neurological symptoms flared up and she was bedridden for two months. Rather than shrink, the tumor grew faster than ever—perhaps because the radiation suppressed her autoimmune system. While she was bedridden, Kai continued to send her absent healing.

Most of his patients report experiencing mental images during healing. Such images often yield information valuable to the healing process. Rebecca was different. She reported few images, thoughts, or past-life impressions. She did, however, report that she felt very relaxed and that her mind went into a state of total peace and serenity.

In early 1995, she experienced a significant image in her altered, dreamlike state of consciousness. Said Kai:

She had the image that her head and brain were split in the middle lengthwise and someone started scraping parts of her brain out. It was an extremely painful and unpleasant experience. The pain was apparently similar to what she had experienced after her radiotherapy (radiation). Following the healing, she told me that the experience was so unpleasant that she wanted to ask me to stop, but she felt she was paralyzed and she could not do it.

After this unsettling experience, Rebecca's symptoms improved rapidly. Her tumor actually increased in size, however. Rebecca continued to have healing sessions with Kai and to do her autogenics on her own. Her self-healing powers improved dramatically as did her emotional frame of mind. Despite her struggle for health and an array of domestic problems, she remained cheerful and optimistic.

By September 1995, her doctor decided she should have an operation, saying that the risk of bleeding could be better controlled now. Rebecca declined.

In December 1995, Kai felt guided to do an active thought surgery on Rebecca during one of his sessions. He didn't say what he had done but asked her afterward how she had felt. She replied that she couldn't say, because she'd been unconscious, just like when she'd been anesthetized for her operation.

During our conversation the following week, she told me that a couple of nights after the healing, she had had a very strange experience. She thought that although she was probably dreaming, it felt very real. In it, she found herself lying on an operating table with six "ghostly surgeons" dressed in white surrounding her. I walked in dressed in the white outfit that I normally wear during healing sessions and instructed the "surgeons" to carry out the surgery on her brain tumor. She then proceeded to describe perfectly what would have happened in that particular type of conventional surgery. The strangest thing was that when she woke up the next day, she found her scalp over the site where the tumor was, was very sore and painful, as if her scalp had been cut. She could not even bear to comb or wash the area and had to ask someone to check her scalp to ensure that it had not actually been cut while asleep.[4]

After this mysterious event, Rebecca improved even more dramatically. She knew her tumor was gone. Spontaneously, her affirmation changed from "My tumor is shrinking" to "My tumor is gone." By November 1996, almost three years after beginning treatment with Kai, nearly all of her symptoms had disappeared. She was left with a mild tinnitus. By June 1997, she no longer had any clinical signs of illness, which astonished her conventional doctor.

Not only was Rebecca rid of the tumor, she literally began a new life—at age 70. She told Kai she hadn't felt as well in years. She was enjoying painting, going out into the sun, and even country dancing in heeled shoes. It was a far cry from the woman who could barely limp around without getting dizzy and losing her balance, and who had to wear dark glasses whenever she ventured into the light.

Was Rebecca's recovery a result of conventional and alternative treatments, or was it a miracle? Did something pivotal occur during sleep?

There are three key events that seem to be related: one, the session in which Rebecca felt as though her head literally was split open; two, the active thought surgery session in which she felt anesthetized; and three, the surgery that took place in the dream.

In my own analysis, the first two events prepared for the third. Some people who have undergone energy healing report feeling a strong physical sensation, like the body being opened, or something being extracted from the body or energy field. Or, they experience the sudden reduction in a tumor. The physical sensations reflect something happening in the etheric body, which is a mirror of the physical body. The etheric body, the layer of our aura closest to the body, will reveal signs of illness that a clairvoyant can see but that have not yet manifested in the body itself.

The dream surgery was a real dream event, involving Kai's spirit guides, who assist him in this way, and himself in astral form. The final healing took place in a realm of spirit that can be better accessed during the sleep state. Had this dream happened hundred of years ago in a Greek incubation temple, Kai would have been seen as the healing god Aesculapius, appearing himself to direct the healing.

It's easy and perhaps tempting to explain away the dream as a dramatization that merely presented a healing that somehow had already taken place. That's how modern psychotherapy would approach this experience. But that explanation robs the dream and the entire experience of power and mystery.

Why did it take three years to happen? The answer, which may depend on numerous circumstances and variables, may never be known. Perhaps a certain amount of preparatory work had to be done—preparation that included the ability of Rebecca to be receptive to the healing. As Kai commented, alternative techniques do not work for everyone, or in the same way for different people.

Working with OBE Dreams

OBE dreams can be induced with techniques similar to those for lucid dreams. Try to remain conscious as your body falls asleep: "mind awake body asleep." Relax the body and allow yourself to begin to drift down. When in the twilight state of hypnagogic sleep, think about becoming lighter and lighter, until you rise up and move away. Monroe called this "lift-off" and said it is the easiest way to separate from the physical body. You may have a sensation of going out through the top of your head, or suddenly being in your subtle body.

Monroe also used a technique that he called "rotation" or "peel-off": while lying on your back and in the hypnagogic state, slowly turn over without using your arms or legs for assistance. When you have turned 180 degrees, think of floating up and away, as though backing up from the body.

Another technique is to raise sexual energy, but instead of releasing it physically, visualize raising the energy as a white dot or globe from the root chakra to the third-eye chakra. Then think of rising up and away from the body.

You may experience an electrical, roaring, buzzing, or vibrating sensation prior to going out-of-body, but not everyone does.

When OBE and lucid in the dreamscape, you can pass through solid objects and go wherever you think. Initially, Monroe recommended, stay close to the physical body in order to learn how to stay in control. Practice leaving and returning to the body.

Then try to visit a place or person where details of your experience can be corroborated later. For example, once I visited the home of my parents, located several hundred miles from me, and in walking through the kitchen, I saw a cake with yellow frosting sitting on the counter. My mother confirmed that earlier in the day she had baked and frosted the cake. The house was dark and they were asleep while I was briefly there. This was corroborated as well.

As you gain confidence about what you experience, corroboration may be less important to you than in exploring distant or exotic locales, either on earth or in another dimension. Like Monroe, you may eventually want to do some interdimensional travel. Set your intention before sleep with prayer, meditation, and affirmation: "In my dream travels tonight, I wish to visit . . ." Always ask to be guided and protected in your journeys. You may be spontaneously pulled to a location by someone else's need or thought, as Kai was summoned for healing. Monroe also found himself virtually magnetized by others.

Like lucid dreaming, OBE dreams seem to be easier for some people than others. Don't be discouraged if one does not happen after a period of experimentation. It's also important to use this gift for the highest purpose: for healing, for illumination, for personal growth.

c h a p t e r s i x

LUCID DREAMS

A LUCID DREAM OCCURS WHEN YOU KNOW YOU'RE DREAMING WHILE YOU'RE DREAMING. NEARLY EVERYONE HAS A LUCID DREAM OCCASIONALLY, AND SOME OF US DREAM LUCIDLY OFTEN. Degrees of lucidity vary. At the lowest level, you awake from a highly realistic dream and realize it was a dream, not waking reality. At the highest level, you are aware of the dream as it takes place, and you can influence its course and outcome. Lucidity can be elusive. Sometimes you lose lucidity or wake up as soon as you realize you are dreaming.

The unusual characteristics of the lucid dream may further our understanding of how dreams can provide us with a more direct experience of the divine. Some researchers believe that lucid dreams hold great potential as tools for creativity and healing. Lucidity itself is not a form of psi, but many dreams containing psi also are lucid. Also, many of the types of dreams we are considering in this book have lucid elements.

What's the allure of lucid dreams? In dream lucidity, one can do almost anything—one acquires "power," as author Carlos Castenada puts it. The freedom one experiences in a lucid dream is fun and exciting.

The initiation of awareness of dreaming can be triggered by various factors, such as the stress of a nightmare, incongruous elements, or a spontaneous recognition that the reality is different from waking reality. Generally, lucid dreams are characterized by brilliant light, intense emotions, heightened colors, images and other sensory experiences, flying or levitation, and a sense of liberation and exhilaration. Intense sexual feelings, including orgasms, occur in some lucid dreams. Some lucid dreams are mystical in nature, involving an apprehension of the divine and a sense of transcendence, bliss, and ecstasy.

Historical Perspective on Lucid Dreams

Lucid dreams have been recognized since ancient times. In the fourth century B.C.E., Aristotle mentioned the existence of lucid dreaming. The earliest extant written account of a lucid dream in Western history is contained in a letter written in 415 C.E. by Augustine, who described the lucid dream of a Carthaginian physician, Gennadius. The purpose of the dream seems to be to convince Gennadius of life after death.

As God would in no wise forsake a man so merciful in his disposition and conduct, there appeared to him in sleep a youth of remarkable appearance and commanding presence, who said to him: "Follow me." Following him, he came to a city where he began to hear on the right hand sounds of a melody so exquisitely sweet as to surpass anything he had ever heard. When he inquired what it was, his guide said: "It is the hymn of the blessed and the holy." What he reported himself to have seen on the left hand escapes my remembrance. He awoke; the dream vanished, and he thought of it as only a dream.

On a second night, however, the same youth appeared to Gennadius, and asked whether he recognized him, to which he replied that he knew him well, without the slightest uncertainty. Thereupon he asked Gennadius where he had become acquainted with him. There also his memory failed him not as to the proper reply: he narrated the whole vision, and the hymns of the saints which, under his guidance, he had been taken to hear, with all the readiness natural to recollection of some very recent experience. On this the youth inquired whether it was in sleep or when awake that he had seen what he had just narrated. Gennadius answered: "In sleep." The youth then said: "You remember it well; it is true that you saw these things in sleep, but I would have you know that even now you are seeing in sleep."

Hearing this, Gennadius was persuaded of its truth, and in his reply declared that he believed it. Then his teacher went on to say: "Where is your body now?" He answered: "In my bed." "Do you know," said the youth, "that the eyes in this body of yours are now bound and closed, and at rest, and that with these eyes you are seeing nothing?" He answered: "I know it." "What then," said the youth, "are the eyes with which you see me?" He, unable to discover what to answer to this, was silent. While he hesitated, the youth unfolded to him what he was endeavoring to teach him by these questions, and forthwith said: "As while you are asleep and lying on your bed these eyes of your body are now unemployed and doing nothing, and yet you have eyes with which you behold me, and enjoy this vision, so, after your death, while your bodily eyes shall be wholly inactive, there shall be in you a life by which you shall still live, and a faculty of perception by which you shall still perceive. Beware, therefore, after this of harboring doubts as to whether the life of man shall continue after death." This believer says that by this means all doubts as to this matter were removed from him. By whom was he taught this but by the merciful, providential care of God?[1]

Many of the incubated dreams in ancient healing temples, such as those described in chapter 15, are likely to have been lucid. Dreamers recorded vivid dreams of being healed or visited by the gods that seemed very real to them.

The cultivation of lucid dreams has not been part of Christian mysticism, though it is part of the Western esoteric tradition. Lucid dreaming is important in Islamic mysticism and in the complex dream traditions of Buddhism and Hinduism. Tibetan Buddhism has a sophisticated dream yoga, part of the Six Doctrines or Truths, in which the yogi learns lucid dreaming at will. Through this is learned the illusory nature of both waking and dreaming states. The Bardo, the forty-nine-day stage between death and rebirth, is described as an extended dream state. Dream yoga teaches how to die and be reborn without loss of memory. Tantric texts from India speak of controlling dreams.

Saint Thomas Aquinas recognized that some dreams are lucid, but he limited them to "sober men and those who are gifted with a strong imagination." Lucid dreams—as well as dreams in general—were not accorded much significance in the West, except to underscore Church doctrine.

More recently in the West, lucid dreams were studied in the nineteenth century, most notably by the Marquis d'Hervey de Saint-Denys, a professor of Chinese literature and language, who documented more than two decades of experiments in learning how to control his dreams. Lucid dreams were named such after the turn of the century during the early days of psychical research, by Frederik Willems van Eeden, a Dutch psychiatrist. Freud acknowledged lucid dreams but had little to say about them.

Lucid dreams often have been associated with out-of-body experiences (OBE), as noted in the previous chapter.

Scientific Research of Lucid Dreams

Research interest in lucid dreams was stimulated in the late 1960s, especially by the publication in 1968 of *Lucid Dreaming,* by Celia Green, an overview of the history of lucid dreams. At about this time, popular interest in dreams in general was rising dramatically, and scientific interest was waning. Despite some researchers who desired to probe the world of lucid dreams, the general scientific establishment was skeptical, believing lucid dreaming to be impossible, or, if possible, that it belonged in occultism.

The state of lucid dreaming was demonstrated in the laboratory in 1970s in independent studies conducted on both sides of the Atlantic. Lucid dreamers were able to give signals with special eye movements during REM stages of sleep, thus demonstrating that they were asleep and aware at the same time. Research has been conducted internationally. Among the major contributors are Keith Hearne, Ann Faraday, Patricia Garfield, Jayne Gackenbush, and Stephen LaBerge. LaBerge has spearheaded much of the research and interest in lucid dreaming and is founder of The Lucidity Institute in Palo Alto, California. As a result of studies done in the 1970s, some scientists changed their minds about the possibility of lucid dreaming.

Lucid dream studies have demonstrated that with practice—using concentration, autosuggestion, and other mnemonic techniques—some, but not all, individuals can cause themselves to dream lucidly or can exert greater control over their lucid dreams. Research shows that women who meditate may be more predisposed toward lucid dreaming than men who meditate, and that people who are easily hypnotized are more likely to dream lucidly. Not surprising, people who have had near-death experiences (NDEs)—which share many characteristics with lucid dreams—also tend to have more lucid dreams than other people.

Slightly more than half of the adult population has at least one lucid dream during life, and about 21 percent have more than one lucid dream a month.

Lucid dream advocates believe that the skill of lucid dreaming can be applied to creativity, problem solving, relationships, health, and the riddance of nightmares. LaBerge's subjects report that with practice, they can increase the number of lucid dreams they experience on a regular basis.

Physicist Fred Alan Wolf has suggested that lucid dreams—and maybe dreams in general—are visits to parallel universes: small holograms within the larger cosmic hologram. Wolf calls the ability to lucid dream "parallel universe awareness."

Characteristics of Lucid Dreams

Brilliant Sensory Input

Heightened colors, sounds, smells, and sense of touch are common in lucid dreams. Colors especially are florescent or electrical.

Says lucid dreamer Michael Moran:

Every now and then I will have a dream in which the colors are very vivid, the sounds are sharp and clear, and my senses are enhanced. In the dream there's a part of me that is lucid and says, "It's one of those *dreams; pay attention!" I shift in and out of being the observer and the participant. This type of dream is usually the precursor of a major shift coming in my life. I get a lot of detailed information. I'll remember the dream very clearly. The change usually happens soon after, within months or a year. Every time I have one of these dreams I am healed. I become a different person.*[2]

Sometimes the very atmosphere seems charged with energy or makes a roaring or thundering. The body might tingle and shake or feel as though electrical currents are running through it. This supercharged nature of the dream leaves a stronger and more lasting impression than nonlucid dreams. Oliver Fox experienced "atmospheric changes" in lucid dreams. He described them as the pressurized feeling that builds before an electrical storm.

Many lucid dreams feature brilliant lights or a general atmosphere of intensely bright background light.

Intense Emotions

Strong emotions of a positive nature occur in lucid dreams: joy, exhilaration, extreme pleasure, and ecstasy. Sexual arousal and intense orgasms can occur.

Mental Clarity

The lucid dreamer often feels mentally alert and sharp, able to see and understand things in new ways. Many lucid dreamers feel their lucid dreams enhance their creativity and problem-solving ability.

Out-of-Body Sounds and Sensations

Lucidity can be signaled by buzzing, rushing, roaring, or whining sounds, or a feeling of tremendous vibration in the body, as reported by Monroe and others. These sounds and sensations may accompany the exit of consciousness from the body. I have experienced both in lucid dreams, such as in the following two examples:

I am in a lucid dream. I am silver, and dressed in flowing silver clothing. I am dancing by myself in a circle. My attention is focused solely on my feet, which are clad in ballerina slippers. I gracefully float through the air, executing beautiful plisses. I notice that I can float higher and higher, and stay off the ground. It is though I am weightless, dancing on air. Suddenly I am in my body in bed. My body is vibrating at tremendous speed, and I feel I am going to leave it. I cry out in a high pitched "eeeeee" of anticipation. Apparently, I make the sound out loud—or a sound out loud—which awakens my husband, who awakens me.

I go back to sleep. The vibrating occurs again, only not as intensely as before. I feel I leave my body. There is a brilliant, blinding flash of light, and I am back in my body. The vibrating stops.

I was aware of my second body in the dream, which appeared as a silvery apparition. Both my OBE and lucidity were short, which happens to many dreamers. In the following dream, I am able to retain both longer:

I have a lucid dream about going out-of-body. In the dream, I am awakened by a roaring sound in my ears and a vibrating sensation. I feel myself go out of my body through the top of my head. I fly around to different places on the earth. I can only recall two. One is a lighthouse on a peninsula. It feels like England, though I have never been to any lighthouses in the U.K. I also go to someplace in Russia.

I return to the bedroom, going through the wall, and then go back into my body. I am not back in very long when the roaring/vibrating starts again and I go out through my head. I feel this time that I can stop it, but I don't want to. The dream ends.

I did not turn and look back on myself, but I knew I was out-of-body. I have had flying dreams of visiting Russia before. I believe I have a past-life connection to Russia. When I actually visited there in 1985, I felt a tremendous connection to the people and literally to the land. It was a body resonance, like I could feel the energy of the country in my bones. Perhaps this is why I visited it in dreams.[3]

In some OBEs, individuals report being able to look back upon their sleeping bodies. This has given rise to the view that seeing oneself is a necessary validation of being out-of-body. Such is not the case, however. Not everyone sees their own body, despite knowing they are out of it. I have yet to see my own form. The frequent out-of-body traveler Oliver Fox reported that he rarely saw his own body, though he often saw the sleeping body of his wife. Both Fox and Sylvan Muldoon concluded that out-of-body projections vary according to the individual.

This is an important point, underscoring the subjective nature of dreamscape experiences. We cannot construct hard-and-fast rules by which to evaluate and gauge our experiences. We can construct general observations based upon collective evidence.

False Awakenings

A false awakening is waking up in the dream only to discover—at some point—that you are still dreaming. Fox experienced numerous false awakenings in his lucid dreams. He learned that if he could recognize a false awakening, he could more easily project himself out-of-body. Recognition of a false awakening can lead to the realization of lucidity—from there we can start directing the dream.

Mind Awake Body Asleep

Mind awake body asleep can occur during any stage of sleep. Most lucid dreams begin as ordinary dreams that suddenly turn lucid. We can attempt to train ourselves to enter mind awake body asleep through concentration, visualization, and affirmations as we fall asleep, such as those given at the end of this chapter.

Sometimes mind awake body asleep occurs during false awakenings: You find yourself "awake" but stuck in a body that will not move. Fox had occurrences of this, in which he "awoke" to find himself curiously paralyzed or unwilling to move. This may actually relate to the physiology of dreams: When we dream in REM, we are in a state of increased heartbeat and temporary paralysis of all voluntary muscles save the eyes and breathing, perhaps to prevent the body from acting out the dream.

My husband Tom has experienced this peculiar state, especially during a period in which he was experimenting with techniques of Eckankar's soul travel and Monroe's dream journeys out of the body.

I had been mulling over the possibilities that dreams could offer you a cheap vacation. I was doing intense mental work finishing engineering school and found myself sleepy at unusual times of the day. This may have led to a heightened awareness.

In the first dream, I awaken from a night's sleep on my bed and cannot move. I think to myself, "God, this is hard to do. Why can't I move!" Getting frustrated, I employ every ounce of willpower I have and finally am able to force myself to my feet and stand beside my bed. I ask my [former] wife, who is in the bathroom, what she is doing. She replies that she is washing her face. I keep asking her again what she is doing and she keeps replying, "Now I'm brushing my teeth . . . now I'm looking in the mirror. . . ."

I then decide to move across the room to the dresser to get dressed. I find it very hard to move. With very great effort, I move over to the dresser and rest my hands on it and stare down at the dresser and the items on the top. I mull over to myself, "Why am I having such a hard time moving? This is weird!" Then it occurs to me that I don't remember waking . . . and before I can say the word up in my mind, I feel a force pulling me backward. My feet fly off the floor and I fall straight back onto the bed with a thump. I open my eyes . . . astonished that I am not standing beside the dresser. I immediately start talking and ask my wife if she remembers any of this, but she does not. She does not even remember talking to me while in the bathroom.

Tom's sudden realization that he was still dreaming ended the dream. Later, Tom was able to increase his control. One evening, he settled into an easy chair and closed his eyes to rest.

Suddenly I hear my [former] wife speaking to me: "I'm going to wake you up!" Immediately, I reply, "No, don't bother me now; I'll get up later." She says, "No I'm going to wake you up now!" Again I respond, "No . . . please, just a little while longer and then I'll get up." She says, "Okay, I' won't bother you now," and she leaves the room.

After this exchange, I relax and suddenly realize that I can't move my body. I am completely awake, yet I am strangely paralyzed. This situation is very uncomfortable, and I manage to calm myself down by thinking pleasant thoughts. I think of a friend and suddenly the friend is at the foot of the easy chair, sitting, and we are talking. The conversation is normal and pleasant. When we are finished, I find that the friend is no longer there. I think to myself, "That was weird, I wonder if anyone I want to talk to will just appear." I decide to try a test. I think to myself, "I wonder if I think of T." [a former brother-in-law] . . . Suddenly, T. walks in the front door of the house and says, "Hi! How's it going?" I say, "Wow, I just thought about you." We talk about school a while and then he leaves.

After this, I remember that this must be the state that Bob Monroe talked about in his book Journeys out of the Body. *I think to myself that maybe it's possible for me to have this kind of experience. However, I don't know what to do. I figure maybe my body will do what my mind wants, so I imagine that I want to float up. I experience an upward movement. I decide that I should try to open my eyes as soon as I can. When I finally get them open, I look at my left arm and see it lying on the easy chair, and another arm, brighter in color, in the position I feel I have floated to. This causes such a shock to me that my heart begins to beat quite fast. I fall back into the chair and immediately wake up and regain total movement control.*

Later, I asked my wife if she was trying to wake me up. She stared blankly at me and said, "Why do you want to know?" I said, "Because you said to me that you were going to wake me up, but then changed your mind, right?" She had me repeat the whole conversation and then told me that she did not say anything to me. She had paused while crossing the room, looked at me, and purposely thought *the same sentences that I heard. She decided not to wake me up. She was a little spooked that I seemed to hear what she was thinking. Evidently, in the mind awake, body asleep state, thoughts can be heard in much the same way as words spoken with the voice.*

In a third dream, Tom is able to do more in the dream state. While lucid dreaming, he uses a mantra chant from Eckankar, *Hu*, called the "love song of God," which expresses the all-that-is in much the same fashion as does *aum*. He also attempts to do one of Monroe's maneuvers of rolling over to facilitate an OBE:

[In the dream] it is about four in the morning and my [former] wife is asleep next to me. I am a lot calmer this time. It is very quiet, but I hear some people having a conversation. When I focus on where the talking is coming from, I can hear the conversation very clearly. There are two females out on my patio deck looking in through the sliding glass door of the bedroom. One says, "Does he know what he's doing?" The other says, "I don't know. I don't think so." When I hear this, I am both curious and somewhat flustered. I feel a little embarrassed that in reality, I don't know what I am doing, but I don't want anyone else to know that.

Eventually, they tire of waiting and watching and leave, and I don't hear them anymore. Alone, I think maybe if I chant a little I can achieve an altered state. I begin a chant of the word Hu. *The first time, I hear a slight echo and then sing* Hu *again. The next time, it echoes back even louder. After the third* Hu, *the echo that reverberates back sounds like the rumbling of thunder, which shakes me somewhat. I immediately stop the* Hu *chant and the sound dies out slowly.*

Still in the state, I try another experiment. I imagine that I want to do a backward roll and immediately feel myself rolling backward. However, again, I get so excited over the feeling of being in two places simultaneously that my heart begins to beat very rapidly, and again I am pulled back into my sleeping position and am very wide awake. I look over at the sliding door, but all is quiet. No visitors.

I am convinced after these experiences that this state of mind awake body asleep is a very powerful state of consciousness that is highly telepathic and may even offer a gateway to realms where other sentient beings live.[4]

Presence of Spiritual Beings

In many lucid dreams, we are in the presence of otherworldly guide and messenger figures, such as angels, religious personalities, or adepts.

One of the most unusual lucid dreamers documented is Saint John Bosco, renowned for his work with young boys at his residential oratory in Italy dedicated to his favorite saint, Francis de Sales.

Throughout his life in the nineteenth century, Bosco had frequent and lengthy lucid dreams, which he often told to others. More than 150 dreams were collected and recorded by his followers. Many of the dreams were prophetic and concerned his boys and the Salesian order. Other dreams were pedagogical and still others were parables. These dreams were in harmony with his religious training and beliefs and concerned the need to follow Catholic doctrine in order to attain salvation.

Bosco's lucid dreams were quite long and involved much specific detail. Unlike most ordinary dreams, they were logical and followed a complete story line from beginning to end. Bosco was usually accompanied by a guide figure, variously an angel, Saint Francis de Sales, Dominic Savio (a highly spiritual boy he knew), or a man he referred to as "the man with the cap." His sensory impressions were so strong that sometimes he would clap his hands or touch himself in the dream to try to ascertain whether he was dreaming or was awake. Sometimes physical phenomena followed him out of the dream and into waking consciousness.

Bosco derived a great deal of guidance from his lucid dreams. He was intensely devoted to his young charges, and his prophetic dreams seemed to have had the purpose of learning about certain boys' spiritual misconducts so that he could try to set them on the right course again. His dreams were uncannily accurate in revealing the secrets of others and also in matters concerning impending deaths.

Bosco would recount his dreams in lectures to his young audience. He would sometimes say that "it was a dream in which one can know what one does; can hear what is said, can ask and answer questions." He cautioned his boys not to speak of his dreams in the outside community, for others would consider them fables. "But we have always this as our norm that, when something turns out for the good of our souls, it certainly comes from God, not from Satan."[5]

Bosco's first lucid dream occurred when he was about nine years old. In it he learned of his spiritual mission in life, which he undertook with great seriousness and from which he never wavered.

When I was about nine years old, I had a dream that left a profound impression on me for the rest of my life. I dreamed that I was near my home, in a very large playing field where a crowd of children were having fun. Some were laughing, others were playing and not a few were cursing. I was so shocked at their language that I jumped into their midst, swinging wildly and shouting at them to stop. At that moment a Man appeared, nobly attired, with a manly and imposing bearing. He was clad with a white flowing mantle, and His face radiated such light that I could not look directly at Him. He called me by name and told me to place myself as leader of those boys, adding these words:

"You will have to win these friends of yours not with blows but with gentleness and kindness. So begin right now to show them that sin is ugly and virtue beautiful."

Confused and afraid, I replied that I was only a boy and unable to talk to these youngsters about religion. At that moment the fighting, shouting and cursing stopped, and the crowd of boys gathered around the Man who was talking. Almost unconsciously, I asked:

"But how can you order me to do something that looks so impossible?"

"What seems so impossible you must achieve by being obedient *and by* acquiring knowledge."

"But where? How?"

"I will give you a Teacher under whose guidance you will learn and without whose help all knowledge becomes foolishness."

"But who are you?"

"I am the Son of her whom your mother has taught you to greet three times a day."

"My mother told me not to talk to people I don't know, unless she gives me permission. So please, tell me your name."

"Ask My Mother."

At that moment I saw beside Him a Lady of majestic appearance, wearing a beautiful mantle, glowing as if bedecked with stars. She saw my confusion mount, so she beckoned me to her. Taking my hand with great kindness, she said:

"Look!"

I did so. All the children had vanished. In their place I saw many animals: there were goats, dogs, cats, bears and a variety of others.

"This is your field; this is where you must work," the Lady told me. "Make yourself humble, steadfast and strong. And what you will see happen to these animals you will have to do for my children."

I looked again; the wild animals had turned into as many lambs—gentle, gamboling lambs—bleating a welcome for that Man and Lady.

At this point of my dream, I started to cry, and I begged the Lady to explain what it all meant, because I was so utterly confused. She then placed her hand on my head and said:

"In due time everything will be clear to you."

After she had spoken these words, some noise awakened me; everything had vanished. I was completely bewildered. Somehow my hands still ached and my cheeks still stung because of all the fighting. Moreover, my conversation with that Man and Lady so disturbed my mind that I was unable to sleep any longer that night.[6]

Bosco shared his dream with his family the next morning. His brothers laughed, and one predicted that it meant that Bosco literally would become a shepherd of animals. Another said he might become the leader of a gang of robbers. His mother said, "Who knows? Maybe you will become a priest." And his grandmother said, "You mustn't pay attention to dreams!"

Bosco's lucid/OBE dream to heaven is recounted in chapter 24.

Transcendence and Divine Light

Some lucid dreams—those called high lucid dreams or ecstatic lucid dreams—involve a sense of transcendence, mystical oneness, and apprehension of the supernatural, brilliant light associated with the divine. These experiences bear a striking resemblance to religious mystical experiences and to near-death experiences (NDEs), in which people find themselves out-of-body, traveling toward a brilliant white light that seems to be the essence of love. I agree with other researchers who see this type of lucid dream as relating to the course of our spiritual evolution.

Oliver Fox, dreaming in the early twentieth century, saw this light as a symbol of the evolution of humankind. More recent researchers such as G. Scott Sparrow see lucid dreams as a means of evolving one's own Inner Light. The light in the dreams represents the divine, says Sparrow, and the purpose of the lucid dream is to help us merge with the divine light. Sparrow compares the lucid dream light to the clear light of Tibetan Buddhism, a state of illumined, pure consciousness beyond image and the material, in which one attains nirvana. Tibetan dream yoga teaches the dreamer to meditate while in a lucid dream. In this manner, the dreamer learns the illusory nature of both waking and sleeping worlds and learns how to eliminate dream imagery or attain dreamless sleep. In Tibetan mysticism, the after-death state, or Bardo, is filled with illusory images arising from the life just lived. If the individual can overcome the illusions, then the chain of karma is broken and the soul goes into the clear light instead of into another incarnation.

Other scenarios of stages of light and consciousness have been developed by other lucid dreamers. In all of them, the brilliant light relates to the dying of the ego and merger with the One, which is why lucid dreams share common ground with NDEs.

All of my lucid dreams contain this brilliant light, usually not emanating from a particular source but permeating the very atmosphere of the dream. I believe that lucid dreams are an essential part of our spiritual development, enabling us to have experiences that would be difficult or impossible for us in waking consciousness. For example, even if we meditate regularly over a long period of time, we still may not attain the transcendence that a lucid dream can give us. The more we have these experiences, the more they happen, and the more they contribute to our spiritual growth.

Sparrow has observed that his own lucid dreaming is responsive to waking experiences of love and deep rapport with another person. The giving and receiving of love and the ability to love unconditionally are paramount to the spiritual path. Lucid dreaming that accompanies love can only expand and deepen us further.

Lucid dreaming plays an important role as an experience of spiritual initiation. As more people learn to lucid dream, this will in turn affect the collective human consciousness, stimulating an increase in spontaneous lucid dreaming.

Interconnected Experiences

Lucid dreams, OBEs, and NDEs also share common ground with the UFO/extraterrestrial experience, another exceptional human experience prevalent in modern times. Many UFO contacts take place in the dream state, and they may be forms of OBE/lucid dreams. Extraterrestrials often arrive in brilliant, blinding light and abduct humans by levitating them, sometimes in shafts of bright light. Medical examinations reported by contactees take place on a spaceship (perhaps related to the astral plane in other dreams) under bright lights. Communication is often by telepathy. These experiences, which seem profound and real to the experiencer, may all be aspects of an underlying reality, a dimension of consciousness shared by all humans and to which we are collectively awakening.

What to Do in Lucid Dreams

As mentioned earlier, sometimes the realization that we are lucid in a dream causes the lucidity to end abruptly. The goal of lucid dreamers is to retain lucidity as long as possible and to direct the action of the dream. Here are ways to enhance lucid dreaming:

Focus to retain lucidity. Focus on an object, such as the ground. Castenada recommends focusing on the hands. Other lucid dreamers have found success with turning their attention away from the visual and concentrating on the feel of objects or on the vividness of sound. LaBerge finds the technique of spinning around like a top in a dream helpful. As you spin, say, "The next object I encounter will be in the dream," and then stop spinning.

Oliver Fox found that if he allowed his emotions to rise too much in a lucid dream, the dream would end abruptly. He would concentrate on staying detached, to be more of an impersonal observer than a participant. LaBerge agrees, noting, "The moment we take a bit too much interest in some facet of the dream, lucidity vanishes. If you are a novice lucid dreamer and have problems maintaining your lucidity, a temporary solution is for you to *talk to yourself* in your lucid dream."[7] Tell yourself, "This is a dream" or "I am dreaming" repeatedly.

LaBerge recommends that if you awaken prematurely from a lucid dream, remain motionless and relaxed, which will enhance your ability to reenter REM sleep.

In the following lucid dream, I use touch to verify that I am dreaming, and then experiment with doing supernormal things such as flying:

A lucid dream. Tom [my husband] and I are in a large office building that is brightly lit. We seem to have just finished giving a workshop together, and Tom is collecting our money at the desk. I wander around the room, which is large and filled with metal office desks. Suddenly I realize I am lucid. This realization causes the focus of the dream to change. Not that it has been out of focus, but things just look different. Also, I am totally alone; Tom no longer seems to be in the dream. The atmosphere in the room seems different, almost as though I am underwater.

I am able to hang onto the lucidity. To prove it to myself, I walk over to a desk and rifle through a stack of papers. I can feel the papers and the metal desk. I say out loud to myself, "I'm lucid, I'm lucid! What do I want to do most?" Immediately, I think, "I want to fly." No sooner than the thought is made than I become weightless and float up to the ceiling, until I can touch it with my hands. "That's not what I meant," I think. "I want to fly out-of-body." *I go back down to the floor, and then suddenly I am rushing up toward the ceiling without being cognizant of a body, and going through it. The dream ends.*[8]

Unlike other lucid dreams I have had, there was no roaring in my ears or vibrational sensation. Flying and levitating are excellent ways to test whether or not you are dreaming. Flying is common in lucid dreams, but not all flying dreams are lucid. According to research, lucidity usually precedes the flying.

Work with the imagery that is present. Upon realizing lucidity, it's hard to resist indulging desires to go someplace or do something radically different than the dream setting. The shift may cause you to lose lucidity. It's much better to work with the dream imagery that is present and see what it holds in store for you. With practice, you may be able to shift without losing lucidity.

Pray or meditate in the dream. This may bring you closer to the brilliant, divine light and will keep the dream centered on mystical illumination.

Convince other characters in your dream that they are dreaming as well. This may lead to some interesting conversations!

Heal fears and phobias. Lucidity offers control by changing dream elements—or avoidance by rising into the air and flying away. Rather than escape, says Sparrow, we should "regard lucidity as an opportunity to *cooperate* with or *forgive* the dream elements rather than an opportunity to exercise control over them."[9]

Heal injury and illness. Lucidity can open powerful healing energies within us. Examples of healing in lucid dreams are given in chapter 15.

Can we do whatever we want in a lucid dream? It may seem so, when the mere thought of flying can cause you to rise up into the air and go wherever your thought leads you. The idea of having lucid dream sex with anyone you choose or having revenge against an enemy may be enticing. However, researchers have shown that there are limits to what we can do in lucid dreams, and those limits vary according to the individual. The conscious mind will not do what the unconscious mind resists. Hypnotists know this, too: a person cannot be made to do anything against his unconscious will. The unconscious will not step over the line of its perceptions of proper conduct. And the other souls in our lucid dreamscape may not share our interests.

Robert Monroe reported that when he would feel a sexual urge in an out-of-body trip and then go looking for a partner, he was often rebuffed; the women he encountered were not always interested. In *Conscious Dreaming,* author Robert Moss reports a similar case in which a male lucid dreamer looks for a sex partner and finds two sexually experienced women. He tells them that this is his dream and he can do anything he wants, but when he tries to embrace them, they push him away. He insists again that this is his dream, and he can make them love him. The women do not believe him. He becomes embarrassed and apologetic—as he would have done in waking life—and leaves the dream.

There are ethical considerations as well. It is advisable, for your own health and well-being, not to do anything in the dreamworld that would not be proper in the waking world. The dreamworld has its own reality, and actions in it have consequences. At the very least, we run the risk of acting against ourselves. On one level, everything in a dream is a piece of oneself.

Thus, researchers also advise against the easy luxury of making monsters, demons, and unpleasant people simply go away in lucid dreams. In ordinary dreamwork, these symbolic figures would be invited to explain their purpose in a dream so that their sources could be identified and healed. A similar approach should be taken in lucid dreams. Rather than conduct the dialogue later, you can have it right in the dream itself. Chapter 9 gives techniques for working with dreams.

Inducing Lucid Dreams

Most of us experience lucid dreams spontaneously. Some people seem to lucid dream more readily and frequently than others. Like dream incubation for guidance, lucid dreams can be induced through a variety of techniques. As mentioned above, hypnotic suggestion has proven effective. But if you don't know a qualified hypnotist to help you out, there are other ways. The following methods are widely used and have been proven to be effective for many dreamers. They can be used in any combination. Through experimentation, find what works the best for you. Results can vary significantly by individual. Some people learn to lucid dream quite easily; others have to devote more effort to it to get results. If you try some of the following techniques and feel you haven't accomplished much, don't give up.

Learning to meditate and doing it regularly also enhances the ability to lucid dream. Meditation with the intent to lucid dream works for some people. Others, such as Sparrow, get more results from meditating for general spiritual growth and understanding.

Set an Intention

Pledge to yourself that you will become aware of your dreams while in them. In the beginning, simply recognizing and holding onto lucidity will take some practice. Tell yourself, "Next time I'm dreaming, I will become aware that I'm dreaming."

As you become more adept, formulate a goal, such as taking a certain action or visiting a distant place. Write your intentions down.

Tell yourself throughout the day and before bedtime that you will be aware of your dreams while you are dreaming. The idea is to prime the consciousness to perform in a desired manner.

Affirmation

Use your intentions as affirmations prior to retiring. Speak them and write them. Repeat to yourself as you fall asleep, "I'm dreaming, I'm dreaming . . ."

Breathwork

As you relax to enter sleep, focus on your breath, drawing it deeply and slowly into your body. See it filling your body with radiance.

Visualization

A practice borrowed from Tibetan dream yoga is to visualize a light at various chakra points. Especially important is the throat chakra, which is located at the base of the throat. This chakra governs our creativity and "voice," which our dreams express. Concentrating on the color of the gods at this energy center can affect dreaming. Visualize a radiant blue light or lotus flower, or a blue lotus flower with a flame in the center, expanding into the throat chakra. Upon awakening, visualize a white light between the brows, which is the third eye chakra, the seat of clear understanding, clairvoyance, and spiritual vision.

Visualization can be combined with a mantra or affirmation.

Use a Cue Symbol

Decide on a symbol that will help awaken you to lucidity whenever you see it in a dream. For example, say to yourself, "Whenever I see a dove, then I know I am dreaming." The symbol should be something that will stand out to your attention.

Dream Devices

Can high tech divices help us to dream lucidly? Available on the market are devices such as masks that flash red lights during REM stages. The red lights are intended to signal the dreamer that he or she is dreaming without waking the person. Like all induction techniques, devices work for some people and not for others. You must experiment for yourself.

A final word: Believe in yourself and your dream experiences. LaBerge observes that lucid dreaming is easier than you might think, but if you think you can't, then it won't happen. Above all, don't allow others to tell you what is or isn't possible, as Juliette B. learned.

Juliette has used a mantra as she falls asleep at night to encourage lucid dreaming. She recognized her first lucid dream at age eleven. She had no idea that there was a such thing as a lucid dream and simply considered it "being conscious" in dreams. She did not think it special, as she hadn't yet discovered that lucid dreaming is not the norm for most people.

The reason I recognized being conscious was because I was doing something in the dream that triggered my "common sense" mechanism. I was running from something, and I was running from it by running around and around a small, square building. Suddenly I realized that (a) it was ridiculous to run in circles like that, and (b) I just didn't run. (In grade school, I was the kid who was always picked last for sports teams.) Luckily, I didn't recognize the magnitude of being able to use reason in my dream, so I didn't wake up immediately, like a lot of people do when they realize they're dreaming. In fact, I didn't think it out of the ordinary at all, but I was pretty impressed with the idea, so every night, before I would go to sleep, I would repeat over and over—out loud—to be conscious in my dreams.[10]

Juliette was so intrigued by her lucid dreams that in school she devoted a science fair project to the subject. Unfortunately, the negativity of a ***sleep clinic researcher*** temporarily killed her ability to dream lucidly.

I went to a sleep clinic in a nearby hospital to interview some of their staff. I asked one of them about "conscious dreaming," and he said that there was no such thing. I even explained it to him, and he continued to tell me it didn't exist. That was the last time I ever had a lucid dream—until recently.

Juliette's experience serves as an example of how much we are affected by the approval and disapproval of others around us, especially those we perceive as being authorities. The sleep clinic researcher should have known better. This experience happened in the 1990s, well after laboratory research has demonstrated the ability of the mind to be aware and sleeping at the same time. Blind skepticism still exists, however. Fortunately, Juliette was able to resume her lucid dreaming.

We all benefit from the insights, wisdom, experiences, and observations passed down to us through the centuries. But only you can attest to your own dreaming Truth.

chapter seven

SHARING THE DREAMSCAPE WITH OTHERS

MOST OF US THINK OF OUR DREAMS AS PERSONAL AND PRIVATE, SOMETHING THAT OCCUR ONLY TO US IN THE DEPTHS OF SLEEP. DREAMS, HOWEVER, ARE NOT ALL THAT PROPRIETARY. Evidence has existed since ancient times that our dreams overlap. Two or more people can share the same dream. It is also possible to enter someone else's dreamscape by sending them a dream. Sharing dreams and sending dreams have been part of our social dreamwork since dreams have first been recorded.

Shared Dreams

One of the earliest examples of a shared dream was documented in the ninth century B.C.E., when King Assurbanipal of Assyria reluctantly prepared to battle an invading army of Elamites. The goddess Ishtar came in a dream to one of the king's priests and promised him victory, commanding him to eat, drink, and be merry and exalt her divinity. Another account of this story says that Ishtar also appeared in a dream shared by members of Assurbanipal's army and assured them, en masse, of victory.

The Kabbalah records cases of dreams shared by groups of people. The *Sefer Hasidim* tells this story.

It happened that a saintly sage was buried next to one who was unworthy. The saint came to all the townspeople in a dream and said, "You did me evil in that you buried me next to a toilet that has a stench. The fumes are hard on me." They placed stones between the grave of the saint and the grave of the evil-doer as a divider; from that time on he [the saint] did not come to them in a dream.[1]

We still share dreams in modern times. Studies show that about one-third of our dreams are shared in some way. The figure may be even higher; unless you tell your dreams to others, there is no way of knowing if others had similar or the same dreams.

Shared dreams, also called mutual dreams, are more likely to happen between individuals who are emotionally linked and in close physical proximity, such as spouses and romantic partners, family members, and close friends. They can occur between strangers, though this is less likely. In the examples given above, the groups had a collective psychic link among members: an army with a collective purpose of winning, and a village with a cohesive family sense.

Shared dreams happen in various degrees:

Mutual recognition. Two or more dreamers see and recognize each other in their dreams, even though the dream action may not be similar.

Mutual dream elements. Objects, settings, actions, dialogue, and other details are the same or similar in shared dreams.

Shared plot, different characters. The dreams are similar in plot and action but do not necessarily include the other dreamers.

Lucid and out-of-body experience. Dreamers experience each other in lucid circumstances or initiate OBEs together in dreams.

Precognition. Dreamers see the same future event.

Shared OBE Dreams

Like lucid and OBE dreams, most shared dreaming happens spontaneously. In the following case, a young woman named Donna (a pseudonym) had spontaneous OBE dreams. Severe emotional trauma and physical illness then brought a sudden psychic opening. Donna began sharing dreams with a neighbor, Anne (a pseudonym), in which they traveled out-of-body together to perform healing work for others.

My experiences with astral traveling (I prefer to call it this rather than just dreaming) started a long time before my spiritual awareness opened, with the spirit of a woman who was brutally murdered. She came to me while I was sleeping and asked for my help. I realized I had left my body and saw myself lying on the bed. This did not frighten me in any way.

Instantaneously, we were in her house where she had been murdered (she needed to show me what had happened). All I felt was the brutality of how she was murdered and all her pain. This I couldn't cope with, or even begin to understand how to deal with, so I just ran and left. I woke to find myself screaming and crying.

The spirit of the murdered woman evidently was stuck on the earth plane and unable to move on. Trapped spirits account for some hauntings. Some mediums specialize in releasement and find spirits naturally coming to them for help. As Donna became more comfortable with her psychic abilities, this avenue of spiritual work developed.

First, however, Donna faced a terrifying ordeal. She had this vivid dream, shared by her friend Anne.

I was lying on what I think now was an altar. It was marble and was covered with a white sheet. Candles were being lit around me, and somebody who I now know to be E. (I did not know him then) was standing close to me. [Note: E. is a releasement medium and healer.] The heat from the candles was intense. Then I saw a wedding cake which also had candles on it.

After this I awoke in tears. Anne came early next morning and asked with some urgency if I was all right, and then told me about her dream. It turned out to be exactly the same as mine. She could feel the heat from the candles exactly as I had. We both took this to mean that through troubled times ahead I would be protected.

The spontaneous, shared dream was lucid for both of them (strong tactile sensations, feeling the heat). Although Anne recognized Donna in the dream, Donna did not see Anne in hers. The dream was precognitive, warning of coming troubles and forecasting the meeting of E., who later became Donna's spiritual teacher.

But Donna ignored the dream's warning. For one thing, she didn't understand the dream enough. She was instead preoccupied with a troubled and deteriorating marriage with an abusive man.

One Sunday night, eighteen months later, a turning point came in the form of a traumatic event.

At dinner with friends, Donna's husband, Jack [a pseudonym] drank heavily. He became aggressive and verbally and physically abusive. His behavior worsened after the friends departed, leaving Donna alone with him, save for their young daughter, who was awake, and a son, who was upstairs asleep. Jack threatened to kill Donna, and beat her for at least an hour. Donna succeeded in breaking away to get her daughter upstairs. She tried to calm Jack down. He pushed her down the stairs. When the telephone rang, he yanked the cord out of the wall. Jack continued his assaults on Donna, three times trying to strangle her. She was afraid of dying during the first two attempts, but on the third felt a strange release of her fear. She fell unconscious and suddenly found herself in a brilliant white light—what she later believed was a full-blown near-death experience.

Vaguely, Donna heard people talking but could see no one. She kept hearing a voice tell her, "I want you to say, 'I love you.'" Suddenly, the strangling stopped, and Donna slowly regained consciousness. Later, she learned that Jack had stopped strangling her because she had blurted out, "I love you." Interestingly, Donna's vocal chords were so damaged that for weeks afterward, she had no voice. She was mystified where the voice came from that spoke the words that saved her life.

Donna knew that she had to make changes. "I was given a new life as long as I willingly gave up my old life," she said. "I did, and the old life went."

Donna divorced Jack. Once free of the abuse, she underwent a tremendous spiritual awakening in which she developed mediumistic and healing skills under the tutelage of E. A change in her dream life happened as well. She began traveling out-of-body frequently at night, often accompanied by Anne.

One such dream episode arose over a case of a haunted house. E. and Donna were called to investigate.

One day E. and I went to a house which the [wife] owner thought was haunted by a dark entity. The family consisted of the wife, her husband, and two children. On entering the house, we found it dark and dismal in both atmosphere and decor. The house held a lot of antique pieces that had been brought in by the husband. We had to decide where the dark entity was coming from. We suspected it had to do with the husband, who was buying ritual objects and bringing them into the house. Before we left, we did some healing with the children. On leaving the house, we only found a couple of energy imprints and were still puzzled about the source of the dark entity. We wished we could have met the husband, but he was not available on this occasion.

I knew I had to go back, but I did not realize that I would be returning in my sleep state. In my dream, I remembered going to Anne to ask for her help. I knew she could see auras and that would be a big help.

We went to the house together and looked into it from the garden. Anne said it was the house that was dark in energy and not the family. In other words, the problem had to do with the things the husband was bringing into the house.

In spite of our task, I couldn't help but notice that Anne was wearing a nightdress that I did not think looked very good on her. I couldn't resist saying, "What are you wearing that silly nightdress for?" She said, "What have you brought me to this horrible dark place for?" At this point, I was pulled back to my house, as one of my children had woken up.

On regaining sleep, I went back for Anne. I had left her at that house, and I knew she would not find her way back home. When I rejoined her, she told me the family's auras were okay. Then we came home.

The next morning, Anne couldn't wait to see me. She said, "Where the hell did you take me last night, and why did you leave me there? By the way, it's a new nightshirt!" She told me everything that had happened in the dream, and it was the same as mine. We had shared the same dream.

A couple of days later, the lady of the house rang me to say how much better the house had been since E. and I had made our visit, and how well the children had slept. By having shared the dream with Anne, it enabled me to answer questions that I couldn't have answered before. We convinced the husband to get rid of some of the objects we thought were causing the problem.

Donna continued:

As I learned more about my spiritual awareness, I found I was leaving my body more and more. I am now not as scared, as the experiences have not been as horrific as the first, and I have learned to trust in my spiritual guides.

I don't always know where I have been, but I do know that I have been somewhere. *For instance, I woke up one morning knowing I had been somewhere. Anne came and asked where I had taken her. She said she was in a lot of pain and dreamed that she called me. She said I came straightaway and told her to go to sleep and everything would be fine. She told me*

I had taken her somewhere dark and that there were nuns present. The place was very therapeutic. After the healing, I had brought her home and her pain had gone.

My experiences of having shared dreams are increasing but only with the same person, Anne. I am not fully aware of the reasons for shared dreams, but I do know in every case in my shared dreams I have found an answer to questions I needed answered.

With all my experiences of shared dreams and astral traveling, as I call it, I have since been able to help release the trapped spirit of the murdered lady. I have released other trapped spirits of the dead as well.

I know that when we help others with healing and releasing trapped spirits, we need our spiritual team to help us just as we need our team on this side to help us. This is the reason I believe we have shared dreams.[2]

Implications of Shared Dreaming

As Donna's experiences indicate, we are able to perform tasks in OBE shared dreams that we otherwise might not be able to accomplish.

Shared dreaming is still an underexplored part of the dreamscape. It has been documented in the laboratory as a spontaneous experience (not part of the experiments). Dreamwork groups have focused on shared dreaming and even mounted international shared dream projects. Results of efforts such as these are documented in *Mutual Dreaming,* by Linda Lane Magallón, an experienced group dreamworker.

What does shared dreaming tell us about consciousness? Magallón says that "mutual dreaming opens the door to more intimate connections with the ones we love. It can also encourage the emergence in dreaming partners of advanced dreaming skills like telepathy, lucidity and astral travel."[3]

Beyond such personal benefits, shared dreams point to the collective evolution of human consciousness. We are powerfully linked to each other through both waking and dreaming states of consciousness. What we think and what we dream can influence the course of human events by changing mass consciousness.

For example, in 1982, Bill Stimson, then editor of the *Dream Network Bulletin,* proposed an experiment in global dreaming. On the winter solstice, nine groups in the United States and Europe met to discuss dreams they had been incubating on the topic of a world dream. Each group selected one representative dream to share with the other groups.

The similarity of images in the networking process was impressive. Themes included a recognition of the importance of the era in which they lived, a realization of the choices they faced, and great hope for the future. There were three mentions of animal and intercultural themes; four references to water, five to transformations or new beginnings, and five to flight or upward movement.[4]

A similar view has been put forth by the Maharishi Mahesh Yogi, the chief proponent of Transcendental Meditation (TM), in which a person achieves transcendental consciousness by meditating upon a mantra. According to the Maharishi, if a minimum of the square root of 1 percent of the world's population collectively did TM, the coherence of their brainwaves would result in a drop of crime, illness, accidents, and aggression. The Maharishi International University attempted to test this hypothesis in 1983 and 1984 by assembling 7,000 persons to meditate. Significant results were claimed, although critics countered that results were selective to support the hypothesis. Thus, group dreaming toward a common theme, such as peace, also can establish a coherence of brainwaves that in turn could affect the physical environment—perhaps by subtly altering the actions taken by individuals.

Psychologist Arnold Mindell has observed that as patterns of a person's life are reflected in their dreams, the same happens on a larger, global scale. Global myths, patterns, and ideologies create our planetary circumstances; thus there are planetary dreams that organize the behavior of large groups of people, such as nations and races. We as individuals can work to change the larger patterns by changing first our own consciousness.

Shared dreaming further maps the reaches of the dreamscape.

How to Share Dreams with Others

While most shared dreams happen spontaneously, it is possible to have them at will. This skill is part of ancient Eastern dream yoga techniques, but Westerners can learn it just as well.

Select dream partners with whom you feel completely comfortable. It's important to establish a zone of trust, empathy, and support. It is possible to share dreams with others long distance, but proximity enhances results.

Do the appropriate inner work to release any personal fears and reservations about shared dreaming. Because we consider our dreams to be extremely private, it's normal to fear a loss of personal control, loss of uniqueness, or invasion of privacy. Be honest with yourself. Unresolved fears will only block your ability to experience shared dreaming. Consider it a bold new opportunity to expand your consciousness.

Shared dreams can be incubated; follow the procedures outlined in chapter 10. Your intentions might be one of the following:

- To meet someone in a dream
- To meet someone in a dream and have mutual recognition
- To dream about a solution to a problem or a choice or decision that must be made
- To share the same dream experience
- To create a shared vision, such as a dream for world peace

Participate in regular dreamwork and dream sharing with your partner(s) to build a psychic field together.

Don't give up if results are not immediate or if they seem insignificant. Shared dreams, like lucid dreams and incubated dreams, improve with practice.

Sending Dreams to Others

In chapter 4, we saw how dreams are a fertile medium for telepathy—the transmission of mental impressions from one person to a recipient who is asleep. What are the possibilities of sending dreams to others so that we can influence their thinking and behavior?

Dream-sending has been practiced since ancient times on the belief that influence is possible. Spiritual masters learn how to enter the dreamscapes of pupils for the purpose of instruction in the dream state.

Ancient Egyptian priests or magicians performed rituals to cause other persons to have a specific dream. Sent dreams figure in the legend of the divine origin of Alexander the Great. According to lore, Nectanebo, the last native king of Egypt, used dream magic to cause the Greek queen Olympias to dream that the Egyptian god Amun would make love to her and she would bear a god. Nectanebo accomplished this through sympathetic magic, by pouring the extracted juices of various desert plants over a wax effigy of the queen and reciting a spell.

Nectanebo then turned his attention to Philip of Macedon. He said a spell over a hawk, which flew to the sleeping Philip and told him to dream that Olympias was going to bear a child who was the son of a god.

The magic was successful, and when Alexander was born, his divine origin was unquestioned.

Egyptian magicians also summoned the dead to appear in the dreams of others. The dead were considered to have great power and thus could enforce a spell or curse. A magician might send the spirit of a dead person to haunt the dreams of an enemy.

In his classic experiments with telepathy and telepathic suggestion, researcher Harold Sherman found he obtained the best results with both sending and receiving impressions when in a relaxed state bordering on the hypnagogic stage. Sherman also discovered that he could use the same exercises to harness the tremendous creative power of the subconscious mind. He would visualize what he desired to achieve, such as meeting someone he needed to see. The subconscious mind would attract the elements needed to materialize the goal. He experimented doing these visualizations when he was certain that others would be asleep and therefore more likely to be receptive to his telepathic images.

However, Sherman cautioned that such techniques would not work if forced.

You cannot "force" anything to happen mentally. When you attempt to force your mental pictures to come true, it is a sign that you are overanxious and afraid that what you desire is not going to come to pass.[5]

Sherman discovered what other dream researchers have also found—that we cannot impose our wills upon others in the dreamscape any more than we can force others to do our bidding in waking consciousness. As Monroe observed in his OBE travels, and as lucid dreamers have discovered, others must first be receptive and willing. You cannot force someone to love you or compel someone to do something for you by attempting to manipulate their dreams.

Dreams are ideally suited for the transmission of healing and love—love that is reciprocal, and love that is for all of humanity.

PART III

High Dreamwork

c h a p t e r e i g h t

THE LANGUAGE OF SYMBOLS

DREAMS SPEAK THEIR OWN SPECIAL LANGUAGE THAT IS AT ONCE BOTH INTRIGUING AND CONFOUNDING. THE DREAMSCAPE IS A LAND OF MYSTERY. THE MYSTERY THAT CAN BE SOLVED DELIGHTS us, but the mystery that resists solution vexes us.

Dreams are fashioned from material of the unconscious. Jung viewed the unconscious as mental contents that are not accessible to the ego and that define a psychic place with its own characters, laws, and functions. Dreams open the realms of both the personal unconscious and collective unconscious to our exploration and understanding.

The Mystery of Symbols

Symbols are potent containers of wisdom, revelation, and insight, delivering to us understanding that goes beyond mere words. Symbols speak to us daily through synchronicities and events. They are revealed to us nightly in the fertile fields of dreams. Understanding the symbols that weave in and out of our lives helps us to better understand ourselves and our interconnectedness to everything.

A symbol is an object or visual image that expresses a concept or idea beyond the object or image itself. It translates the human situation into cosmological terms by both concealing and revealing with an element of mystery. Symbols are the language of the unconscious, especially the collective unconscious, where reside the accumulated archetypal images of humankind. Jung, who devoted a great deal of his life to studying symbols, said that objects and forms that are transformed into symbols become endowed with a great psychological and redeeming power. This especially pertains to the realm of dreaming, where our symbolic images help us to heal and to grow.

The beginnings of symbols date to late Paleolithic times, when nomadic hunter/gatherer societies expressed their magico-supernatural beliefs in rock carvings and paintings. As civilization developed, symbols became integral to all esoteric teachings, containing secret wisdom accessible only to the initiated. In all mystical, magical, and religious traditions, symbols play an important role in the alteration and transformation of consciousness.

Anything can become a symbol: natural and man-made objects, numbers, the elements, animals, the earth, the sky, the heavenly objects, deities, myths, folktales, and even words. The human being is one of the most ancient and profound of symbols: in the Hermetic tradition, it is a divine reflection of the macrocosm. The circle is a universal symbol of great power, representing the sun, illumination, wholeness, the wheel of life-death-rebirth, the Word of God, Truth, and the philosopher's stone of alchemy. In the East, the circle often is expressed in the lotus shape and in mandalas. In Jungian thought, the circle represents the self, the totality of the psyche.

Symbols express our inner reality. They contain far more than can be expressed by an equivalence of words, which makes them very powerful in their effect on us. Symbols change in our dreams as our consciousness changes.

When Symbols Are Archetypes

Many symbols are archetypal and thus carry a larger-than-personal-life meaning. For example, the tree plays a prominent role in mythologies as the anchor of growth, fruition, life, wisdom, and knowledge. The Tree of Life forms the blueprint for Kabbalistic mysticism. The Tree of Knowledge stands in the Garden of Eden. The World Tree is the *axis mundi* connecting the three cosmic spheres of spirit (branches), earth (trunk), and underworld (roots). Jung considered the tree as an archetypal symbol of the self and its process of individuation, as represented by growth and branching out. On a personal level, a tree represents our life, especially family life. Branches spreading into the sky represent growth, seeking, and higher understanding, while roots can symbolize things buried or unrecognized potentialities.

Not long after I became self-employed as an author, I found myself in the enviable position of having almost more work than I could handle. What's more, my natural curiosity about many things led me to a wide range of subjects. Before I realized it, I was spreading myself rather thin, working on a diverse array of projects. I had this dream.

A huge, beautiful tree grows on my property, but it spreads too much and needs pruning. I worry about how much it will cost, but I know it must be done. Neighbors assure me that it is a good idea. I hire a crew to come out and prune the tree.

The tree represents my work, which is spreading in too many directions. The tree needs to keep its shape. However, it cannot be done without cost—that is, not pursuing or stopping some activities that are putting too much energy into shoots and branches and not enough into the main trunk.[1]

I also interpreted the dream on a spiritual level. At the same time that my career was expanding, I was pursuing an equally diverse spiritual path. The result was that my energies on all fronts were scattered rather than focused. I decided which professional and spiritual pursuits were most important to me, and I trimmed the rest.

Another example of a tree dream comes from a woman I'll call G.G. She grew up in a dysfunctional family. She lost her father at a young age and has had difficulty with her mother all of her life. She has struggled with issues of self-esteem and speaking out for herself. Prior to her dream, she made the difficult decision of severing her relationship with her mother.

In the dream, G.G. and her son are in a car, driving into the countryside. They turn around and head back into town.

As we get into the city, we see there has been a storm. The electrical trucks are there, and the men are working on the electrical lines. Back to our left, a huge tree is completely uprooted. It is suspended in the air at a slight angle. I see the green of the leaves, the trunk, and the complete root system spread out. As it is raised, plugs of cylindrical blond wood fall from the trunk. It is as if the cylinders were previously cut and left in there because "they" knew this storm would happen. I think, "Someone has gone in and prepared it."

What the dream meant to me: The storm that had just passed is my emotions that had just passed, but some repair work is still left to be done. My son represents sharpness, intelligence, and creativity, which I have within me. I need to clear up some things before I can move on: quit believing those negative voices I hear at times that say I am not smart enough, that I am "different" (as Mother used to say). The uprooted tree: I think this decision about my mom has been coming for years. I do feel uprooted, as if I stand alone, as a woman, not that little girl within who has always had some degree of fear of my mom. The new cylindrical pieces coming out of the tree, that had been prepared to weather the storm, are the new growth gained by letting go, as well as the strong, sturdy parts within me that I have been preparing along the way. The life lesson is that something good can come out of something bad.[2]

The dream shows G.G. that she has within her the strength to weather the turbulence. The electricians repairing the power lines are also symbols of her inner power, especially mental, and the ability to be more outspoken.

Symbols act upon us whether or not we are aware of the process. The symbols in our dreams have an impact upon us. The more we are aware and the more we understand the nuances of symbols, the more we enrich our spiritual and personal lives.

The Four Elements in Dreams

In deciphering our dreams, we can derive meaning from the four elements of nature. Aristotle ascribed characteristics to the elements: earth is cold and dry, water is cold and moist, air is hot and moist, fire is hot and dry. Each element shares one characteristic with one other element. In alchemy, the elements can be transmuted from one to another by working with the unshared characteristics. In addition, the elements have masculine or feminine aspects: earth and water are feminine, and air and fire are masculine. Each has magical attributes, too. In the mystery traditions, candidates must undergo trials by the elements in order to be initiated into understanding of the higher worlds.

Elements in dreams can reflect our emotional, psychic, or spiritual frames of mind. They often show us what we are facing or processing or need to face or process. The masculine or feminine properties of elements may relate to the animus and anima as well.

Upheavals of the elements, such as storms, earthquakes, tornadoes, hurricanes, tidal waves, rampant fires, volcanic eruptions, and so on, can reflect inner upheaval due to stress or upset in life, especially a sudden or serious loss. These symbols also may relate to awakenings of the kundalini energy.

Fire

The potency and devastation of fire can make it a frightening element in a dream. We tend to view fire as a destroyer. It does destroy, but it also purifies and transforms in the process. It eliminates the old and obsolete so that new life can spring from the ashes.

In alchemy, the process of the Great Work begins and ends with fire, which purges impurities from the substances it touches. Similarly, fire in a dream can represent a purging in order to make way for renewal.

In the mystery tradition, fire is the first trial, and pertains to the burning away of the veils to our perception of the higher worlds. We become aware of Truth.

Fire also represents passion and sexual power that, like fire itself, must be controlled so as not to run rampant. Fire is the source of creativity and new ideas. It also illuminates our vulnerabilities.

Fire has strong associations with lightning (creativity) and with blood (sacrifice and ordeal). Fire tests the stuff we are made of. We can be strengthened by fire, like a blade of steel tempered by the flames.

In terms of spiritual awakenings, fire is the most likely element to relate to kundalini activity. When aroused, kundalini is like an inner fire, bringing sensations of intense heat and images of flames. Thus in dreams, fire can represent or presage bursts of kundalini activity.

In the following dream of a young woman, fire represents a series of stresses.

I dreamed that my sister and I were running around trying to put out a house fire. When I woke up, I told my boyfriend about this. He's superstitious, and that day he packed up and left early for a job in Florida. The next day, I received a phone call from a woman claiming that she had been dating him for two months and was also pregnant by him! Then, a month later, my father had a heart attack while driving on the freeway and died before impact. My aunt and uncle were passengers. My aunt was okay, but my uncle had to have a couple of operations.

I feel that all of these things that happened in a month's time are the fires that my sister and I were trying to put out. She is the eldest of seven children, and had always been a take-charge type of person.[3]

The house in the dream represents the dreamer, and the fire presages a series of unhappy events threatening her. Her sister's help represents the sister's longtime family role of handling situations and helping to solve problems. The events have tested the dreamer's mettle.

Water

Water dreams are among the most common, perhaps because water relates to emotions, and dreams help us come to terms with emotional issues. Water represents the hidden depths, where emotions reside. To be overwhelmed by water, such as a downpour or a tidal wave, can symbolize a situation that is emotionally overwhelming. Drowning can represent being pulled under by emotions.

Water also represents the unconscious. Traveling across large bodies of water can represent spiritual journeys in which one must traverse the unknown. In ancient times, people believed that the seas were populated with great monsters; the farther away one sailed, the greater danger one had of encountering these fearsome beasts. Monsters can lurk in the unconscious as well, representing uncoalesced fears and shadow material.

Pregnancy can bring on dreams of swimming or being lapped by gentle waves.

In alchemy, water has associations with baptism, which represents the birthing of the new. In the mystery tradition, it is the second trial, and it pertains to our ability to act and demonstrate self-control according to the principles of the higher worlds we can now perceive. It is akin to swimming in deep water.

Initiation by water can be by journey or by baptism. The latter may take the form in dreams of a dunking, a bath, or diving into a pool of water.

Soon after I began my spiritual work in earnest, I had this clear and vivid dream.

I am swimming in the ocean to the Edge of the World. There really is such a thing. The ocean is vast and black, cool but not cold. Beyond the Edge is a ring of white mountains, looking like an unreachable fantasyland. The Edge is marked by a line of pontoons that stretches into infinity. I feel comfortable in the water, confident. I wonder how many thousands of feet of black water are beneath me. There are others in the water—I don't know who.

Sometime later, I had another similar dream.

I am swimming in the ocean, very far out. There are monsters deep in the water, and I worry about one coming up, grabbing my legs, and pulling me under.[4]

In the first dream, the spiritual search is represented by my swimming out into the far reaches of my own unconscious. Its territory is vast and uncharted, its depths unknown. Its color is black, which I associated with the void, primal chaos, and the unknown. In alchemical terms, it is the stuff of the *prima materia,* the first matter from which all else is created. The ocean is cool (comfortable) but not cold (uninviting). Other swimmers are making their journeys out. The white mountains off in the distance are the spiritual goal—the sacred ascent to the land of the gods. They seem unreachable because I am but a beginner, just starting out.

The ring of mountains calls to mind the image of Shambhala, the secret, legendary kingdom of enlightenment in Tibetan Buddhist mysticism. According to legend, Shambhala lies deep within rings of mountains, and only two kinds of travelers ever find it: the unaware who stumble upon it, and the adepts who know precisely where to look for it. Inside Shambhala, people enjoy the gold of enlightenment, represented by precious metals, jewels, and abundant fruits. They have learned the secrets of the Kalachakra, the Wheel of Time—the alchemists' immortality.

In this dream, I am like the Fool of the Tarot—the innocent who steps into the unknown, unaware of any dangers or pitfalls.

In the second dream, fear shows. On any journey, after a time, we begin to think about dangers that might be around us. Perhaps we see the dangers or experience them. The spiritual path involves going into the unconscious, where we must confront the fears that form the monsters within, or else risk being pulled under by them.

This dream reflected anxiety about losing my center by going too deeply into the mystical. In the dream, I no longer have the firmness of distant earth as a safety or point of orientation, but I am free-floating in the unknown. Working with the dream enabled me to recognize the anxiety and realize that it was groundless.

In the following dream, water takes on a more personal meaning for a woman, T.

Toward the end of my ten-year marriage, I dreamed I was in the ocean and waves were overtaking me and I was drowning. My husband heard me choking [in my sleep] and had to shake me to wake me up. I really thought I was drowning. At the time, my marriage was going sour, and it ended in divorce.[5]

The emotional turbulence of the disintegrating marriage is represented by the overwhelming waves, and the dreamer fears drowning in her own emotions.

Air

The element of air represents mental effort, thoughts, intellectual pursuits, logic, and left-brain activities. It has a masculine energy. Air also represents freedom or escape, especially if we fly in the air. Other types of air dreams feature solving puzzles or mysteries; holding authority positions such as teacher, judge, or police; being students; taking tests; and processing papers. Dreams involving organization of materials and activities (having to be somewhere on time, do a presentation, give a lecture, etc.), and riding up and down elevators also are air dreams.

The quality of the air in the dream can provide information. Is it crisp, clean and pure, and easy to breathe, or is it fogged, polluted, stifling, stagnant, and difficult to breathe?

Air initiations often involve scaling the heights: going up a mountain (a spiritual ascent using the intellect), ascending a tower (the ivory tower of the intellectuals and academes).

In the mystery tradition, air is the third initiation and pertains to finding our inner strength and to attuning ourselves to always listen to the voice of spirit. Thus we are able to enter the temple of wisdom.

Earth

Earth dreams often relate to our foundation in life. We think of the earth as firm and stable. The earth also represents materiality; our possessions, things, and physical well-being. It can also represent the body.

Earthquakes occur in dreams during times of upheaval, when we feel we have lost our firm foundation and are suffering a shakeup, especially due to loss or the threat of severe illness. Earthquakes may mirror anxieties relating to changes of residence or finances. Volcano eruptions may relate to bottled-up anger threatening to explode.

The initiation of the earth is the fourth trial in the mystery tradition, and it pertains to going within oneself. In dreams, this is represented by the entering of wombs, caves, tunnels, and dark spaces. Because earth has a feminine energy, earth initiations also have to do with recognizing and expressing our feminine side, such as through nurturing or intuition.

This dream of mine involves both earth and air and features a change in the spiritual journey from one phase to another.

There is a huge, snow-covered mountain, which represents some kind of test or initiation. People ski down its huge face. I am skiing down, and along the way, lose my sword and a long, serrated carving knife, both of which are in sheaths. I try to go back along the trail to look for them, but I can't find them. I can either go back up the face of the mountain or go another way, which is through the mountain. I take the inner way back to find my things.

Suddenly I am deep inside the mountain, walking on a narrow, twisty wooden catwalk suspended in space. It is very treacherous. All around me it is dark. Somewhere below me, I know there is swampy water of an unknown depth. Along the catwalk are plumbing pipes, like in a basement or the inner workings of a house or building.

I am accompanied by my two dogs from waking life, Tessie and Honey Dog. One is ahead of me and one is behind. I worry about any or all of us falling off the catwalk, but the dogs are unafraid, surefooted, and know where they are going.[6]

The mountain (earth) is the spiritual ascent made through the masculine intellect (air). Here I am undergoing an initiation from one phase of the Great Work to another. After reaching the top, I must go back down, that is, bring the spiritual into the material, like Moses coming down from the mount. I must integrate the spiritual insights I have learned into daily life. I don't ski with typical poles, however, but with a sword and a knife. These are tools of the warrior and the quester. Both cutting tools, they represent discernment: the ability to cleave right from wrong. Instead of making another intellectual ascent, I decide to try another route. Going inside the mountain represents a feminine going within, probing the depths, entering into the womb of the Great Mother. It is the unconscious, dark and mysterious, possibly dangerous; the swampy water suggests the possibility of monsters lurking in the depths. The plumbing that suggests the basement of a house further reinforces the image of the unconscious, but with a more personal twist. There is a path through this unknown territory, and I am going to have to trust that I will stay on it. The dogs are chthonic symbols, that is, in mythology they belong to the gods of the underworld. Dogs are archetypal symbols of protection, guidance, guardianship, and instinct. That I have two represents balance, especially between the masculine and feminine. The dream assures me that I will be correctly guided by my instincts and intuition.

Mysterious Symbols

Dreams that have special archetypal and spiritual content sometimes feature mysterious symbols, such as writing in unknown languages or alien-looking shapes. In the dreams, we may feel that we know what these symbols mean, but we can't explain it when we awaken. Or, we may be perplexed in the dream as to what their meaning is. Dream guides sometimes give us symbols and explain what they mean.

In 312 C.E., the Roman emperor Constantine was given a symbol that led to a military victory and paved the way for the spread of Christianity throughout Europe. Constantine was proclaimed emperor by his troops in 306, but he had to defend his position against rivals. He was forced to fight Maxentius, and prepared to engage him at Mulvian Bridge near Rome. He prayed to God for help and was given first a waking vision and then a dream that convinced him to invoke the name of Christ. As a result, he defeated Maxentius and retained his crown. Some twenty years after the death of Constantine, the historian Eusebius recorded an account of the experiences, saying that Constantine had related them personally to him.

Accordingly [Constantine] called on [God] with earnest prayer and supplications that he would reveal to him who he was, and stretch forth his right hand to help him in his present difficulties. And while he was thus praying with fervent entreaty, a most marvelous sign appeared to him from heaven. . . . He said that about noon, when the day was already beginning to decline, he saw with his own eyes the trophy of a cross of light in the heavens, above the sun, and bearing the inscription, CONQUER BY THIS. *At this sight he himself was struck with amazement, and his whole army also, which followed him on this expedition, and witnessed the miracle.*

He said, moreover, that he doubted within himself what the import of this apparition could be. And while he continued to ponder and reason on its meaning, night suddenly came on; then in his sleep the Christ of God appeared to him with the same sign which he had seen in the heavens, and commanded him to make a likeness of that sign . . . and to use it as a safeguard in an engagements with his enemies.

At dawn of day he arose, and communicated the marvel to his friends: and then, calling together the workers in gold and precious stones, he sat in the midst of them, and described to them the figure of the sign he had seen, bidding them represent it in gold and precious stones.[7]

The sign was the two Greek letters *chi* and *ro* combined. Called the labarum, it became the symbol of the Roman Empire until its demise in 1453.

Mysterious symbols and languages, such as unknown hieroglyphs, pictographs, geometric shapes, and cursive writing are part of the revelatory tradition, in which the initiate receives information direct from a divine, or at least nonhuman, source.

Joseph Smith, Jr., the founder of the Church of Jesus Christ of Latterday Saints (Mormonism), had a nighttime dream/visionary experience in which he was visited by the angel Moroni. The angel told him that he had helped write and then bury a history written on gold plates by his father Mormon of an ancient people descended from Israel who had lived and died in America. Moroni said God had chosen Smith to find the plates and translate them. The angel revealed the hiding place of the plates and the seer stones of the Urim and Thummin, and ordered Smith to dig them up in four years' time. Smith followed the instructions and translated the plates with the help of two men. The resulting *Book of Mormon* was published in 1830 and became the bible of the new religion. Smith said the plates were covered in a strange hieroglyphic writing that combined Egyptian, "Chaldiac" (Chaldaic) and

"Assyric" (Assyrian) languages. Moroni reclaimed the plates, Smith said.

In kabbalistic lore, the angel Raziel, whose name means "secret of God" or "angel of mysteries," placed all of the secrets of the cosmos in *The Book of the Angel Raziel.* Raziel was ordered by God to give the book to Adam so that he could gaze into the mirror of all existence, see the face of God, and see himself as an image of God. The book contained all celestial and earthly knowledge, as well as the secret to decoding 1,500 keys to the mystery of the world, which were not even explained to the other angels. Jealous at being left out of the cosmic secrets, the other angels stole the book from Adam and threw it into the sea. God ordered Rahab, the angel of the sea, to retrieve it and return it to Adam. It later was passed to the prophet Enoch, where much of it was incorporated into *The Book of Enoch.* Although the keys in the book are not understood by any other angel, Raziel nonetheless is said to stand on the peak of Mount Horeb every day and proclaim the secrets to humankind. The teachings of this book may actually have a medieval text written by Eleazar of Worms.

Persons who are extraterrestrial experiencers (contacts and abductions) often say they are shown or given mysterious writings as part of their instructions from aliens. Typically, this coded information—which may come in a dream or a visionary contact experience—pertains to apocalyptic warnings about dire consequences to the earth as the result of human negligence, or to secrets of advanced alien technology. Many symbols remain unknown to the experiencer.

Mysterious languages or symbols, such as in papers or books shown to us in dreams, also carry personal messages: We are being alerted to something we know but that we haven't yet acknowledged, such as a realization, an awareness, or a need for action.

We can also draw mysterious symbols out of the data bank of the collective unconscious. In the late nineteenth century, the chemist Friedrich A. von Kekule made a revolutionary contribution to organic chemistry because of a dream. Kekule had attempted without success to discover the structure of the benzene molecule. One night he had a dream in which atoms formed long, snakelike chains. One snake grabbed its own tail and began to rotate. From this, Kekule was able to create a model of a closed molecular ring. The symbol of the snake biting its own tail was unknown to him, but it exists as one of the most important symbols in Western alchemy. It is called the *ouroboros*, and represents the unity of opposites, wholeness, oneness, and eternity.

It is often possible to decipher the meaning of unknown languages, scripts, and symbols by meditating upon them or incubating a dream for the revelation of their meaning.

Vivid dreams containing strange symbols have visited me for years, such as this one from my dream journal.

I am at a convention and someone introduces me to the comedian Steve Allen. He is very young, much younger than in real life. When he hears about the books I've written, he is very impressed and invites me to have breakfast with him the next morning. Flattered, I accept.

When I arrive at the table, he tells me that overnight he read some of my books and is impressed. He has written a little something up for me, something he knows I will understand. He hands me a sheaf of papers. They are covered with geometric symbols arranged in horizontal lines like some sort of hieroglyphics. Every now and then, my name in Arabic letters, "Rosemary Guiley" (no middle name), is interspersed in a line. The lines are different colors. There are several lines of symbols in red, then green and blue.

I am embarrassed that I cannot readily understand the symbols—and this is supposed to be based on my own work! I will have to study them later.

I recorded my thoughts in my dream journal:

Steve Allen is a brilliant comic, and is known for his high IQ and sophisticated intellect. As a comic, he is a prankster. In the dream, he personifies Hermes the trickster, who comes to deliver esoteric information. I believe that I have absorbed this information on some level of my consciousness.

Later, in browsing through Gayle Delaney's book, Living Your Dreams, *I found a reference to Steve Allen. Delaney wrote to him in 1983 about his dreams, and he answered that he is extraordinarily interested in dreaming, that he uses dream-generated ideas for much of his work, and that his most successful song, "This Could Be the Start of Something Big," came out of a dream. I feel that even though I did not know this information at the time, I pulled it clairvoyantly out of a collective data bank. Thus the dream underscores on yet another level the vital importance of mining my own dreams—and my need to understand them better. I've got my own name written all over them. "This Could Be the Start of Some-*

thing Big" may refer to a shift in my own work that has been inaugurated with the publication of my book, Angels of Mercy.[8]

In fact, *Angels of Mercy* did inaugurate a new phase of my work, turning my focus from the paranormal to the spiritual and mystical.

But what if I had not had Delaney's book to tell me about the title of the song? Certainly, this was not known to me consciously. Without it, could I have gotten the same meaning from the dream?

Whenever we engage in dreamwork, we are always led to the information we need to illuminate the dream. Often, this comes through synchronicity, such as finding or leafing through a book or hearing a casual remark. If I had not had the book, I would have been given some other source that would have augmented the dream—perhaps not from the same angle, but resulting in similar insights. Even without the book, my association of Steve Allen to the trickster provides the same conclusion: The trickster is known for surprises (that "start of something big").

Working with Mysterious Dream Symbols

Make drawings of unknown symbols in dreams, then meditate upon them for additional information. Sometimes mysterious symbols will remind you of symbols familiar to you, and you can make associations. With a little research, you may discover the same or similar symbols from literature on archaeology, symbology, religion, mysticism, alchemy, and esoterica.

Dreams reveal what is hidden to us; we are meant to understand them, even parts of them that seem indecipherable. Mysterious symbols may not yield up their meanings immediately, but may do so over time or perhaps in subsequent dreams. Remember that symbols are not necessarily translatable into words. Your understanding of them may be more of a knowing.

chapter nine

INTERPRETING DREAMS

THE TALMUD SAYS THAT AN UNINTERPRETED DREAM IS LIKE AN UNREAD LETTER. THUS, IF WE ARE TO LIVE TO THE FULLEST, WE MUST UNDERSTAND OUR DREAMS. IT'S NOT ALWAYS EASY. FRAGments, disconnected scenes, and bizarre imagery often confound our efforts. If our dreams are meant to be understood, we ask, why can't they be more direct and straightforward?

No one knows exactly why dreams are the way they are. But we cannot deny that they are bearers of information that is important to us. Jung viewed dreams as a part of nature that has no wish to deceive but expresses something as best as it can, just as a plant grows or an animal seeks its food.[1]

In ancient times, people often sought help from professional dream interpreters; this practice still goes on around the world today. In the modern West, the professional dream interpreter is often a psychoanalyst. However, rather than tell people what their dreams mean, the psychoanalyst helps people to make their own interpretations.

Dream interpretation is a subjective art. If two persons were to have exactly the same dream, each would interpret it differently, based upon their own unique experiences, beliefs, and worldviews. What's more, dreams seldom have just one meaning but come with multiple messages and nuances. The meaning of a dream is also likely to shift over time as new insights are realized. Sometimes dreams or parts of them do remain mysteries.

Though the ancients relied upon professional dream interpreters, they also recognized that the meaning of a dream is not necessarily fixed but is open to multiple interpretations. In the Talmud, the canonized teachings of Judaism's early great rabbis, the story is told that Rabbi Bana'ah took one of his dreams to the professional dream interpreters of Jerusalem. There were twenty-four interpreters, and each one offered a different interpretation, all of which were fulfilled. The rabbi said his experience confirmed the adage that "all dreams follow the mouth," meaning, as a dream is interpreted, so it comes to pass.

There may not have been exactly twenty-four actual interpreters in Jerusalem—the number twenty-four seems to refer more to "many" than a specific number—but the rabbi's story does illustrate that there is no one right interpretation to a dream. In fact, there can be many interpretations, each one valid. This becomes evident in group dreamwork where many viewpoints are offered for a single dream.

Rather than be problematic, however, the open-endedness of dream interpretation proves to be a great strength. Each of us has considerable latitude in which to explore a dream and discover its truth. An interpretation is right when it rings true to you.

Making a Commitment

Before beginning any program of dreamwork, whether it be alone or with others, there are two important commitments to make: honor your dreams and record your dreams.

Honor Your Dreams

Dreams are part of our core essence. When we take them seriously and honor them, they respond accordingly by revealing more information. By honoring dreams, we make a commitment to remember, record, and interpret our dreams. Initially, this means as many dreams as possible. Dreamwork is like learning a foreign language; you have to practice it and immerse yourself in it to become proficient. As time goes on, you will become more selective, recording and working with the dreams that seem charged with the most energy.

Honoring dreams acknowledges their power and benefits. Sometimes dreams are frustrating or frightening, making us reluctant to tackle them in dreamwork. They seem to be a Pandora's box of trouble if we open the lid. Dreams *do* ask us to resolve, reconcile, and face feelings and situations that we often seek to avoid. We must bear in mind that dreams come to us as a service and as a tool for healing, enlightenment, and self-empowerment. Our dreams do not ask us to deal with anything beyond our inner resources or capabilities. Our dreams are under the guidance of the higher self, which is concerned with our path of fulfillment and wholeness.

Record Your Dreams

You can't work with dreams if you don't have the details. Dreams are like little wisps of fog that evaporate in the morning light—we forget them quite easily. Although we have multiple dreams throughout the night, we're likely to remember only the dream we have prior to awakening—and even that one can go fast from memory. Consequently, you must commit your dream to writing or tape as soon as possible. Even speaking the dream out loud, to yourself or your partner, will help to set it in your memory.

The ancients suffered the same difficulties that we do in remembering dreams and their details. Numerous spells that the Egyptians used for incubating dreams admonished the dreamer to always have a writing tablet handy for recording the dream immediately upon awakening.

Today we still do the same thing. Some people like to sleep with a notepad or tape recorder beside the bed so that they can record a dream whenever they awaken, even in the middle of the night. It's a good idea to set the alarm clock a few minutes earlier than you would otherwise so that you have time in the morning to record a dream without being rushed. Once you get it down, you can go back to it later when you have more time to work with it.

When I'm home, I like to type my dreams directly into a computer file. I record the dream and add notes, including associations and interpretations that come immediately to mind. Later, I go back and review what I have written and add new thoughts to the file. When I'm traveling, I put dreams on a tape recorder and transcribe them into the computer file when I get home. I like having one master file rather than dreams scattered over bits of paper, because I can see patterns and themes over periods of time. Keeping dreams in a notebook serves the same function.

Record all the details you can recall, no matter how bizarre, no matter how inconsequential they may seem. Do not edit as you record. Often it is the strange and "inconsequential" that prove to be the most important factors in interpretation. Include emotions, colors, sensations, "atmosphere," and numbers.

Do not discount imagery that seems to be based upon activities from the previous day or days. For example, if you see a movie and then have a dream with elements of the movie in it, you might be inclined to toss off the dream as some sort of reenactment of the movie. Such imagery is called *day residues*.

In fact, dreams often make ample use of day residues in order to get some other point across. It's as though the Grand Dreamweaver borrows whatever stage props are available for a presentation. That can include day residues, events from the past, and otherworldly settings.

Record dream fragments. Many people think that dreams with meaning have to be like stories, with a beginning, a middle, and an end. In fact, most dreams are not complete. We seem to jump into the middle of a story that abruptly ends before a resolution. Fragments can be as big a gold mine of wisdom as dreams that seem to last the entire night.

Pay attention also to the dreams that occur in the twilight zones between wakefulness and sleep. As we fall asleep, we enter a state of consciousness called the hypnagogic state; when we rise up out of sleep to wakefulness, we go through a similar stage called the hynopompic state. Both are characterized by dreams with fleeting, often jumbled imagery and sometimes voices and sounds. Lucid and OBE dreams can occur in this state as well as other dreams with important messages.

Is a dream still a dream if we wake up and the dream continues or another experience begins? For example, some people who report contact with the dead or visits by angels and otherworldly beings say they are awakened from sleep to see visitors in their room. They distinctly feel awake. While it is possible that some of these experiences may be lucid dreams that involve false awakenings, I do believe that dream experiences can spill over into waking consciousness. Our consciousness is better able to penetrate dimensional boundaries when we are asleep. The dream state opens a door. Sometimes the encounter remains within the dream state and sometimes it emerges into waking consciousness.

Dreams Have a Punny Sense of Humor

Our dreams speak to us in a language of symbols and metaphors. At times, this language can seem mysterious and impenetrable. In fact, it's rather simple. Once we get the hang of it, our dreams explain themselves quite clearly.

The symbols and metaphors in dreams come from our activities and experiences in life and what we know about the world around us. They also come from the deep realm of archetypes and myth, which is formed by the collective unconscious. But we often overlook one of the richest sources of dream meanings: the pun. Sometimes the real, deep meaning of a dream is couched in a silly play on words. It's as if the gods of dreaming have a great sense of humor. One can virtually hear Hermes the trickster chortling from the heavens as we puzzle over strange imagery in a dream.

Take the example of a dream involving a bear. Our personal association might be ferocity, strength, or a formidable opponent to be feared. The archetypal association is protection. A pun suggests something we can or cannot bear.

Why puns? Dreams make artful use of the raw material of the way we think and communicate in waking consciousness. Puns play a significant role in how we describe our world. Sometimes a pun brings home the dream message in a way more powerful than direct language. And sometimes puns may be a way of relieving stress in dreams, by getting us to laugh and see a lighter side of things.

The ancient Egyptians, who paid great attention to the meaning of dreams, based many of their interpretations largely on puns. Many involved homonyms. For example, to dream of a harp (bnt) meant something evil (bint) would happen to you. To dream of a donkey (az) meant you would be promoted (saz). Some of the early Egyptian dream interpretations found their way into popular dream books that have been passed down through the ages. Because the puns don't make sense in other languages, these seemingly strange and arbitrary meanings can seem puzzling.

Homonym puns still appear in dreams today. A deer may represent something that is dear; a worn-out shoe sole may express something that is wearing down the soul.

There are several ways that puns occur in dreams. One of the most common is the visual pun, in which a picture expresses the pun. Dream expert Ann Faraday tells in her book *The Dream Game* of dreaming about a man in long white underpants shooting her down with a machine gun. Later she found herself on a live radio show hosted by a man named Long John Nebel, who allowed a critical guest to verbally "machine gun" Faraday and "shoot down" her expertise on dreams.

Proper names can be dream puns as well. A person dreams about comedian Bob Hope jumping down a street on a pogo stick. The dreamer's interpretation: "Hope springs eternal!"

Dreams also make ample use of slang terms, especially for references to sexual matters and body parts.

In dream language, nothing is too outrageous or ridiculous for a meaningful pun. If the message of a dream is puzzling you, try puns and plays on words. The answers you seek may suddenly appear.

Recurring Dreams

Sometimes a specific dream recurs over a period of time. Many people have repeating dreams that happen for years. A recurring dream is the higher self trying to reach waking consciousness with a message to take action. Recurring dreams often address repressed material and unresolved emotions. Because the material is repressed, recurring dreams often are frightening, such as being chased by a monster or a dangerous and shadowy person. Repeating dreams can be brought to an end by asking the dream what it is trying to tell you and confronting whatever is frightening. Caution: It may be best to work with a therapist in these situations so that proper integration and resolution can take place.

Recurring dreams usually stop when the issue they are addressing is resolved, as in this experience of Mary D.

When I was a young adult, I had a recurring dream that was quite frightening. I was in a house with an upstairs (very dark and ominous). In the dream, I would climb the stairs, and at the top there would be a door that was slightly open (a light shone from behind the door). When I pushed the door open, a rope hung (inviting me to grab it and swing outside, through the door). I could not see what lay below the door. I had this dream many times until I ended a marriage that was very painful.

After I left him, the dreams stopped. In fact, in the last dream, I grabbed the rope and swung out of the door. I was surrounded by light and had a wonderfully free feeling. I felt it was a confirmation that I had made the right decision.[2]

Sometimes repeating patterns have to do with old fears or anxieties about us not measuring up. In fact, the majority of dreams deal with anxieties of varying degrees. Sometimes we find upon examination that the fears are groundless or should have been laid to rest long ago. Or, by doing dreamwork, we discover ways to overcome the fears and anxieties.

Recurring nightmares can be part of pathological conditions and post-traumatic stress disorder. Work with a therapist is recommended in these situations.

Patterns and Personal Signatures

The longer you work with dreams, the more you will observe patterns in imagery and themes. These may be clustered (reflecting a particular situation in life) or ongoing throughout life (reflecting life themes). Patterns can be quite revealing about how you are going through life. For example, perhaps over a long period of time you have occasional dreams of driving in your car and getting lost or traveling and getting lost. The car often symbolizes the ego, or how we see ourselves "driving through life." Dreams of getting lost in your car might be prompting you to reexamine what you are doing. We often tell ourselves that everything is fine and that we are perfectly happy, but the higher self knows otherwise and sends dreams to tell us so.

Dreamwork will also reveal to you your own personal dream signatures. Everyone has them; they comprise a personal dream dictionary of sorts. When they show up in dreams, you know what they mean specifically to you. Personal signatures can be emotional tones, physical sensations, or certain imagery. As noted earlier, personal signatures play an important role in alerting us to precognition.

One of my own personal signatures is the black-and-white dream. I usually dream in color, as do most people. Whenever I have a dream in black and white, I know that this is a signal to pay extra attention.

Robert D. has a personal signature relating to the directions of left and right in a dream.

In my dreams, I pay attention to the movement of people, animals, or objects from right to left, or left to right in dream scenes. If the movement is from right to left, the meaning has a negative cast to it, indicating difficulty, danger, stress, disappointment, or hardship of one kind or another. If the movement is from left to right, opposite meanings are indicated, such as fulfillment, satisfaction, victory, happiness, avoidance of danger, the lessening or avoidance of pain, etc. These effects have been examined many times over the years in my dreams, and in every case that I can remember, they have worked out as I have described. In most cases, the meanings are pretty obvious and straightforward. In a few, the symbolism had to be studied carefully to get to the true meanings.

Seventeen years ago, I was laid off. I was in great perplexity as to what to do and where to turn for suitable, satisfying work. In this time period, I had a dream where I was standing by a long bridge that spanned a dry stream bed. Mountains were to my right. The left was not in view. I climbed to the top of some packing boxes to get onto the trestle, to my left, underneath the roadway of the bridge. This was a narrow space, and I had to crawl with some difficulty on beams and supports to get across the bridge. Once on the other side, I walked off the bridge on the left side and started down a road going left from the bridge.

This seemingly negative dream was encouraging to me. The mountains to my right indicated difficulties to overcome. The dry stream bed revealed the dryness of my spiritual life. The crawling across the bridge on the trestle beams was to be accomplished by determination, perseverance, hope, and faith in the future. Getting off the bridge meant that the worst would soon be over, and that lesser problems would be encountered on my trip down the road to my left. This was a premonitory dream of what happened.[3]

Seven Keys to Interpreting Dreams

Over the years, I've tried many methods for working with my dreams in a variety of formats: working alone, working with a therapist, and working in a group. Each format offers different nuances. I've found them all to be successful in helping me get to the core of my dreams. Dreamwork is highly subjective. My advice to beginners is to sample various formats and techniques until you click with one or more.

I've developed my own system for analyzing my dreams. Its seven steps help me get to the meat of the dream quickly and focus my attention on the messages. I say *messages,* not *message,* because a dream is seldom about one piece of information. It resembles an onion: There are different layers, each one unique to itself, but all are part of the whole. Remember that there are three levels to the dream:

- The personal level, in which everything in a dream expresses a part of ourselves

- The archetypal level, in which some images are drawn from the archetypal realm of the the collective unconscious
- The transpersonal level, in which we experience other realities

I like the resonance with the number seven. In numbers mysticism, seven is the hero's journey, the alchemical Great Work, the search for treasure, which is wholeness. Seven is the number of magic and wisdom about the unseen.

There is but one rule when it comes to deciphering dreams: Only the dreamer can truly interpret his or her own dreams. Others can help and may indeed provide suggestions that hit the mark, but dreamwork is subjective and unique to the individual.

The Seven Keys are:

1. Determine the high concept.
2. Dissect the dream.
3. Make personal associations.
4. Make archetypal associations.
5. Look for the spiritual dimension.
6. Expand on the dream.
7. Take action.

Let's look at each one in more detail:

Determine the High Concept

The high concept of a dream is the distilled essence or theme of the dream. If you had to summarize your dream in a sentence, what would you say? Even a complicated dream with disjointed activity and scene changes can be boiled down to a sentence. The high concept will help you find the important thread or theme of the dream. Giving the dream a title helps to focus the high concept.

Dissect the Dream

Take the dream apart and examine its elements. Look for emotional tone within the dream and upon awakening. Are there characteristics of lucidity? Dominant colors, sounds, textures, smells? Who are the cast of characters? What activities are going on? Is this a recurring dream, or does it have a theme that shows up frequently in your dreams?

Freud's technique of free association can be quite helpful in getting a handle on a puzzling dream. Take a particular element in a dream—such as a person or an object—and offer spontaneous associations that come to mind. Spontaneity is the key here; if you pause to analyze or think about associations, you are allowing judgment to screen the process. Free association liberates the right, intuitive side of the brain. Don't worry about how silly some associations may sound. The results can surprise you: Sometimes the offbeat proves to be the key to unlock the mystery.

Make Personal Associations

What do all the elements in the dream tell you about yourself? What associations can you make between the dream and your waking life, present or past? Look for simple associations first. Consider puns and plays on words. Look for any of your personal dream signatures.

Make Archetypal Associations

Dreams that are lucid, highly charged with energy, contain the number three or personal dream signatures, or have otherworldly elements in them will need extra attention for archetypal associations. These dreams are drawing significantly on the mythical realm and are likely to have big messages.

A good dictionary of dream or mythological symbols is essential for learning archetypal associations. Many dream researchers disdain dream dictionaries. This attitude is most unfortunate, because it cuts dreamers off from a rich source of ideas. It is true that a dream dictionary cannot dictate—and should not dictate—the meaning of any dream. The meaning of a dream is always within a context of a life.

However, when dream symbols have an archetypal role, such meanings are more universal, because they are drawn from the collective unconscious. Unless you have an extensive knowledge of mythology, many of these associations will not be readily apparent to you, but you *will* feel the click when you look them up in a symbols dictionary. A whole new level of the dream opens up when you see it from an archetypal perspective.

There are many dream dictionaries available on the market. Select one with care. Some are merely reprints of centuries-old dream books that date back to Artemidorus's efforts from Greece and Rome. Their associations, once appropriate for society in Artemidorus's day, are now obsolete. If you leaf through a dictionary and find many definitions not making much sense, it may be Artemidorus repackaged.

I use several reference books in my own dreamwork: my own dictionary, *The Encyclopedia of Dreams: Symbols and Interpretations,* and several books on mythological symbols.

Look for the Spiritual Dimension

Every dream has something to tell us about our spirituality; some dreams speak to this more loudly than others. Remember that symbols contain and convey more than do words. Our understanding of symbols in dreams awakens a knowingness within that is often hard to describe.

Expand on the Dream

Techniques abound for getting information from dreams. Here are a few tried-and-true ones:

Conduct a dialogue with the various elements of your dream, whether a person or an object. Ask the person or thing what its message is for you. Write out the answers you get. This type of dialogue is called gestalt, and was pioneered by the Freudian-trained analyst, Fritz Perls.

You can also describe everything in the dream as though you were explaining it to someone who knows nothing about you. Use a real friend, an imaginary friend, or write it down or tape-record it.

If the meaning of the dream eludes you, try finishing it as a daydream. Get relaxed, retrace the dream, and then allow it to continue on its own. Or, you can take a more assertive role by changing the dream.

A dream about a turtle followed by a daydream exercise inspired Christian scholar Morton Kelsey to study mythology, which had a profound impact upon his work.

I stood at the ocean and a great big, very old turtle came out of the water. It said something very important to me, but as I awoke, I forgot what was said. So I reconstructed the dream in my imagination and began to fantasize. (It is most interesting to note that one can return to the dream world almost as if it were real.) I asked the turtle what it had said, but it did not answer; rather, it climbed out of the water. It went to a rock wall and knocked on it three times with its beak. A door opened and I went inside. Two years and 80,000 words later I came out; in this time I had lived through many of the myths of humankind with my weekly ventures into this fantasy-land. Before this I had never studied ancient mythology, but now I myself had looked into this world and its images.[4]

(Note the number three: the turtle knocks three times on a door, the magical charm to gain access to a hidden realm.)

You can also meditate on a dream or symbols within a dream, which invites the higher self, through intuition, to give you a flash of insight. This insight may not come immediately but will happen later, typically when you are involved in a routine activity and are allowing your thoughts to wander. Carl Jung often meditated upon dreams whose meaning perplexed him. Sometimes the illumination came only after a long time and much thought, he said, but was always worth the effort.

Another way Jung explored the nuances of his dreams was to paint them. This impressed the dream upon his memory, making it easier to access for meditation. Painting and drawing dreams often reveals what has been or cannot be expressed by words. You needn't be an accomplished artist to benefit from this exercise. Even the most modest drawings can yield big treasure of insight.

A popular dreamwork exercise is to start the drawing from inside a circle. The circle creates a mandala, representing oneness, unity, and wholeness.

If you wish to get creative in a bigger way, try mixed media to express your dream. Take colored paper, string, ribbons, sticks, glitter, clay—whatever captures your fancy—and build a three-dimensional picture from your dream.

These exercises release creative energy that can suddenly show you your dream in a new and exciting way.

Take Action

Our dreams present information in order for us to act. It is important for us to honor the dream by taking an action based upon our understanding of the dream. If we do not act, the entire dream mechanism remains incomplete, and our dreams will keep reminding us of the same message until we do act. By acting, we bring the spiritual (the insight from the dream) into the material (our waking life).

Action does not necessarily mean major changes in life, although sometimes that's the case. Action can be as simple as acknowledging the gift of insight from the dream. Acknowledgment is part of the integration of the individuation process.

I find that making the acknowledgement physical in a small way helps set it in consciousness. Make a little ritual of it by writing it down in your dream journal or giving thanks for it aloud in prayer.

Dreamwork in Groups and Families

The collective importance of dreams has been recognized since ancient times, when professional dream interpreters helped others find meaning in their nighttime experiences. Various societies have practiced and still practice forms of community dream-sharing, in which dreams are placed before the public for interpretation and action.

Participating in a dream group is stimulating and exciting. Bear in mind that week after week, the group will hear and discuss topics of a highly personal nature. It is important that everyone in a dream group feel comfortable that members will keep personal matters confidential and will not be judgmental.

It is also important that the personal integrity of a dream be maintained. A dream belongs solely to the dreamer, who is the final arbiter of its meaning. Observers listen and filter the imagery according to their own ideas. When contributing ideas for interpretation, don't tell the dreamer what the dream means. Better to phrase your suggestions as, "If that were my dream . . ." or "In my dream, I . . ." This enables the dreamer to easily accept ideas that have a resonance and discard those that do not.

An effective group dreamwork technique called the Dream Helper demonstrates just how connected we are through our dreams. It was developed by Henry Reed, a psychologist affiliated with the Association for Research and Enlightenment (A.R.E.) in Virginia Beach, Virginia, and prominent dream researcher Robert L. Van de Castle. It is a modern version of a very old and honored technique used by many peoples around the world. In the ancient Western world, for example, dreaming by proxy was practiced at incubation temples: a person could be hired or appointed to dream for someone else.

In the Dream Helper, the group dreams for one of its members. The exercise is simple. One person who has a problem or decision to make volunteers to be the focus. The matter is *not* disclosed to the group. Instead, the entire group tunes in together through prayer, meditation, or ritual in order to establish a psychic cohesion. Everyone then sleeps on it with the intent of having a dream that will help the focus person. The resulting dreams are compared the following morning or at the next meeting. The focus person reveals the problem or situation. The dreams are discussed and interpreted.

This technique consistently surprises participants with a high incidence of shared dream elements and telepathy among participants. Two or more persons may have the same or strikingly similar dreams. Invariably, dreamers hit on different perspectives of the issue, providing illumination for the focus person.

Other researchers exploring the group-shared content of dreams find that families have common links in their dream imagery. Edward Bruce Bynum, one of the leading researchers in this field, observes that family dreams offer a potential for healing that is often ignored by both medicine and clinical psychology. "Working with dream imagery and dream symbolism in a family or a larger group situation greatly expands one's own boundaries, yet maintains a sense of external cohesiveness and integrity," says Bynum. "This often stimulates similar processes in others. One can begin to see how an issue in one's own life is stimulated and unfolds systematically in the lives of others with whom one is intimately involved. This occurs on both a psychological and a somatic level."[5]

Dreams can also provide a safe way for family members to express themselves. Parents especially can benefit from the dreams of their children, who often are reluctant to communicate verbally.

Look for the Positive

Dreamwork should be an empowering experience. No matter how obscure or troubling a dream seems to be at first glance, working with it should release positive energies. Our dreams speak to us in order to help us grow, expand, and heal. Interpreting a dream should be directed at finding guidance and solutions. In its highest aspect, the dream initiates us into a new level of consciousness. It reveals our *becoming*.

chapter ten

THE ANCIENT ART OF DREAM INCUBATION

DREAMS HELP US SOLVE PROBLEMS AND OBTAIN GUIDANCE, BUT WE NEEDN'T WAIT FOR THE DREAM MUSE TO GRACE US WITH AN ANSWER TO A PARTICULAR QUESTION OR SITUATION. SINCE ancient times, people have asked and commanded dreams to help us. Techniques for inducing specific dreams are called incubation practices. Incubation, which is derived from the Greek term *incubatio* ("sleeping in") is the keeping of something under conditions favorable for development. We incubate dreams by impressing and holding a request for information within consciousness, so that a desired dream is born into our awareness.

For example, in her book *Living Your Dreams,* Gayle Delaney describes a struggling artist facing a major decision about his career. His income is erratic and comes primarily from students who pay him twenty dollars a month for drawing lessons. He wonders if he should give up trying to make a living as an artist and get a salaried job. He asks for an answer to this question in his dreams: "Should I get a job to earn money, or is there a better way for me?"

I see a twenty-dollar admission ticket to financial well-being. I somehow understand that this will hold me over until bigger things come my way. In the dream, I think this means I should continue to teach my drawing classes even though the going will not be easy.[1]

The artist decides not to give up his classes for a salaried job. Within eighteen months, he is more popular than ever and is charging more money, and his work is being shown in prestigious galleries.

Lura L. had a question of a different sort. A student of dreamworking, she finds herself opening to exciting new inner vistas. One night prior to going to sleep, she asked the angels to bring her a spiritual dream.

I know there was a lot more to the dream, but all I can remember is that there seemed to be a lot of water sprites governing the water. The moonlight was very strong, clear, and bright. This one little water sprite told me, "Every *drop of water has purpose and meaning."*

She was six to eight inches in height, with opaque wings. She was shimmery, shiny, and as if a manifestation out of Star Trek.

It gave me such an uplifting feeling. Every time I thought about that little water sprite, I got prickles on the back of my head and neck. It was very profound and seemed so real.

Sprite *is not in my vocabulary. When I looked it up in the big dictionary, it said "spirit" or "soul." That fits; that seems right.*

Now I really believe that there are such things as sprites. Now I truly know that anything is possible. I can tap into that universal mind or universal consciousness. I am not afraid anymore. It was a spiritual healing for me.[2]

Two very different requests, one dealing with a career decision and one with spiritual growth, were both answered by dreams.

Historical Dream Incubation Practices

Dream incubation is done around the world and has been an integral part of the Western tradition of dreamwork. The ancient Egyptians so believed in the importance of dreams that they practiced elaborate incubation rituals for healing, prophecy, and information. When one needed help from the gods via dreams, it was customary to travel to one of the many temples where incubation rituals were performed (see chapter 15, on healing). If travel was not possible, many other rituals could be performed privately. A person could spend the night in a cave and perform a magical ritual involving a lamp with magical words and figures inscribed upon it. The lamp was placed on a brick and then on sand. Frankincense was placed in front of the lamp. The person lit the lamp and gazed into the flame until a vision of a god appeared. He then went to sleep on a rush mat without speaking or asking any questions. The summoned god would appear during a dream and answer questions.

Spells were recited aloud in the Egyptians' incubation of dreams. Speaking the words rather than merely thinking them was of crucial importance, as were tone and pronunciation. A statement attributed to Imhotep, the god of medicine incubated at the healing temples, held that "the very quality of the sounds and the intonation of the Egyptian words contains in itself the force of the things said."[3] Spells were often repeated seven times.

The following Egyptian spell to incubate a dream involves both writing and speaking.

Take a clean linen bag and write upon it the names given below. Fold it up and make it into a lamp-wick, and set it alight, pouring pure oil over it. The word to be written is this: "Armiuth, Lailamchouch, Arsenophrenphren, Ptha, Archentechtha." Then in the evening, when you are going to bed, which you must do without touching food [or, be pure from all defilement], do thus. Approach the lamp and repeat seven times the formula given below: then extinguish it and lie down to sleep. The formula is this: "Sachmu . . . epaema Ligotereench: the Aeon, the Thunderer, Thou that hast swallowed the snake and does exhaust the moon, and dost raise up the orb of the sun in his season, Chthetho is thy name; I require, O lords of the gods, Seth, Chreps, give me the information that I desire.[4]

The Greeks and Herbrews used dream incubation as well. Not only can we control our dreams, we must, said Plato in *The Republic*. He advocated an incubation technique for seeing truth in dreams: Before going to bed, concentrate on noble thoughts rather than on the lower passions. This will ensure dreams that see clearly into the future, rather than dreams that produce misleading visions.

The *Sefer Hasidim* (Book of Devotion), a medieval kabbalistic work, does not directly encourage dream incubation but acknowledges the use of various incubation practices. Some examples are vague and tell only of "asking" for a dream. In one case, a *Hasid*'s disciple stretches himself on the grave of his master and asks for the answer to a question. The disciple wants to know if he is being punished or rewarded concerning his ascetic practices. The master comes to him in a dream and says, "Come, I will show you," and takes him to paradise.

In another example, the incubation is an oath between two friends, who promise each other that the first one to die will inform the other of what the afterlife is like.

A seventeenth-century Jewish dream book, *The Interpretation of Dreams,* by Solomon Almoli, offers a version of a *she'elat chalom* (dream question) ritual, which was used for questions of a theological nature. The ritual calls for fasting for a day, purification by bathing, and refraining from eating meat or drinking wine on the night of the incubation. Before retiring, one washes the hands, recites a bedtime prayer, and reads silently selections from scripture. The dream question is written, read, and placed beneath the pillow. After these observances, the incubant goes to sleep, being careful not to have any conversation or sexual stimulation or intercourse. In fact, the incubant must sleep on his or her left side alone in bed and alone in the house, on clean sheets and dressed in clean bedclothes. All efforts go to concentrating on the dream request as one falls asleep.

Other dream incubation practices are similar in calling for ritual purification and cleanliness, prayers, and abstention from sex, alcohol, meat, and sometimes all food. By purifying the body, the spirit is purified as well. Meat, heavy foods, and alcohol (as well as other drugs) potentially interfere with the sleep cycle and the ability to remember dreams. Sexual activity diminishes energy that needs to be directed to the incubation. (Recall that the techniques for inducing lucid and OBE dreams make use of raised but unreleased sexual energy.)

Dream incubation officially fell out of favor in Christianity in the early centuries of the new religion. Saint Jerome, who so profoundly influenced the Christian view on dreams in general, discouragèd "pagan" incubation practices and said that this was not a way to reach God. People cannot summon a transcendent God, he said; rather, it is God who initiates all communication with people. The populace, however, had different ideas about accessing the divine and preserved the custom of visiting holy places—such as shrines to the Virgin Mary and archangel Michael—and sleeping there in hopes of incubating healing dreams.

In tribal societies, dream incubation is similar to the vision quest, in which a person seeks contact with and guidance from the spirit world. Vision quests traditionally are undertaken by males at times of war, disease, death, initiation into manhood or a career (such as hunter or shaman), and childbirth (to seek a name for the child). They involve purification, followed by a solitary trek into the wilderness to a sacred place for several days and nights. The incubant fasts, thirsts, smokes tobacco, prays, and meditates for a vision. There may be self-mortification or mutilation or the use of hallucinogens. In a successful vision quest, the individual falls into a trance or experiences a lucid or OBE dream in which his guardian spirit manifests or he receives the sought-after advice from the spirits or Great Spirit. Successful vision quests are considered essential for success in life.

Modern dreamwork has brought a comeback to dream incubation, adapted to modern lifestyles. With a modest amount of effort and practice, we can put our dreams to work for us. Dream incubation can be simple or elaborate. It's not necessary to retire to a sacred place or temple to undergo involved procedures. Dream incubation can be done in your own home with a minimum of distraction.

Regardless of its form, simple or complex, dream incubation is essentially a ritual.

The Importance of Ritual

Ritual has played an important role in the development of human consciousness since the beginnings of our history. When we think of ritual, we tend to think of religion, but ritual actually exists in all facets of life. It is part of the cosmic fabric that weaves everything together in a harmonious whole. Daily life is structured around rituals: personal habits, meals, activities at certain times, and so on.

By definition, a ritual is a prescribed form of ceremony to achieve a goal. Thomas Moore, author of *The Care of the Soul*, calls ritual the "soul's work." Ritual helps the human consciousness tap into unseen forces: forces of the inner self, forces of nature, forces of the cosmos. Hsun Tzu, a Chinese philosopher of the third century B.C.E., said that ritual makes for harmony in the universe and brings out the best in human beings; it is the culmination of culture.

When we engage in ritual, we are activating forces associated in mythology with the divine feminine, the creative aspect of the universe. Ritual gives birth to new awareness and holds space for growth. The divine feminine balances the divine masculine, which is the active principle of the universe: doing, building. The masculine is associated with left-brain linear thought and logic, and the feminine with right-brain intuition and visionary thinking. Each of us, man or woman, has aspects of both within the psyche.

A ritual by itself does not incubate a dream. Ritual changes consciousness, which creates a space for inner knowing to come in. This may arrive in a dream but also can come in other ways, such as flashes of inspiration. Once our consciousness is changed, we do not go back to our former awareness.

The most effective rituals, even if they are simple, engage the senses as much as possible. Involving the senses alters consciousness and opens the gateway to visionary thinking. The Egyptian spell described above engages sight, sound, touch, and smell. We accomplish the same goal today with different activities: we write or speak a question, petition the Divine or the higher self for an answer, and perhaps burn a candle or incense.

Guidelines for Dream Incubation

Here are ten steps to incubating a dream.

1. Choose an important matter and be willing to explore it.
2. Phrase a question you would like your dreams to answer.
3. Write the question in your dream journal.
4. Prepare the body, mind, and soul.
5. At bedtime, do an incubation ritual.
6. Write and say the incubation question again.
7. Follow guidelines for improving dream recall as necessary.
8. Give extra attention to dream interpretation.
9. Watch for extra information that comes later.
10. Don't give up if success is not immediate.

Let's look at them in detail.

Choose an Important Matter and Be Willing to Explore It

Dream incubation is an activity of the sacred. The ancients undertook dream incubation when something important was at stake, such as healing or a major decision. Approaching dreams for answers to questions is akin to pilgrims approaching the oracle at Delphi—one does not come to the temple with trivial questions. So, we go to our inner temples with questions that have weight.

It is also important that, in choosing a question, we are completely clear on our willingness to have it examined by the truth that is expressed in dreams. There is always the possibility that we will receive answers that we might rather not hear.

If you are not clear in your intent, your dream oracle will not be clear, either.

Phrase a Question You Would Like Your Dreams to Answer

Keep the question short, simple, and direct. The more complicated the question, the higher the risk of receiving ambiguous answers. Ask for specifics. If you're trying to decide between two courses of action, it's best to inquire about one course. Ask, "Should I do Plan A?" and not "Should I do Plan A or Plan B?"

Here are some examples of effective phrasing of questions.

- Should I (proposed action)?
- How can I heal myself?
- How can I solve (problem)?
- What is the status of my relationship with (name)?
- How can I improve my relationship with (name)?
- How can I make (project or venture) a success?
- How can I manifest abundance and prosperity?

Incubation questions can also be more open-ended. If you're new at dream incubation, however, it's best to acquire some experience with simple questions first, in order to learn how your dreams respond. Some open-ended questions are:

- What shall I do now?
- Show me my path.
- Why . . . (do I . . . am I . . .)?
- What is the divine purpose for me?

Write the Question in Your Dream Journal

Writing down the incubation question helps to set it in consciousness and start the alchemical process of incubation. The question cooks away on the back burners of your mind. Writing down the question also helps to crystallize focus and intent. Don't be surprised if you get ideas for improving the question—or even decide to ask something else.

Prepare the Body, Mind, and Soul

Dream incubation should be undertaken when we have the time to devote proper attention to it. Choose a day and night when you will not be stressed, hurried, or involved with activities close to bedtime. During the day, follow the ancient wisdom of eating lightly or fasting; abstain from alcohol.

Pray or meditate on the question, which continues the alchemical cooking. Be sure to give thanks for the answer that will come, which prepares the way for receiving the answer. Think about the question throughout the day.

At Bedtime, Do an Incubation Ritual

This can be as simple or as elaborate as you like. It's not necessary to be alone, but anyone else present should be respectful of your incubation. Create a special atmosphere by lighting a candle, burning some incense, or playing some soft, meditative music. You may wish to take a ritual bath, which will relax you. Spend a few minutes in prayer or meditation to still your mind. If you wish to read, choose something that is inspirational or spiritual—this is not the time to read a novel or news magazine.

When you feel ready, turn your attention to your question. Repeat it aloud three times* followed by, "I give thanks for the answer, which will be in a dream that I remember." Visualize yourself awakening, remembering, and receiving an answer. Make the image as vivid as possible.

Why is it important to speak the question out loud rather than just thinking about it? For the same reason that the ancient Egyptians—and others—spoke their dream spells out loud. Sound is an effective way to set forces of the universe in motion.

Sacred sound is the basis for all creation. Cosmogonies—stories of creation—from around the world tell of the world and its features and creatures being spoken or sung into existence. The Gospel of John says in its opening line, "In the beginning was the Word and the Word was with God, and the Word was God," telling us that God-in-speech is God-in-action, creating. In the Eastern traditions, we find the concept of *shabda,* or sacred sound, which is harnessed by the power of the mantra, a sacred word, name of God, or phrase that is repeated in order to unleash certain cosmic forces in the consciousness.

If saying the question out loud is not comfortable or feasible, rest assured that you can still do the incubation if you repeat the question silently. Mystical traditions teach that thoughts are things

---

*The significance of the number three is explained in chapter 12.

and are the parents of all action. Thoughts also set forces in motion.

Write the Incubation Question Again

This adds to the buildup of energy that is fertilizing the field of your dreams to address your question. Follow the age-old tradition of placing the question beneath your pillow. At this point, you should be ready for sleep, so refrain from the distractions of conversation, the media, or reading.

As you fall asleep, try the Eastern visualization of placing a blue light at the throat chakra. Breathe into the blue light.

Follow Guidelines for Improving Dream Recall As Necessary

If you have a tendency to lose dreams easily when you wake up, give yourself extra time the morning after an incubation. Follow the recall tips in chapter 14. Perhaps you might want to use an affirmation for remembering dreams prior to going to sleep. Or, use some of the techniques for recall upon awakening.

Give Extra Attention to Dream Interpretation

Even though you've incubated a dream, your answer may not be readily apparent. Sometimes answers are buried in the layers of a dream. You may need to devote more time to a postincubation dream, especially if the dream does not obviously address your question.

Watch for Extra Information That Comes Later

Dream alchemy sometimes seems a peculiar process, operating by its own rules and timetables. The answer to your question may not be in the dream you have. Or, perhaps you do the incubation process, but do not recall a dream the next morning. Sometimes the answer pops up later. It may come in a dream the next night, or even weeks later. It may come via intuition—a sudden flash that hits you while you're not thinking about the situation. It may also come via synchronicity, or "meaningful coincidences." Synchronicity can come through things other people say to you in which a message seems to be hidden, or something you read, or some other seemingly chance event, such as an opportunity.

Don't Give up if Success Is Not Immediate

If you do not receive an answer in a dream, repeat the entire incubation process again the next day. If you still have no results, repeat it a third time. If three tries produce no results, there may be one or more reasons why.

- You are not clear on the question or your willingness to examine it.
- You have received the answer but haven't recognized it.
- You will receive the answer at another time.

If you have remembered dreams but do not feel they answer your question, reexamine them for clues you may have missed. Remember that dreams are often subtle in their messages.

Many times, answers must come at the appropriate moment. Trust in the process and allow yourself to ride with the flow. Be observant for signals. Pray and meditate for insight.

If a long period of time elapses without an answer, try the incubation process again. Or, try another question. Dream incubation is learning a skill, and practice improves the process.

Incubation Without Ritual

Ritual enhances dream incubation, but actually we can incubate dreams whenever we have an intense desire for a solution to a dilemma. The intensity of emotion and desire for a solution can help the higher self break through in a dream. In the following example, Alexis B. incubated a dream in this fashion. Her recognition of the answer involved a bit of sleuthing, demonstrating how answers are sometimes veiled in dreams.

In June 1996, after receiving news from my father that Mom had suffered a sudden cardiac arrest, I was on a plane from New York to Boston.

There followed a tumultuous several weeks of listening to repeated negative prognoses from the doctors as to my mother's recovery. Dad and I (who have always taken an optimistic view toward healing, often through unconventional methods) kept up our spirits and tenacity with regard to my mother's recovery. We worked extremely hard to find alternative approaches to act as an adjunct to the conventional route the doctors had been taking in my mother's care.

As she lay in a deep coma, or "vegetative state," as the doctors labeled it, Dad and I were busy doing research on coma arousal; meeting with various holistic doctors; buying all sorts of herbal supplements that helped to strengthen the heart, brain, and any other organ affecting Mom's condition, and of course, seeking out spiritual support.

On one very frustrating morning after a sleepless night, I sat helplessly in Mom's favorite chair in the living room, combing my thoughts as to what, if anything, I could do to help her. I had resorted to some way-out methods, including the process of dowsing, to try to reach her through clairvoyance and perhaps gain some insight on how and why this awful event happened. While sitting in the chair, suddenly out of sheer desperation, I shouted aloud, "If there is anything I can do to help my mother, show me in my dream!" That was it. I then took a few deep breaths, and tried to calm myself, trusting that my request would be granted.

The next morning, as I puttered around the house, getting ready to make the trip back to the hospital, I remember saying to myself, "Oh well. Guess my request was not fulfilled. In fact, I don't even remember what I dreamed last night." Then, seemingly, as soon as I got busy thinking of something else, sketchy details of last night's dream started to come back to me. Like many of my dreams, the one that I started to recall at first made little sense and certainly didn't seem to pertain in any remote way to my request. As the day went on—and it could have been more than a day, more details started to flow about the dream, like scenes from a movie, first taken out of context, then slowly being put in the right order. The very fact that the dream (over time) was returning to my conscious hinted to me that perhaps there was some significance to its message after all.

In the dream, I was visiting a publisher's office and speaking with someone who worked there at the front desk. She must have been a friend of mine, because I remember asking her for some freebies (extra copies of magazines and promotional stuff from around the office). She complied and gave me all sorts of things to take with me. I saw a table with loads of fashion magazines (all different titles), but one stood out from the rest. It was a magazine with a picture of model Linda Evangelista on the cover. There were several details of this magazine cover that stood out to me: white background, model with blond hair, the model's expression, and most importantly, the date of April 1995. Then I mentioned the name of another model to my friend at the publishing house: Elle MacPherson.

Alexis dissected the dream—publishing house, model, magazine—and determined that it was telling her that important information was contained in a magazine. But what magazine, and where? She used pendulum dowsing on magazines she found around the house, asking her "dowsing angel" if each was the right one, and receiving a "no." At last she quit and busied herself with other activities.

She went upstairs to her parents' bedroom, where she found some of her possessions she'd left behind when she moved out: old books, records, photos—and magazines.

I had my back facing a shelf in which there were several magazines and was not consciously thinking about them when suddenly something told me to turn around and look. Lo and behold, there was the fashion magazine [from the dream], complete with model Linda Evangelista on the cover, white background, and the date of April '95 in the lower left-hand corner. The magazine's name? Elle. *Just like the name* Elle MacPherson *in my dream. Of course, my heart raced when I discovered that this had to be the magazine.*

Alexis looked over the table of contents. Her attention was drawn to an article entitled, "Meditation Can Make You Happy, Yes," in a section called "Inner Happiness." The article included an interview with a psychiatrist.

I proceeded to read the article and was able to narrow down my message to one paragraph:

"Yes. If we can't control the environment or, in other words, if we can't control our parents' depression—which as children we can't; we can feel our parents' depression, but we can't control it—all we can control is ourselves. . . ."

I knew, unequivocally, that this little line was meant for my eyes. In fact, it sounded like it came directly from my mother, something she would definitely say. Most importantly, I took it to mean that all I can do for her (to make her happy) was to continue to take care of myself. God will take care of her. Furthermore, I believe that there was significance to the reference of depression, as my mother had suffered with depression so long, out of feelings of hopelessness with her ills. Throughout her heart condition and other complications that ensued, she, although tenacious by nature, still became tired and despondent about her overall condition. All along, I played an integral part in trying to seek out the underlying (psychological) role that led to my mother's physical disorder and thus I perhaps tried to control her depression. *She, in fact, would sometimes remind me that she was the only one who could attempt to solve this problem and that I should stop trying so hard to solve it for her. Ultimately, she would be telling me to not worry about her and to take care of myself.*

My mother passed away about two months after the cardiac arrest. I feel she is still trying to impress upon me the importance of taking care of myself. Somehow, she is having a profound effect on me now more than ever, and I will never take her or these intuitive messages for granted ever again.[5]

Alexis asks for a dream and then, like many people who try dream incubation, awakens feeling that no answer has been forthcoming. Yet, she does remember a dream, although it doesn't seem to address her problem. Only in analyzing it does she realize that it did indeed provide the answer. But still the answer is not obvious, and Alexis must allow her intuition to keep guiding her until all of the pieces fall into place.

Note that twice Alexis feels stymied and so stops thinking about the dream and turns her attention to something else. This is a common technique of alchemically cooking the intuition. Frustrated concentration creates a barrier between the higher self and waking consciousness. If we engage in another activity, the intuition is free to cook until it boils over into awareness with a breakthrough insight.

Whenever you are stuck with dream interpretation or with any creative problem, set it aside for awhile. Go about your daily business. Some of the great artists and thinkers of history knew that their greatest inspirations would come when they were pleasantly engaged in a light activity. Beethoven and Mozart would go for carriage rides; Albert Einstein liked to go sailing. Gardening, puttering around the house, running errands, and similar activities provide excellent alchemical cauldrons.

Interestingly, the dream is very specific about the type of magazine (fashion), its cover (white), a model (Linda Evangelista), and even the publication date (April 1995). Yet the dream obscures the title of the magazine (*Elle*) in a person's proper name. Why be specific about all details but that one—and a crucial one at that? We cannot fathom the answers to such questions. This is but one example of the mystery of dream language—a mystery that requires us to always be the investigator.

c h a p t e r e l e v e n

THE MEANING OF COLORS

WE HAVE KNOWN SINCE ANCIENT TIMES THAT COLORS HAVE SPECIFIC EFFECTS UPON THE BODY, MIND, AND SPIRIT. THE ANCIENT INDIANS, CHINESE, TIBETANS, EGYPTIANS, GREEKS, Persians, and Babylonians ascribed various qualities and attributes to colors: for example, red, the longest wavelength of visible colors, was associated with the physical and material, while violet, the shortest wavelength, was associated with spirituality and enlightenment. Pythagoras corresponded colors to the notes of the musical scale. And colors have been used in healing since at least 3000 B.C.E. in the belief that their vibrations are absorbed and utilized by the body. Healing temples of light and color existed in Heliopolis in Egypt.

More recently, color healing has been used in the West since the late nineteenth century as a therapy to correct imbalances in the body. Color therapy is a supplemental treatment of a wide range of physical, mental, and psychological disorders, including fatigue and depression.

Modern research has reaffirmed ancient wisdom by demonstrating that different wavelengths of light act on the biochemicals of the body, the reproductive system, and circadian rhythms.

With color an important aspect of our holistic health, it's no surprise that colors have significance in our dreams. Brilliant, electric, or florescent colors are often characteristics of lucidity and otherworldly contact. Colors also express emotions. The appearance of colors should be interpreted along the same lines as other elements in a dream. Look first for personal emotional associations that you make with a particular color: red, for example, might always mean power or passion or anger to you. Is a color a favorite or a least favorite? Does it remind you of something from your past or some activity with which you can make further associations? If yellow was a childhood favorite, perhaps that leads to a vision of your old room or a toy, which in turn brings up associations with people and feelings. What is the context of the color to what's going on in the dream?

Carl Jung held that red, yellow, blue, and green are four "psychological primaries" and represent inner balance. Thus, if three of the primary colors are present in a dream and one is missing, then the associations with that color are what is needed to achieve inner balance.

It's an interesting idea and may have a bearing on some dreams, but it does not explain the meaning of color in dreams in general. Often in dreams just one color stands out, and it may not even be one of those primaries. What then?

Dream researcher Bob Hoss categorizes four ways to examine color:

- Color is a symbol unto itself, like the images in a dream, and must be interpreted accordingly.
- Color amplifies an image by expressing the same things as the image.
- Color complements an image by working with it to give a complete message.
- Color modifies an image by painting over it and thus possibly points to repressed or conflicting emotions.

Colors have a positive and a negative side. Sometimes our associations with colors are based upon language, such as being blue or depressed, or green with envy. These language associations change with time and also vary by culture.

How does a color express an imbalance? Perhaps a lot of red is telling you that you need to be more assertive, or it may be an indication of a need to cool down. It may direct your attention to a chakra (see below). The context of a dream and your intuitive interpretation will guide you in making the correct analysis.

Colors also have esoteric significance, so we should consider the meaning of colors on a spiritual level in a dream. When red and white appear prominently together in a dream, they may have an alchemical significance, for red and white express the masculine-feminine opposites, respectively. Another alchemical color symbol is a rainbow or mother-of-pearl swirl. In alchemy the latter is called the *cauda pavonis* (peacock's tail). It is a shimmer of color that appears in the alchemical brew, signifying that the attainment of the philosopher's stone is at hand. In my dreams, this iridescence has appeared on the face of an angel.

The rainbow also has other meanings. It is the path to the gold, which can be a new level of awareness or understanding, enlightenment, or, on the mundane level, accomplishment or happiness. In the Eastern alchemical traditions, adepts who achieve immortality acquire a new, indestructible body called the rainbow body, body of gold, body of glory, Buddha body, or light body. The rainbow is also the path to otherworldly realms; its presence in a dream may signify another dimension. In myth, rainbows are the roads to the otherworld for the souls of the dead and also to the kingdoms of the gods.

Whenever colors appear in a dream, notice their clarity. Clear, rich colors generally have positive overtones; colors that are dirty, muddy, or unclear generally have negative overtones.

Here is a list of colors and their meanings. Not all colors have specific alchemical meanings; those that do are noted.

Red

Positive: blood, life, the life force, fertility, passion, activity, energy, courage, willpower, ferocity, wounds (initiation), death (transformation)

Negative: lust, materialism, greed, anger, rage, war

Alchemical: masculine and kingly energy; sublimation, suffering, love

Orange

Positive: harmony, balance, ambition, pride, artistic expression, purification by burning away impurities

Negative: excessive ambition and pride, excessive appetites, egoism, cruelty

Yellow

Positive: the color of the sun, warmth, illumination, light, intellect, generosity, purification by burning away impurities, beginning of spiritual ascension

Negative: cowardice, fear, low self-esteem, sickliness, narrow-mindedness

Alchemical: transition, especially by heating up

Green

Positive: growth, hope, renewal, freshness, lushness, health, youth, vigor, harmony, refreshment, abundance, prosperity, soul of nature, the midpoint

Negative: rot, mold, slime, overripeness, decay, suffocation, overgrowth, neglect, death, envy

Alchemical: beginnings

Blue

Positive: the spirit, the spiritual and spiritual ascent, the heavenly, the numinous, inspiration, devotion, religious feeling, godliness, contemplation, inspiration, tranquillity, relaxation, truth, peace, clear thinking

Negative: depression, isolation, loneliness, coldness, numbness

Violet

Positive: sanctity, religious devotion, knowledge, temperance, authority, power, nostalgia, memories (**Indigo:** advanced spiritual qualities or wisdom, psychic faculties, intuition)

Negative: sorrow, grief, mourning, excessive or abusive power and authority

Purple

Positive: the color of the gods, royalty, imperial power, pomp, pride, justice, truth

Negative: excessive imperial power, pomp and pride, penitence

Alchemical: final stage of the Great Work

White

Positive: purity, holiness, sacredness, redemption, mystical illumination, timelessness, ecstasy, innocence, joy, light, life, transcendent perfection, brilliance of the Godhead, wholeness, transformation and renewal

Negative: blank, featureless

Alchemical: feminine and queenly energy, beginning of the ascent from darkness

Black

Positive: the unconscious and processes in the unconscious, womb, gestation, inner planes, descent into the unconscious, high sacred authority

Negative: fear, darkness, the unknown, the shadow, demonic agencies, destruction, threat, danger, decay, depression, death, mourning, hatred

Alchemical: dissolution necessary to begin the Great Work

Silver

Positive: the color of the moon, magic, mysticism, psychic nature, emotions, intuition

Negative: illusion

Alchemical: reward of the Great Work, the feminine principle of the cosmos, the affections purified

Gold

Positive: the sun, divine light, illumination, enlightenment, the Godhead, the highest state of glory, Absolute Truth, attainment, riches, treasure, fruition

Negative: greed, hoarding, falsehood (fool's gold)

Alchemical: reward of the Great Work, the masculine principle of the cosmos, youthfulness

Brown

Positive: the color of the earth, earthy qualities, groundedness, stability, firmness

Negative: coarseness, lack of clarity (muddiness), spiritual death and degradation

Gray

Positive: humility, neutrality, wisdom, transformation from material to spiritual

Negative: lackluster, dull, penitence, limbo

Pink

Positive: the flesh, sensuality, robust, emotions, the material, love

Negative: naive

Colors of the Chakras

The seven primary chakras of the body's energy field, or aura, each have a color. An intuitive senses the chakras in different ways. This person might get a visual impression of a chakra's appearance, envision colors, or feel flows of energy. Clear colors indicate balance and vibrancy, and muddy colors indicate blockages. As an intuitive, I feel the energy flow of the chakras and, if they are blocked, receive visual impressions relating to the causes of the blockages.

Colors in dreams may relate to the chakras, especially if a particular color is pronounced and recurs. Again, context and intuition will tell you if dream colors point to the chakras.

Root chakra (Four Spokes)

Color: red
Physical: adrenals, spinal column, kidneys
Psychological: vitality, will to live
Spiritual: grounding in the material world, stability

Spleen chakra (Six Spokes)

Color: orange
Physical: gonads, reproductive system
Psychological: sexual energy and power; quality of love
Spiritual: expression of personal power, assertiveness

Solar plexus chakra (Ten Spokes)

Color: yellow
Physical: pancreas, stomach, liver, gallbladder, nervous system
Psychological: emotions, sense of place and purpose
Spiritual: emotional balance, intuitive sense, self-esteem

Heart chakra (Twelve Spokes)

Color: green
Physical: thymus, heart, blood, circulatory system
Psychological: love, sense of connectedness with all life
Spiritual: unconditional love, forgiveness, compassion

Throat chakra (Sixteen Spokes)

Color: blue
Physical: thyroid, bronchial apparatus, vocal chords, lungs, alimentary canal

Psychological: will, expression, communication, creativity, profession

Spiritual: self-expression in alignment with divine will

Third eye chakra (Ninety-Six Spokes)

Color: Indigo

Physical: pituitary, lower brain, left eye, ears, nose, nervous system

Psychological: abstract concepts, visionary ability, psychic perception

Spiritual: faith, discernment, vision, wisdom

Crown chakra (Nine Hundred Seventy-Two Spokes)

Color: violet white

Physical: pineal, upper brain, right eye

Psychological: spirituality, integration, transcendence

Spiritual: oneness

Higher Chakras

There are higher chakras than the primary seven. These higher chakras deal more with subtle realms of consciousness. The eighth chakra, which is located a few inches above the crown chakra, is called the *higher self* or the *oversoul.* This chakra opens when we expand our awareness into a bigger frame of reference than the limits of time and space. The oversoul sees past, present, and future as one, the entire line of our incarnations, and the soul's path. The ninth, tenth, and eleventh chakras penetrate into the realm of the angels and masters. The twelfth chakra is at the level of the light body or body of ascension (twelve is the number of resurrection).

Colors that represent these levels of awareness are magenta, magenta gold, turquoise, turquoise silver, gold silver, and hues of purple and purple violet, which may appear in rainbows, swirls, tapestries, or streams of light. Often in otherworldly dimensions, the brilliant colors are simply beyond words—"Like nothing I've ever seen on earth" is a common description.

Tips for Dream Color Analysis

Consider these questions in analyzing the role of color in a dream.

- What are my personal associations with this color?
- What are my archetypal associations?
- What are my spiritual associations?
- Is the color a symbol in itself?
- Does the color amplify, complement, or modify another image in the dream?
- Could this color reflect an imbalance in life, in terms of excess or deficiency?

As part of your action plan for a dream, you might want to do some creative work with colors. A guidebook on colors will give you in-depth information. Here are a few suggestions.

- Change colors in your environment or wardrobe.
- Meditate on colors.
- Breathe colors by visualizing the breath as filled with them.
- Eat colors by making food choices.

Colors are an important part of the story of the dream. Sometimes they hold the key to unraveling the dream's mystery.

c h a p t e r t w e l v e

THE POWER OF NUMBERS

EVER WONDER WHY CERTAIN NUMBERS SEEM TO PLAY A ROLE IN YOUR LIFE? IN THE MYSTERY TRADITIONS OF BOTH EAST AND WEST, NUMBERS ARE NOT QUANTITIES, THEY ARE IDEAS OR forms that constitute the building blocks of all things in the universe. Each number has it own vibration, character, and attributes, which in turn influence the physical world by attracting certain energies. Seven, for example, is a lucky number of magic, and four is the number of solidity, practicality and work.

Every word can be reduced to a numerical value to reveal its vibrational nature. In the ancient science of numerology, names, words, birth dates, and birthplaces are translated into numbers that reveal personality, destiny, and fortune. It is not uncommon for people to choose personal and company names that vibrate to a desired cosmic frequency.

The Babylonians, Persians, Arabs, Greeks, Gnostics, Hebrews, and early Christians used systems of numerology variously to decipher the hidden meaning of sacred texts, make decisions, and hide the secrets of alchemy. In the eighth century B.C.E., King Sargon II of Babylonia used the numerical value of his name to determine the size of city walls.

Numerical values were assigned to letters of the alphabet, and words with the same numerical value were examined together. In this manner, sacred texts were read according to their numerical correspondences. For example, Genesis 18:2, which states "And lo, three men . . ." was interpreted as referring specifically to the angels Michael, Gabriel, and Raphael because both "and lo, three men" and "Elo Michael, Gabriel Ve-Raphael" added up to 701. By the Middle Ages, kabbalists had developed this into a sophisticated system called gematria.

Pythagoras is considered the Western father of numerology, due to his discovery that the musical intervals known in his time could be expressed in ratios between the numbers 1, 2, 3, and 4. Pythagoras reasoned that the entire universe could be expressed numerically, creating a mystical system that was expanded by other early Greek philosophers. He observed that the numbers 1 + 2 + 3 + 4 add up to 10, which begins the cycle of numbers over again, for 1 + 0 = 1. Thus, 10 is the number of perfection and the All, and automatically returns to the number 1, or creation and beginnings.

In the Pythagorean system, a numerical value of 1 through 9 is assigned each letter of the alphabet. Odd numbers are masculine (active, creative), and even numbers are feminine (passive, nurturing). The numerical values are as follows:

1	2	3	4	5	6	7	8	9
A	B	C	D	E	F	G	H	I
J	K	L	M	N	O	P	Q	R
S	T	U	V	W	X	Y	Z	

To find the numerical value of a name, all the numbers of the letters are added together and reduced to a single digit. For example, Mary equals 4 + 1 + 9 + 7 = 21 = 2 + 1 = 3.

Strings of numbers and dates can be reduced similarly to find their core value by adding them together until they are reduced to a single digit.

There are exceptions to the reduction in the form of *master numbers:* 11, 22, and 33 are numbers of high spiritual vibration and are left intact.

Numbers in Dreams

Carl Jung paid attention to numbers in dreams. He viewed numbers as archetypal symbols representing the self, the dynamics of the psyche, and its stages of growth and development. Numbers regulate both matter and psyche, and are an archetype that has become conscious, he said.

As with other symbols, numbers in dreams must be examined according to the three levels of the dream: personal, archetypal, and spiritual. Not all levels may apply.

Personal. A number might relate to a time, period, or age in life. Here numbers are not necessarily reduced to a single digit. The numbers 7 or 12, for example, might point to a time in life 7 or 12 days, weeks, months, or years ago, or to yourself at ages 7 or 12. Is a number an old address of yours? Look for associations related to that place or time period.

Archetypal. Reduce numbers to a single digit to examine correspondences and associations that click.

Spiritual. Relate archetypal numbers to your spiritual consciousness.

The following meanings of numbers relate to all three levels of the dream. Odd numbers are masculine, and even numbers are feminine. Included are the nine basic digits of the Pythagorean system plus master numbers and other numbers that have special significance.

Zero

Zero is nothingness. It can be seen as emptiness or worthlessness, or as potential—the unformed and unmanifest that has yet to become defined and filled with meaning. Zero has associations with the circle, the symbol of wholeness, perfection, and eternity.

One

One stands for beginnings, independence, strength, initiative, originality, leadership, the ego, oneself. It is the beginning of all things, unity, oneness, the source of all creativity and creation, and oneness realized with all good.

Two

Two symbolizes partnership, balance, cooperation, agreement, diplomacy, beauty, duality. On the higher planes, it is the joining of opposites, the descent of spirit into matter, the polarity of opposites, and the dawning of something new into consciousness.

Three

The product of 1 + 2, three is creation, growth, generation, forward movement, imagination, and artistic creativity. It is spiritual synthesis, harmony, and sufficiency; also prudence, friendship, justice, peace, virtue, and temperance. Three is the number that opens doors to the higher planes. It is a powerful number with a substantial presence in dreams (see special section below).

Four

Four represents solidity, stability, practicality, earthiness, responsibility, dependability, and industriousness. Four is a follower rather than a leader. It is the "eternal principle of creation," according to Pythagoras, since it is the final number that brings everything to unity (1 + 2 + 3 + 4). It describes the universe (four elements, four quarters, four directions). It is a principle number of alchemy and represents a transition or initiation of consciousness from the three-dimensional realm to the fourth dimension.

Five

Five is the number of energy, change, freedom, cleverness and resourcefulness, and the midway point. It expresses the fifth element of spirit, the *quinta essentia,* and stands for the resurrected Christ (there were five wounds upon the body of Jesus). It also stands for humankind (four limbs and the head) and the microcosm. Five represents the victory of the spirit over matter and the awakening of the I AM consciousness, the realization of God within.

Six

Six symbolizes love and harmony in relationships, as well as generosity, domesticity, and humanitarianism. Esoterically, it pertains to the interrelationship of the human and the divine and is a working and building number aimed at illumination. Six relates to the beauty of the soul that emerges from the alternating light and shadow of life. It concerns the transmutation of physical love into spiritual love.

Seven

Seven stands for investigation, research, analysis, discovery, philosophy, charm, and luck. It is the number of rest (God rested on the seventh day of creation) and spiritual realization. It is mysticism, the psychic and occult, introspection, intuition, magic, and the hero's quest for spiritual truth.

Eight

Eight is material success, setting priorities, toughness, tenacity, executive ability, administration, judgment, supervision, and satisfaction with work. Eight is a cosmic number of regeneration and birthing into the new. It is cosmic knowing, exaltation, the essence of the life force, secret wisdom, and consciousness that spans the physical and spiritual.

Nine

Nine represents philanthropy, compassion, service, tolerance, broadmindedness, and the capability of living a largely divine life. It is spiritual and mental achievement and completion of a phase. Nine is the number of the spiritual evolution of humankind: The numbers 666 and 144,000, expressing spiritual opposites in the Book of Revelation, both reduce to a nine. Thus nine synthesizes the ego's entire journey, or the philosopher's stone of alchemy.

Ten

Ten is the number of completion and return to one. It is the number from which all things come and to which all things return. It is the divine inhalation and exhalation of creation.

Eleven

Eleven is the first master number that does not reduce to a single digit. It expresses a high level of humanitarianism, intuition, inspiration, prophetic ability, and illumination. It amplifies the power of the number one and is the resurrected lightbody demonstrated by Christ. Eleven brings the merger of the individual with the universal, and the transmutation of earthly urges into the spiritual light of compassion, brotherhood, and universality.

Twelve

Twelve turns the wheel of the heavens and represents the cosmic order of things. It is the number of regeneration, representing the New Jerusalem. It concerns extension, expansion and elevation, and liberation from the bondage of time and space.

Thirteen

Most people regard thirteen as a number of bad luck, misfortune, and mishap. In esotericism, however, thirteen is the number of mystical manifestation. The teachings of Jesus are centered on the formula of 1 + 12 (Jesus plus his twelve disciples). One added to twelve creates the unlimited number of thirteen, according to Pythagoras. It is through this formula that such miracles as the multiplication of the loaves and fishes take place. Thirteen is the all-or-nothing cosmic law of destiny: death through failure and degeneration, or rebirth through regeneration. It is also the number of the Great Goddess, represented by thirteen lunar cycles to a year.

Twenty-two

Twenty-two is the second master number that does not reduce to a single digit. It is the mastermind, high capability, wisdom. Twenty-two is the spiritual master, a luminary. It is the number of the angelic kingdom and amplifies the power of the number two.

Thirty-three

Another master number, thirty-three is the level of avatar or bodhisattva, a human incarnation of the divine who functions as a mediator between humans and God and serves the spiritual evolution of humanity. Thirty-three is self-realization, the product of intense spiritual devotion and practice.

Forty

Forty is the number of spiritual incubation, trial, and initiation. The Bible makes references to forty: the period of the deluge, the reign of David, the days Moses spent on Mount Sinai, the years the Jews wandered in the desert, the days Jesus spent fasting in the wilderness, and the elapsed time between the resurrection and the ascension. In alchemy, the initial phase of the work, the *nigredo,* the blackening, takes about forty days to complete. Spiritual awakenings sometimes take place over a forty-day period.

The Number Three in Dreams

The number three plays a prominent role in myth, mysticism, the mystery traditions, folklore, alchemy, and the dynamics of spiritual growth and change. In my dream research over the years, I have noticed that three occurs frequently, as a digit, a quantity, a series of actions, events, themes or patterns, or even a series of repetitive dreams.

Three is the numerical vibration that opens the gateways to the higher planes. Dreams themselves are the gatekeepers and thus vibrate to the number three. The role of the dream is to open us to new and higher awareness and expand our consciousness so that we live life more fully and express our highest potential.

Pythagoras said that three is "a triple Word, for the Hierarchical Order always manifests itself by Three." All the great religions recognize the expression of the Godhead in trinities. For example, in Christianity it is Father–Son–Holy Spirit. In Hinduism the trinity is Brahman-Shiva-Vishnu. There are three pillars to Zen Buddhism. The ancient Egyptians' holy trinity was Osiris-Isis-Horus. The Great Goddess has a threefold expression of Virgin-Mother-Crone. In Jewish mysticism there are three pillars to the Tree of Life, which is a blueprint for the descent of the divine into matter and the return ascent to the Godhead. The top three *sephirot,* or stations, of the Tree of Life are the mystical steps to unity: understanding, wisdom, and humility. In the *Sefer Yetzirah* (Book of Formation) of the Kabbalah, three is expressed in the Three Mothers, Aleph, Mem, and Shin, which form the foundation of "all others." Aleph, Mem, and Shin are letters of the Hebrew alphabet that mean, respectively, breath or vital spirit; seas or water; and life-breath of the Divine Ones or Holy Spirit.

The Western mystery tradition and alchemy are based on the legendary teachings of Hermes Trismegistus, or Thrice-Greatest Hermes. Three is the ascent of consciousness, represented by the upward-pointing triangle and the face of the pyramid. It represents the unification of body-mind-spirit and heart-will-intellect and eyes-ears-mouth (what we see, hear, and speak as products of our spiritual consciousness). The Three Wise Men of the Bible represent the enlightened consciousness. The Great Work of alchemy takes place in three main stages.

The Greek philosopher Anatolius observed that three, "the first odd number, is called perfect by some, because it is the first number to signify the totality—beginning, middle, and end." Thus, we find in mythology, folklore, and fairy tales the recurrent motif of the triad: three wishes, three sisters, three brothers, three chances, blessings done in threes, and spells and charms done in threes (thrice times the charm). Three is also the number of wisdom and knowledge in its association with the Three Fates and the past, present, and future, and the ancient sciences of music, geometry, and arithmetic.

When events or synchronicity happen in threes, it is time to pay attention, for this is how the world of spirit, intuition, and the higher self knock upon the door of waking consciousness. Thus, when three shows up in a dream, it is a signal that requires attention.

People have experienced the power of three in dreams since ancient times. A poem from Babylonia dating from about 1700 B.C.E. describes how a nobleman became ill due to demons and how a series of three dreams led to his recovery. In the months prior to the start of World War I, Carl Jung experienced three dreams presaging the war, despite the fact that he was not thinking about the prospects of it.

Numerous examples of dreams given throughout this book feature the number three in them. Look for three as you read along.

Three Angels

In the following dream, the number three represents the angelic kingdom, based on the account in Genesis of three angels disguised as men who visit Abraham. The dream also involves archetypal symbols of the tree, the house, and an earthquake, as well as direct audition (disembodied voice). There is an element of prophecy, which can be associated with the Three Fates of time. The dreamer is Robert Wise, an Episcopal clergyman and coauthor with Paul Meier of a book on dreams, *Windows of the Soul.* At the time of the dream, Wise was entering a period he described as "considerable personal loss and trial" and "overwhelming turmoil."

In the dream I was asleep in my own bedroom on the second floor. . . . Three men awoke me and pointed out of the window. One man said, "Everything that can be shaken will be shaken." I was aware the statement was like a biblical passage and the three men were holy. I remembered the three men who visited Abraham by the oaks of Mamre. Even though I wasn't sure of the meaning of the moment, I knew I was being given a very special message.

Suddenly the house began to quiver. As I looked out the window, the land began to move up and down in waving motions, like carpet being shaken. Trees started flying out of the ground, and I knew I was in the middle of a terrible earthquake. The entire house began to sway violently. My large waterbed lifted off the floor, and I was so terrified I began to scream at the top of my lungs. Even though I was still asleep, I could feel my heart pounding. The three men disappeared, and I remember thinking, "I will not survive the ordeal." From somewhere a voice answered, "Oh, but you will. You are coming to the greatest time in your life." The house turned on its axis and faced a new direction.

The tremor subsided and the house settled on a new foundation. I looked out the windows at the fields beyond the edge of my property and was amazed that the terrain had completely been rearranged. Trees, lakes, and roads were totally different. Everything was peaceful and well ordered.[1]

The literal shake-up in Wise's life is forecast by the three angels, whose presence also is a reassuring connection with God. The direct audition of the disembodied voice can be interpreted as the higher self and the voice of God. The dream shows that the eventual outcome of the upheaval will be good. According to Wise, events occurred just as the dream predicted. The dream was a source of "profound inner knowing" that God was directing his life and leading him to a place that he had never before been. It also was a great source of assurance that the ultimate outcome would be for the better.

Three Pills

An archetypal dream involving three that left a lasting impression on me occurred during a phase of my spiritual work in which I found myself at the threshold of plunging deeper into my interior:

I am at a conference. A young man, sparkling and electrical and having blond curly hair, comes up to me and holds out one hand. In his palm are three pills: a green cube, an orange oval (like a football), and a white circle (like an aspirin). "Take these," he says. I say I do not take anything without knowing what it is. He says he has been on a special diet, and the pills are vitamins.

I take the pills and put them inside my mouth, and they begin to dissolve immediately. The young man laughs, and I realize I have been tricked. He says the pills really are hallucinogens. I spit them out, but it is too late—they are already half-dissolved. I try gagging, but I can't throw up. Even if I could, I know it wouldn't help, because I have already absorbed part of the pills.

I report the young man to the authorities, and they take him into custody. He has a reputation as a trickster, I am told. I steel myself for the onset of psychedelic effects, afraid, but it never comes. When the pills I spit out are analyzed, they are found to be harmless. I am tricked again.[2]

At the time, I had a fear of losing my center or becoming ungrounded if I experienced too profound a change in consciousness in terms of psychic openings. And yet I was determined to pursue the spiritual path, meditating and studying the esoteric teachings, all of which would lead—or so I understood—to just such a thing. While I knew intellectually that psychic phenomena were not the object of the path, I was still fearful of creating a change in my awareness, my perception, that might prove to be unwelcome but would be irrevocable. The dream reflects my desire to change consciousness and my fear that it will be out of control once I do so. Even though I must be tricked into taking another step, I see from the dream that my fears have no basis.

The trickster archetype is not an evil figure but one that uses cunning and trickery, if necessary, in order to accomplish a goal. In Western myth, the trickster is associated with Hermes/Mercury and the healing gods Aesculapius of Greece and Serapis of Egypt. Both gods appear in myth—and in dreams—in trickster guises.

The three pills evoke the gateway symbolism of the number three: By taking them, I will be propelled into another state of consciousness. The pills also represent my self-imposed blockage. I can't progress unless I am forced (or tricked) into taking my medicine. I considered the shapes and colors of the pills. The cube represents foundation and the cosmos. Its green color is growth, renewal, youth, and abundance, symbolizing the fruits of pursuing the Great Work more deeply. Green in alchemy is beginnings; here it is the beginning of a new phase. Green rules the heart chakra: The higher stages of the Work require an opening of the heart center.

The oval reminded me of a *vesica piscis* or mandorla, a shape formed by the intersection of two circles. The *vesica piscis* is a feminine symbol representing the doorway to the great mystery. Orange is a solar color and represents a stage of alchemy closer to completion of the Work. Orange rules the spleen chakra, the seat of personal power. Here it refers to the confidence to move ahead.

The white aspirin-like tablet symbolizes the circle, which represents wholeness and eternity. White is purity of spirit, transcendence, and ecstasy—the fruits of the Work.

If I consider the youth as a personification of Aesculapius, the dream means that I need to heal my fear and proceed with my path. In the dream, the process of healing has already begun; the medicine has been swallowed.

The pills show that I have nothing to worry about. By swallowing them, I take their symbolic energy into my being. The authority figures in the dream—my fears—have no power to stop the process.

Ultimately, the dream points to my need to let go of unfounded fears and move forward. The trickster youth is also that part of me that seeks to get the action going.

Three Women

Romance author Zita Christian had periodic dreams in which black women or girls played a role. Some of the dreams involved lucidity. They seemed to lead to a past-life dream. The black women made their first appearance as a threesome.

I am in someone's house or apartment. Dick [husband] wants to go for a drive. The car is old and dented. He puts a surfboard in the back. We both realize this is not his car at all. He goes across the street where the steps are and gets his own car. It's new. We go for a nice ride.

Scene changes. A corporate attorney in the law firm where I work has become a foreigner. He wants me to go to Italy with him and a group of other people. I don't want to go to Italy, but he says it's important that I do and he will pay me to go. The group is composed of mostly Italians and blacks. Almost all of the black people are women. There is an elderly black couple; they are married. He has heart attack but survives. She collapses. She's cold. Needs a blanket. Knows she is going to die.

Scene changes. I am in my living room with my daughter, Laurie. Three black women are there. I think they were with the group going to Italy, but not sure. One woman is a wedding planner. One does public relations; she says her name is Zita! The third one is a singer. I recognize them as the Pointer Sisters. [Go lucid: This means "Point her."]

The singer stands in the center of the room and sings "Amazing Grace." When she is finished, she and the other two women go outside. I follow and say, in front of witnesses, "Be sure to sing Amazing Grace three *times at my funeral.* Three times. Important."

One month later, Zita's daughter met the man she later married. Near that same time, Zita sold her second book. The black women have multilayered symbolisms. They resemble the triple aspect of Fortuna, or the goddess of Fate: Past, Present, and Future. Their black color represents hidden wisdom. They are aspects of Zita—one is even named Zita. And as the Pointer Sisters, they carry the play on words of pointing something important out to Zita.

About ten months later, Zita had this dream.

I am with my writer friends Leslie and Linda. We are at a bookstore, reading aloud from our current releases. I had felt well-prepared earlier, but now I'm nervous. I fear my work is lousy. I start to read, lose my place, frantically flip the pages, looking for a good part.

A parade of black women and girls comes in. The girls are around nine or ten years old. They're smiling at me as I continue to search through my book.

I decide to go to the beginning. I open the book to the first page. Something strange. I didn't write this. I'm sure I didn't write it because right at the beginning is a poem about black slaves—women and children—and it's written in a language I don't know.

One of the children—a child of someone to whom I had extended hospitality—used a blue magic marker and colored all over the pages of my new book. I'm upset, then I realize the child is just being creative. I should be glad she wants to express herself in my work.

ↄ ↄ ↄ

Another dream occurred six months later.

I'm riding a little scooter. I stop to give an old black woman a ride. She has no shoes. I have all my belongings in a plastic laundry basket. She has only a few things, so I find a place for her things with mine. We go riding along back country roads. I like this woman.

ↄ ↄ ↄ

And about two weeks later, Zita had a dream she identified as a past-life dream.

I am a mulatto in the South prior to the Civil War. A white man my age wants to help me. It is the dead of night. I scurry around to locate what few personal items I have—only three or four things, each hidden or buried in separate places. Each pertains to herbs. One special item is wrapped in oilcloth and buried in the backyard. The light of the full moon helps me find it.

I'm ready to go. Assume the man is taking me from the small shack to the big mansion, but he says no. I can't go there because I'm half black. I'm stunned. Have never known such prejudice.

I leave with the man. I know I'm about to escape, but don't know where I'm going.[3]

ↄ ↄ ↄ

Perhaps the three black women—the "point-her sisters," appeared as the gate openers to an emerging past-life memory. Preceded by three vivid dreams involving black women—including slaves—the way was prepared for Zita to pay attention to and understand the past-life dream.

In your dream journal, start making note of numbers in dreams, especially the number three. Numbers are powerful keys for opening the doors of perception and understanding.

c h a p t e r   t h i r t e e n

MESSAGES FROM ANIMALS

DREAM ANIMALS TELL US ABOUT OURSELVES AT A PRIMAL, INSTINCTUAL LEVEL OF BEING. THEY CORRESPOND TO PHYSICAL, SEXUAL, SENSUAL, EMOTIONAL, AND SPIRITUAL NEEDS THAT the conscious mind needs to address. In psychological terms, they represent the unconscious. They also represent the self and symbolize stages of psychic growth and development.

In mythology, animals are often invested with an awareness of spiritual reality that is keener than that of humans. Thus they become messengers of wisdom. In mythologies, cosmologies, and folktales, animals are archetypal images that arise from the characteristics observed by humans. For example, a bear represents protection and nurturing, because the mother bear is observed to be one of the fiercest protectors of its young in the animal kingdom. The fox is sly, the dog is protective and guiding, the bird is the soul or spirit, and so on. These animal traits may be ones that we need to develop or acquire or call upon during times of stress. They speak to our instinctual layer of consciousness and stimulate the creativity that resides at the wild core of being.

Animals in dreams are great teachers. Simply by being themselves, they speak volumes to us. When animals create fear in a dream, they also show us where to look in our lives for the source of the fear. An animal known for its predatory powers, for example, may relate to something or someone that is attacking us in life.

Being devoured by an animal occurs in dreams and is a widespread archetypal motif in legends, myths, and fairy tales. It symbolizes a descent into the underworld, the sinking of the consciousness into the unconscious. Such a descent precedes a spiritual renewal.

Pregnancy elicits dreams of newborn animals—especially puppies, kittens, and seals—and small, furry mammals in both men and women. They symbolize the vulnerability of the newborn.

Power Animals

We enter into a personal and deeply spiritual relationship with the essence of animals through the power animal, also called the medicine power or totem animal. A power animal represents the collective power of an entire species or genus and customarily has magical powers than enables it to perform extraordinary feats, such as a wolf with the power of flight. They almost always appear in animal form but may shapeshift into human form. In animal form, they can converse with humans and use various magical powers of strength and flight.

In shamanism, power animals are alter egos of the shaman and are a source of magical empowerment. In his visionary work, the shaman is accompanied on his trips to the underworld or heaven by his power animals, who communicate via telepathy or the magical power of speech. He also becomes his power animals, assuming their form, which gives him access to their animal nature and abilities. Power animals are protective and instructive, and they change as the shaman grows in his craft.

Power animals traditionally are acquired during a vision quest, a solitary ritual in the wilderness in which one prays for one's powers to make themselves known. Initially, power animals must be invited to appear. Once manifest, they become a part of the consciousness of the person and can be summoned. Many people today undertake vision quests or training in shamanic journeying in order to connect with their power animals. Power animals can also make themselves known in dreams and can be summoned in dream incubation.

Sometimes animals, especially power animals, move out of our dreams and visionary consciousness to have encounters with us in waking life. Such an experience happened to jeweler and artist Heyoka Merrifield, who has a close relationship with animals in his work. Heyoka is renowned for his stunning jewelry and sculpture with spiritual, mythical, and alchemical themes. Meticulously crafted, imbued with the energy of the gods, his pieces are collected by celebrities, exhibited by galleries, and prized by many. Heyoka modestly says that his art mirrors himself and his "limited" understanding of the cosmos. But looking upon his work and wearing his visionary pieces, one feels his deep-heart connection to the Great Mystery. Dreams are a part of that connection, enabling or strengthening Heyoka's attunement with the spiritual.

I made a necklace for a friend of mine whose medicine power is the black panther. The piece was very strong when I finished it. Within about two months, I heard about someone who had exotic pets across the river. I went to see them. She had lions, a wolf, and a black panther that she had raised from a baby. After everyone left, she said I could go in the cage with the panther. I jumped at the chance. I had this wonderful relationship with the panther. I was petting it and it was purring. It put me in an altered state for weeks afterward. The woman said that no one had ever had that relationship with the panther before, and she wanted to videotape it sometime.

The experience showed me that something in my work had manifested in the physical. Then, a few months later, I had this dream. I had to fight a huge lion. There was no way I was going to win this battle. My main medicine power is the jaguar. In the dream, I said, "Okay, if that's the way it is—a fight to the death—then I'll do it. But you're going to have to fight me as a jaguar." I turned into a jaguar and started walking into battle. Then I realized that I was *a black jaguar. I awoke.*

The black panther started out in my jewelry piece, then came into the physical, and then moved into the dreamworld.

What these symbols meant for me: I have a relationship with animal powers—they help me bring down power into my work. Many animals have helped me, but the jaguar is my primary animal. When I was a young boy, though, the black panther was my totem animal. My bike was the black panther, and my imaginary "whatever" was always the black panther. I realized from the dream that although my medicine power animal is the jaguar, my feminine aspect, or my anima, is the black panther. My anima also has its own power animal, which is the shadow side of the jaguar.

The lion represents the primary purpose of life, the most passionate part, which for me is medicine and jewelry. I definitely have found the king in my life. My career has been taking off and consuming me a lot, not only the making of the jewelry but also the business end that I have to deal with. My ceremonial life is taking a second seat. My career is a competitive, masculine thing, and my ceremonial life is feminine energy. I see that

I have to rearrange things so that my career is more in balance with the ceremonial side.

When I connect with something in the dreamworld and I bring it into the physical in a [jewelry] piece, the piece has more power to it. I wanted to celebrate this dream with another piece of jewelry, so I made a piece with a jaguar on one side and the black panther on the other.[1]

Magical Animals

In the mythical realm, animals—like the power animals of shamanism—often have magical powers. They possess wings and can fly, which represents the ascent of the spirit to heaven or higher consciousness (see chapter 20). They are fabulous beasts not known in the natural world, or they have the ability to become invisible. They have the gift of speech and make themselves understood to those who are awakened enough to hear the message. Such animals are guides into the realm of spirit.

Animals appear in dreams as bearers of important information. They may convey it by their mere presence, by their actions, or by the magical gift of speech, as in the following case. The dreamer is a young woman who was having difficulties in her relationships with her parents.

I was skiing with a very accepting friend. I was wearing scanty shorts and having a great time being myself when the friend disappeared and my parents appeared . . . .I picked up a shotgun and threatened the family if they came closer. I even shot at the ceiling to scare them, firing until I ran out of shells. Finally, a dog and bird started telling me how my family felt so I could help them.[2]

The dream shows that the young woman wants to be accepted for herself by her parents, and is threatened by their disapproval. The dog and bird, two friendly animals representing protection and spirit, act as intermediaries. The dream enabled the young woman to heal her strained relationship without sacrificing her self-identity.

For Shawn Shelton, a rabbit communicated an important message about how she was steering her life. The rabbit visited first her in waking consciousness and then hopped into her dream life.

This is the first time I've had this kind of experience with a dream. The afternoon before I had it, I was walking through my parking lot. The hugest, most gorgeous, most beautiful big brown rabbit hopped across the lot. It had huge ears and a beautiful face. It stopped, got up on its haunches and tilted its head and looked at me. It was not scared of me at all. I started talking to it. It hopped over to the grass and sat there eating and watching me. I must have stayed there about ten minutes with it before I had to leave.

That night, I had a dream where I was walking by my apartment complex along the sidewalk. All of a sudden, a car came speeding down the street. It alarmed me because it was going so fast. I noticed that this rabbit was running alongside of the car. I was worried because I thought the rabbit would get hit. The rabbit ran in front of the car, jumped onto the lawn, jumped into my arms, and put its head on my chest. I woke up and thought, "What an amazing dream!"

I went back to sleep and had the exact same dream again. I've never had a dream twice.[3]

Shawn knew the message the rabbit had for her. "Rabbits have always meant innocence and warmth to me," she said. "The speeding car seemed to be indicative of how my life has been lately, not taking the time to smell the roses, not taking time for myself because I'm so busy all the time with work. The rabbit was trying to get my attention to focus more on myself and on the earth and the things that I love."

The message actually was delivered in the encounter with the rabbit in her parking lot, but Shawn was too distracted about getting to work to become aware of it. Her dreaming self followed up quickly with a reinforcement—not just once but twice in a repeat of the same dream.

Animals As Creativity

Animals can represent our primal urges of creativity. At one point in my career, I went through a stressful time that sapped my energy and left me feeling rather dried up creatively. I had this dream.

B. [my former husband] and I live in a house surrounded by woods. For some reason, we give refuge to a fawn and a small goat, who come into the house. (We also have our two dogs in the dream.) Looking out the window,

I see a mountain lion, and now I know why the wild animals sought shelter. When the mountain lion is gone, we release them; the fawn bounds across the road in supernaturally high leaps in which it literally floats through the air.

Then I see a bear outside. We get the fawn and goat back in, and some strange dogs come along with them. Soon we are giving refuge to many animals, both wild and domestic, all the time, whenever a danger is present outside. Word of this spreads, and people start bringing us their unwanted pets. Soon we have a house full of animals.

A man brings a steel bowl containing a litter of newborn sheepdog pups. There is a shallow layer of water in the bowl. I take the bowl and put it in a room while I tend to the other animals. When I go back to get the pups, I find they have all drowned in the water. The shock is enormous and I am devastated. How could I be so negligent? I should have taken them out of the bowl immediately. I tell B., and he is very upset, too. I am awakened and the dream ends.[4]

I was quite emotionally distraught over the image of the drowned puppies, so much so that it was difficult for me to work with this dream. When I did and was able to see the true meaning of the dream, the results afforded me a great deal of relief. The animals represent deep, unexpressed creative urges. I especially saw this in the fawn who virtually floats through the air. The animals are magical, like creativity. They come in out of the woods—the unconscious—and seek refuge and nurturing. Similarly, ideas must be nurtured. These images symbolize the incubation that an artist must allow for new ideas to spring forth.

However, I wasn't allowing that incubation or expression to happen. I was too preoccupied with events in daily life to give time to my writing. I was allowing all sorts of things to crowd into my house and was putting my art on hold. The mountain lion and the bear represent the threat to my creativity. Yet they are creativity, too: It's my own creativity turning in on itself.

As for the last part of the dream, I drew these associations:

Man who brings the puppies: higher self presenting unformed ideas
Newborn puppies: ideas, creativity seeking to be born
Bowl: womb of consciousness where ideas are nurtured
Water: emotional distractions

I saw how I had been taking my newborn ideas and then neglecting them. Neglected, they can only die. In the dream, I do tend to other ideas [animals], but the message is to focus myself, pay attention to my art, and listen to what my creative side is trying to tell me.

My action was to make a commitment to devote time daily to exploring and developing new ideas. Initially, I felt painfully blocked, and I even wondered if I had assessed the dream correctly. Soon I experienced a breakthrough and began to feel creatively productive again.

Snake Dreams

Dreams of snakes are common and pack a powerful impact. Usually, snake dreams are frightening due to fear of snakes or religious beliefs about the snake representing evil. Often we can't get past such associations to look more deeply into the archetypal and spiritual meanings of the snake, which is where lies its true power: a power of transformation.

The snake represents renewal of the personality, regeneration, and change. It is also a symbol of kundalini, the serpent power.

In alchemy, the snake is the *serpens Mercurii,* the quicksilver that represents the constant driving forward of psychic life forces: living, dying, and being reborn. The snake is the *prima materia,* the unformed and dark chaos, from which order and life spring. Alchemical art often shows the snake wearing a gold crown, gem, diadem, or light to depict its expanded spiritual consciousness, which, like kundalini, arises from the same energy as sexuality.

The snake is an important symbol of healing. Aesculapius, the Greek god of healing, had a snake as an animal totem. In dreams he appeared with a snake or in the form of a snake. Domesticated snakes were kept at the sacred healing temples of the classical world. The healing power of serpents is cited in the Bible as well: Numbers 21:8 describes God instructing Moses to set a fiery serpent upon a pole, so that all who look upon it shall live. A single snake entwined on a stick is the symbol of Aesculapius. As we saw earlier, double snakes entwined on a pole is the magical wand or caduceus of Hermes/Mercury. Both have been official symbols of the modern medical profession. The caduceus also demonstrates the double path of kundalini as it travels up the chakra system from the root chakra to the crown chakra.

For Roger Jahnke, a snake dream clinched his decision to study

Chinese medicine. Jahnke attended medical school in the 1960s, but left to become a student of comparative world literature. In the 1970s, he became interested in pursuing a career in Chinese medicine, which perplexed his family. At the time of the dream, Jahnke was studying the trance readings of Edgar Cayce, founder of the Association for Research and Enlightenment (A.R.E.).

One of the really strong supporters for taking this step was my friend, Charles Thomas Cayce [grandson of Edgar Cayce], who had recently visited a school of Chinese medicine in Vancouver and been to China to work with psychic Chinese children. I was at the A.R.E. Camp at Rural Retreat, Virginia with [Native American medicine man] Rolling Thunder when Charles Thomas said to me, "Chinese medicine is right for you. I believe you're going to Chinese medicine school." Later that week I dreamed of chasing a snake all night. At the end it climbed a tree and turned into a pouch hanging over a limb. Rolling Thunder interpreted the dream: "You are a healer. The snake pouch is your medicine bag."[5]

Interestingly, Jahnke was also reading at the time an ancient book on Chinese medicine that described the flow of energy in the body: the Chinese version of kundalini.

In mythology, snakes are powerful magical and mystical creatures. Jung termed them a potent archetype of psychic energy, power, dynamism, instinctual drive, and the entire process of psychic and spiritual transformation. He also observed that in myth, snakes are often the counterpart of the hero: he has snakelike characteristics (such as snake eyes), is related to a snake, or becomes a snake after death.

Snakes are universal symbols of renewal and rebirth because of their unique ability to shed their old skin for new. The ouroboros, the snake that forms a circle by biting its own tail, symbolizes the eternal cycle of life, death, and rebirth. Snakes embody both masculine and feminine energies. The snake represents a phallus, the creative life force, sexuality, and sensuality. The resulting pregnancy (feminine) represents a state of psychic transformation: pregnant with ideas, possibilities, changes, events about to happen.

Snakes also express the feminine because they crawl along the earth and live in holes in the ground. Thus, they have connections to the underworld, the unconscious, the intuition, and instinct. Mythical snakes guard the sleep of both the living and the dead; they are creatures at the gateway to new consciousness.

In dreams, the snake may indicate a transformative process already under way, but it more often calls attention to the need for us to move to a new level of consciousness. We may fear the snake as we fear change itself, but the snake must be seen as a positive sign and not a negative one. Even a snakebite in a dream benefits us by a forcible infusion of wisdom and awareness which, if acknowledged and integrated, will heal and transform. To be stalked or pursued by a snake intent on biting indicates that the unconscious is attempting to bring something into waking awareness.

When we face periods of intense spiritual change, dreams of snakes are likely to occur. More than any other dream animal, snakes are also likely to come out of the dream and into physical life. The realms of spirit and matter interpenetrate, and the message of the snake is not to be ignored.

Alice Yeager is an artist and healer with mediumistic abilities who found snakes visiting her first in dreams and then in waking consciousness as part of an awakening of kundalini.

I awaken from a dream about an encounter with a snake in my face, touching my face with my eyes closed. It brushed my skin, starting at the forehead, and descended down my face to my chest. Earlier, it crossed over my bare legs as I sat on the floor in a room with F. and J. J. had massage oil on, but the snake left her and F. alone. We had followed [author] Deepak Chopra into a multiroomed, arty dwelling (with other cultural and barren rooms).

The snake also curled between my legs as I sat in a lotus position, motionless.

Three foreign women (from India) entered and laid out button symbols on the floor and then interpreted the symbols left to right in two rows. It was the first of two readings for two of us.

I awakened hearing the words, "You seek oneness, but experience separation."

Earlier in the dream, Deepak spoke facing away from an audience. A woman interrupted him. He allowed her to speak (she spoke of the need for medical schools to offer choices of study including the healing arts).

Deepak stayed with us in my mother's house for several days. He had several conversations with me.

Alice was unsettled by the snake and associated it with an omen of change, but she was uncertain whether the change would be good or not. The Indian elements (Chopra and the three women) are possible references to kundalini, Eastern mysticism, and healing. The three women, who give a reading, call to mind the Three Fates of Greek mythology. They read from left to right, or past-present-future. The message of the reading is in the words Alice hears upon awakening.

Alice continued her spiritual pursuits, increasing her clairvoyant sensitivity and healing ability. A year later, she had series of three snake dreams:

A silent scene with a young, brown-haired woman as guardian observer standing behind me as a three to four-foot, dark snake came up and bit me in the back at my waist to the right side parallel to my pinched nerve at the left.

I awakened from the dream with my back still stinging from the bite.

While I was in the dream, and afterward while I was reviewing it, I was aware that the experience represented a test of trust or some form of initiation where I allowed myself to trust that it was all right for the snake to bite me. I was to go through the experience as a test of faith and trust in my own inner guidance to allow it to bite me, and trusting the observer/guide's presence as appropriate.

The second and third dreams came about nine to ten months later.

I was lying on a stone path made out of large river rocks that had a cement-edged border. A gamekeeper was in observance, watching in silence, similar to the snakebite dream. He watched as a large, golden python crawled up me, starting at my feet and legs to my torso, then across my right arm outstretched above my head and to the right (at about the two o'clock position facing up, or ten o'clock from the observer's point of view). I lay perfectly still trusting that it was okay for the python to travel up my body. I watched its head travel up my arm past my head. I awoke once its head reached the end of my right hand.

Ten days later, a real snake actually showed up at my office. It was dark and about three and a half feet long. I encountered it at the bottom of the stairs outside. Cornered, it hissed at me.

I asked in meditation for the meaning of this, and was told that the snake signified a messenger of higher spiritual knowledge. The areas of my body that the snake crawled across were areas of pain. "It was telling you the root (and route) of the lessons to be learned." The head going up my right arm was a clear directional indicator of how the energy is flowing en route to cleansing and clearing the body, mind, and spirit.

"Keep focused on the head for further indications. You may want to continue the dream in waking state and dialogue with the snake (python) and the gamekeeper (your guide that represents bad)."

This dream, as well as ones about levitating, had elements of teaching, serving, overcoming, making a difference, having trust and confidence, and demonstrating higher consciousness awareness. It also was about initiation and a test of trust in a higher source of purpose and guidance. "Be aware of the signals and indicators in your wakeful state to help you awaken further."

The actual snake encounter "was a manifestation of the superconscious by bringing into reality that which you aspire for your life's purpose work, that is, overcoming challenges and turning them into good. The snake was a messenger about love, abundance, and forgiveness."

Three nights after the actual encounter with the hissing snake, I had a dream that I had a house with three levels. Other people were with me at each level. Numerous dark snakes infested each level and curled together like the snakes in [the movie] Raiders of the Lost Ark, *though not quite as many.*

I saw this again as stages or levels of initiation of awareness. My ability to accept the snakes' presence and ignore them was part of the test as I moved with others up and down the three levels.

I was aware that I was not the only one undergoing the experience and that there were multiple snakes as well as people. They were mostly females about my age—some seemed familiar but can't remember who (perhaps they were costudents or I met them in classes or groups).[6]

Note the repeated appearance of three in Alice's dreams, reinforcing the spiritual nature of the dreams' meanings.

Three animals, a snake, a wolf, and a llama played significant roles in a dream for Dennis K. At the time, he explained, "I was going through the process of separating physically and emotionally from a relationship of eighteen months. I still hadn't finally resolved my divorce, and a lot of personal inner work was still needed; I could not go any further in the relationship. I was planning a trip to California soon to work on the final details and see my children. I was also dealing with some post-traumatic stress from the Vietnam conflict. On top of all this, I had to find a new place to live."

Dennis's dream is rich with archetypal symbolism related to his emergence into a new phase of life. All three animals are message-bearers. Dennis's account is as follows.

Setting in a house with a basement.

Began upstairs . . . I was with a woman named D. and her mother, L. (I am connected to them from a past life—strong emotional connection to D. and strong physical connection with L. Both are healers and very enlightened.)

I saw D.'s face and it spoke to me without saying any words. I felt joy seeing her face. I saw someone who resembled her mother and felt it was her throughout the dream but couldn't be totally sure.

Walked downstairs and as I approached the stairway, I knew I was going to face something pretty scary. Also, as I approached the stairs, I realized that I had no clothes on and I was talking to D. I don't remember if there were words or it was only telepathic. I think both, but more of an awareness of information between us. I felt she was supporting me in where I was going.

When I arrived in the basement, another woman was waiting for me, but I didn't fully recognize her. I sort of wanted it to be L., but I wasn't sure. She didn't have any clothes on, either.

I was nervous and I told the woman I had to find the bathroom. She told me to do it here, as she extended her hand holding onto an Easter basket.

I began to get aroused (I felt embarrassed about it, but she smiled) and I didn't feel comfortable about urinating in an Easter basket so I kind of just stopped and looked into the basket. It was a weathered weave with a ribbon on the outside. There was a wooden slat in the bottom of the basket and I thought it wouldn't hold any liquid because it didn't fit squarely or cover the entire bottom. She then said to go ahead and do it and it will be okay. She said she would urinate in the basket after I was done. She held the basket as I went.

Then I was told (without words) that I had to face my fears now. I remembered I had no clothes so I couldn't leave but just as I thought that, a black snake with a red stripe slithered over the edge of the basket. The lady said it came from inside of me. She was urinating into the basket as the snake came out.

She told me it was very dangerous and I had to touch it and learn how to live with it without fear. I felt as if I was expected to know how to handle the snake. I did have fear, but I was willing to deal with the snake. Then I heard this troubling noise outside.

The basement had a walk-out of a few steps upward to the ground level, and I could see outside clearly. I saw this white wolf just standing there and it literally said to me I had to get past it and everything would be as it should. I didn't know what it meant, but I felt eager to get past it—but I was fearful. Then a strange-looking white llama with a brown face began running around the wolf. It was making frightening noises as if something was terribly wrong. It scared me because it looked deformed. Its head and neck seemed to be on a hinge atop the body. It freely and erratically fell and jerked around. The wolf didn't seem to notice. I kept seeing D.'s face, resting on her hands on the kitchen counter, just smiling at me. I felt secure in the smile. She was wearing Native American jewelry. I looked at the wolf's eyes and as I began to walk toward the doorway, I woke up.[7]

At the time of the dream, said Dennis, "I was in a very emotional state, but I was pleased with my progress. I was feeling a good amount of fear, stress, and sadness."

The matrix of the dream is the subconscious, represented by the basement. Symbols of healing show early in the dream in the form of healers D. and L. The two of them indicate the dawning of something new into consciousness. The unknown woman is Dennis's anima, part of the self that is hidden to him. They are both naked, that is, revealing their essential selves to each other. Urination often represents creative or emotional expression. The Easter basket is significant as a symbol of resurrection and renewal. Both masculine and feminine sides of Dennis seek to share in the renewal; his anima offers support to see him through his doubt about the process holding water, or being valid.

The black and red snake that emerges from the waters of inner creation has a high alchemical significance. Black is the first stage of alchemy (*nigredo*), representing the death of the old. Red is the last stage (*rubedo*) just before the attainment of the philosopher's stone or wholeness or enlightenment. Thus the snake represents the entire Great Work, the beginning and the end. Dennis has a natural fear of this profound and uncertain change, but his anima tells him he must release the fear, which can be accomplished by handling the snake.

But up and outside—above the subconscious—stands a white wolf which is both obstacle and gatekeeper to the integration of inner change into waking life. Associated with the wolf is D. (healer) who wears Native American jewelry. Thus we must look at both alchemical and Native American nuances concerning the wolf.

In alchemy, the wolf and the dog represent the dual nature of Mercurius or Hermes, messenger of the gods, whose magical staff is the caduceus of entwined snakes (kundalini). The wolf is fierce and devours; it represents the element of earth and the realm of the underworld (the unconscious). In Native American symbolism, the wolf is the teacher and pathfinder, the forerunner of new ideas, and the connection to personal medicine power. Its white color in Dennis's dream indicates its spiritual nature. It is at once an inner demon and the way-shower to freedom from the inner demon.

The llama with the bobbing head symbolizes distractions. The wolf demonstrates to Dennis the need to stay focused: Don't look at the distractions and get sidetracked from this important change in life. He heeds the call and sets out to cross through the doorway, a symbol of transition.

The dream brought inner material to greater awareness for Dennis. Months after the dream, he reported that he "continued to progress and heal at an accelerated rate." He was in a relationship that was deepening spiritually. And, he said, "My relationship with my children and former wife is turning toward forgiveness, and I have a clearer sense of loving without condition."

Dreamwork with Animals

Approach animals in a dream as friendly guides and teachers, even if they are fearsome or arouse fear. The fear itself is part of their lesson. Remember that frightening animals are a common motif in dreams, and their presence may indicate an inner battle between the conscious mind and the deeper instinctual nature. To dream of being pursued by a frightening animal may indicate that something has become separated from consciousness and needs to be reintegrated. The more dangerous the animal, the more urgent the need to address reintegration. The type of animal may provide clues to what has become alienated.

Follow interpretation guidelines for making personal, archetypal, and spiritual associations outlined in chapter 9. Then try communicating with the animal or becoming the animal. Use the incubation guidelines in chapter 10 for calling your power animals into the dreamscape.

chapter fourteen

IMPROVING DREAM RECALL

One of the first questions asked by anyone who begins dreamwork is, "Why are dreams so hard to remember?" Surely, if dreams were important, we would have an easier time recalling them.

Every now and then a vivid dream leaves such a impact upon us that we still remember it in detail years later. But most dreams slip quickly out of our grasp. If you have trouble remembering your dreams, take solace in the fact that you have plenty of company. Some people have difficulty remembering any dreams. Others have difficulty periodically.

We all dream, and dream profusely throughout the night, with anywhere from several to many dreams of varying durations (dream researcher Jeremy Taylor has documented as many as twenty dreams in a single night). During the sleep cycle, we have periods of rapid-eye movement (REM), which occur about every ninety-two minutes and last for about three to fifty minutes, getting longer as the night goes on. The average person spends about two hours a night in REM. We dream during both REM and NREM (non-REM) periods, but if we are awakened from an REM state, we are more likely to remember a dream. REM dreams are often characterized by more brilliant and bizarre imagery than NREM dreams.

Despite all this dreaming, we are likely to remember only one dream, if any at all.

Interestingly, chemicals in the brain that govern long-term memory—norepinephrine and serotonin—are suppressed during dreaming. Meanwhile, acetylcholine then allows electrical signals to be sent to the cortex, beginning a dream. Thus, dreams by themselves do not enter long-term memory. The only way we can store dreams in our long-term memory is to record them and work with them. That's why it's so important to keep a dream journal.

Perhaps there is a divine purpose in our natural forgetfulness of most dreams. With many dreams every night, we would be completely overwhelmed with them if we remembered all of them. Rather, the dreaming mechanism is selective: The dreams we need for inner work are the ones remembered. You might ask why, then, do we have so many dreams if we don't need them all?

I meet a fair number of people who insist that they do not dream because they never remember any dreams. Science, however, has demonstrated that not only do we all dream, we *need* to dream. Volunteers in laboratory experiments who are deprived of their REM dreams develop physical, mental, and emotional difficulties. They become irritable, fatigued, more susceptible to illness, and have difficulty concentrating. If you didn't dream, you'd be seriously ill.

The act of dreaming may have an even bigger purpose than the health of the individual. In chapter 27, we explore the role of dreams in relation to the survival and evolution of the human species and the collective unified consciousness.

Various factors can affect our ability to remember dreams:

Stress and fatigue. Dealing with worldly affairs takes energy that might otherwise go to dream recall. I find that whenever I go through periods of intense concentration on a project or I am distracted by stress, my dream recall drops temporarily.

Medications. Some medications stimulate dream imagery; others depress dream recall. If you are taking a medications, especially those that alter mood, ask your doctor what he or she knows about its effects on dream recall.

Alcohol. Liquor interrupts sleep patterns and can have an overall effect of hindering dream stages of sleep as well as recall in the morning. If you are seeking to remember your dreams, it's advisable to stay away from alcohol, especially in the evening.

The ability to visualize. People who are vivid imagers may be able to better remember dreams than people who are more oriented to sound, touch, and smell.

Unconscious fear of dreams. Fear of or an aversion to dreams, perhaps from childhood or religious training, may create an unconscious desire not to remember.

Guidelines for Improving Dream Recall

To enhance your ability to remember dreams, put this ten-step program into action.

1. Take dreams seriously and respect them.
2. Meditate or pray daily.
3. Keep a dream journal and record dreams upon awakening.
4. Frequently imagine yourself remembering, recording, and interpreting your dreams with great enjoyment.
5. Make a ritual at bedtime to focus attention on dreams.
6. As you go to sleep, use a dream affirmation as a mantra.
7. Upon awakening, hold the body still.
8. Think about people, animals, and objects familiar to you in waking life.
9. Try vitamin B (especially B_6) before going to bed.
10. Try backward recall. As you go to sleep, recall in reverse order the things you did during the evening and day. As you awaken, do likewise: "I am awake, and before that, I was dreaming. . . ."

Let's look at each point in more detail.

Take Dreams Seriously and Respect Them

The number-one rule for working with dreams applies to improving dream recall. If you think dreams are unimportant, they will be less likely to impress themselves on your memory. The more attention you pay to dreams, the more you will notice them.

Meditate or Pray Daily

Meditation stills the mind, improves focus, and alleviates stress. What's more—and what's most important for dreams—is that meditation alters our state of consciousness, making it easier to access the intuition, the higher self, other dimensional realities, and the voice of God, all of which speak through dreams. A few minutes of meditation a day will reap big benefits. Start the day and end the evening with quiet time.

Prayer is equally effective. It's more conversational, but even the chattiest of inner prayer eventually settles into profound zones of peace and quiet. Once you get into the habit of going within, you will notice a change in your dream life: You will remember dreams more easily, and the nature of your dreams will change to include themes and imagery of a more spiritual nature.

Compose your own prayers specifically about dreams. Here are two that I use with students.

> *Dear Creator,*
>
> *I know that you speak to me through my dreams. My dreams are messengers of your divine light and unconditional love, revealing your will to me. It is my heart's purpose and soul's desire to heal that within me that must be healed, and to express your will to the best of my ability. My dreams show me the way. I give thanks for the loving guidance you give through my dreams. Help me to remember my dreams and to understand them, so that I may grow.*

> *Dear Creator,*
>
> *I want to receive your guidance in all the ways that I can, but I am having difficulty remembering my dreams. I am putting forth my best effort, and I ask for your help in removing the obstacles to the path of clear wisdom and insight. Please send your angels of dreams to assist me in my endeavor. I give thanks now for the bounty of wisdom and healing that I receive.*

Always give thanks for the gift of remembering your dreams, even if you have not yet realized it. By assuming you already have what you seek, you bring it into manifestation. This is one of the principles of effective prayer.

Keep a Dream Journal and Record Dreams upon Awakening

The prophet Habakkuk admonishes us to record our visions (Habakkuk 2:2–4). The ancients evidently understood how fleeting dream/visionary experiences are if left to memory. As mentioned before, the Egyptians stressed recording of dreams as well.

The act of recording dreams stimulates the recall of dreams. If you awaken remembering nothing, record that in your journal. Document the smallest dream fragment, including feelings. Over time, you will coax your dreams into greater awareness once waking consciousness arrives.

Frequently Imagine Yourself Remembering, Recording, and Interpreting Your Dreams with Great Enjoyment

Failure to remember dreams is frustrating, and frustration in turn can hamper recall efforts. This is a little exercise of the imagination to counteract frustration. It establishes the expectation that you will—of course!—remember your dreams. Do it throughout the day. Practice it until you believe it deep down in every cell.

Make a Ritual at Bedtime to Focus Attention on Dreams

Flopping into bed exhausted or watching television to the point of sleep are counterproductive to good dreamwork. You will still dream, but you may not remember. The dreaming mind may need to be coaxed to yield up its nightly treasures. Give yourself some time before bed to relax, meditate, or pray, and concentrate on dream prayers or affirmations. Set up the expectation within you that you will remember your dreams.

As You Go to Sleep, Use a Dream Affirmation As a Mantra

Dream affirmations or mantras act like incubators to program the consciousness. In the following examples, note that only the first two specifically address the recall of dreams; the rest address the benefits of dreams. Like prayers, dream affirmations fertilize the consciousness to make it more receptive to working with dreams. Here are some examples:

- I remember my dreams.
- I remember my dreams in detail.
- My dreams show me God's guidance.
- My dreams reveal myself to me.
- My dreams show me what to do.
- My dreams help me heal.
- I appreciate my dreams, which helps me attain health and wholeness.

Upon Awakening, Hold the Body Still

Once we're awake, holding onto dreams becomes difficult. By keeping the body still, you will minimize the impact of wakefulness. Try to remember all that you can, even fragments of dreams. It may be helpful to return to a favorite sleeping position.

Think about People, Animals, and Objects Familiar to You in Waking Life

These thoughts trigger associations, which can help reclaim dream memories.

Try Vitamin B (Especially B_6)

Studies show that vitamin B, especially B_6, enhances the vividness of dreams. It won't by itself improve recall, but if imagery is more vivid, you may be more likely to recall it. If I'm in a dream recall slump, I will occasionally take about 50 mg of vitamin B_6 before retiring. High doses of vitamin B can be harmful, so be sure to stay within the recommended daily doses stated on the containers. You can also add vitamin B–rich foods to your diet. In addition, you might try an herbal tea formula designed for dreams. Saint John's wort, for example, has long been used in herbal dream mixes, perhaps because it enhances imagery, like vitamin B.

Try Backward Recall

Remembering things in reverse order to stimulate dream recall may sound strange, but it works. As you go to sleep, recall in reverse order the things you did during the evening and day: "I'm going to sleep, and before that I read, and before that I watched television . . ." and so on. The next morning, as you awaken, do likewise: "I am awake, and before that I was dreaming, and I dreamed . . ."

If results do not happen immediately, do not give up, but keep trying. Time and persistence may be needed to renew dream energy. Think of it as water flowing down a riverbed. If the riverbed is dry, it takes a while for water to fill it. So don't be frustrated—have faith!

PART IV

Mastery of Life

c h a p t e r f i f t e e n

DREAMS THAT HEAL

DREAMS ARE ONE OF OUR RICHEST SOURCES OF HELP FOR HEALING. THE HEALING POWER OF DREAMS COMES IN MANY WAYS: THE HEALING OF THE BODY, THE HEALING OF INNER WOUNDS, and the healing of setbacks, losses, and griefs.

Dreams have been revered around the world as a source of healing for thousands of years. In the ancient world, dreams had three primary purposes: to forecast the future, to provide the guidance of the gods, and to facilitate healing. The ancients knew dreams could forecast and diagnose health problems as well as become the medium for physical healing itself. Records report that all kinds of ailments and conditions were cured with the help of dreams, from chronic illnesses to blindness and lameness. Therapeutic dreams were often incubated in special temples or groves with the help of priests.

In ancient Egypt, special priests known as Masters of the Secret Things and Scribes of the Double House of Life were trained in dreamwork and practiced out of temples. The greatest temple was at Memphis, near Cairo, which was dedicated to the god of healing, Imhotep.

Imhotep originally was a mortal who lived during the third dynasty (his dates vary, ranging anywhere from 2980 B.C.E. to 2570 B.C.E.). He was highly regarded in his time. He was a physician, an astrologer to the priests of the sun god, Ra, and also a skilled architect—he designed and built the step pyramid and the healing temple at Saqqara. After death, Imhotep was buried at Saqqara and was elevated to the status of god of medicine. Memphis became an important center of dream incubation for healing, its activities lasting nearly until modern times. The pyramid and ruins of the temple can be visited today.

By the first millennium B.C.E., dream incubation was a widespread practice in Egypt. Other temples were famous as centers of healing, among them the temple of the goddess Hathor at Dendera near Thebes; the temple of the goddess Neit at Sais; Queen Hapshepsut's temple at Deir el-Bahri; and Sety I's temple of Osiris at Abydos. Pilgrims poured magical water over statues with healing incantations carved on them and then drank or bathed in the water. They slept in small crypts to incubate dreams in which they sought to speak directly with the gods concerning a cure.

The Greeks, who borrowed from the Egyptians, also revered the dream for its therapeutic value. Incubated dreams for healing were directed to Aesculapius, who, like Imhotep, was a mortal elevated to the status of deity. In his mortal life, Aesculapius (whose name means "unceasingly gentle") may have been a healer who lived during the eleventh century B.C.E. According to his post-deification myth, he first became a chthonic (of the underworld) demon or hero, and then the son of Apollo (god of the sun, music, healing, and prophecy) and the mortal woman, Coronis.

One version of the story goes that Coronis, pregnant with Aesculapius, was unfaithful to Apollo. Apollo learned this from a raven. At that time, all ravens were white. But Apollo flew into such a rage that he turned all ravens black from then on. Apollo sent his sister, Artemis, to slay Coronis by shooting her with an arrow. Her body was placed on a funeral pyre. Just before the body burned, Apollo snatched the baby from her womb. He gave Aesculapius to the centaur Chiron. The centaur raised the boy in the mountains and taught him the healing arts.

Chiron bore a permanent wound from a poisoned arrow shot by Hercules. Both he and Aesculapius were wounded in different ways and in need of healing. This is the basis for the archetype of the wounded healer—that we must heal our own wounds before we can heal others.

Aesculapius became a revered healer, so adept in his work that he could even raise the dead. This threatened the immortal gods, so Zeus struck Aesculapius down with a thunderbolt and killed him.

Zeus then placed him in the sky, where he became the constellation Orion.

The cult of Aesculapius was powerful and spread throughout the classical world. At its peak, some four hundred temples were devoted to the god. He was also worshiped in sacred groves and caves.

Long after the establishment of Imhotep and Aesculapius as major gods of healing, Serapis was introduced in Alexandria, Egypt, in the fourth century B.C.E. by the first Ptolemaic ruler of that country, Ptolemaeus Soter. Serapis was a composite god of Osiris and Apis, the gods of the underworld and the earth, respectively. Historians speculate that the cult of Serapis may have been a calculated attempt by Ptolemy I to blend Egyptian and Greek beliefs in order to appease both segments of the population.

The cults of Serapis and Aesculapius were quite strong and managed to survive Christianity by about four hundred years—the only cults of ancient healing gods to do so.

Guises and Symbols of the Healing Gods

Aesculapius was depicted as an aged man with a beard, carrying a staff entwined by a single snake. He was accompanied by a dog and by a boy dwarf, Telesphorus, who was associated with the phallus (regeneration) and fullfilled dreams and prayers. Serapis was accompanied by a dog, which was associated with Sirius, the companion of Isis, goddess of healing. He was sometimes shown as having a bull's head and wearing a solar disk and uraeus, a fire-spitting cobra that sits at the third eye and gives protection and clear insight. Like Aesculapius, Serapis was accompanied by a boy dwarf, Harpocrates, the posthumous and weakly son of Isis and Osiris, and also associated with regeneration by virtue of his large genitals. Both Telesphorus and Harpocrates were keepers of the mysteries.

The snake is a complex symbol of regeneration, wisdom, and inspiration from the gods, and of the kundalini energy. Records show that the ancients had an understanding of the dynamic unconscious and of cognitive states, emotional reactions, and subtle endocrine system functions, all of which were brought into play in the rituals of the dream temples. Rituals involving snake images may have had the purpose of stimulating kundalini.

The dog is guardian of the underworld and guide of souls, and thus is associated with death and rebirth.

All of these images were important in the healing dream incubation practiced at the temples.

Dream Incubation Practices

Serapian rituals closely followed those set by the cult of Aesculapius. For the sake of simplicity, we'll focus on the better-known of the two, Aesculapius.

Persons who sought healing through dream incubation made pilgrimages to a temple. In the classical world, the largest and best-known of these was at Epidaurus in Greece. Today, the temple lies in ruins, but a nearby stadium is intact and still used for public performances.

A pilgrimage was a sacred and serious matter, requiring a purity of mind, body, and spirit. Pilgrims stayed in a dormitory while they underwent purification rituals of diet, exercise, bathing, prayer, offerings of food and money, and even animal sacrifice (usually of a ram). Augury (divination) was done to determine if pilgrims could go on to the next step.

If the augury was favorable for a cure, the pilgrims were admitted to the *abaton* (place not to be entered unbidden), a building just for the purpose of incubating dreams. There, they were given ointments or potions designed to induce sleep or were given autosuggestion by dream priests. They stretched out to sleep on the skins of sacrificed animals next to a statue of the god Aesculapius. In the morning, they reported their dreams to a priest, who interpreted them.

Dreams were most auspicious when the god himself appeared in them, either as a bearded man or as a radiant youth. Sometimes the god appeared in the form of his animal totems, the snake or the dog. He often was accompanied by one or both animals, and by his female companions: his wife, Epione (the gentle one) or one of his eight daughters, most notably Hygieia (health), and Panacea (heal-all). If the patient was touched in the dream by the god—or better yet, one of his totems, the dog or snake—it meant healing had occurred during the dream. A dedication plaque discovered on the island of Kos shows a patient lying on a bed being licked by a snake while he is operated on by Aesculapius.

Sometimes dreams were interpreted from a prescriptive point of view, with instructions to the patient to take certain medicines or measures that would then result in healing.

If a person did not have a dream on the first night, his condition was likely to have been judged incurable. Sometimes priests gave instructions for the pilgrim to go home, follow certain dietary or spiritual practices, and then return again.

The priests sometimes indulged in questionable, perhaps even fraudulent, practices, such as dressing up in the guises of the god to appear before someone as an apparition in the middle of the night. If someone were too ill or unable to travel to a temple, priests would dream for them by proxy (sometimes a substitute person came to the temple instead). We have little way of knowing whether or not such dreams by proxy were fabricated.

Nonetheless, numerous cures were experienced at the dream temples. Everyone who experienced a cure was required to record it at the temple. These testimonials provided great inspiration to the arriving pilgrims, thus contributing to an expectant state of consciousness.

The fee for a cure was based upon a person's ability to pay. Aesculapius was believed to prefer an offering of a cock.

Healing Dream Incubation Practices into Modern Times

The Christianization of the European world brought first cosmetic, and then substantial, changes to the practice of dream incubation. Sacred caves, groves, and temples were replaced with healing wells, springs, shrines, and churches. People were encouraged to pray rather than dream for healing. They addressed their prayers to the archangel Michael (who absorbed many of the characteristics of Hermes and Apollo), patron saints, Mary, and Jesus. The serpent, so potent a symbol of healing and enlightenment, was demonized as a symbol of Satan and evil.

As the dream became increasingly disparaged in Christianity as either fantasy or something demonic, dreams disappeared as a medium between humanity and the gods. Encounters with saints, angels, and Mary were explained as occurring in visions or were couched in ambiguous language. To say they came in a dream meant derision or even questioning by church inquisitors. Since many of these encounters happened during intense and long periods of prayer or meditation, it is possible that they may have actually been hypnagogic dreams.

Dream incubation for healing is still practiced around the world, as formal rites and as informal and highly personal measures. It is being rediscovered in a popular sense in the West.

Dreams That Diagnose and Forecast Illness

The ancients also recognized the diagnostic value of dreams in relation to illness and healing. Hippocrates (469–399 B.C.E.), the Greek physician credited with being the father of medicine, believed that discordant and unharmonious dreams could diagnose physical ills, especially imbalances of the bodily humors. Aristotle, who was skeptical about the value of dreams in general, acknowledged that we are more sensitive to the onset of illness when we're asleep than when we're awake.

Galen, another prominent Greek physician born much later (c. 130 C.E.), believed similarly in dreams and was guided by them throughout his life. When Galen was twenty-seven, he became seriously ill with a subdiaphragmatic abcess, in which infected fluid collects in the abdomen under the diaphragm and over the liver—a potentially fatal condition. Following the custom of the time, Galen traveled to an Aesculapian temple to incubate a dream for his cure. He had two dreams in which he opened an artery located between the thumb and forefinger and let it bleed until it stopped naturally. He performed this procedure on himself, which drained his infection, and he was healed. (His dreams undoubtedly made use of his medical knowledge; most of us would not be wise to perform self-operations.)

Galen did many operations on his patients based on information obtained from dreams, and he claimed to have saved many lives as a result. He said that it is necessary to examine dreams in order to "prognosticate and heal satisfactorily."

Dreams that forecast the start of illness before actual symptoms appear are called *prodromal* dreams (from the Greek *prodromos,* or "running before"). The Greeks observed such dreams. But after the fall of the classical world to Christianity, such dream wisdom was lost, until Carl Jung and others revived it in the twentieth century. "The dream does in fact concern itself with both health and sickness, and since, by virtue of its source in the unconscious, it draws upon a wealth of subliminal perceptions, it can sometimes produce things that are very well worth knowing," Jung said, adding that dreams often helped him to distinguish between organic and psychogenic symptoms.[1]

Jung noted that some patients who dreamed of destruction or injury to horses—an archetypal symbol of the human body—subsequently were shown to be in the early stages of serious illness, such as cancer. In at least one case he documented, the illness was caught early enough to be treated successfully.

Numerous cases have been documented in modern medical and dream literature about dreams forecasting serious illness. For example, Bernie S. Siegel, a cancer surgeon who has authored best-selling books on the interaction of mind and body (*Love, Medicine & Miracles* and *Peace, Love & Healing*), recognizes the significance of dream imagery. He tells about a case involving a man who dreamed of hot coals placed beneath his chin, their searing heat literally gnawing his larynx. On the same night, his girlfriend dreamed of him in a bed filled with blood. The man had another dream in which medicine men stuck hypodermic needles into his "neck brain." Certain that something—perhaps cancer—was wrong with his throat, but suffering no other symptoms, the man sought out a doctor. The doctor was skeptical about the dreams. Tests revealed early stages of cancer in the man's thyroid gland (also called the "neck brain"), which is near the larynx.

Siegel asks patients to draw themselves, their disease, their treatment, and their white cells eliminating their disease. The spontaneous images are similar to those that arise in dreams, reflecting a deep wisdom. These images can provide invaluable guidance to health care professionals.

Using the Healing Power of Dreams

Our dreams play a more important role in our overall wellness than most of us realize. Patricia Garfield is among researchers recognizing the connection between dreams and health. "Your dreams can help keep you healthy, warn you when you are at risk, diagnose incipient physical problems, support you during physical crises, forecast your recuperation, suggest treatment, heal your body, and signal your return to wellness," she said in her book, *The Healing Power of Dreams.*[2] Of course, dreams should not be a substitute for medical treatment but should augment it, especially in the areas of prevention and diagnosis.

Garfield's rediscovery of the role of dreams in healing began in 1988 when she fell and broke her wrist. She later realized that the night before she had the accident, she'd had two dreams warning her of "too much frenzied activity and a lack of protection." At first, the injury was diagnosed as a sprain. Garfield experienced continuing severe pain. About ten days later, she dreamed that her arm was broken. She went back to the doctor. X rays confirmed that there were two breaks. Because of the lapse in time, the bones were already healing improperly, and correcting the problem was no longer a simple matter. Garfield faced surgery to rearrange the bones, with a metal plate to hold them in place, followed by months of physical therapy.

Her recuperation was slow and painful, with some unexpected complications. She soon realized that her dreams were undergoing a radical transformation during this process, dramatizing each phase of the recovery. Through her research and work with patients, Garfield began to understand the many symbolic metaphors dreams use to communicate information about wellness and illness. Dreams, she found, contain crucial bits of information about the condition of the body. Dreams also deliver information about remedies and treatments.

Garfield identified seven phases of dream metaphors that occur around the occurrence and recovery of physical injury and illness. Here are some of the imageries related to each phase. (Please note that these are not definitive in that they *always* represent stages of illness. The same images can relate to psychological factors in dreams as well.)

1. *Forewarning dreams.* Imagery that warns us we are vulnerable, such as going too fast, breaking down, collapsing, being battered by storms.
2. *Diagnostic dreams.* Dominant themes are damage and impaired function, such as through extreme heat or cold, excess water or dryness, rampant fire, pain, injured animals or plants, damaged or destroyed buildings or equipment.
3. *Crisis dreams.* Severe images such as rotting flesh, polluted water, vermin infestations, burning sensations in parts of the body, bloody accidents, violent blows or wounds to the body.
4. *Postcrisis dreams.* Images that reflect operations, fear of dying, replay of injury, dead animals and people, lost and stolen objects, physical assault.
5. *Healing dreams.* Images that indicate a restoration of energy and feelings of support can include beautiful scenes (especially gardens), happy children and animals, successful navigation of obstacles, being with friends and loved ones.
6. *Convalescent dreams.* A gradual shift from healing dreams involving similar imagery, and an emphasis on a new body

image, such as new clothing, or optimism, such as having a baby or attending a ceremony.

7. *Wellness dreams.* Imagery that is clear, bright, and in which we are attractive and functioning well.

Paying Attention to Dream Signals

Clearly, we need to pay more attention in general to dreams and their role in our wellness and healing. Dreams that may be relevant to health matters should be shared with doctors and other health care practitioners. Unfortunately, many doctors still dismiss dreams as meaningless, especially if there are no apparent indications of the presence of disease. Find a doctor who is willing to listen.

Attention to dreams is especially important when it comes to forewarning dreams. We should be most alert to signals that warn us in advance of illness or injury, so that we can take preventive or therapeutic measures. How can we distinguish these dreams from others?

Certain clues can tip us off: unusually vivid imagery, a distinct emotional tone, recurring imagery (such as an accident happening over and over again), a feeling of the dream being prophetic, and imagery involving communication (representing our body trying to tell us something). If at least several of these factors show up in a dream, it may relate to future illness or injury. *Again, these imageries can have other meanings, so their presence should not be assumed to always relate to health matters.* Rather, the entire dream needs to be evaluated.

When Healing Occurs During a Dream

Physical healing can take place during dreams. Dreamers dream themselves whole from accident and illness and report miraculous or tremendous improvement after a dream, such as the following testimony from a woman: "I had a lump in my breast which I took apart inside my body in a lucid dream. It was a beautiful, geodesic cathedral-like structure! A week later the lump was gone."[3] Such results are similar to those reported after prayer.

Characteristics of in-dream healings include bathing the body in light or love, applying energy healing techniques, and being healed by mysterious, otherworldly beings. Carlie P. suffered severe chronic pancreatitis, which created cysts that had to be removed surgically. Six weeks after surgery, another large cyst appeared suddenly, and Carlie had to return to the hospital for another operation. The night before surgery, she was in intense pain:

I said my prayers and went to bed thinking that I would not be able to sleep due to the pain. Well, I did sleep, and while I was asleep, I had this dream.

I was walking along the beach at sunset and came upon a young woman. She smiled at me and told me to lie down and rest. I did as I was told. I remember feeling warm and very comfortable. The woman then walked around me and walked away.

I woke up at four A.M. on the dot and knew that my grapefruit-size cyst was gone. I had been able to cup it in my hand before I went to bed. I was absolutely pain free. I ate for the first time in months. I had been on a liquid diet up until then.

I still have pancreatitis but was spared an operation that night. My doctor could not believe that the cyst just disappeared overnight and said that if it had burst, I would have definitely been rushed to the emergency room.[4]

Carlie associated the woman in the dream with her guardian angel who had transmitted healing while circumambulating her. Her story parallels the types of dream cures recorded at Greco-Egyptian incubation temples.

Cellular Restructuring

P. M. H. Atwater, a leading near-death experience researcher and author, had a lucid dream that not only resulted in a physical healing, but a spiritual healing as well that helped her launch her professional career as an author.

For three years, I had been forced to deal with the pain of ribs that refused to stay in place. It was my fault for trying to lift furniture too heavy and for compounding that injury by another such lift the following year. Then a man hugged me too hard, popping the ribs out once more. Before the comedy of errors was over, I could neither lift a glass of water to my mouth or bathe myself or even breathe without excruciating pain.

It was a nightmare of unbelievable proportions that led to a total restructuring of every behavior habit I had ever formed. I played the if-this-were-a-dream-what-would-it-mean game. I explored every facet of forgive-

ness and prayer I had ever learned. I earnestly pleaded for clarification: Why had this happened and what could I do about it? Yet nothing worked.

Then one night the answer I wanted came. It was another one of those the-minute-your-head-hits-the-pillow-and-until-the-alarm-goes-off-in-the-morning, nonstop, continuous dreams. Only this time, it really was a dream: a collage of symbols that illustrated how what seemed to be the result of my stupidity was actually an opportunity for me to restructure my entire body. Why? So I could move past my former role as amazon, a woman who could outwork most men, to the next phase in my life where intellect would be more valuable than muscles and the realms of mind and spirit would overlay the physicality of labor.

The vividness of how each image in the dream flowed into the next as if creating a seamless stream of molecules and cells rearranging themselves was simply awesome. And it went on and on until morning. I awoke tired, with a clear sense that I had worked all night long helping my body ready itself for the shift my life would soon take. And I was grateful, for I came to regard my so-called "chronic condition" of dislocating ribs as a rare and wonderful gift, a reminder that would prevent me from reverting back to habits that no longer served me.

Because gratitude replaced the anger of feeling cursed with a senseless disability, I was able to repattern behavior responses and stabilize my ribs. This dream enabled me to do that, to be hopeful instead of helpless. My first book, Coming Back to Life, *which contains my initial findings from researching the near-death phenomenon, was the result.*[5]

A Golden Light Healing

Tom A. served as a Marine fighting in the Vietnam war. He was nearly killed, an experience that deeply traumatized him. After his return home, he suffered for years with post-traumatic stress disorder that took a terrible toll on his personal life and marriage. He sought the help of a psychiatrist. He took tranquilizers, carrying them with him wherever he went in case of panic attacks. He lived in fear that he would go crazy and end up in a mental institution.

During this period, Tom heard a news event about a Vietnam veteran who went beserk and killed a number of people in a shooting spree with a machine gun. This event had a great impact on him.

I told my wife she'd better be nice to me or I could do something like that, too. It was a joke, but not a very nice one. That night, I had a dream that

I was in the mall shooting people with an M-16 machine gun. It was a matter-of-fact thing to do. The police showed up and shot me. I was shot five times, in both arms and both sides and once in the stomach.

Then the ambulance showed up. The guy who ran the ambulance didn't put me on a cot and take me to the hospital. Instead, he sat me down in the back of the ambulance and started to talk to me like we were old friends. He talked and talked, and after awhile I wondered what was going on, where this guy was leading. I said to myself, "I must be dreaming, because if this keeps up, I'm going to bleed to death."

At that moment, I realized that I was dreaming. Also, that very second, the dream became a hundred times more vivid and more real. The wounds actually felt real, and I hurt.

Then a golden light came down over my head and down around me and healed me of the pain. It got as far down as my hips. I felt a wonderful joy from the golden light, and a beautiful sensation. I felt freedom and healing. I interpreted it as one of God's graces. It was something I didn't deserve, but it was being given to me.

I had a false awakening and thought I was awake. I closed my eyes and woke up again, and I was really awake. I remembered that the last week that I was in Vietnam, I had heard about this fellow who had a fat body. He had been shot in the stomach and died from his wounds. He was very proud to be in the Marines. We'd always had to encourage him to finish his goals, however. That stayed with me, and I knew that it had to do with the illness that I was trying to get better from.

I felt that there was now hope for me, that I could have some control over my panic attacks. I didn't feel completely cured—I felt the golden light should have completely covered me, instead of just down to my hips. But that indicated that there was still more work that I had to do.[6]

After the dream, Tom improved dramatically and was able to stop taking tranquilizers. "I've pretty much gotten my life back together," he said. "But my psychiatrist didn't think much of the dream!"

It is interesting that Tom is shot five times in the dream. Remember from chapter 12 that five is the number of energy, change, freedom, spirit, the resurrected Christ, and the victory of spirit over matter. It also represents the midpoint. In Tom's dream, five reveals a dramatic turning point in his healing.

Forgiveness in the Cosmic Lounge

Lucid dreams happen to Michael Moran when something major needs to be resolved in his life. On one occasion, his dreaming self traveled to the Cosmic Lounge, a place where healing happens.

The dream came during an intense time in my life. Within about a three-month period, my divorce happened, and my mother died. My career changed, and my whole identity associated with that career was swept away. Shortly after this, I started a relationship that was very intense and passionate, but it was one I really struggled with. It was a love-hate relationship. We brought out the best and the worst in each other. We both knew it wasn't going to work, as much as we wanted it to. We tried to make it work. It was important to both of us, but it wasn't the one.

We lived together for about three years and then broke up. There was a lot of anger and hurt on both of our parts. H. met someone else and got married within a couple of months. I met Faith.

I went through a period of real anger and resentment. I couldn't let go of it. It was stopping me from fully entering into my relationship with Faith and even from enjoying life. I knew that I had to forgive myself and H.

I started asking for the ability to just being willing to forgive. I struggled with it. One night I had this dream. Suddenly, I was aware that I was dreaming. Everything was brilliant white. I was going somewhere to meet people. I came to a white building that had one door with a porthole window. To the left-hand side was a green neon sign that said Cosmic Lounge.

I opened the door. It was very dark inside. It was a cocktail lounge. The light broke the darkness. As my eyes adjusted, I saw the barman, who was drying glasses. Obviously, I was a regular in this lounge because he said, "Oh, hi, Mike, they're right over there." He pointed to a corner where there was a big round table. Sitting around it were friends and people who'd been a part of our lives when H. and I were together. They were having a great time. I could tell it was a reunion, and I was the one who had brought everyone together. I'd arrived late, and so I got a good-natured ribbing. They kept asking me, "Are you sure this is the day?" I said that it was.

Then, a part of me knew that we were all dead, and everybody had come back just for this reunion. Part of me wondered what was going on. Suddenly there was this bing! *noise. All of us turned. An elevator had just opened, and there stood H.*

The love that I felt for her in that moment was one of the purest loves that I had ever experienced in my life. I got up and walked over to her. I hugged her with this unbelievable love pouring out of me. She looked at me with a sense of wonder and said, "What does this mean?"

I said, "H., you were magnificent. You were perfect. It was an Academy Award performance. You played your role perfectly." We hugged. She said, "And you were perfect, too. You were magnificent."

We went back to the table and we all hugged and laughed and reminisced.

Then I woke up and sat straight up in bed. My face and chest were wet with tears. I said, "My God, so that's what this is all about!" Suddenly there was nothing to forgive. The anger and poison were completely wiped away and replaced with profound love. I also knew that the person I needed to forgive was not her, but me.[7]

That everyone in the dream was dead represents the dead past—a phase in life that had come to an end. The people were more like mourners at a wake, celebrating the life that was over.

Healed by love and forgiveness from his own heart, Michael was now able to engage fully in his relationship with Faith, and the two were wed. The intensity of the emotion experienced in the dream was so great that Michael could not speak about it for quite some time. Even years later, the memory of it still brings tears to his eyes.

But there is a light side to the dream, too, said Michael. "Now whenever I'm in a difficult situation, Faith and I will joke, 'I wonder how this is going to play out in the Cosmic Lounge?'"

Angel of Healing

Bobbie B. was recovering from surgery for a mastectomy and breast reconstruction when she had a dream that facilitated her healing.

I was in a dream state and a woman appeared to me. She was ethereal and I seemed to sense her presence from above and to the right. She may have been wearing long, flowing white garb. She placed an orange crystal in my right hand and the moment she did so, an exact duplicate of the orange crystal appeared in my left hand.

I interpret the orange to be representative of the spleen chakra and associated with healing energy. The woman is clearly from another realm and may be my higher self, a guide, or an angel. She gave me one crystal, but the other one came of itself through me. I interpret that to mean that I will get healing help, but I will also have to heal myself.

The dream was very uplifting for me. I did heal very well, and people were amazed at how well I looked during my recovery period. I had had quite a bit of difficulty sleeping during the first few weeks after the surgery, and after this dream, I was able to sleep for longer and longer periods of time and get the rest I needed.[8]

Dreams have much to offer the expanding field of complementary therapies and healing. Practitioners of the healing arts, as well as medically trained physicians, should pay attention to the dreams of their patients and should encourage dreamwork as a way to assist the healing process.

One of the best ways we can use our dreams for healing is to incubate them for information that will facilitate the recovery from illness or accident. Follow the guidelines in chapter 10. Pay close attention to your dreams throughout your entire recovery.

c h a p t e r s i x t e e n

ENHANCING CREATIVITY

PLATO RELATES IN *PHAEDO* THAT SOCRATES, WHILE HE WAS IN PRISON AWAITING EXECUTION, HAD A RECURRING DREAM IN WHICH THE SAME DREAM FIGURE URGED HIM TO "SET TO WORK and make music." The expression in Greek could refer to any creative art, but Socrates had definite ideas about his interpretation of it in his dreams. He believed that he had been "making music" for years through his philosophy. However, he also believed that the dream was urging him to expand his creativity by writing poetry. During his final days, Socrates put Aesop's fables to verse. "God has ordered me to do this, both through oracles and dreams and in all the other ways used by divine providence for giving its commands," he stated.

The ancients called this type of dream either *admonitio* (command) or *chremastismos* (oracular response). In such a dream, a respected authority figure, such as a god, priest, ruler, or even a parent, appears to the dreamer and commands them to take a specific action. Numerous examples in Greek literature show that people paid careful attention to such dreams and acted upon them; Plato commented in *Laws* on the frequency of such dreams. Evidently, people often were directed to commemorate the dream with a plaque, statue, or chapel. Archaeological digs have uncovered inscriptions such as "in accordance with a dream" and "having seen a dream."

As Socrates and others were commanded by their dreams to

express their creativity in new ways, we in modern times are guided—and even commanded—by our dreams to do likewise. The authority figures may be aspects of ourselves or may be visits by the dead or guides. They can be represented by human figures, otherworldly beings, animals, or disembodied voices. Sometimes no specific authority figure directs us in a dream, but the dream has a clear message of instruction.

Dreams have always provided inspiration for solutions to problems, ideas for inventions, and artistic expressions. For example, artist and poet William Blake found dreams to be a continuing source of inspiration as did Salvador Dali and other artists of the surrealistic schools. The idea for *Dr. Jekyll and Mr. Hyde* came to author Robert Louis Stevenson in a dream; Stevenson would often converse with brownies, a type of house fairy, when he was in a hypnagogic state. Numerous composers, including Richard Wagner and Beethoven, dreamed some of their masterpieces. Einstein conceived of his famous theory of relativity while in a hypnagogic dream state. Elias Howe, inventor of the sewing machine, solved the riddle of where to put the hole in the needle from a dream. In it, he was captured by savages who threatened to kill him if he couldn't find an answer to his problem. He noticed in the dream that their spears had holes in the tips. Upon awakening, he knew he had been given the answer to his dilemma. The list goes on.

I have received numerous ideas and artistic guidance from dreams. Some come spontaneously and unexpectedly, and others are the result of incubations. Even the ones that seem spontaneous really are the products of incubation in terms of thought and concentration during waking consciousness. Dreams have a marvelous way of sorting everything out.

Becoming a Heyoka

Artist and jeweler Heyoka Merrifield, whom we met in chapter 13, took the name Heyoka after it was revealed to him in a dream. He was born Edward Merrifield. His art matured as his connection to spirit deepened, primarily through direct experience in meditation, communion with nature, and vision questing. As Edward, he was introduced into the Native American ways of the sweat lodge and the pipe ceremony, both of which opened the door to his transformation as a medicine man.

Edward began to feel that he needed a new name that was better suited to this medicine man energy. Many medicine animals came to him in dreams and vision quests—the jaguar, owl, eagle, deer, rattlesnake, coyote, and others—but none seemed to click as his new medicine name. Rather, he was drawn to the energy of the *heyoka,* or contrary, someone who functioned as a sacred clown.

According to Native American tradition, governance of a tribe was a democracy based on a council circle. The members of the council discussed and decided all new laws. The formal introduction of a proposed law to the council was done by the heyokas, who usually were the artists and creative persons in the tribe. The heyokas would help the examination of the effects of proposed laws by acting them out, often in hilarious ways.

Edward saw artists as the modern-day heyokas—people who bring attention and criticism to the way we rule our lives. The heyokas also help to reunite us with myth.

In certain Native American traditions, a person realized his calling as a heyoka if he dreamed of lightning. In his pipe ceremonies, Edward meditated upon receiving a new name and awaited a sign. Soon it came in a lucid dream:

In my dream I was growing long eagle wings. As sometimes happens for me, my conscious mind was awake while I slept. I was very elated because flying dreams are my favorite kind. After a flying dream I wake up feeling exhilarated and energized. I soared through the sky and then I saw a huge thunder cloud. I flew into the middle of the cloud and then remembered that a heyoka dreams of lightning. Lightning shot out of my body in all directions, and when I awoke I knew that I had been given my new name, "Heyoka."[1]

Early in his career, Heyoka was inspired by a dream to begin making harps. At the time, he was immersed in Eastern Indian music.

One night, after an especially meditative music session, I had a dream of a wonderful harp. I was playing this harp that was part sitar and part ancient Egyptian harp. The next day I started building my first harp and when it was finished it sounded as beautiful as its form.

I made musical instruments, mostly harps, for several years. Very few people seemed to understand the visionary musical instruments I was creating.[2]

One who did appreciate them was Donovan, the popular folk singer. Donovan had a dream in which he played a special guitar. He contacted Heyoka to bring it into physical reality. Heyoka had never before made a guitar. Given a sketch by Donovan, he executed the dream instrument.

It was in the shape of a swan whose beak held six fish that were the tuning pins. The swan's toes were a bridge that held the strings and the sound hole was its heart. When finished, this guitar from the dream world sounded as magical as it looked.[3]

Truly a visionary instrument! The guitar was the first such instrument that Heyoka had ever made. Guitars require far more precision than harps. Crafting it was a real "rite of passage," said Heyoka.

Dreams are a source of great artistic and creative inspiration. For Heyoka, dreams reach into the realm of the Sacred Void, or the unconscious, a deep inner place where imagination, inspiration, and intuition are born.

When I return from the Sacred Void with an idea that wants to become a work of art, it is like a spark of inspiration. Somehow this spark needs to become a raging fire in order to be manifested. Many people who have connected with the source of creation and have come back with a vision, let it fade into forgetfulness. The vision needs to be nurtured to become the fire that turns into passion. Passion has a life of its own and together we create the work of art.[4]

When our dreams bring our inspirations to us, we can ignite that spark into a raging fire by working with the dream: recognizing its message and acting upon it.

A New Identity

Heyoka's dream-given name is in itself a source of creative energy. Names have great power; they carry our essence. All esoteric traditions recognize the power of the name. A name has a certain vibration. The ancient Egyptians, Greeks, Hebrews, Assyrians, and Gnostics knew that incredible power could be unleashed by the sound vibrations of names, as well as sacred words. The Egyptians invented names of power for magical rituals. In Judaism, the most powerful of all names is the Tetragrammaton, the personal name of God in the Old Testament, usually expressed as YHWH, the Hebrew letters *yod, he, vau, he.* So awesome is the Tetragrammaton that for centuries it was seldom spoken, but was whispered only on Yom Kippur by a high priest. In the scriptures, substitute words were used, such as Adonai or Adonay or Elohim. The exact pronunciation of the Tetragrammaton is not known; the most accepted is Yahweh. A common variation is Jehovah. In Eastern mysticism, the principle behind the mantra is that the names of God invoke protection and also imbue the consciousness with divine attributes. In many spiritual traditions, especially shamanic, it is customary for the initiate to take a new name that expresses his or her new identity as one reborn to a new level of consciousness.

Many people change their given names specifically to bring new vibrations into their lives. Numerology is often consulted. Dreams play a role. Such was the case for author and near-death experience researcher P. M. H. Atwater.

When I was about to marry for the second time, I became consumed with what I would call myself. I had been a numerologist since the mid-sixties, and I knew well the power of names. I wanted to honor my first marriage, even though it ended in the tragedy of anger and despair. Three children claimed their place in life because of that marriage, and two parents rediscovered theirs. Tragedy need not overshadow the worthiness of what can be learned from it, and I wanted the numbers in my new name to show that. Plus, in the area I now call home, I could fill out certain forms with the state that would formally legalize whatever name I chose.

Yet every combination of letters left me cold. Nothing felt right. With the wedding barely two weeks away, I was running out of time. In frustration, I gave the situation to God. Ego preferences would have to take a backseat to wisdom: Thy will, not mine.

A few days later, a most unusual thing occurred. While fast asleep, I woke up to the fact that I was dreaming. I was still asleep, yet I was fully conscious and completely aware. Before me spread a vastness of sparkling black, so alive it shimmered with a warm and wondrous sense of presence. Suddenly, huge, gigantic block letters arranged themselves to spell out a name. The letters were of a white brilliance so bright it glowed of its own light. The name suspended before me was—P. M. H. ATWATER. This so shocked me that I jumped straight out of bed and landed in the middle of my bedroom floor, eyes facing a blank, white wall. And there, floating near my nose, was the same name, only in reverse color; now the block letters were of the warm, living blackness that had comprised the backdrop of the lucid vision I had just had. I was aghast!

I stood there, looking at the letters, until they faded away. Then I ran out my door and told the friends I was renting a room from about what had just happened. It was as unbelievable as it was uncomfortable. Me, wear three initials for a name? No way. It seemed egotistical to me, loud and brash, in defiance of what I wanted to respect. I couldn't accept the name. Still, I had asked God for help; I had invoked wisdom. *Thus, I committed the name to prayer, affirming that if this name was truly right for my highest good, I would be so shown. After seven days of prayerful contemplation, the name took on a life of its own, embracing me within a vibration of love.*

After the wedding, I changed all documentation to reflect the legality of my new name. Seventeen years later, I have grown used to people questioning it, confused by the three initials and wondering why I would ever take on such an odd combination of letters. My answer is always heartfelt: "My name was revealed to me in a most unusual vision and I wear it with joy."[5]

Social Change

Artist Helene Huber was galvanized to use her art for social change by a dream charged with high energy. She relates the unfolding of events.

The Dream

We seemed to be in a high school auditorium, and I was asked to participate in an experiment for the military. A tube was put into my mouth, which extended into a tank full of some liquid. I was told (by telepathy rather than the spoken word) to create pressure by blowing through the tube, so that the level of the liquid in the tank was kept as high as possible without spilling over.

By concentrated effort I did so well that the military representative conducting the experiment complimented me. Suddenly, I lost my concentration and the liquid boiled over. I was surprised at the effect. A stream jetted high into the atmosphere and a mushroom cloud developed. I was shocked, realizing that this meant I could sooner or later be subject to horrible suffering from the fallout.

This made me very angry, and I expressed my anger, saying that nuclear defense made me angry from the very beginning. I was told, "You should have spoken up sooner. If enough people had protested in the beginning" they would have done differently.

The Effect Upon Me

I woke up knowing that I had work to do and I felt eager to get started. I was reminded then of my prayers the two previous mornings concerning watching to see what emotions would arise so that I could acknowledge them and either express them or convert their energy into creative expression and healing.

So I immediately acknowledged that the military-industrial complex angers me with what strikes me as the disgraceful waste of Earth's and humanity's precious resources in the ungodly name of national defense. Instantly, I knew intuitively that this anger, this energy could serve, by being transmuted, to help break up the old pattern of an eye for an eye, anger for anger, hostility for hostility. By being transmuted through the divine power of Creative Spirit, the energy could help bring forth on Earth the pattern of love, intelligence, harmony. I felt elated knowing I would be guided, "inspirited" to cocreate bits of art as effective peacemaking.

What I Am Caused to Do

As a consequence of all the above, I am using the talents and resources the Creator invests in me to focus on art making that conveys the energy of which it is composed. The art making that is not other than lovemaking—the making of love to the One and to all the One includes.[6]

A nuclear explosion, a mushroom cloud, and fallout are symbols that often appear in dreams that presage a kundalini awakening or a tremendous burst of creative energy. Our inner circuits are loaded with energy, and the dream tells us the energy needs to be released. In her dream, Helene is given specific guidance for how to channel her artistic energy to serve her sense of purpose. There is a high level of emotional involvement, as evidenced by her immersion in a tank of water which she, by her own pressure, must keep high but level. She experiences anger in the dream but has a constructive outlet for it, one that stimulates her to follow through in waking life to refocus her work and begin new projects.

Dreams can serve not only artists but scientists and the corporate world as well. Intuition training has already become vogue in the corporate world; dream incubation practices should be added to business brainstorming tools.

Simply by doing dreamwork, you will unlock more of the creative power of your dreams. For specific help, follow the guidelines for dream incubation in chapter 10.

c h a p t e r s e v e n t e e n

GETTING GUIDANCE

WHEN WE ARE FACED WITH IMPORTANT DECISIONS, SUCH AS CHANGES INVOLVING OUR HOME, JOB, AND RELATIONSHIP, OUR DREAMS RESPOND WITH GUIDANCE THAT LITERALLY helps us navigate our way. Maps, paths, and instructions from voices and guide figures point out to us the road ahead. Unusual lights over places, landscapes, and signs also mark the trail. Magazines tell us what we need to know. It's as though the dreamworld is saying to us, "Here—this is the way that has been prepared for you." Sometimes the dream guidance confirms what we already know and helps to end vacillation or second-guessing. Sometimes the guidance is unexpected—and we are put to a test of faith.

Career and Relocation Decisions

Choices at the Dream Airport

Carol Parrish-Harra is a renowned metaphysical teacher and the founder of Sancta Sophia Seminary and the Light of Christ Community Church in Oklahoma. The school and church are part of an intentional community called Sparrow Hawk Village, located on Sparrow Hawk Mountain near Tahlequah. The Sparrow Hawk community and its church and school exist because

Carol was guided to Oklahoma by meditation, dreams, and waking visions.

In the late 1970s, Carol and her husband, Charles Harra, were living in Sarasota, Florida, where Carol had a thriving ministerial preparatory program and a spiritual community, called Villa Serena, an apartment complex in which residents gathered for communal meditation and study. More than one hundred students were in the program and were setting up study groups in other cities.

Although Carol and Charles loved Sarasota, Carol was feeling an inner urge to move to another location to create a safe haven in preparation for Earth changes. In 1979, Carol was told in a meditation that in five years she would not want to be in Florida. It was hard for her to believe, but she also believed in following one's guidance. She considered moving to Sedona, where one of her teachers, Torkom Saraydarian, was relocating, and to Rapid City, South Dakota.

In 1981, while she was still debating her options, Carol had these experiences:

I had a clear guidance dream. I was in an airport and about to go through security check. There were three gates from which to choose. The first to the left, wide and attractive, was labeled "Sedona." The far right, again wide and attractive, was labeled "Rapid City," the middle was small and plain. The sign over it said "Other." With a feeling of resolve I lowered my head and went through the middle check area. I awakened knowing it would be neither of the places I was considering.

Soon thereafter the guidance came. In my vision I was in a large room with maps on all four sides. In front of me a map of the U.S. filled the entire wall. My inner teacher stands behind me and reaches over my right shoulder, his finger directly on a spot on the map. It seems I am standing too far back to see where he points. I step up closer. I am stunned as I see the state of Oklahoma with the name printed clearly across the state. His finger is in the northeastern corner of the state. My heart seems to stop. I cry out, "Oh, no, not Oklahoma . . . not OKLAHOMA!" I snap out of the vision. My heart aches. I can't believe it. I've never been in Oklahoma in my entire life.[1]

Carol's guidance also gave her the name Tahlequah as the place to find. She'd never heard of it. A check on a map confirmed that Tahlequah, a town of about 10,000 persons, did in fact exist. "My heart was the heaviest," Carol acknowledged, "because I thought that Sarasota was at least on a par with heaven. But I knew this was an opportunity to do something in keeping with a plan that I had envisioned."

Carol and Charles traveled to Oklahoma. When they saw Sparrow Hawk Mountain, located in the Ozarks foothills, they knew they'd found the right place. They purchased 332 acres and began to build Sparrow Hawk Village.

It took time for Carol to make the adjustment to living in the country, but she came to prefer Sparrow Hawk Village to any other place to call home. "Something very fine is happening here," she said. By 1996, the village had about 90 residents; more than 140 students were enrolled in the seminary program.

Perhaps Carol was led to Sparrow Hawk Mountain because of the strong Indian energy there—it is located at the end of the Cherokee Trail of Tears—and because of the earth energies. When plans for the village were laid out, the area was dowsed by noted dowser, Sig Lonegren. The sanctuary was built over a spot where five powerful ley lines converge. Its design is intended to heighten spiritual awareness. A huge amethyst crystal anchors the Ray of the Ascended Master Saint Germain over the intersection of the lines. The energy inside this sacred space is palpable, and it varies even around the room, depending on which side of the lines one sits. The nature spirits have a presence at Sparrow Hawk as well. Many visitors, including myself, have walked along the dirt roads at night and tuned in to the sparkling lights of the nature spirits, which many of us call fairies, sprites, or devas.

Master Guide

One of the long-time residents of Sparrow Hawk Village, Barbara Barber, was led to the place by guidance from her dreams.

I got to Sparrow Hawk Village through my own inner guidance. At that time I didn't know anything about the seminary or its founder, Carol Parrish. My religious background was with the Episcopal Church. I was pursuing a career as a professional artist, painting and teaching others how to evoke creativity from the soul. Friends told me I was a Christian mystic and one suggested I contact Sparrow Hawk Village Bookstore for information on the subject. I did so. The year was 1986.

A few months later, a series of dreams brought to my consciousness that there was a window of time in which I could prepare for my soul's work. My sense was that this was my last chance for this life. Fifty years of my current life had already passed. So I called and set up my first visit to Sancta Sophia Seminary and Sparrow Hawk Village.

In 1990, another series of dreams started. I had a sense that I was to leave my island home off the coast of Georgia and move—but where? Another series of dreams began. They were all the same setting in which I was outside the home I owned at that time. In each dream there was someone with me who I call a guide. Each time the setting was the same and the guide was pointing out specific topographical locations. In the first dream, we walked a little way down the side of a hill. It was heavily wooded. In the second dream, we did the same thing only this time the trees were not as thick. It was as though a clearing was being prepared. I could see the surroundings more clearly. From my perspective, things were becoming clearer.

The third dream occurred four days before I was to go to Sparrow Hawk Mountain to look at houses to rent or perhaps build, but not wanting to do the latter. The dream setting was the same, a mountaintop, trees, and the guide. This time, the view was even clearer as though someone had removed the trees halfway down the mountain. This guide was pointing things out to me again, saying, "Now look at this, that, and that." As I stood on a lot on top of a mountain, I saw a panoramic view with hills across a valley. The guide pointed, saying, "Now, look down there." My gaze followed his outstretched arm, and I saw a river winding its way through the valley. The dream ended.

Four days later I arrived at Sparrow Hawk Mountain and the small community located in its valley and on top of the mountain. There were no houses to rent. One of the lots I was shown was located at the southwestern edge of the village. I stood on the lot for awhile and felt an urge to walk down the side of the mountain alone for a short distance. The hill was heavily wooded but, being early spring, the trees were still barren of new growth. I looked down the mountain and across the valley to the foothills beyond. I let my gaze follow the rim of the distant hills. It was a panoramic view. I dropped my eyes toward the valley below and saw what looked like water. Can this be? Memory of the dreams flashed into recall. Returning to my companions, I asked about the water. I was told that this is the only lot in Sparrow Hawk Village that has a view of the Illinois River.

I bought the lot and built a home.[2]

The experiences of both Carol and Barbara share some interesting similarities. There are guide figures present, geographical locations, and pointing as instructions for where to look. Interestingly, the number three appears: three gates at the airport for Carol, and three dreams in a series for Barbara. Both were facing major life changes that ultimately completely reoriented their lives. Dreams (and for Carol meditation and waking vision) enabled the high spiritual guidance to come through.

Answer in a Magazine

Jeffrey Mishlove's name is synonymous with intuition and psi. Mishlove, who holds a doctorate in parapsychology and is a clinical psychologist, is the host and coproducer of a popular national public television series called *Thinking Allowed,* in which he interviews the leaders of consciousness exploration. In 1993, Mishlove became the director of the Global Intuition Network, an association of diverse professionals who are interested in the practical application of intuition. He also serves on the editorial advisory board of *Intuition* magazine, writes books, and lectures. His book, *The Roots of Consciousness,* first published in 1975 and since revised and expanded, is considered a classic.

Intuition, psi and consciousness, and broadcasting were not his original choices for a career. In fact, Mishlove's career choice was influenced by a guidance dream he had in 1972, while he was a graduate student in college. He was studying criminology.

My interest in criminology reflected my fascination with human deviance. However, I was feeling very uncomfortable studying only negative forms of deviance. I deeply wanted to reorient my career focus. One evening, I felt inspired to tell myself and to accept without a doubt that I would have a dream that would provide an answer to my career dilemma. Then I did have such a dream.

I dreamed I was visiting some friends in Berkeley, who were not at home. Knowing where they hid their house key, I took the key and let myself into their apartment. I walked into the living room where I found a magazine sitting in the middle of the floor. In the dream it was called Eye *(a popular magazine at the time). I picked it up and began paging through it. While I was dreaming, I had a distinct feeling of elation. I knew that somehow the answer I was seeking existed in that magazine.*

I awoke early in the morning and . . . felt drawn to act on the inspiration of the dream. Immediately I dressed and ran four miles across Berkeley to the apartment I had dreamed of. My friends were not home, but I did know where they kept their key. Breaking the bounds of conventionality, I let myself into their home. To my delight, there was a single magazine in the middle of their living room floor. It was not called Eye, *it was called*

Focus. *And this magazine literally brought focus to my life. It was the magazine of listener-sponsored television and radio in San Francisco.*

As I sat there, paging through Focus *magazine, I was struck with the idea that I would redirect my career through involvement with public broadcast media. I applied to volunteer at KPFA-FM, Berkeley's listener-sponsored radio station, and within three weeks, I was asked to host and produce a program twice a week called* The Mind's Ear.

Suddenly, I found that my life was transformed. Every Tuesday and Thursday I had the opportunity to hold intimate, hour-long, uninterrupted discussions with leaders of the human potential movement, yogis, scientists, psychics, psychologists, visionaries, humorists, etc. I felt as though I had found my home in the universe.

This experience gave me the confidence to pursue a unique doctoral diploma in parapsychology at the University of California, Berkeley, and to write the first edition of The Roots of Consciousness. *The inspiration of that dream still motivates my life twenty years later as I produce the* Thinking Allowed *television series.*

My own dream experience certainly does not reflect a contact with higher intelligence in the romanticized or stereotyped manner characteristic of theosophical and Rosicrucian legend. It does suggest a synchronistic connection (which implies some higher intelligence) that has been integrated into the movements and actions of my life pattern.[3]

By asserting that he would have a dream that would address his career dilemma, Mishlove initiated a dream incubation. His resulting dream has elements of lucidity: the elation and the realization in the dream that his question is answered. Furthermore, Mishlove took the most important step: he acted on the dream.

If not for the dream, would Mishlove have taken this course? Might-have-beens are impossible to predict. But the dreamscape responded immediately to his need, and laid out the answer clearly so that he could proceed without delay.

On the Map

Some years ago, a map dream helped me to move forward with a decision about moving to a new home.

I am given certain items of jewelry—they are ones I already own, but have been transformed somehow. The gold ones—earrings, ring—are shinier and have a brighter glow. Most significant is my watch, which was black and is now all gold, including the band.

In the dream, I see these pieces laid out on a map that shows what appear to be Connecticut townships. The pieces are on top of one of the townships where we have been looking for a new house. I take the pieces of jewelry and put them on. The watch feels the most special.[3]

I interpreted the dream as both predicting and confirming my feeling that my then-husband and I would move to a particular community. We had looked at many houses in several communities, including the one depicted in the dream map, but I was afraid of making the wrong decision. The watch symbolized that time was at hand for a transition. The shiny gold jewelry also gave me the feeling that the move would bring about a spiritual renewal. There is an alchemical symbolism here in the transformation of the watch from black to gold. In alchemy, the *nigredo,* or blackness, must come first before the gold of enlightenment can be attained.

Slot in Life

Writing opened as a second career for romance author Zita Christian. Although successfully published, Zita felt that she had yet something else to do in life. She was answered with this dream.

I was in the office of a friend of mine who works at a law firm. She was showing me the billing system and offered to demonstrate the new billing computer. She took me over to the machine, punched a few buttons, and the computer produced a printout, which she handed to me. My name was at the top. Underneath was a slot for my occupation. Instead of having one slot, I had two. Slot B said, "Romance." Slot A was empty. To me, that's an indication that I have yet to find my niche, or perhaps I've not yet fulfilled my mission in life. Either way, I know the dream is significant because of how I was pointed, both to the machine and to the printout.

In the ensuing months, Zita had several experiences that filled out this dream. She had three dreams of a familiar woman's voice speaking or conveying messages. In the first dream, the voice exclaimed, "Nine!" so emphatically that Zita woke up suddenly. In the second dream, Zita worked with a blank sheet of paper and the voice said, "Expand your margins." In the third dream:

My hair is pulled away from my face and held back with combs. All along each comb are lush, deep purple flowers. The message comes as a feeling instead of a voice, but it is very clear: I am to communicate with the dead.[4]

Nine is the number of wisdom and completion, a vibration in which we pull together the sum of our knowledge and experience. The command to "Expand your margins" relates to pushing out creatively into new territory—the product of nine. Zita was puzzled about how she would communicate with the dead. Then, unexpectedly, a new book project materialized in which she was telling the story of a deceased man, and was researching his life and personal papers. Also unexpectedly, she was invited to teach a class on writing romance novels, which allowed her teacher energy to express itself from within.

And she had several dreams with a Chiron theme. Chiron, you recall from the chapter on healing, is the wounded centaur from Greek mythology who raises Aesculapius and teaches him the healing arts. Chiron represents an archetypal energy that concerns the healing of our own wounds in order to open our ability to heal in general. Chiron also is the name of an asteroid that figures into one's horoscope. The placement of Chiron at birth indicates the type of wounds we have come into life to heal.

All of these dreams and experiences were illuminating for Zita. "I suppose the Slot A part of my dream is to be a teacher, but not in the traditional sense," she said. "I can see the connection between teaching and healing and moving back and forth between the two worlds." Writing, she said, has always been part of her soul since earliest memory. "I can't remember *not* writing, though it wasn't until the early 1980s that I thought it was possible to write for a living. Even then, it was another ten years before I sold my first book. But I have felt that writing would somehow be a bridge, not to another career, but to another dimension.

"I've always had the ability to see the underlying pattern in a situation, whether from events themselves or from the words of a conversation, or as in the case of the [deceased man's] letters and diaries, the words between the lines. I don't know what you'd call a person who moves between two worlds, but whatever it is, that's what will fill my Slot A."

A Bridge

L. K., a college student, made a difficult decision to change career majors, which meant changing colleges as well. Even though she was certain about it, the change caused a lot of personal upheaval.

I was experiencing a lot of pain and uncertainty in my life, regarding what I want to do with the rest of it. I will still be involved with music, which is my original career choice, but I will also get to major in what I really wanted, which is psychology. I really want to go into research psych and counseling. Most of the people who were skeptical were immediate family members, like my mom. But as I was more definite about what I wanted to do, she even accepted it.

During this period, L. K. had her first lucid dream.

I think that this dream was a spiritual revelation for me of sorts. It involved me being on a high bridge, which was sent very high into the sky so that people could observe the area from it. The one stipulation to this was that when the bridge was lowered, into a large body of water, the person must jump off very quickly while still above the ground several feet. I was not aware that the reason the observers must jump off the bridge was because it would be lowered into the lake several hundred feet. Thinking I could jump at the last minute and be safe, I was too late. While I was being pulled under at sixty miles an hour, I suddenly realized I was dreaming.

While I usually wake up from my dreams when in danger, I did not try to awaken myself. In my dream I thought, "I can get out of this one, God is here." I found myself swimming up to the surface, or being assisted by some higher power to the surface, some forty feet above. Upon reaching the surface, I was given a hero's welcome, being told I performed a feat that should not have been humanly possible. I was given the understanding that it wasn't humanly possible, but that I was spiritually assisted.

This was the first dream that ever had a spiritual link involved. This dream made me realize that although some people think I may not be able to handle my decision of switching careers, I believe that this dream was a message from God telling me it is possible, especially with His help. Lately I have realized what a potential I have to achieve my goals in life!

Despite the reassurance of the dream, L. K. continued to feel uncertain about her transfer. Once again, her dreams responded.

I said a prayer and asked God if He could give me any guidance other than that I am receiving from my family. Since then, I have had about four different dreams that encourage me to go ahead and follow my desire to do this transfer. Many times I will be talking to people in my dreams who I know and who attended the school I would like to go to. A former teacher I had who went to this school was in my dream and said to me, "It's a great school—you'll be very happy there." I don't know how much more positive my signs could get![5]

When our dreams offer guidance, they keep up the message until we accept it. L. K. needed more than one assurance, and her dreams obliged.

The bridge is an important symbol of transition, representing the move from one career choice and college to another. In a sink-or-swim situation, L. K. discovers not only her own powers to swim, but the presence of a source of spiritual help that she can call on as well.

Life Directions

River of Life

The river is often a dream symbol representing the course of life. It is tranquil or turbulent, reflecting events and choices. It runs high or low, reflecting our energy and zest for life. It can be clear and sparkling or shrouded in fog and mist. In the following stories, rivers are key symbols in dreams that bear important messages of life guidance.

Myrtle Fillmore, the cofounder with her husband, Charles, of the Unity nondenominational Christian movement in the late nineteenth century, was sick much of her early life. She suffered from tuberculosis and believed that her life would be limited and perhaps cut short by illness. When Myrtle was a young student, she studied geology and took trips into the countryside to study rock formations and waterfalls. During this period, she had a profound dream, the meaning of which did not reveal itself for many years.

One night in my dream I took a wonderful trip all by myself, and this is what I found—the bed of a stream that must have been active at some time. It was beautiful, with white sandy bottom, but all the water it held was in a few bowls of white rock—apparently a dried-up stream. Stopping to investigate I could find no source. A very high ledge of rock crossed its bed at the south, and looking to the north I could see only a continuous bed of like character as that before me. In my astonishment, I voiced the question, "From whence the source of this stream?" And for the answer there came a sudden voice, more of waters than anything else, "I will show you," and over the ledge of rock came pouring a regular Niagara. I had to get back in the woods away from the spray. It ceased when the bed was filled. As I stood looking at the clear waters of the stream, beautiful flowers sprang up.

Many years later, when doctors had pronounced Myrtle's health to be beyond help and predicted she would soon die of her tuberculosis, Myrtle discovered the power within her to heal herself through prayer. She suddenly realized the meaning of the dream.

When my life stream was so low and I was about to lose it, there came pouring into me this Truth. I saw more clearly the meaning of my dream. I remembered where the source of my life was, and how it came over the rock that was higher than I.[6]

Myrtle's road to recovery was not an easy one. She did not experience a miraculous healing overnight; nonetheless, she did experience a miracle, recovering fully from an illness that doctors had declared was terminal. The healing power of prayer and the ability to achieve wholeness through positive thought and affirmation became cornerstones of the Unity philosophy.

In her prayer, Myrtle sought to replace negative thoughts with positive ones. She attuned her consciousness to that of the Creator, bringing in divine light throughout her body and establishing within her the conviction that perfect health is our God-given, natural state.

Her recovery took about two years to complete. During that time, she was frequently plagued by doubts and despair. When those low times struck, she would resolutely pull herself together, release the negative, and focus on the positive. She paid attention to her dreams, recognizing them as valuable sources of guidance.

Changing Streams

Cas P. had grown up Catholic. But in 1981, well into adulthood, her inquiries into spirituality had led to conclusions and beliefs that did not fit within Catholic dogma. Cas dropped her belief in many of the church's tenets and began to question whether or not she should leave the church altogether. It was not an easy matter to resolve. Cas sat on the fence, and her inner struggle went on for years. In 1988, she had two dreams that galvanized her into action.

I had been fighting with myself since 1981 about whether to stay with the Catholic Church or not since I no longer believed in many of its tenets. I was reluctant to do so because there is much beauty in its teachings, music, art and literature. It had provided my moral foundations, but I felt a need to break away. I had the following two dreams two weeks apart in 1988.

In one, I am coming to a major intersection on the outskirts of W. [town]. I meet a policeman, an older man I've seen in other guises in my dreams. He asks if he can take me home. I reply, "No. It's not allowed. Besides you have to help her." I point to a shadowy figure in his police car.

The scene changes, and I'm standing on the other side of the intersection. I see a new housing development with white houses. The houses have black rooftops and are large and ordinary looking. Landscaping has not been done. I see a few tufts of green grass in the newly spread-out dirt. There is also a rather dried-up stream at my feet. I know somehow that I must follow this stream in order to get home. Suddenly there is this pounding, insistent thought: "Because this is what I've agreed to." As I stand there, I'm aware of being totally alone and lonely, but I'm not sad; that this is something I want to do. No one made me. The feeling is one of matter-of-fact acceptance.

Scene changes again. I'm in the new downtown B. [city]. There are no people here at all. I can see the little parks and benches, new buildings and walkways. No traffic is present. I'm standing on a grassy bank with lovely trees and a rushing, clear, sparkling water/stream at my feet. On the opposite bank is a wall of small stones, light pink, tan, gray, and white. Water pours down the stones and into the stream. I am incredibly happy and know that this stream and the one outside W. are connected. I just go back there to continue because "this is what I have agreed to." Again, there is this pounding insistence. End of dream.

This dream came two weeks later. I'm in a church. It seems very square. Along two sides of the church are clear, ground-to-ceiling windows. Enough light comes in that artificial lighting is not necessary. At the front of the church is a marble altar and in front of that is a long marble kneeler and a rich mahogany railing. There are very few people present. I am standing in a pew waiting for the service to commence. Suddenly, a woman's voice announces that the service has been canceled. I put my head down and sob, heartbroken.

Suddenly, from my right side, an arm comes around my shoulders and hugs me. I look up and slightly downward. There is an elderly man who looks as if he stepped out of the Old Testament. He has gray, black, and white long hair that joins a moustache and beard that has grown down his chest. He wears an off-white robe (unbleached muslin) and over that a beautiful, black velvet mantle. He has a somewhat sad, half-smirk and the most beautiful dark brown eyes. He doesn't say a word; he doesn't have to because there is all the understanding in the world in those eyes. He moves ahead of me and I see the back of the mantle is covered with gold embroidery. His yarmulka is also black velvet with concentric circles of gold that end in a little gold knob on top. End of dream.

Three years later, in 1991, I left the church. The second dream was a great comfort.[7]

The first dream confirms to Cas that her spiritual tradition, Catholicism, has dried up for her, symbolized by the dry stream. However, she knows the stream will lead her to her next spiritual path, symbolized by the sparkling stream. The authority figure of the policeman offers to "take her home," that is, back to her traditional roots. The shadowy figure in his car is an aspect of Cas that needs help in order to be liberated.

In the second dream, Cas waits for a traditional church service to begin, but there will be none. It symbolizes her break with tradition, which she knows must happen, but that nonetheless causes her much sadness. She receives angelic comfort from a mysterious Jewish wise man. "The second dream gave me a great deal of comfort and told me I was on the right track," said Cas.

As a Catholic, Cas had had very little exposure to Judaism, and so the Old Testament wise man puzzled her. Wise men and women often are archetypal figures that symbolize deep inner wisdom and the wisdom that exists in the collective unconscious. The Jewish appearance perhaps symbolizes the universality of all spiritual paths: they are diverse but all take us to the same place. Later, she shared the dream with a friend who suggested that she had been visited by an angel.

After Cas left the church in 1991, she began following an

eclectic, independent path that has been a source of great spiritual nourishment and happiness.

Relationships

Finding New Love

Most of us desire to spend our life in a loving relationship with a partner. When a relationship ends, it's often hard to envision how or when we will find someone else, especially if the breakup was particularly painful. We fear loneliness and being alone. If we turn to our inner guidance, optimism rather than pessimism takes the upper hand. Our higher self can even show us what's ahead.

After recovering from a difficult divorce and enduring unsatisfactory dates, Amy (a pseudonym) decided to marshal her inner resources to find a new love. She put together a plan of action that included prayer, affirmation, and visualization. She conducted dream incubations, asking to be shown how to find the man who would become her next husband. Nothing happened for awhile. When discouragement set in, Amy would shake it off and resolve to keep trying. Meanwhile, she was engaging in activities where she hoped to meet available men.

One night, Amy had this dream.

I am late for a meeting or a conference. When I enter the crowded room, everyone else is already seated and the program has just started. As I look for an empty chair, my eyes are pulled almost as though they are magnetized to a dark-haired man who is looking at me. His gaze is intense and seems to go very deep into me. I am startled and almost paralyzed. I have a sense of elation, that this is meant for me. I wonder if anyone else will notice.

The dream convinced Amy that she was going to meet the man of her dreams at one of the many spiritual meetings, workshops, and conferences she attended.

Every time I went to something, I had high expectations that this would be it. Though I met some interesting men and went out with them, none of them clicked with the feeling that I had in the dream. I was ready to pass the dream off as a wish fulfillment. One night I made a last-minute decision to attend a program on intuition. There were some unexpected traffic problems, and I wound up being late. I sort of raced into the room, a bit disheveled and not even thinking about my dream. Suddenly I found myself in a replay of the dream, my attention drawn to this man who was looking at me. I took at seat at the edge of the room. At the first break, he came right over and introduced himself. I had this same feeling of elation. Everything just sort of fell together after that. We're getting married in six months.[8]

There is a psi element to this dream, forecasting the circumstances in which Amy will meet her future partner. What's more, the dream provided a source of inspiration that buoyed her up when she became discouraged. An interesting touch is the program on intuition in the dream. It's as though the higher self is reminding Amy that paying attention to intuition pays off.

Letting Go

For Laura B., a dream of a talk with a wise man enabled her to crystallize her growing anxieties about her marriage and take action. The wise man was someone she knew, but who in the dream assumes an archetypal role.

In 1977 I had just completed my Ph.D. in religious studies and was teaching as a one-year visiting assistant professor. I had been married for three years to a struggling young lawyer who was unemployed at the time. While I loved him deeply, I was beginning to sense that there were deep differences between us that could not be spanned. Then I had the following dream.

I was in a large, old, dark house. In every room there were parties going on. I would wander into a room and try to enjoy the party. But after a little while, something bad would happen and I would have to leave. I don't remember what the events were—perhaps just a drunk getting out of hand or a sinister mood descending. In each room I would get the feeling that I had to leave right away. So I careened from room to room, each time being driven out by something painful or vaguely evil.

Then I found myself in the very center of the house, in a room where I hadn't been. It was stark white, with a single bare lightbulb hanging from the middle of the ceiling and reflecting off the white, glossy walls. It was a small room, like a bathroom, but I remember only a single wooden chair, in which was sitting a college professor of mine, a Jewish professor who had taught ancient Near Eastern studies and Old Testament. While I had not been his student, I had admired him and thought very highly of him.

He looked at me and said simply, "Don't you realize you are married to two people?" In the dream at once I realized that he was right. How could I have forgotten? That was why I couldn't linger in any of the rooms. I had to go back and put myself/house/life back in order.

I woke up then, with the sure knowledge that I was going to have to leave my marriage. It took a year and was nasty and painful all around, and I cried regularly for an hour a week for three years before I could heal the pain and guilt of leaving. But a few years later, I remarried, left the state, had children, bought a house, got the kind of teaching job I had always wanted, had a religious conversion, and started on the spiritual journey I am still on.

At the time, I thought that the dream meant that I was "married" to both my husband and my career. After twenty years, I think that interpretation was mistaken. I didn't have to choose career or marriage. I ultimately chose both, although neither one was the sort I had fantasized about. Instead, I think the dream meant that I had made incompatible commitments to two people: to my husband and to myself, and in the end I could only honor my commitment to self. I had to find someone who could commit to loving the self I was committed to becoming. Fortunately, I did. We've been married for nearly seventeen years now.[9]

Laura's dream wisdom could apply to any of us: We must honor our commitment to ourselves in order to honor commitments to others and to our perceived purpose in life.

Our dreams provide us with constant guidance, whether we consciously seek it or not. Regular dreamwork will ensure that none of your inner wisdom will be overlooked. Our dreams show us Truth. We may not always rejoice to receive it, but our lives will always be better for acting upon it.

chapter eighteen

VOICES OF AUTHORITY

IN THE LANGUAGE OF MYSTICISM, AUDITION IS THE EXPERIENCE OF A VOICE THAT SEEMS TO COME FROM BEYOND ONE'S OWN SELF AND SPEAKS IN ONE'S OWN LANGUAGE. THIS VOICE MAY SEEM TO FLOAT in the air, audible to the ears, or emanate from within. It seems to be a connection to the Divine—a direct hot line to God—and it brings illumination and transformation. Typically, the voice is clear and powerful and speaks with great authority: a stand-up-and-listen voice.

Audition usually occurs in waking consciousness or in meditative, contemplative, or distracted states of consciousness that skirt the borders of sleep. This powerful source of spiritual wisdom also comes in the sleep state through dreams. Sometimes the voice *is* the dream, without imagery. Sometimes a disembodied voice accompanies imagery. Such dreams are called *audition dreams.*

Audition has a time-honored place in mysticism as one of the first phenomena to occur as the mystical life deepens. Saints and sages the world over have experienced it. Audition, said Evelyn Underhill in her classic work *Mysticism,* is one of the means by which the "seeing self" approaches the Absolute. Mystical auditions bring sudden calm, flood the personality with new light, initiate or accompany transformation and conversion, resolve indecisiveness, confer knowledge, deliver spiritual stimulation, and stimulate creativity.

Audition is not limited to mystics. Artists, scientists, and inventors experience it. In fact, everyone experiences audition at some point in life, frequently a turning point. One does not have to live the ascetic life of an adept or mystic to be graced with audition in either waking consciousness or dreams.

The Bible contains innumerable references to the voice of God addressing people in visions or dreams. Most accompany imagery. A dramatic example of a near-imageless audition is the conversion of Saul, related in Acts 9:3–7. Saul despised the new Christians and was bent on destroying them. His conversion took place as he journeyed to Damascus.

. . . suddenly a light from heaven flashed about him. And he fell to the ground and heard a voice saying to him, "Saul, Saul, why do you persecute me?" And he said, "Who are you, Lord?" And the Lord said, "I am Jesus, whom you are persecuting; but rise and enter the city, and you will be told what to do." The men who were traveling with him stood speechless, hearing the voice but seeing no one. Saul arose from the ground; and when his eyes were opened, he could see nothing; so they led him by the hand and brought him into Damascus. And for three days he was without sight, and neither ate nor drank.

After three days (note the number three), Saul received a laying on of hands and was healed. The scales fell from his eyes as he was also healed to truth. He was baptized and became Paul, the greatest evangelist of Christianity in the ancient world.

Audition that emanated from a brilliant light also occurred to Saint John of the Cross in 1578, when he was in prison. One night a heavenly light descended into his cell, from which a voice said, "John, I am here; be not afraid; I will set thee free." The voice said, "Follow me," and the light moved before him. Suddenly, John found himself outside the prison. His vision was weak for several days, he said, because the light was like looking into the sun.

Saint Teresa of Avila, a Spanish Carmelite nun and contemporary of Saint John of the Cross, was governed by voices throughout her mystical life. Said Underhill:

They advised her in small things as well as great. Often they interfered with her plans, ran counter to her personal judgment, forbade a foundation on which she was set, or commanded one which appeared imprudent or impossible. They concerned themselves with journeys, with the purchases of houses; they warned her of coming events.[1]

The voices also told her to begin a reform movement, the Discalced Carmelites, which she did.

Voices still urge people to action in modern times, as we will see in the story about voice-over dreams in this chapter.

Teresa, like other mystics and adepts who had frequent encounters with the spiritual realms, advised giving visions and voices careful evaluation—sound advice that still holds today.

Big Dreams, Big Changes

For Susan E. Mehrtens, a series of audition dreams ushered in a major life change, completely reorienting her worldview, occupation, and place of living.

Prior to her first "voice-over dream," as she calls them, Susan was a college professor in Maine, teaching history and environmental studies. She was an avid sailor, a self-described "rugged individualist," and a no-nonsense intellectual. She explained in her autobiographical account in the journal *Exceptional Human Experience:*

Typical of the Eastern Ivy intellectual, I was very skeptical of anything that smacked of "new age," dismissing stuff like astrology, intuition, parapsychology, and channeling as "woo-woo" nonsense from weird places like California. I was sure I had not an intuitive bone in my body, and I was quite content to operate in the rational, analytical, Cartesian world in which I had grown up. At fleeting moments I was aware that my life had an aridity, or sterility—I couldn't quite articulate what it was, but the creativity just wasn't there, yet when the grant proposals had to be written, or the college handbook faced revision, I could be counted on to produce suitable prose. So this hint that not all was well remained tiny enough for me to feel quite content with myself and my life.

Susan didn't know it, but she was about to have an awakening that would begin with a dream.

It was the morning of the day after Thanksgiving—November 25, 1983—that I had the dream that changed my life forever. Like other people, I had

had dreams before, but I never thought anything of them, and they were not like this. There was no action, no story line, nothing but blackness, and then this extremely loud voice, like a megaphone going off in the bedroom:

"Friends will die. Relatives will die. You will give up everything, and your life will be transformed."

And then, while I was still asleep, these words reverberating in the ethers, I experienced the most incredible ecstasy, an ineffable joy or peace, a feeling of being loved and accepted—very like what I later learned is common in the near-death experience (NDE). As many who have gone through the NDE say, this is something words are inadequate to describe. All I can say is that the memory of this final piece of my "Big Dream" has been enough to sustain me through some really bizarre and trying times over the last decade. But I didn't know back then just what I would be facing, nor did I realize that I had just had the first of what I would come to call my "voice-over" dreams (dreams with no narrative or action, just a loud message giving me guidance or direction).

Susan awakened and shared the unusual dream with her husband, Ed—and then forgot about it, never thinking that the dream might be precognitive.

Five days later, she was notified of the sudden death of a close friend. A chill ran through her. She remembered the dream, and that it had spoken of multiple deaths, and giving up everything.

About a week later, Susan heard of the death of another friend. She began to worry about the dream.

Then my Aunt Harriet died very suddenly, and Ed and I fell out, and the emptiness of my 30-month-old marriage became clear. Within six months of the dream, I had lost two friends, two aunts, an uncle, and had gotten a divorce.

By the summer of 1984, Susan's life was in chaos. It seemed she was in a free fall into darkness. Dreaming every night was a terrifying experience. She knew she had to get her life back together. She consulted a series of counselors. She discovered the work of Carl Jung—of whom she knew nothing—and began to understand her dreams. But Susan was still in fear of the other shoe ("give up everything") that waited to drop.

When a friend set up an astrology reading for her, Susan was initially furious to be subjected to "mumbo-jumbo from the new agers." She heard the reading out and was astonished to see her life reflected accurately in it. In astrological terms, Uranus was conjunct her mid-heaven. Translation: archetypal midlife crisis. Her initial voice-over dream had forewarned her of the upheaval.

Susan left her job and began what she described as "a life of research" through projects that came her way via a network of personal contacts.

I still had dreams, and was beginning to recognize three types. There were the ordinary dreams I had every night—action, narrative, people I knew, or didn't, usually with some strange element that held clues to my growth or healing, the sort of dreams we all have. Then there were the "numinous" dreams, which wouldn't necessarily have any action, but reminded me of the last section of my first dream, where I felt so loved. These dreams put me in touch with the divine (hence "numinous"), and they always left me feeling renewed in hope, strength, courage. I had them perhaps once or twice a year. And finally there were the "voice-over" dreams, which came at odd intervals. I could never anticipate them, call them up on demand, or control what they said. All I could do was learn how to react to them.

A series of three voice-over dreams in 1985 and 1986 directed her to leave Maine, go to California, drive there herself in a truck containing a small amount of her belongings, and use her personal network to find a research job.

This was a most bitter pill! For years I had castigated California as "fruit 'n' nut land," and here I was being told to move there! It was as if the Universe was grabbing every one of my prejudices and blowing them away!

Susan spent twenty-nine months in California essentially reinventing herself. She learned to trust her intuition, pay attention to her dreams, and live more in the moment. Her dreams continued to clarify her new path and identity as well as give guidance about practical matters. When dreams told her to set up a business (including what to name it), but not advertise it because all of her business would come via word of mouth, Susan followed through, though she did not initially understand how a business could survive without advertising. She was successful in attracting word-of-mouth business, just as the dreams had predicted.

Another voice-over dream told her to develop her intuition more. Susan plunged into courses and workshops, eventually becoming a channel.

I came to learn that intuition development is a natural part of spiritual advancement, and in time my focus shifted from intuition alone to the wider goal of general spiritual growth and soul work.

Besides addressing the big picture of Susan's life, the voice-over dreams also took care of little matters.

My "voice-over" dreams were not above dealing with humdrum practicalities. In March 1988, I was told in a dream that I would get a new car, and the whole process would be very rapid, so I should prepare for it. That led me to read up on the various models and their safety ratings, etc. Two months later, the dream was right: The entire process took less than 24 hours, and the car was just what I wanted. Two years later, when I was determined to leave California and had earlier that day put earnest money on a house in Oregon, I had a "voice-over" dream telling me that I would not buy that house. As it turned out, I was sent by my dreams to Washington, D.C. instead, and when the time came to find housing there, I was told in a dream that the house would have a four-digit address, be on a terrace, and in a town with a "-ville" suffix. Locating the right house became a simple matter of choosing the one with these features. I was very happy in that house.

But, as one might imagine, things get sticky when conventional American reality confronts a life lived according to dreams—as when I tried to explain to the Oregon realtor that I would not be buying the house. The fact that I had had a dream telling me otherwise just would not register with her. It was all finally settled only after two attorneys were brought in, months later.

After twenty-nine months in California, Susan returned to the East Coast, to New York State.

The frequency of the "voice-over" dreams has lessened. I'm on the path the Self intended; my image of myself is more in line with who I really am, and I am more open and watchful for guidance on the conscious plane.

I certainly am happier and more creative than I ever was before my "wake up call." I know I can rely on my psyche as a source of inspiration and guidance. Between my dreams (which are very interactive: I can write a request for direction or guidance in my dream journal and get a reply in my life or my dreams without fail) and my channeling, I have written several books in a matter of days. I also have come to understand a dream I had seven years ago, as I was leaving teaching.

I love teaching. I have always thought of myself as a teacher, and still do. The dream told me I would return to teaching eventually, but not full-time, not in academia, and I would not teach history, marine or medieval studies, Latin or ecology, as I had before. Rather, I would teach who I had become. That made no sense to me at all then, but it does now, because I realize that my living the last 10 years has taught me lessons others need to hear.

Susan's conclusions from her experiences are these:

- Sometimes life gets so out of whack that extraordinary or paranormal experiences are necessary to set it right.
- Personal growth usually comes through development of our Achilles' heel, a part of life that causes us trouble.
- Life improves when we take the time to heal our neuroses.
- The Jungian belief that we dream to wake to life is true, and paying attention to dreams can provide invaluable guidance.
- Your vocation is literally your divine calling, or that which is right for you. In Susan's case, she had to be called in dreams because she was closed to her intuition in waking consciousness.
- Our conventional view of reality is flawed because science rejects the intangible, psychic, and spiritual. We need an extended science that encompasses the full range of human reality.

"So this has become my vocation," said Susan, "to teach who I am as a challenge to convention, toward fostering the global mind change that lies on the near horizon of our culture."[2]

And it all started with a voice in a dream.

A Change in His Ways

Michael Moran is respected in his two careers of radio broadcasting and the ministry, but he stirred up a lot of trouble as a youth. His beloved father, whom he had idolized, died when he was twelve. His grief turned into anger, and he "went nuts" for a couple of years. "All of my emotions shut down," said Michael. "I waged war on the world." Michael especially looked for fights. Taught how to box by his father, he used his ability aggressively on anyone he thought was acting like a bully.

A run-in with the police for inciting a disturbance put Michael in jail. Embarrassed and feeling very much the victim, Michael had plenty of time to think. He thought a lot about his mother. "I felt powerless, like I didn't have a voice, and no one would listen to me," said Michael. "Even though I fought a lot, I really was very shy." While in jail, Michael had a significant dream that forecast his path in life.

I am a disc jockey, which would be out of character for me, though my sister was dating one, and I thought he was the coolest guy in the world. I'm taking phone calls from kids. I'm their advocate, giving them their voice, taking up their cause.

After his release from jail, Michael went home to a house heavy with pain. He was depressed and didn't know what to do with himself.

One night, I was sitting on my bed looking at a picture of my dad with a crucifix by it. I started swearing and cursing. I felt abandoned. I threw something at the picture and hit the crucifix. The picture fell and broke.

I laid down in bed and must have fallen asleep. Suddenly, I heard a voice call my name. It sounded like my father, but it couldn't have been. I sat up and turned on the light and called out, "Mom?" She was two floors above me. I woke her up, but she didn't answer me.

I sat on the bed feeling really sad. Then I heard my name called in a deep voice a second time. I still thought it was my mom's voice rumbling through the heating duct. I got up and said, "Mom?" She shouted, "What!" I went back to my bed.

I heard the voice call my name a third time. This incredible peace washed over me, and somehow I knew everything was going to be okay.

I woke up the next morning totally different. At the time, my grade point was about a 1.2. I stopped hanging out with the bad crowd. The vision of the disc jockey stayed with me. I enrolled in a speech class. I was terrified, but I excelled.

That dream set the whole direction of my life, to go into broadcasting. People told me I had a gift. Spirit put me in that jail cell, because that's where it got my attention. It was the turning point from being from an angry victim to having a sense of direction. From that moment, I never questioned what I was going to do with my life. I knew I would go into broadcasting to help people.[3]

Michael's dream in jail showed him what he was to do with his life and how he could have a voice. Although the dream impressed him, it wasn't until he experienced the audition dream, the voice that said only his name, that everything fell into place for him. The audition dream also came out of the dream consciousness and into waking consciousness the second and third times. Was it the voice of God, his father, or his higher self? Perhaps all three.

What's in a name? A name contains the essence of who we are. It contains the "I Am That I Am." In mystical traditions around the world, names carry vibrations by which the forces of the universe can be navigated. Calling upon the name of an angel brings us into contact with the angelic realm. Calling upon the name of God brings divine energy to our consciousness.

We all need to be addressed by our names, our unique vibrations in the All-That-Is. We are soothed, angered, brought to attention—the entire range of human emotions—simply by the way someone calls our name. In Michael's case, the voice was calling him to attention—to pay attention to the disc jockey dream, to who he was and what he was to do in the world.

Both of these cases feature the number three: a series of three dreams for Susan and three calls of his name for Michael. Thrice times the charm—the door to Spirit flies open!

Release of Creativity

Not all audition dreams relate to spiritual transformation. Some come to help solve problems in daily life. Nonetheless, they retain the aura of guidance from on high, something that comes from beyond the self.

Early in my writing career, I was invited to give a workshop at a prestigious writer's conference. I accepted gladly, and set about preparing my two-hour presentation. I developed an outline, transparencies, and handouts. Although I did not have a lot of public speaking experience, I was not daunted by the prospect, as are many people. I'd discovered at a young age that I liked to stand up and speak to an audience, and I'd been an award-winning debater in school. I was seldom nervous and never at a loss for words.

Since this was a new presentation, I planned to rehearse it once or twice to set it in my mind. Then, I would be able to speak fluidly and extemporaneously with just a few notes for prompts.

To my dismay, I found that I could not get through the talk. Ten minutes into it, I completely shut down, feeling like my tongue had turned to cement. I wrote a more detailed outline. I still could not get through the talk. I would stop cold, forgetting what I wanted to say. I wrote a still more detailed outline. It didn't work.

The day of the conference presentation drew closer, and I became increasingly nervous. For the first time in my life, I suffered from stage fright. I worried that I would look like a complete idiot.

I arrived at the hotel still not knowing what I was going to say and how I was going to say it. The extensive notes seemed useless. The night before the talk, I went to bed worried, but somehow managed to get to sleep. I had a dream in which a disembodied male voice spoke in one ear: "You have your material well in hand."

I awoke and saw that it was morning. Strangely, I felt completely at ease, even though the moment of reckoning was at hand. I even felt elated. I had not the foggiest idea what I was going to do, but I no longer worried about it.

The workshop was full. I was not daunted by the expectations of the standing-room-only crowd. I laid out my stack of detailed notes and outline. As I began to speak, I felt a profound shift of consciousness, as though "I" was shoved off to the side. It seemed that I was both speaking and watching myself speak at the same time. I felt a presence that seemed to sit on my shoulders. I felt charged with an unusual energy.

Two hours later, I wrapped up the talk for an enthusiastic and appreciative audience. I had not used my notes once, and I had covered all the ground I had originally envisioned.

I attributed this experience to angelic intervention: the voice, the entry of energy, the presence on my shoulders.

Undoubtedly, I did have my material "well in hand," since I'd done extensive research. But the dream was significant for me in three ways: (1) I never again experienced paralyzing anxiety before a talk—the inner resources respond readily; (2) I became more aware of the presence of the angelic realm in my consciousness and paid more attention to it; and (3) I received yet one more validation of the way dreams work to bring us guidance.

c h a p t e r n i n e t e e n

TURNING POINTS

MAJOR CHANGES IN LIFE ARE MARKED BY SIGNIFICANT DREAMS—DREAMS THAT REASSURE US, FILL US WITH HOPE AND RENEWAL, OR SHOW US A NEW PATH. THE FOLLOWING stories are examples of dreams in three different turning-point situations: life-and-death, religious/spiritual change, and professional upset and rebirth.

Perseverance

Sandra (a pseudonym) experienced a life-saving turning point OBE dream during a time when she was so low and depressed that she decided to commit suicide. She had suffered from severe bouts of depression since a troubled childhood that included violence and being the victim of a stalker crime. In long-term denial over the fall-out of such events, Sandra struggled to keep her head above water, but she had a difficult time forming close relationships. The final blow was the loss of a job that jeopardized her ability to support herself.

I was only thirty-one years old, but I felt I'd had enough—I was in the process of checking out. I had made my plans on how I was going to go. I was clearing my papers out. I went to lie down. As I was lying there, I suddenly had a knowledge that instead of doing something overt to end my life, I had the power to choose brain cancer as a way out. I could check out within six months and not harm people the way doing something overt would do. It was a sad choice, but it was the one I made.

I started apologizing to God. I had grown up in the Catholic tradition, but I thought that I had been a very fortunate person, that I was luckier than most, I had a very high IQ, I was physically very strong and athletic. On the surface, I had a lot going for me. I said, "You've given me all these things, these gifts, and I've screwed them up in every way possible. I don't see any way out. This is what I want [brain cancer] unless you can change it for me."

I was on my back, feeling totally surrendered and very peaceful. All of a sudden, the room changed. I went into a temple. The walls were a white-on-white mosaic. It was very simple and beautiful. At the end was a man who had a shaved head and was wearing white. His eyes were very dark and intense. I had no idea who he was. He talked to me. He told me that in this lifetime I had chosen a harder path because I wanted to get "there" faster. "You're on the right path and you're going to get what you want, but you have to stay here, you can't leave," he said.

Suddenly I was back in my body. I went into a hysterical sobbing. A friend had given me the name of her counselor. I immediately called that person and started a counseling process.

However, things got the worst they'd ever been in my life! It took me a long time to understand what the man was saying. For a long time, I felt his presence.

I had a series of dreams like that. I was in denial and refused to go back and experience the impact of some of the violence in my life. Then my little dog died, killed by another dog. When I saw my little dog with his wounds, I went into flashbacks for two days of sheer hell, reliving the violence I'd experienced years earlier. It took several months to process it.

A year later, I was in bed and not quite asleep when I saw his little face come up. It was huge. I heard a voice say that a spiritual being had been embodied in my dog because at that point I was not able to interact with people. The only way to get through to me was with the dog. But I had to go through the trauma of losing him in order to stand on my own. The voice said that the dog was fine and the being was fine now. After that, my feeling about the whole experience changed. It was real powerful.

Sandra's dream/visions seem to have occurred in the hypnagogic state. Later, she had an equally powerful experience while in

prayer meditation, an altered state that can be similar to the hypnagogic state.

Whenever I prayed, I prayed to know love, to be loved. I became aware that I was seeing a face that I interpreted to be Jesus. He said, "You can have this experience." Suddenly it was pink around me. I had an experience of total, unconditional love. In that moment, I knew that there was nothing that we could do as humans—that we were such children—that would make us less than totally loved. Just like a two-year-old can do nothing to make you love them less. It was a total understanding that what a two-year-old is to us, we are to this unconditional love. Everything was totally forgivable. Everything. *That experience totally changed me. I was able to tap into that energy and handle any situation without getting angry or feeling vulnerable.*[1]

Sandra's visionary experiences helped her to find her inner strength and rebuild her life. She had an expanded perspective on the purpose and path of her life, seeing it from the point of view of the greater whole, and understanding the lessons she faced. The experience of the unconditional love is one of a mystical nature that transcends words but comes to reside in the heart as a knowing that pours out into everything else.

Letting Go and Moving On

Major course changes in life require releasing the past. Profound shifts in religious and spiritual values, life philosophy, worldview, and values turn our attention in totally new directions. As we embrace the new, we may feel the need to repudiate or reject the past. But all of our experiences contribute to who we are. We learn from everything. Moving forward is about building upon what we have already experienced, acknowledging the gifts that come from all that we do.

Michael Moran titled this lucid dream about change, letting go, and integration "The Young Monks Danced."

I was in ministerial school, having a spiritual crisis with my roots in Catholicism, which were very deep. I was the first in the family to break away from the church, and it disturbed them. Early on, my concept of God changed—I could not stand exclusivity, regardless of where I saw it, religious, racial, or whatever. Culturally, however, I'm still very Catholic.

When you change, part of you wants to revert back to what is familiar. The ministerial school was challenging my belief system. To help this crisis of consciousness, I was allowed to do a directed study on mysticism.

I started teaching a class on Thomas Merton, the Trappist monk and mystic. At the end of it, the class visited a monastery. We did chanting with the monks, prayer, and a lot of contemplation. I felt so at home—a sense of peace and security and familiarity. A part of me did not want to go back. I just wanted to stay in this familiar womb and chant the Psalms. I just wanted to accept and not question.

While I was there, I had this dream. The dream opened with vivid sounds and colors, crackling with energy. My friends and I are sitting in a circle, laughing, with an incredible sense of community, love, and spirit. There are two doors to the room. Suddenly one of the doors flies open and these young monks come in, almost like whirling dervishes. They have guitars. They whirl around the room, singing and laughing. We're all delighted. I'm thinking, "This is the way it's supposed to be!"

The door opens again and a monk with a basket comes in. The other monks reach in and take out little heart-shaped bits of brown bread. They throw them up in the air, saying, "Receive the body of Christ! Receive the body of Christ!" We're grabbing them. I pick up one and tear it and taste it. It is rich and moist and chewy. It really has substance.

Another monk comes in with a huge chalice, swinging it. The wine splashes. It is the sweetest, most wonderful wine I've ever tasted in my life. So deep red. I'm getting it all over me and loving it. Everyone is in ecstasy: "Receive the blood, the life of Christ!" It is a genuine sharing of God, a complete celebration of the sacraments. I am so moved, I say, "Thank you God for this experience!"

Suddenly there is a shift and this presence comes into the room. The monks stop, look, and hang their heads, like they are afraid and ashamed. A rage starts welling up inside of me. I think, "No, don't stop!" Fear comes into the room. I turn to look. There is an old priest in a formal garment holding a chalice and the host. It is like what I remembered from my days as an altar boy: thin wine and a dry, brittle host. He is glaring at everyone, shaming them. All of the joy leaves. There is shame, guilt, and awkwardness.

I awakened and sat up in bed and thought to myself, now I remember why I left the church. I left because of the shame, the guilt, the sourness of their wine, the whole brittleness. But I left behind a lot of richness, too. I needed to make peace with my former spiritual path. I knew I had to take all of the richness from my past and integrate it into what I was doing now. I left the monastery with a great sense of peace.[2]

Michael completed his new ministerial training. The dream enabled him to bridge the past and present and bring the spiritual riches of his past into his new life.

Resurrection

Sometimes we are dealt such abrupt and major changes that we truly experience a death of sorts and must regroup and resurrect ourselves to a new life. Unexpected losses of loved ones, jobs, homes, and financial security register big shock waves on our personal Richter scales. Suddenly we are faced with the threat of going under or the task of rising like the mythical phoenix from the ashes of our defeats or sorrows.

Sometimes dreams forewarn about such upheavals, but we may not realize the message until the disaster hits. If we pay attention to our dreams, however, we find a tremendous source of wisdom, strength, and healing to help us in the recovery.

A series of significant prophetic, lucid, and healing dreams aided Beverly Rubik through a time of professional crisis and personal upheaval. Rubik has a long list of scientific and academic credentials and is renowned for her work in the interrelationships between matter, mind, and spirit, and alternative/complementary medicine. A Phi Beta Kappa with a doctorate in biophysics, she has been at the leading edge of research in these areas.

In 1988, Rubik left her faculty post at San Francisco State University and moved to Philadelphia, where she became the founding director of the Center for Frontier Sciences at Temple University. The mission of the Center is to facilitate global information exchange, networking, and education on the frontiers of science and medicine. The first of its kind in the world linked to a major university, the center spawned others in Mexico and Italy.

The vision is lofty, but a difficult one to navigate through the often rigid channels of academia and science. In the mid-1990s, Rubik's work at Temple came to a sudden end.

Here is Rubik's account of the events and the dreams that were interwoven in them.

Beginning in September 1995, I had several extraordinary dreams, some of which puzzled me at the time, but in the end, predicted a major life event that ended my career at Temple University in Philadelphia. In early

September I dream that I am in a big castle, and powerful villains with machine guns are chasing me. They shoot everyone around me, except somehow I am still alive, cowering in fear and anguish lest they detect my panting and fill me with bullets, too. They see me and come over to try to kill me, now with large swords. I escape, find my way out of this castle, and discover another castle even more beautiful down the road. It is empty, and I occupy it. However, the villains catch up with me and try to kill me with their swords once again, but I escape their blows by flying up and around the castle interior. I am amazed that I can fly, and delighted that the ceiling is high enough so I am safe from their swords. But I grow tired of flapping my arms; I cry out for help. No one comes to rescue me. The villains were just waiting for me to fall down from fatigue so they could kill me. But just when I am nearly exhausted, I discover I have a new power: I point my index finger at them and tell them to be gone, that they have no place here in my castle. They begin to shrink and end up the size of rats. Someone enters the room then and takes them away, dumping them in the moat outside the castle. I am elated and soar through the air, like a big bird. I am safe again and free.

The castle in this dream represents academia to me, the "ivory tower" as it is frequently called; the villains, my various political enemies in academia. The dream foretold of a violent and brutal battle that I was about to face. As I hardly ever dream of violence, I felt this dream was significant, although upon waking, I did not know what to make of it. I felt it was related to academia and big battles, the territorial "serfdom and turfdom" that I had encountered, and the potential threat my work posed to others in academia such as those in conventional medical schools. Only later did I realize this dream was prophetic in that I had to go out and find a new "castle."

A month later I had another dream of consequence that involved many [people] that I have known over the years. In this dream I am camping on the flat top of one of the Mayan pyramids at Chichen Itza (that in Chinese I was told means, "energy mouth of the universe"). I wake up and walk down from the pyramid very carefully, as it is so steep that each step below is invisible. At the bottom of the pyramid, there is a lot of activity with many people milling around preparing for a ritual and feast in which I am to participate. Many of my friends and relations are there, as are many of the long-time participants of this conference. Somehow I am not involved in the ritual preparation, although everyone else is. I see the altar being decorated for the ritual, and it is elaborate and beautiful. Then I see my severed head sitting on a platter at the foot of the altar! I am shocked and shudder in fear and awe. I grasp my neck and am relieved that it is still intact. I ask those around me what this means, and they say it is "good medicine" and not to worry. Everyone seems so nonchalant about my head being on a platter! The ritual begins and prayers are offered for healing. I woke up disturbed and puzzled about this dream, but immediately wrote down the details for future reference. It was indeed a powerful, prophetic dream, and I would come to understand its meaning in the near future.

A few days later I was abruptly dismissed from Temple University on Friday, October 13th (the day witches were burned in former days). A letter handed to me by my superior revealed that my position was eliminated due to a projected budget shortfall. I had had no review whatsoever, and there had been no discussion of the Center's situation. Needless to say, the usual procedure under a projected shortfall is to ask the director what cuts they would make in their programs or which staff positions they would eliminate. In this case, the university retained my staff and cut off the head!

The fact is that a small projected budget deficit at the beginning of the academic year is not uncommon, as funding is raised throughout the year. I had ended each academic year with a surplus. In fact, I had no deficit at the present time. I was horrified and shocked. I immediately phoned my largest donors to inform them of this action and to see if I could get a commitment from them that might save my position. One of my philanthropists assured me that he would work with my other donors to spearhead a coalition that would make up any projected budget shortfall. He faxed me a note saying that he would make a further contribution if I were retained as director of the Center. I marched into the dean's office with this advice, hoping to negotiate with the Temple administration. However, I was told it was a "done deal," and once again I was stunned. A locksmith arrived at five P.M. and changed all the locks on the doors of my office, so I had to evacuate. A few weeks later, all those listed on my database, about 3,500 people worldwide, got cryptic letters from the university telling them that I was no longer director of the Center for Frontier Sciences at Temple University as of October 13, 1995, without any explanation.

After the panic was over, I reflected on my dreams in relation to my ordeal at the university. Although I did not understand the meaning of the dreams earlier, immediately it was clear that I had anticipated my ultimate battle and beheading. The dreams led me to believe that prayers and rituals were already under way in the spirit realm, and this consoled me. However, this was so abrupt a change, unanticipated, and it was so unusual for an academic position to be terminated in this way, it took me time to recover my composure. I suffered insomnia and then became ill with a bad cold and cough followed by several weeks of a lingering laryngitis. I was literally speechless in more ways than one at the way the university had dealt with me. These were all appropriate symptoms for a "lachesis" type, my homeopathic constitutional type, which is "snake venom." In relation to this, the most vulnerable spot on the body of a snake is its neck, the only place where you can restrain it, and it can't bite you. Thus, a "beheading" followed by throat problems is a deep constitutional transformation in homeopathy as well as alchemy. Unable to deal with the hundreds of phone calls from people who wanted to know what had happened, I sat silently and reflected on the meaning of being "headless." I reread the Zen book by D. E. Harding, On Having No Head, *which describes the path of the eight stages of the Headless Way in Zen Buddhism. Two weeks later, when I was still sick with laryngitis and a bad cough and taking codeine, I had a third dream that was relevant. I dream of having a terrible discomfort in my neck and throat. I start to cough violently, and I can barely breathe. Suddenly, I am aware that something solid is stuck in my throat. Coughing even more violently, I reach in my throat and yank out several black raven feathers and then a writhing earthworm. Finally, I am relieved of the cough. Over the years, the raven has been my power animal in several shamanic journeys. It appears from this dream that I have merged with this animal or that the raven was sacrificed on my behalf. Recall that in my first dream . . . I was empowered to fly like a big bird and escape the villains trying to kill me. The earthworm is also a sign of transformation, a sign of vitality by its writhing movement and shape shifting. Soon after this dream, my illness finally went away.*

Shortly thereafter, I had a fourth dream of a headless dragon dancing before me, full of fire and passion. Later that week, I was walking along a commercial street in Bethesda, Maryland, with a friend and saw a dragon in a shop that attracted me. Its vivid colors reminded me of the dragon in my dream, although it had a head. I went in and bought the most appealing dragon. Later, we performed a ritual in which I cut off the dragon's head. I put the headless dragon on my ritual altar at home. There it remains today as I experience the path of headlessness while I slowly start to regenerate a new head.

After my beheading at the university, I gave myself the luxury of time to recover. It was liberating to enter into emptiness and headlessness, after being overworked and exhausted. I "wandered in the woods" for several months before I decided what to do. In February 1996, I decided to establish an independent nonprofit corporation, the Institute for Frontier Science (IFS). In March I incorporated IFS, and in April I obtained my first start-up grant. As people learned what had happened at the university and what I was trying to build, several unsolicited donations were sent to me as well.

The purpose of IFS is to foster and maintain research, education, and information exchange in science, health, medicine, consciousness, and the mind-body-spirit relationship. It focuses on frontier areas of science and medicine that challenge the dominant biomedical paradigm and hold the promise of future breakthrough. However, one main focus is on public education and information exchange rather than academia. The people make the paradigm, not the scientists, at least at the present time. The people's revolution in health care is a clear example, as people march with their feet and their pocketbooks, spending over thirteen billion dollars annually consulting with alternative and complementary health care practitioners, demanding something more than conventional biomedicine can provide. Furthermore, IFS will conduct research on subtle energies and subtle energy medicine. IFS will also provide an "umbrella" for independent scholars and administratively manage their research funding. IFS will set up a home page on the world wide web and an electronic journal. In addition, an ongoing computer conference is being established on the internet to discuss frontier issues in science, medicine, and technology. Lastly, I would like to reflect on the lessons I learned in relation to all this. I established a maverick academic center in a difficult setting, and it grew and flourished. Now I have the confidence and expertise to be an independent entrepreneur. I can and will build another institute that can be more effective without the extraordinary burdens of the conventional academic setting.

Contrary to my earlier beliefs and expectations, I learned that new data in itself doesn't convince anyone. No matter how much scientific data we might accumulate that challenges the mainstream scientific or medical paradigm, nothing much would change. Changing science or changing the world is about transforming ourselves. People need an inner experience that is extraordinary and paradigm-shaking, and furthermore, they need to say "yes" to try to integrate it into their whole being. The paradigm shifts one life at a time.

I learned that what we see in science depends on our attitude, orientation, and how we choose to interact with nature. I would like to study how the beholder of nature interacts with that which she or he holds. If nature is held in fear or loathing, then I would expect different results would be obtained in science than if nature is held in love and esteem. The same is probably true for life in general. Once again, transforming the world out there starts with changing ourselves inside. It is interesting that this could be put to the test scientifically, but I doubt whether such data in itself would change things!

In August 1996 I was in Italy and bought a large platter that reminded me of the one in my prophetic dream where my head appeared on a platter. I set it empty on my altar at home. That night I had a wonderful dream. I dreamed my platter was full of tiny "Venuses on the half shell." The goddess of love appeared naked in full glory, similar to the one in the famous painting by Botticelli, The Birth of Venus, *but there were many of them, each one beautifully posed on a white half shell, presented to me on a platter at my table. I had just visited Florence and had seen this work in the Uffizi Museum. Perhaps this is a special food for the soul to nourish me on the next phase of my journey.*[3]

It's hard to add any comment to the artful analysis that Rubik has made of her dreams and the meanings of the various images in them. Her account serves as a good example of the way dreams help guide us through the trials of life. They provided her both a forewarning of the trauma and also the seeds for healing and renewal.

All of the dreams recounted in this chapter occurred spontaneously in response to crises. They all played an important role in the reestablishment of equilibrium. Turning-point dreams can be incubated as well. Whenever we find ourselves at a crossroads, in a difficult spot, or turned upside down, we can ask our dreams for help.

PART V

Spiritual Initiation

c h a p t e r t w e n t y

SPIRITUAL AWAKENINGS

PURSUIT OF A SPIRITUAL PATH, WHETHER WITHIN A RELIGION OR WITHIN AN ESOTERIC TRADITION, BRINGS PROFOUND CHANGES IN DREAMS THAT CALL FOR A NEW UNDERSTANDING. THE DREAMS OF the initiate become increasingly transpersonal, reflecting a deepening awareness of higher realities. The contents of our dreams shift, and we have experiences that are inaccessible to us in waking consciousness.

Rudolph Steiner stated that the higher soul is actually born during deep sleep, when we are in a world different from the sensory one and better able to perceive the spiritual world in its own character. "Our dreams lose their meaningless, disorderly and disconnected character and begin to form an increasingly regular, lawful and coherent world," he said. "As we evolve further, this new dream-born world not only becomes the equal of outer sensory reality with regard to inner truth, but also reveals facts depicting, in the full sense of the word, a higher reality."[1]

As we progress on our spiritual path, the dreamworld unfolds a higher reality. We become aware of the spiritual world, wherein dwells the soul. The soul is quite active in this world at night when we sleep. Through our dreams, we learn that what happens in the spiritual world is the cause of what exists in the physical world. Thus, it is the task of the initiate to bring the truths of the inner realm into expression in the outer realm, said Steiner. We must become conscious of our dreams and carry what we learn into waking life.

In *How to Know Higher Worlds,* Steiner lays out seven basic requirements for entering onto the spiritual path. They apply to serious dreamworkers as well, for dreamwork is its own spiritual path.

1. *Improve physical, mental, and spiritual health.* Sound understanding and perception of the higher worlds occur when we are healthy.
2. *Feel yourself to be a part of the whole life.* Cultivate a sense of connection to others and a sense of responsibility to better the whole. An interest in and love for humanity is necessary for the spiritual path.
3. *Recognize that thoughts and feelings are as important as actions.* Everything that happens in the world originates from thoughts and feelings.
4. *Know that your true nature lies within.* We are not products of the physical world; rather, the physical world reflects who we are.
5. *Follow through on resolutions that you make.* Resolutions should be based on the principle of love. Act accordingly.
6. *Have gratitude for all that you receive.* Without gratitude, we cannot love.
7. *Understand life as these conditions demand.* In so doing, you will live in more harmony and unity with the whole.

Kundalini in Dreams

The kundalini life force energy becomes activated in spiritual awakenings and manifests in dreams characterized by psi, lucidity, out-of-body travel, ecstasy and bliss, transcendence, union with nature and the cosmos, interaction with snakes, and contact with otherworldly beings and realms. Sometimes intense flows of kundalini are symbolized by explosions (especially nuclear), and natural cataclysms such as earthquakes and tidal waves. Swimming with, riding, or becoming a dolphin also can symbolize kundalini; dolphins represent Christ, or the culmination of the Great Work of alchemy.

Dreams of flying high and ascending to heaven parallel mystical experience and the state of shamanic consciousness. In shamanism, the shaman enters a dreamlike state that is both lucid and controlled and travels to heaven or to the underworld in order to divine information and heal. The flights are done by shape-shifting into power animals, by riding mythical horses or the spirits of sacrificed horses, by traveling in spirit boats, and the like. Muhammad, the founder of Islam, rode a mythical, eight-legged horse called the Buraq to heaven. The entire Koran was dictated to him in states of trance, beginning with the "Night of Power," when he was forty years of age. According to lore, the angel Gabriel appeared to him in a dream as the Messenger of Allah with the first revelation.

Ravindra Kumar, a university professor and founder of the Academy of Numerology and Kundalini-Yoga in New Delhi and Copenhagen, has experienced numerous transpersonal dreams, including mystical flight, since awakening kundalini. He describes some of them as follows.

Some time around the year 1980, I dreamed of flying higher and higher in the sky until I reached the summit of a hill surrounded by beautiful lakes, meadows, and gardens. Reaching the top of the hill, I saw a beautiful temple, absolutely white in color and shining with equal luminosity from every side. It gave me an instant feeling of happiness and bliss and a longing to have further visits to such a place. This increased my love toward God and led me to regular practice of yoga and meditation. It was the beginning of the withdrawal of my interests from the affairs of the world. Now I know that it was a temple on one of the astral planes.

Since then I have had regular dreams of a similar nature: flying over places similar to those on earth but without the negative attributes of earth. Lakes, mountains, rivers, gardens, fruits, and flowers so lovely and soothing that you cannot describe the derivative happiness. I can fly over streets, colonies, and houses, stop and descend down on the ground if and when I like, and take off and fly again.

Once I saw myself standing in front of a translucent fortress having two gates and a water canal in the middle. People were entering one gate and coming out of the other. People appeared to be circles of light, not in the form of physical bodies. There were people moving on the bank of the canal and also on the grass; they, too, were either in the form of a point of light or a circle of light. I could see three persons on the ground; one of them instructed me telepathically to move forward. Soon I found myself crossing a very broad river like an ocean of clear blue water. I had no dimensions to my body, just a point of awareness. Having crossed the river, I found myself in front of a group of mountains. I was trying to look at one of the mountains when suddenly the dream came to an end. Perhaps it was an out-of-body travel and I returned to the physical body on the earth. It gave me a firsthand experience of the astral planes under the guidance of an invisible helper or a guru. It could be the Eckankar Master Sri Harold Klemp or else Pythagoras. Next day, I was full of happiness and my faith in yoga and meditation was further increased. This was the year 1987.

I had several visits to such planes, which were the source of happiness and bliss on one hand and detachment from the world and its relations on the other.

I had several dreams of snakes around me in different forms, without any feeling of fear—it was almost a daily feature while I was asleep. I saw snakes with open hoods in different situations. Sometimes a snake would be looking at me in a friendly way, at another time it would be crawling on my body, and at yet another time it would fly with me in the sky. These were the dreams indicative of the awakening of kundalini.

In 1995, while I was in San Francisco, I dreamed of a big gathering in which I could see a person with an outstanding physique and a glow on his face and in his eyes, looking at me in a very affectionate way. He was moving in one direction, and I read the name "Bapu" written on his chest. Next day, I came to know from my mother that it was the nickname of the present-day saint of India, Asaramji. As I understand now, it was my higher self coming in the form of a guru to initiate and bless me.

I saw a special kind of dream in which I felt that supernatural powers had been bestowed on me and I was testing those powers. For example, I saw something like an electric pole at a distance. I moved and rotated the fingers of my hand, pointing toward the pole, and the pole was twisted. Similarly, I could stop a moving vehicle and could throw a big stone from one place to another, simply by the gestures of my fingers. I could travel anywhere and do anything by the power of thought and gestures of hand.[2]

Ecstasy and the Ineffable

Dreams that are part of spiritual awakening bring intense feelings of ecstasy, joy, and an understanding of the ineffable. Sexual orgasm can occur during such dreams, a by-product of kundalini.

Catherine G. had an intense spiritual dream she titled "Second Coming." The dream followed a period of depression and low feelings due to personal and professional moves that left her feeling unsettled. "I think it was just too much and it ruptured so much in my life—my feelings of security and feeling at home in myself—my Self as Center," said Catherine. In addition, there were issues sim-

mering below the surface: feelings of being deserted by God or that she had been duped into believing in a God that doesn't exist.

I am working part-time or freelance for my old employer, who in the dream is a hypnotherapist (I am also a hypnotherapist), but my old employer is not a hypnotherapist, but an agrochemical company. She has given me some tasks to do and I am doing them, but at the last moment she throws in one more task: making ten copies of regulatory reports (as a technical writer I used to write regulatory reports for my past employer). She gives me a long list of all the reports that need to be copied. The print is so tiny I can hardly see it, although a few of them on the list are printed a little larger. I go down the list trying to decipher which ones she wants ten copies of. I see that most of the ones she wants copied are recent, numbered by year: RR 97, RR 98, and RR 99. I stay late to finish the project, which I do not enjoy doing; it seems like stupid busywork. Now we are fixing sandwiches for a party or luncheon of black rapper people. We get the food together, baskets, picnic blankets, etc., and drive out to the luncheon site. It's way out in the country, down beautiful long country dirt roads. The roads are lined with tall trees, golden fields to each side as we approach the site. We arrive and there are many, many, long, long tables set up for the luncheon. All have white tablecloths on them. They are put side by side so as to create one very long table.

I am now standing back against the trees, observing. I see before me many, many men, perhaps 600 or 1,000, gathered around the tables. Jesus Christ is supposed to be one of the guests, but no one knows which one he is. There is much anticipation and excitement as the men eat and talk, knowing that he is present, but not knowing who he is. I am aware of the light—beautiful, soft, golden light around everyone, matching the golden fields, the blond hair of many of the men.

Next I am in a building that appears to be a modern office building with a large two-or three-story lobby made of glass. There's talk of a second coming. There's an energy and a hubbub everywhere. (I have a strong orgasm in my sleep here!) I am with a coworker and we are now running because everyone's in a panic. The building seems to be shaking; everyone is afraid, but I see that it's not an earthquake. It is God making himself/itself known. It's as if the earth and building are shaking but without the movement. I'm aware of only light everywhere. The most beautiful shimmering light is all around me and everyone, filling the entire space. The shimmer is God's presence. We follow the light and I then have a vision of being inside a huge cathedral with the same light filling its space, reflecting the beauty of the stained glass windows—lots of blues here. We try to make it through the panicked crowds. Then we both are hit with over-

whelming ecstasy in God's presence: It's like a wave hits us—mentally, emotionally, physically—intense and utter ecstatic joy, which lasts a few moments—the most wonderful feeling I can remember, physically and emotionally. A sense of well-being, love, pure ecstasy, pure joy.

Catherine said she interpreted the report numbers as referring to years that (at the time) were still ahead; perhaps there was a personal significance associated with them. She observed that the dream demonstrated that God is made of the same stuff we are: "life energy, sexual energy."

My spiritual view is that we are cocreators with God. That our spirit and soul live on forever. I have been interested in everything metaphysical for many, many years and am still in awe and wonder about the universe. My hypnotherapy practice is another avenue for expressing my spiritual interests. Now, at age forty-eight, I realize that the mundane can be as much a spiritual experience as the profound.[3]

Catherine added that she did not have a personal belief in a second coming of Christ (although it would be exciting), and so that image in the dream must be interpreted for other symbolic content. It may herald her own personal and spiritual second coming in the second part of her life. As noted, earthquakes are often symbols of kundalini arousals. The earthquake in this dream also is related to the orgasm Catherine experiences, which is a powerful release of energy. Here, Catherine understands within the dream itself that the shaking is really the presence of God, which is where kundalini takes us when it reaches the crown chakra.

Connecting with the Gods

Shawn Shelton felt blessed with a dream in which she experienced being a part of divine creative energies.

I am somewhere looking out and watching the sun come up over the horizon. I realize that I am looking out through two gigantic paws—the paws of the Sphinx in Egypt. I am in a chamber inside the chest. I am with another being. We are in the middle of a ritual that is Tantric in nature. We are circulating energy through our hearts and up over our hearts, and then down through our spines and through the base [root] chakras, and back up again through our hearts. This forms the energy of an ankh over both of us. The energies are then rippling out over the delta of the Nile and reawakening the soil. It is springtime, the equinox. This is a ritual to reawaken the Nile delta for fertilization to grow the food that supports the culture. I am aware that the other being with me is Geb. I say to Geb, "Isn't this the most blissful moment?" Then I realize that I am Nut.

At that time, Shawn did not know that Geb is the ancient Egyptian god of the earth. She did know that Nut is the goddess of the sky. Geb and Nut are children of the sun god Ra. Husband and wife, they bear the gods Isis and Osiris. They represent primal creative forces of the divine masculine and feminine.

As goddess of the sky, Nut swallows the sun each night and rebirths it each morning. The sun traverses the length of her body. Nut's body represents a world that exists purely internally, yet simultaneously with the realm of the manifest. The ancients called this mysterious, invisible realm of the inner world the Duat. The Duat is the realm of psychic energies and also the underworld of the dead. It is not so much an actual place as a condition of being.

Becoming Nut in the dream is not so much becoming a goddess but experiencing all that the goddess represents and embodies: an ineffable realm from which creation springs forth. The ankh is the Egyptian symbol for the life breath (*chi, prana, ki*), and represents immortality and resurrection. The energy pattern made by Geb and Nut through the chakras is similar to many esoteric techniques of moving the kundalini force through the chakra system by using the breath and visualization (sound is also used). Energy is circulated in patterns as a way of stimulating the chakras, increasing vitality, and improving spiritual vision. In the dream, the energy spills out onto the earth and rejuvenates it as well, demonstrating the interconnectedness of all things.

A week later, Shawn participated in a group past-life regression led by Brian Weiss. Shawn returned immediately to Egypt.

I am walking around a ledge that is shoulder high with the Sphinx. I am on the left-hand side. I walk all the way around to the right side. A door behind the Sphinx's face opens and I see an initiate standing, fully clothed in the clothes of a pharaoh, holding an ankh in one hand. His arm is outreached for me to come inside. As I step inside, he closes it. I'm back inside the same chamber that I was in with Geb. I turn around and look through the heart of the Sphinx, and here is the sun coming up once again through the paws.[4]

This experience, as well as other imageries of Egypt, enabled Shawn to reconnect with the power of her dream.

Learning from Spiritual Content and Messages

Dreams that carry big messages deserve extra attention in dreamwork. Even though they may be vivid and powerful, record them immediately to preserve all details. Be thorough in working with symbols and images. Spend time in meditation on the meaning of the dream. Ask yourself these questions:

- What does the dream show me about my spiritual awareness?
- What spiritual lesson is embodied in the dream?
- What is the dream asking me to do about my spiritual path?

I keep a dream journal of all my dreams, but I also keep copies of big dreams in a separate file. These dreams especially bear periodic reexamination, for they yield new insights as I progress along my path. They also fit together in their own special picture that emerges over the course of time.

chapter twenty-one

WORKING WITH MASTERS AND GUIDES

THE SPIRITUAL MASTERS ARE AVAILABLE TO US IN THE DREAM STATE TO ASSIST IN THE TRANSITION FROM ONE LEVEL OF AWARENESS TO ANOTHER. MANY OF US IN THE WEST UNDERTAKE SERIOUS spiritual searches but have no inclination to seek out a guru or withdraw into an ashram. However, we can in the dream state receive the teachings and guidance of a master. We do not necessarily have to consciously ask for such encounters. They happen when we are ready for them. Our dreaming consciousness is more open and able to absorb large amounts of intuitive learning, or knowing, because the waking mind is out of the way.

The dream master may be a great teacher who is living, such as Sai Baba or Sri Harold Klemp, or someone who is no longer incarnate. The great masters learn while they are incarnate to teach in both the physical and spiritual realms, and they continue to teach after leaving the earth plane.

Dream masters may be archetypal figures, such as the wise old man or wise old woman, or shape-shifted animals. They also may be beings unknown to us. A healer I know was called to his path unexpectedly and spontaneously when beings dressed in flowing robes appeared to him while he was in the hypnagogic stage of sleep. They invited him to come along with them. Suddenly, he was flying out-of-body over desert sand and found himself at the Great Pyramid in Egypt. He knew that people—or beings—were inside in the apex. Instantly, he was in the apex, in the company of white-robed beings whose humanlike forms were not as dense as physical bodies. He was told telepathically that they were members of the Great White Brotherhood, and they resided in the pyramid's apex. The beings said he would be given instruction that would make him proficient in certain skills.

He awakened to a brilliant white light that filled his room and a roaring sound. Later in the day, while he was at work, he had a spontaneous out-of-body experience in which he was taken up into light and "cradled in the arms of God." It was so wondrous he did not want to return to his body.

Then began instruction and conditioning. At night, he felt his consciousness go out his window to a spaceship that had physical form, and he was transported to a nonearthly (astral) school where he was instructed. The experiences were interwoven with his dreams. At times, he felt flooded with too much information to process. The Great White Brotherhood also took him in their ship to hover over hydroelectric plants, which somehow were involved in the raising of his own vibrations, his own energy field, so that he could accommodate the tremendous energy that he would use for healing.

Transmission of Power

My healer friend experienced phenomena associated with kundalini activation: brilliant light, roaring sounds, and out-of-body projection. The electrical energy in the dream images is especially interesting. Kundalini activation sometimes makes the body feel as if it is vibrating with electricity. These phenomena also are associated with opening of healing powers.

In the next dream, electrical shock is part of an encounter with a master as a young woman's spiritual search is just beginning.

Bobbie B. considered herself an agnostic, but was open to exploring various religions and spiritual traditions. Soon after she had finished reading *The Autobiography of a Yogi* by Paramahansa Yogananda, she had this dream.

I was in a large room. I felt it was very high up, but there was nothing in the room to indicate such height. Along the back wall, there were men sitting on pillows, wearing loincloths. I entered the room from the left and as I stood there, a Hindu spiritual master came toward me from the right. He was of average height and a bit chubby. He wore traditional Hindu dress. When he reached me, he said, "I will help you to know God." Since I was in my agnostic phase at that time, I started to say, "I'm not sure if I believe in God." Before I could get the words out, he touched my forehead and an electrical shock ran through my entire body.

The next day, I was shopping at a five and dime store and I found a book entitled How to Know God, *a translation of the Hindu Vedas, edited by Christopher Isherwood. Needless to say, it was one of many books I read over the years on my spiritual path to mysticism. This dream is very important to me and I have told it to very few people.*[1]

Bobbie's encounter with the master is the dream version of a waking-life encounter with a guru in which *shaktipat* occurs. *Shaktipat* is a transmission of psychic power (*shakti*) from guru to student, which accelerates the spiritualization of the student. Traditionally, it is only done when a student has advanced sufficiently in order to properly receive the power. *Shaktipat* stimulates kundalini over the course of time. The objective of raising kundalini is to achieve God realization.

Shaktipat can be considered a door-opener to another, higher level of consciousness. Within this broad context, a certain level of power can be transmitted to a novice as a way of prompting someone onto a spiritual path. *Shaktipat* is transmitted by a touch, a look, or by intent of will. Followers of Sai Baba have reported feeling electrical shocks at his touch.

Jesus delivered *shaktipat*. "The Gospel of Truth," a Christian Gnostic text in the Nag Hammadi literature, describes how Jesus transmitted power through his breath (the life force) and voice (the instrument of creation), which was received by others as light.

> *When he had appeared instructing them about the Father, the incomprehensible one, when he had breathed into them what is in the thought, doing his will, when many had received the light, they turned to him. . . . When light had spoken through his mouth, as well as his voice which gave birth to life, he gave them thought and understanding and mercy and salvation and the* powerful spirit *[author's emphasis] from the infiniteness and the sweetness of the Father.*[2]

Look of Power

The masters Peter Deunov and his disciple Omraam Mikhael Aivanov of the Universal White Brotherhood were renowned for their looks of power. (The Universal White Brotherhood, not to be confused with the Great White Brotherhood mentioned earlier, was founded by Deunov in Bulgaria prior to World War II.) The eyes are the conduits of the life force and are linked to Truth. In the following dream, the look confirms the identity of a master.

I was walking along a street in London, and my wife came hurrying up to me. She looked very excited and said, "I have found a Master" (a saint or holy man). I was very skeptical and told her so. Nevertheless she insisted, and asked me to come and see for myself. We walked to a printing firm nearby, where a few people were already waiting for the Master. I reviewed my skepticism, thinking that this was probably a man who was very clever and spoke much occult nonsense, and so everybody thought he was godlike; or at least, all those who desperately wanted to find a godlike man. Just then a man walked down some stairs from the building and said quietly to those waiting outside, "He's coming." Outside the building was a loading bay a few feet high. Onto this walked a slim man of middle height, in his thirties. He seemed very ordinary and was bald except for the sides of his head, where his hair was a sandy ginger color. He appeared a very passive man, and began to talk quietly, with little emphasis, his gaze above our heads, as if looking beyond us. As he talked, I thought to myself that I had heard all this before. I had read it in the Bible and a number of other books, but it hadn't done me any good. Neither could I see myself even beginning to live up to it. In fact, I dismissed the man as a dreamer. He didn't talk for long, however, but soon finished and came down from the bay. We all walked slowly along the street, some of the people asking him questions. When we neared the end of the street he stopped. We also stopped, and were facing him in a small, irregular semicircle, there being about six of us. He didn't speak, but looked at the person on the extreme left for a few moments. Nobody said anything, and he then looked at the next person. I watched him but had no idea what he was doing until his gaze turned to me. Suddenly it was as if a bolt had struck me and pierced me to my inmost being. I knew this man understood every fragment of my life—more than that—he loved me as I have never been loved before. A floodgate opened in me and a torrent of emotion and love swept over me. I stumbled forward impelled by the current of my feelings, and embraced this stranger with a fervent love. As he held me the turbidity smoothed and became a calm love, and I stepped back. His gaze turned to my wife and I saw her expression change under the impact of his eyes. Now I had no doubt—he was a Master.[3]

Third Eye Look of Power

I received *shaktipat* from a master in a lucid dream. At the time, I was making a transition in my work, going deeper into the mystery tradition. I knew immediately that a transmission of power had occurred during the dream.

Tom [my husband] and I are in a spiritual class led by an Indian yogi or guru. He looks very young, is slight in build (about five foot six) and has loose, long dark hair. His eyes are sometimes dark and sometimes blue. He has an electric presence about him that is very alluring. He comes around to each of us, placing his hands on our shoulders. When he does this to me, I make direct contact with his physical eyes and the third eye. He says telepathically to me (in a playful way), "Oh, so that's what you want, you're ready for that now?" Suddenly his third eye becomes visible as a brilliant white, crystalline light that pulls me into it like I am on a tractor beam. I go deeper and deeper into all three eyes, and then we are literally fusing. There are no bodies, no physical boundaries. In this fusion of energy I am filled with bliss and ecstasy. I awake from the dream with heart pounding, gasping for breath. I am charged with energy.[4]

This dream was so intense that I knew I would remember it for years.

I didn't know who the master was in the dream, but I felt certain that I would recognize him if I saw a picture of him. I shared the dream with a friend who was on more familiar ground with the particular attributes of various ascended masters. "Sounds like Babaji," she said. A few weeks later, I was at a conference and saw an array of drawings of ascended masters. A shiver went through me. One of them looked exactly like the master in my dream. I turned the picture over to see if there was a name on the back. It was Babaji.

In Eastern mysticism, Babaji is among the ascended masters, or "deathless ones," whose spiritual advancement enabled them to transmute their physical bodies into subtle bodies, thus escaping the wheel of birth-death-rebirth. The masters live in another dimension (geographically sited as the Himalayas), and have the ability to manifest in our dimension whenever they choose. They are dedicated to helping the spiritual advancement of other souls. When they appear to mortals, they may be as a youth or a wise old man. They may seem solid, like flesh and blood, or diaphanous. Their alchemically transmuted bodies are called light bodies, buddha bodies, bodies of gold, bodies of glory, and rainbow bodies. According to esoteric philosophy, all of us have the same potential ability, through spiritual development, to transmute ourselves into a higher realm and take on light bodies.

It is not uncommon for students of the spiritual path to experience encounters with ascended masters, sometimes in waking consciousness, but often in the dream state. Like angels, ascended masters usually have brilliant and compelling eyes, especially blue or alternating between blue and dark brown. Their appearances may be accompanied by sweet smells. They appear to someone who is ready for illumination.

The story of Babaji was first told to a Western audience by Yogananda Paramahansa in *The Autobiography of a Yogi,* translated into English in 1946. Since then, other books have told his story as well. Babaji reportedly was born on November 30, 203 C.E. in an Indian village now known as Parangipettai. At an early age, he was drawn to the spiritual path and began studying with a guru. He purified himself through diet, meditation, yoga, and prayer. At about age fourteen, Babaji attained *soruba samadhi,* or the "deathless state."

Babaji transmitted to selected mortal initiates the knowledge of Kriya Yoga, a yogic path to God. *Kriya* means "action and awareness." The yoga is designed to systematically awaken the chakras and the kundalini *shakti,* which leads to God or self-realization.

My dream with Babaji was a catalyst for various changes, which have continued as of this writing. It seemed that a greater charge of kundalini began moving through me in relation to my creative work in writing, speaking, and healing. Initially, I could feel the heat of it while I worked, and would be drained at the end of a session. Clairvoyants saw changes in my aura—more green for healing energy, more gold and white around the crown. Over time, I became more accustomed to this energy and assimilated it physically. It no longer tired me out; it energized me.

Soon after the Babaji dream, I had a dream that validated my feelings of working with higher energies.

I am a major presenter at a religious conference. People have high expectations of me. At one session, I am asked to give the opening prayer. I am surprised, because nobody warned me in advance. I begin to give an impromptu prayer. My voice comes out very high, as though it has been raised an octave. I worry that people will think I am nervous, but I can't get the voice to go lower.

The prayer goes on and on—a real kitchen sink. I invoke a bit of

Saint Francis, asking for the "brotherhood and sisterhood of the animals," and end with "In the name of the Father, the Mother, the All That Is, the Holy Son, and the Holy Trinity." At which people say, "Amen." Afterward, I try to cover up my high voice with a lot of coughing. As I cough, I realize that I have a very real obstruction in my throat—it feels like a huge ball of phlegm about to break loose.[5]

This dream told me that what I had to say through my work was going up in vibration, symbolized by the higher pitch of my voice. This involved a clearing of the throat chakra, the seat of expression of creativity, symbolized by the obstruction that I am coughing up.

It is interesting to note that both my and Bobbie's dreams involved the third eye, located slightly over and in the middle of the brows. The third eye becomes activated in spiritual work, especially meditation and prayer. It is the center of clear seeing, enabling one to perceive and understand the realms of the unseen. Through the third eye, we experience faith, the fuel of invention, and perseverance. Jesus referred to the third eye as the lamp of the body: "Your eye is the lamp of your body; when your eye is sound, your whole body is full of light; but when it is not sound, your body is full of darkness." (Luke 11:34) In other words, when we follow a spiritual path, we fill ourselves with divine light. When we follow the path of materialism and lower desires, the third eye does not function well, and we are spiritually dark inside.

Bobbie was charged at her third eye as a wake-up call to get on the path. I was pulled through the third eye of an ascended master into cosmic consciousness—a sort of graduation experience from one level of awareness to another.

Power through Initiation

The same night that I had the Babaji dream, a friend of mine also dreamed of him, and received *shaktipat.* Prior to going to sleep, Toni G. Boehm, founder of Awakening Hearts ministry, had participated in a women's group, which had raised a lot of powerful energy. Toni had been questioning her own power; the group experience was beneficial for her. Her dream was lucid; she described it as being "both awake and asleep." Ascended masters change their appearance as necessary, and Babaji appears as an old man, which is also a symbol of wisdom.

I dreamed I went somewhere and walked out into a hallway, where there was this older gentleman. He said, "I have something for you." I held my hands out, and he placed into them what looked like a cup and saucer.

I went around to show different people the cup and saucer. I asked them, "What do you think of this cup and saucer that this man gave me?" Several people said, "I don't see any cup and saucer." Other people would say, "Oh, wow, that's great!"

I went back, and he was still in the hallway. I said to him, "I think this is so beautiful, but some people don't see it. I really appreciate this cup and saucer." He said, "Toni, that's not a cup and saucer. It's a teapot." "A teapot!" I exclaimed. He said, "Yes. A cup is that which you contain and drink from for yourself. I gave you a teapot so you could share it with the world." I said, "Who are you?" He said, "My name is Babaji. I have come to teach you how to manifest from the interior realms, on the inner planes." I told him how much I appreciated it. That was the end of our scenario together.

Somehow I felt that he had told me to take a bath. So I went to a bathtub and took a bath. When the water went down the drain, it wasn't water, it was blood! I thought, "Isn't this strange? I've been taking a bath in blood, and I thought it was water."

Next thing I'm in front of a bathroom stall, but I'm totally dressed, and Babaji shows up again. A friend of mine, J., was standing beside me, kind of at the back, pulling on my coat and talking to me and Babaji, saying, "But Toni, Toni, I want to learn, too. Can't I be a part of this?" Babaji turns to him and says, "Yes, my son, you can be a part of this. I will name you a master novice or novice master."

That was the end of it. I felt waves of radiating energy pulsing up and down my body, filling me with happiness. It wasn't quite ecstasy, but it was pure pleasure, just radiating.[6]

As Toni awoke, her first thoughts were on Babaji, of whom she knew nothing beyond his name as a spiritual teacher. She was also struck by the bath of blood. "I thought I was being baptized into new life—truly a cleansing of consciousness, a lifting to a new level," she said.

Blood is a potent symbol, not only in dreams, but in myth, the mysteries, and sacred rites. Blood represents the emotions, the soul, and the vital life force. It is one's essence, and is connected to matters of the heart. It represents one's ideals. Baths are symbols of baptisms, and to bathe in blood is to undergo a spiritual purification and rebirth.

A baptism is an initiatory experience, and it can take place in the medium of any of the four elements. A baptism by water represents an immersion in the unconscious and emotions, and is a cleansing and dissolving process. A baptism by wind (air) represents a blowing away of chaff, especially involving the intellect. A baptism by going inside the earth represents gestation inside a womb. A baptism by fire represents a purging or burning away of what is no longer needed.

Baptism by blood is comparable to baptism by fire, for both blood and fire are symbols of intense purging. Blood has the additional dimension of redemption. When blood is shed, especially divine blood, the sacrifice is redemptive. Dream baptisms by either fire or blood may refer to experiences in life that are taxing the ego and bringing about changes (sacrifices) for the betterment of the individual. Toni was caught up in such experiences that were challenging some self-imposed limitations.

"The teapot made me feel that there was something that I had to give to the world," she said. "Maybe I was only giving by the cup. It had to do with owning my own wisdom and power. Babaji was telling me not to be afraid to pour, because there is an unlimited supply. The manifestation from the inner realm is knowing that there are no limits. Whatever it is you are manifesting, there will always be an unlimited supply. You just have to keep it flowing."

Toni floated through the day on lingering feelings of "pure satisfaction and happiness." The dream was a gateway experience, an initiation into a higher level of awareness. "Over the past year I've had numerous initiations," she said. "Each is a culmination of having learned something. In an initiation, you own what you have learned—you realize your own wisdom."

As she sat in prayer that day, Toni received a message about her spiritual mission in life: "I am a midwife for the birthing of the soul's remembrance."

Dreams such as these, featuring an advanced guide figure and charged with energy, expand the horizons of our creative potential.

Transmission of Knowledge through Mysterious Symbols

The presence of mysterious symbols in dreams increases when a person enters onto the spiritual path for Truth. After we learn to perceive the higher worlds, we are given a language that speaks to us as all knowing and that manifests in figures, colors, and sounds. Rudolph Steiner mentions this occult or hidden script as part of the process of spiritual initiation.

This occult script is inscribed forever in the spiritual world. Once the soul has attained spiritual perception, the script is revealed to it. But we do not learn to read this occult alphabet in the same way that we learn to read an ordinary human alphabet. Rather, it is as if we grow toward clairvoyant knowing, and while we grow, there develops in us—as a soul faculty—a force impelling us to decipher, as if they were the characters of a script, the events and beings of the spiritual world present before us.[7]

Mysterious symbols or languages in dreams involving guides, otherworldly places, lucidity, out-of-body experiences and other elements of high spiritual content deserve special attention. Use meditation, prayer, incubation, and active imagination to deepen your understanding. Recognize that a direct translation may only hint at the full meaning.

The following dream gave me a symbol to use in my meditation and work.

I am in a class that is teaching esoterica. An instructor, a wise old man, is teaching us about a new Tarot deck. He shows cards that replace some of the traditional cards. They have new names and symbols. There is one card that stands out to me. It is called TRUTH, and its symbol is a pyramid, made out of four horizontal bars with spaces between the bars, and topped with a flame.[8]

I was so deeply impressed with this symbol that I described it to Robert Michael Place, my artist partner who designed and developed our two Tarot book and deck sets, *The Alchemical Tarot* and *The Angels Tarot*. I asked Bob to draw it for me. My request in turn stimulated a current of creativity for Bob. He designed it as a Tarot card—a twenty-third trump of the major arcana. A hierophant holds a card bearing the symbol. The card is titled TRUTH.

Bob's comments to me were:

I think the image of the pyramid is brilliant. It illustrates the entire Hermetic philosophy. The universe flows from the One, the good—the flame. As it descends, it forms the seven tiers of the dense physical world—the four elements and the three imperceptible spiritual layers or three principles. This in turn demonstrates that the physical world is permeated and supported by the spirit. It also relates to the mythic mountain in the center of the world, the place of ascent to heaven.[9]

Bob found a seventeenth-century alchemical drawing of the Emerald Tablet, the symbol of the Hermetic teachings (Truth), showing the tablet as a pyramid of stone with a flame on top! I was unfamiliar with the drawing.

What I was given in the dream by a spiritual master was a symbol that contained the whole and essence of the Western mystery tradition. It can be explained in words only by a lengthy discourse, but the symbol makes it understood in its entirety at a deep level of consciousness. Both Bob and I now use it in our work with others.

Guidance and Instruction

An encounter with a guide figure in a dream can push out into waking consciousness. The ascended master El Morya has been a guide for many years to Carol Parrish-Harra (see chapter 17). Her first encounter with him came in the middle of one night in 1972 when she awakened and sensed a presence in her room. Opening her eyes, she saw a tall man elegantly dressed in an Oriental robe and turban of aqua blue silk. The smell of roses wafted through the room. He looked at her with calm but piercing eyes. Carol felt that she knew him, yet did not know his name.

The man identified himself as El Morya, and he had come to give her a message. "Take your pencil and pad and write down what I say; otherwise, in the morning, you will think this is all a dream," he said.

El Morya proceeded to dictate a long message about Carol's spiritual mission and some of the obstacles she would face. "My name is whispered daily in your ear—it comes to you to help you to grow wise and strong," the master said. "For this you have come into the body."

He also told Carol that she would be asked "to go where women rarely go and to practice bravery and courage." She was to aid all persons in the healing ministry, for healing is needed for the world. He also told her that she would carry "a harsh message" that sometimes would be difficult for others to understand and accept.

Carol did not remember the end of El Morya's visit. The next thing she knew, she was waking up in the morning, remembering an exciting dream. Then she saw her notepad filled with notes. The dream had been real.

El Morya is Lord of the First Ray. In esoteric tradition, there are seven primary rays, or emanations, expressing qualities of God. These vibrations make up everything that exists and also express themselves in the incarnations of all life forms. The First Ray is the will or power aspect of God. People who incarnate under the influence of this ray tend to have strong willpower; their challenge is to use those qualities to bring the manifestation of God's will into the world. First Ray people tend to be leaders.

In his message, El Morya told Carol that in this lifetime she was a first ray person on loan to the second ray. The Second Ray is love-wisdom, and seeks to instill the quality of love in all forms. People born under the influence of this ray tend to make good teachers and ambassadors.

The experience with El Morya threw her into high gear. She read about the masters; she consulted spiritual advisors. At the time, Carol was a recently ordained minister, conducting services, teaching classes, and doing private counseling. She felt she was firmly on her spiritual path. But the encounter with El Morya pushed her in new directions. She received guidance that Agni Yoga was to be her way. She visited ashrams and teachers around the U.S., including Torkom Sarydarian, who taught her about Agni Yoga. The Yoga of Fire, as it also is called, seeks expression of the divine fire within, the inner fire of the true self.

In the late 1970s, Carol made a pilgrimage to India, where she met and was blessed—or given *shaktipat*—by the avatar (incarnation of God) Sai Baba and by Babaji. The latter reportedly had manifested a physical form in order to conduct teachings at his ashram.

Carol's first encounter with El Morya was so powerful and personal that for years she kept it largely to herself, occasionally discussing it with people close to her. She told the story publicly for the first time in her autobiography, *Messengers of Hope*, published in 1983. Her activities and renown as a spiritual leader and teacher—people from all over the world seek her out—have borne out El Morya's message.

Follow Your Own Guidance

In his adolescence and young adulthood, my husband Tom was a follower in two spiritual organizations that had strong founder figures who served the role of a master; one has a continuing line of masters. But in his early adulthood, Tom began to question his own inner wisdom versus that of a master. Wasn't his own Truth just as valid as the Truth held by a "more spiritual" person such as a master? This issue created a deep inner struggle. A dream answered the question.

As I gaze at my surroundings, I suddenly see that I am in a temple. I think to myself that this is a place where spiritual answers are often found. The temple is quite beautiful and peaceful. I then notice that before me are two indi-

viduals in what seems to be a line. All of us are wearing long, flowing robes of various colors and are here for the same purpose. We are each waiting our turn in line to meet with the master at the temple and receive a spiritual name. I become quite thoughtful, however, when I realize the purpose. The receiving of a spiritual name bothers me at a very deep level. I cannot seem to understand how my inner essence can be labeled, and I wonder how the master justifies the naming of it. My inner essence is undefinable.

When the two individuals before me are through meeting with the master, it becomes my turn, and I walk into the inner chamber. The master has a Chinese appearance with soft, brown eyes. I voice my concerns to the master as to the purpose of the naming ceremony: "Master, how can I be named when 'I AM that I AM'?" The master then replies to me, "The true purpose of any soul is to follow the dictates of his inner self." He then instructs me, "Go in peace, my son."

Relieved that I have completed the ceremony without being named, I turn happily away from the master's presence, clench my fist, and say, "Yes!" I awaken in my bedroom, quite satisfied with myself.

This was a spiritual initiation for me. I believe that this dream was a test of my spiritual independence. It resulted in a healing of having to accept someone else's opinion over my own, even if I perceived that person to be of a high spiritual quality.[10]

Spiritual guides and masters appear when they are needed. We do not command them to appear, but we can ask, in dream incubation, for them to provide guidance. Guides and masters work in many ways through dreams and in events in waking life. Even though they may not make an appearance in a dream, they may send guidance to us through dreams. Once a master appears, the presence remains in our energy field.

chapter twenty-two

ENCOUNTERS WITH ANGELS

ANGELS ARE BEINGS WHO MEDIATE BETWEEN GOD AND MORTALS. THE TERM *ANGEL* COMES FROM THE GREEK *ANGELOS*, WHICH MEANS "MESSENGER." SIMILARLY, THE PERSIAN TERM *ANGAROS* means "courier." In Hebrew, the term is *malakh,* which also means messenger. One of the angel's chief duties is to take human prayers to God and bring God's answers back. Angels also mete out the will of God, whether it be to aid or to punish humans. Angels are specific to Judaism, Christianity, and Islam; however, they derive from concepts of helping and tutelary spirits that exist in mythologies the world over. The Judaic-Christian-Islamic angel owes much to the supernatural lore of the ancient Babylonians and Persians, which was absorbed into early Hebrew lore.

We place angels in a celestial realm, but they exist in other dimensions more subtle than ours. They are incorporeal, but have the ability to assume form and pass as mortals. When they make themselves known to us, they appear as ordinary people, as beings of fire, as lightning, and as brilliant light. Sometimes we perceive wings or the suggestion of them; however, few reported anecdotes of modern times feature angels with wings. Technically, angels don't need them; they simply are wherever they need to be.

A monotheistic religion needs a being like an angel. God is imageless, formless, and thus remote. Angels, onto which we have projected our idealized human form, help to make God more accessible and personal.

Angels have a long tradition of appearing in dreams, as documented in the Bible and non-canonical texts. They are dispatched by God to appear in dreams and visions to warn, inform, and aid. Throughout the history of the Christian church, numerous saints, theologians, and holy persons have recorded their interactions with angels. Since the church had discouraged dreamwork, it is not surprising to find, in the ensuing centuries, few accounts of angels in dreams. Rather, angels manifested during intense periods of prayer, meditation, and contemplation—altered states of consciousness bordering on the hypnagogic stage of sleep.

Now that angels have enjoyed a renaissance in popularity, the reporting of angelophanies—the experience of an angel—has increased, including within dreams. Angels are part of numerous dreams with various themes in this book.

Angels have been a particular interest of mine since about the mid-1980s, when I had my first angelic encounters—in dreams. At the time, I did not have any strong feelings about angels, and yet there was no other term that fit the being who entered my dreamscape from time to time: a female presence dressed in luminescent silver, flowing clothing, but with no human features on her face—simply a swirl of iridescent color. These were always big dreams, involving out-of-body travel to other realms, communication by telepathy, and much spiritual instruction, although I could never either put words to it or remember it when I awakened. Silver Lady, as I called her, acted as a dreamscape travel guide and as a conduit of information from a higher source.

Silver Lady's role in my dreams ended with *shaktipat,* in which she transmitted power in the manner of a spiritual master. I awakened to see her beside the bed. A strong current of energy was streaming out of her hands and into my heart and third-eye chakras. It was rather like being downloaded through a cosmic modem. When I was pumped full, the connection was broken and Silver Lady disappeared. Later, I felt I had been infused with an alchemical blueprint that would unfold itself throughout the course of my life.

From these dream experiences, I began to contemplate angels, and I discovered them to be quite an active spiritual force in the affairs of our earthly realm. They become part of us through the function of the oversoul, the expanded part of us that is aware of the unification of all things.

In dreams, angels are most often associated with healing, comfort, and transcendent awareness. Barbara relates this story about illness, healing, and comfort.

I very seldom dream, or maybe I very seldom remember my dreams, but this one was so vivid.

I was raised Catholic, but grew away from the church; I did not attend mass weekly, maybe six times a year and on Easter and Christmas, even though I continued to pray. I learned to pray to my guardian angel as a child, but I don't think I was ever sure that I had one.

When the symptoms of my condition began to worsen, I became more devout, attending mass regularly and going to healing masses at churches in other towns, and to one by Father R., convinced that I would be healed. I prayed to God, the Blessed Mother, to Saint Anthony, Saint Theresa, Saint Jude, and to all the angels. But that was not to be. After three years, I realized that brain surgery [to correct a benign condition] was my only option.

I was in the hospital. The first surgery was not successful, and I had agreed to undergo the procedure again six days later. The night before the surgery I was quite distraught and extremely frightened, thinking that I would not survive another surgery of this nature. I cried myself to sleep, sobbing and sobbing. During the night, I had what I think was a dream, but I'm not sure whether it was some sort of visitation. I was walking in an area with no vegetation; everything was a nondescript color—beige or white. I was crying as if lost, and then suddenly Jesus was carrying me and holding me close. I said, "I'm too heavy for you." Then a baby angel appeared and said that he would help. I knew that this angel was the baby that a friend had lost days before he was due to be born. The baby angel helped me through the night, and the next day, my surgery was successful. I had a complete recovery with no recurrence of my symptoms.

After my recovery, I told the mother about my experience with my little angel, K. She told me that it almost made her feel that (s)he had not died in vain. I now realize that God let me survive two serious operations because I am on this earth for a reason. I am not sure yet what that reason is, but someday He will reveal it to me, and I will do what He asks of me. Now I know I have a guardian angel. I don't know if (s)he is K. or not, and I don't know how I will find out if (s)he is. I just know that I am more open-minded about the spiritual world and a much more positive-minded person as a result of my dream/encounter.

I thank God and my little angel every day. Sometimes, when I am praying myself to sleep, I think I see the faces of other angels. I know that they exist and that they can be a source of great comfort.

I have not shared this dream/experience with more than a few very dear family members and friends. It moves me to tears whenever I remember it. It made me a much more spiritual person, and I hope to have another encounter someday.[1]

Like my series of dreams with Silver Lady, Barbara's dream renewed her belief in angels. More important, it strengthened her connection to God—which is the purpose of angelic intervention.

Angelic Protection

Besides acting as messengers, angels provide protection. The Bible tells us this in Psalms 91:11–13.

For he will give his angels charge of you to guard you in all your ways. On their hands they will bear you up, lest you dash your foot against a stone. You will tread on the lion and the adder, the young lion and the serpent you will trample under foot.

Numerous angel stories tell of people in danger from hostile persons or the elements who were miraculously rescued or protected by mysterious strangers they can only say are angels. These stories are compelling and make for good drama. But angels also provide ongoing spiritual protection, as demonstrated in the following case.

Linda (a pseudonym) is an administrative employee at Unity Village, the world headquarters campus of the Unity School of Nondenominational Christianity, located near Lee's Summit, Missouri, just outside of Kansas City. For about a century, Unity has offered a prayer service called Silent Unity. Anyone can call or write for whatever prayers are needed. A telephone prayer room is staffed around the clock by specially trained people who pray with callers. The room is a special place; only certain persons connected with the prayer ministry are allowed to enter it.

One night, Linda had this dream.

I exited my body, flew over my house, and headed for Unity Village. I saw an angel floating over the prayer room and also over the administrative area. It was the colors of the sunset, shaped like a human but not in the sense of having a nose, fingers, and toes. It was more like a shadow or silhouette—like the patterns of our dimension were repeated in it.

The angel had a consciousness that I was able to communicate with. I wanted to go to the prayer room, where the people were. This entity blocked me. I was surprised, because I work there at Unity. The angel led me to my own office, and I knew this was where the work I was being called to do would take place. I had an understanding that all of the administrative area of Unity Village is sacred space and protected space.

I have spent a lot of time in prayer and meditation at Unity Village. I realized the meaning of what the angel said—that prayer and meditation at the village is protected. You can have certain spiritual awakenings there without taking any risk. I also realized that this was one of the main purposes of the village—to be a protected place on this planet. The angel is there to make sure that no energy that doesn't belong there goes in.[2]

The power of this dream left a lasting impression upon Linda. She felt she had been given divine guidance concerning her work. The portrayal of prayer and meditation as sacred acts protected by the angelic realm is a remarkable image.

Out of Dreams

In my Silver Lady dreams, the last one I had involved a merger of the dreamscape with waking consciousness, when I awoke and found the angel in my physical environment, giving me the *shaktipat*. I have found that many angelophanies occur this way when we awaken to a visionary experience. It is possible that false awakenings may account for some of them. In others, I believe that we awaken but remain in an altered state of consciousness that enables us to perceive other-dimensional realities. Our dream and visionary experiences have a purpose: to advance our spiritual consciousness.

Stacy gives this account of angels upon awakening.

Just last night, my daughter, an asthmatic, was sick and was sleeping with me. I awoke in the middle of the night, opened my eyes, and above her only a foot or two were at least three, maybe five angels floating around her in a circle. They were wisps of white with a few other colors showing through. I had been very worried about her, but when I saw them watching over her, I went back to sleep and slept peacefully the rest of the night.[3]

In the next example, a waking vision warned a woman of her mother's undiagnosed but grave medical condition. Valerie R. tells the story.

May 18, 1993, seemed like any other day for me, typical in every way; that is, until I was met by a guardian angel who helped me save my mother's life and in so doing, changed my own.

It all began when I was softly awakened out of a sound sleep when the most wonderful feeling of love entered my being. I experienced an intense flow of supreme divine energy blending with mine; I felt one with it and instantly I felt a connection to the universe. Basking in the light of this true joy, I wanted to be part of it forever.

This supreme energy showed me the importance and uniqueness of my spirit—of everyone's spirit. Each person's existence played an integral part of the workings of the universe. I had a special role, a unique role that only I could fill. I was bathed in feelings of worth, value, and complete love. Instinctively, I knew that I had just been cradled in the arms of the divine.

Something very important happened to me that day; a messenger of the divine spirit—an angel of God—expressed its love to me. I had experienced the highest level of connectedness with God and his world.

To my surprise, that feeling made way for an immediate fear of impending doom. My intuition told me that I was being given a message of utmost importance. Very vividly, I saw shining white clouds sparkling magnificently against a brilliant blue sky. Emblazoned in a golden aura on the clouds and flashing on and off like a neon sign was the date, December 19, '93 (my mother's birthday).

This scene had an indescribable heavenly nature to it. Everything was glittering and shimmering and had a strange, surreal, 3-D presence. This vision was further enhanced with an audio and sensory dimension.

To my right, I heard voices strongly affirming the word "maternal." In my left visual field, my mother's face, surrounded in black, flashed before me. Death, darkness, and impending doom tore through my soul like a lightning bolt. I was struck with the eeriest uneasiness and despair. I had an inner knowing that she was going to die!

Upon the vision ending, I was shaken and panicked, but I vowed that I would fight for her life. Not knowing exactly when she was going to die, I just hoped that there was time to take life-saving actions!

At once I alerted my mother of the message I had been given, urging her to revisit the doctor whom she had just seen three weeks prior, being given a clean bill of health.

Valerie's mother, however, resisted going back to the doctor. Valerie descended into a state of emotional turmoil, certain that without medical help, her mother could die at any moment. Valerie sought the help of Dr. Bruce Goldberg, of Woodland Hills, California, who runs a full-time hypnotherapy practice specializing in past-life regression, future progress, and conscious dying. Goldberg holds a doctorate in dentistry and a master's degree in counseling psychology, and is the author of *Past Lives, Future Lives, The Search for Grace, Peaceful Transition,* and *Soul Healing.* He began treating Valerie for prebereavement.

During the course of her treatment, Valerie was able to finally convince her mother to see a doctor again. She was found to have a large kidney stone seriously impairing her kidney functions.

The doctor couldn't believe that she didn't have any pain or symptoms before now. We were told we were lucky. Had this gone on any longer, it was very likely that she would have suffered kidney failure—probably would have been put on dialysis, and even worse, could have died. In addition, her high blood pressure, which had been medically monitored for years, was now dangerously out of control.

Within minutes of the diagnosis, her blood pressure medication was properly adjusted and her kidney procedures were immediately scheduled. We caught in time what could have led to her premature death. All thanks to the message that the angelic energy desperately conveyed to me.[4]

Angels appear in dreams as guide and comfort figures, roles also played by people in dreams. Their angelic status, however, has a greater impact than does a person—they are an ultimate authority figure arriving straight from the Source. The appearance of an angel in a dream demands our attention, and calls us to look within.

PART VI

Beyond the Veil

chapter twenty-three

CONTACT WITH THE DEAD

DREAMS HAVE ALWAYS SHARED A STRONG LINK WITH THE REALM OF THE DEAD. SLEEP HAS BEEN CALLED THE LITTLE DEATH, AN OBSERVATION ECHOED IN THE TALMUD: "SLEEP IS ONE-SIXTIETH part death."

One of the greatest ways that our dreams help us is in dealing with the death of a loved one. The most frequently reported encounter dream involves a deceased person. In the majority of cases, the purpose of the dream is to offer consolation and assurances that the deceased one is all right. The dead also offer advice, especially pertaining to matters of the estate, and warnings about impending mishaps to the living. They ask for attention, such as details for a proper burial, prayers, or alms. Sometimes the purpose is to provide a sense of protection and companionship, as if the deceased has assumed the role of a guardian angel.

The ability of the dead to visit us in our dreams has been accepted in many cultures since ancient times. Relationships, especially with family, are seen as continuing after death, with the recognition that the ancestral spirits have the ability to intervene in the lives of the living. Most spiritual traditions around the world accept dream contact with the dead as positive, having a beneficial effect for both the living and the dead.

In the modern West, we tend to view dreams of the dead purely from a psychological perspective. We say these dreams traditionally are part of the grieving process, in which we seek to assure ourselves that someone we love has survived death and is indeed in a better place. We also say these dreams are expressions of wish fulfillment—we wish the dead were still alive—or expressions of unresolved guilt or anger.

True, many dreams of the dead are just that: grief processing, wish fulfillment, and repressed emotions. These dreams do help us through our grieving.

However, other dreams of the dead are different. They are charged with energy and carry a realism that distinguishes them from our other dreams. We awaken from such dreams wondering if we were asleep or awake. These dreams are real events. In waking consciousness, the dead are, for the most part, beyond our reach. But in the dreamscape, the souls of the departed can meet and communicate with the souls of the living.

These dreams have a high spiritual content, bringing tremendous power to affect us as deep levels of our being. Through them, we confront the great mystery of life and death.

Linda T. was deeply saddened by the death of her grandfather. A dream helped her to accept his death and move through the grieving process.

My grandfather died of emphysema, and watching him die, as you can imagine, was very hard. I was getting married on May 16. My grandfather died on May 3, thirteen days before my wedding. I took it very hard; I had made special arrangements for him in the church—he was going to have the best seat in the church!

My wedding came, and it was a beautiful, warm sunny day. I just knew my grandfather had something to do with it! I knew he was smiling down on me and the whole family. My grandfather loved to get the whole family together; there wouldn't be a minute of that time without a smile on his face.

A few weeks after my marriage, I sat down and wrote him a letter, a letter I should have written him years ago. I just wanted him to know that I loved him and wanted to tell him things I should have told him while he was alive. Needless to say, I cried through the whole thing.

That night, after crying myself to sleep, I dreamed of my grandfather. It was one of the strangest dreams I have ever had to this day. One wall of the bedroom looked like a movie screen, and it was showing me a movie of my grandfather when I was a very small child. He was at the lake in his bathing trunks, holding the raft for one of us to get on. He called to me, and as I looked at him, he told me, "Linda, don't worry, I am all right and

I am happy." I laid back down. When I woke up in the morning, I was finally able to accept his death.

I believe to this day that my grandfather came to me in my dream to let me know that he was finally okay, and that I had nothing to worry about.

The number thirteen played a big part in my grandfather's life. In the war, he was stationed on a boat—number thirteen. On the thirteenth day on the thirteenth hour, his ship was hit and went down. Only thirteen men survived—my grandfather being one of them. My father was born on October 13, and in the end, my grandfather died 13 days before my wedding. His birthday was May 1, and he died on May 3, but those two numbers put together are thirteen.

I think of him often and wish he would come back to me in my dreams, but I know he is watching over me and my family and that he is happy and healthy in heaven.[1]

Most big dreams of the dead occur soon after death, usually within a few weeks. Linda's dream, occurring within weeks of the death, also may have been incubated by her exercise of writing the letter prior to going to sleep. It is not uncommon, however, to experience powerful dreams of the dead years later. Dream encounters with the dead can be stimulated by what we're going through in life.

Historical Perspectives and Themes

In the West, the history of our views of dreams of the dead reflects divergent opinions and the influences of religion and science. Some of the early church fathers were skeptical of dreams of the dead. Saint Augustine drew distinctions between ordinary and nonordinary humans when it came to dreaming of the dead. He was well aware that his admired friend, Saint Ambrose, had been visited by the dead saints Gervasius and Protasius. This, Augustine said, was God's will concerning saints. However, ordinary people did not return in dreams—these were delusions. In the Middle Ages, some theologians said that dreams of the dead were merely masquerades of the devil. Despite such opinions, popular belief generally has supported the appearance of the dead in dreams.

During the high Middle Ages, much attention was focused on the doctrine of purgatory. There were many accounts of the dead in purgatory appearing to exhort the living to mend their ways while alive or to pray for the release of the dead from purgatory. Among the Jews, dreams often focused on communication between the living and the dead. The *Sefer Hasidim* notes that many recurring dreams dealt with questions of proper burial. The dead were not shy about appearing in dreams to demand better interments, as we saw in chapter 7.

The concern of the dead over their burial is a universal motif in folklore, called the *grateful dead.* The typical story goes that a hero starts out on a journey and comes upon a group of people who will not bury a man who died before paying his debts. Or, the group is abusing the man's corpse. The hero gallantly gives all his money to either pay the man's debts or pay for a proper burial. He goes on his way. He is quickly joined by a mysterious companion (usually a human but sometimes an animal), who brings him great fortune, saves his life, helps him accomplish a seemingly impossible feat, finds a princess for him to marry, and so on. At the end of the story, the hero learns that the mystery companion is really the grateful dead person.

Besides their burial, the dead also return with other grievances. One account from the Middle Ages tells about a dead canon who came to a colleague in a dream to complain about his effects being kept. It had been the canon's policy to donate clothing of the dead to the poor. The next day, the colleague had the canon's cape given to a beggar. That night, the canon appeared in a dream again, dressed in the cape.

Another common purpose of the dead appearing in dreams is to impart warnings. In the first century B.C.E., Cicero told the story of a man named Simonides who buried a stranger. Later, as he prepared to sail away on a voyage, the dead man appeared to him in a dream and warned him not to go. Simonides decided against going and then learned that the ship sank and everyone on board was drowned.

Whether this story is fact or fiction is not certain. It was an old story even at the time of Cicero. Nonetheless, it contains elements that have continued to appear in dreams on down through the centuries. Rose Anne K. experienced a modern version, in which a favorite uncle appeared in a lucid dream years after his passing in order to give her a warning.

I had always loved him best and missed him dearly. In 1992, he appeared to me in a dream. I was beside myself with joy at his appearance. It was so real, not like a dream but as though I were awake and in my living room. He told me he had something very important to say but very little time. "You must be very careful this year; you are in danger." I reached out my hand and touched his cheek, I could feel him and I ached to embrace him, but he pulled away and walked out of the room.

He was right. I hesitate to elaborate, but suffice it to say vigilance made the difference.[2]

The situation does not involve repayment of the favor of burial, but perhaps the favor of joy during life as the favorite uncle.

Cases of Dream Contact with the Dead

Permission to Die

Lillian Hernandez has been spiritually gifted from childhood, seeing the dead and spiritual guides. She can feel the touch of invisible guides and hear them call her name.

I always have loved my God, and I was reared in the Catholic church. Up until 1993, I taught catechism to young children. I have always worked, first as a practical nurse, then as a preschool teacher, and currently as an administrative assistant at a university. My life has not been easy, but I have always kept my faith, and I guess that's what keeps me going. Now I feel compelled to tell about an event that is very personal to me.

In August 1990, my dear mother, may God bless her soul, was diagnosed overnight with cancer in the left hemisphere of her brain. The doctors told me to talk with my peers, because she needed surgery stat [immediately]. The doctors said that if we agreed to surgery, she might survive nine months. If we didn't, she might survive three months. My peers and I agreed on the surgery.

Within three months of the surgery, the radiation treatments started causing her seizures which left her paralyzed and speechless. Finally, the cancer took her whole brain. I would run from work, run home to cook for my family, and rush to the hospital every day.

This one night, when I went to the hospital, the doctors were waiting for me. They wanted to talk to me regarding her impending death. They felt that we were suffering too much, and that if she should go into cardiac arrest or respiratory failure, I should sign the forms allowing them not to put her on a machine or to resuscitate her. I called my sister from the nurses' station. She was hysterical on the phone. Finally, she agreed that I should sign the papers.

Immediately after that, I requested a Catholic priest to come and give my dear mother her last rites and blessings. As I stood there with the priest, praying while he blessed her, all I could see were deep tunnels in her eyes. When we finished, the priest told me that my mother was dead, but her soul would not leave her body because she didn't want to leave me and my peers. He said that I should find it in my heart to give her permission to leave and allow her to go.

"Father," I said in tears, "I can't do that." He said I must find the way to let her go. He walked with me out of the hospital.

When I got home, I called my sister and, crying, explained what had happened. I asked her if she could find it in her heart to allow my mother to leave us. Crying, she said she couldn't. That night, I went to sleep and had this dream:

I had gone to the hospital to visit my mother as usual. When I went to get the elevator, some nurses and doctors were running because there had been a cardiac arrest. Intuitively, I knew it was my mother. However, when I got to her floor and I reached her door, instead of her private room, I was in a room full of beds with people who were dying. I looked for my mother until I found her. She was in a bed, yet she was fenced in with a door on the top. When I looked at her, she was completely naked on the bed. She turned her head toward me and she said, "God bless you, my daughter." I said, "Mommie, what are you doing here, naked?" She said, "Please my daughter, let me go, open up this door and let me go." She stood upright on her tiptoes, with her arms extended toward the ceiling, and she said, "Please, Lillian, help me to go!"

I took her out of the bed, because I feared she would fall. But again, she stood on her tiptoes, with her arms extended toward the ceiling and said, "Please, my daughter, help me to leave, please let me leave." At that point, I woke up hysterical.

Lillian was deeply shaken by the dream, but she knew what she had to do.

The next evening, I went to the hospital after work. I knew that I had to allow her to leave. I took my prayer book and started praying. When I finished praying, in tears, I told her that we loved her and we would always love her. I explained that she had to leave this life, because her physical body was no longer good. I explained that her spirit would be going to a place where she would feel no pain. I told her that when she left her body, she should go toward the light, go into the tunnel and follow that light. I told her there would be other spiritual guides and angels that would be waiting for her. I told her I would always love her and never forget her and that someday we would be together again. That was the hardest thing I have ever done in my life.

The next night, the doctors called me at four A.M. *to tell me that my mother had died in her sleep, and that she did not suffer in her death. When we went to the hospital to see her, she looked so peaceful, and I knew she had found that peaceful place with God.*[3]

One explanation for Lillian's dream is that her deep distress became dramatized as a visit from her mother. Lillian knew what she must do, but the advice was externalized through the figure of her mother, making it more acceptable to her.

Another explanation, and one that I would make if this experience had been mine, is that Lillian had a true encounter with her mother, made possible by the dreamscape. Though paralyzed and speechless in her body, her mother's consciousness nonetheless could still reach out to communicate with Lillian in a reality that is not bound by time, space, and physicality. She has accepted her impending death and is more than ready to go, but the energy of family resistance literally holds her back.

Because the medium of communication is the dream, the imagery carries the symbolism characteristic of dreams. The mother is in a cage (the reluctance of family to let go) with a door on top (the path of ascent of the spirit to the afterlife). She is naked, symbolizing her readiness to be birthed into a new existence. She is among other souls about to make their transitions as well.

Those who work with the dying know just how strongly the feelings of the living can influence the dying process. Unresolved problems, unfinished business, and loved ones who don't want someone to die can all contribute to delaying the dying, usually to the discomfort of the one who is about to pass on. A dying person often comes to terms with death before loved ones do. However, once impending death is accepted, it is important to the dying to make the transition as peacefully as possible, and with the support of loved ones.

Even when a dying person is comatose, they still can be aware of impending death on some level of consciousness. They can also be aware of what others around them are saying, thinking, and feeling. Knowing that loved ones are suffering great distress can cause the dying to hold off death as long as possible. If we remember the mystical tenet that thoughts are things, we can see how powerful emotions and thoughts can build up in walls of energy to imprison a soul that seeks to be liberated into a new life beyond the body.

In *Final Gifts,* authors and hospice nurses Maggie Callahan and Patricia Kelley tell of numerous cases they witnessed in which peaceful dying could not be completed until the right circumstances were in place. "Sometimes the right circumstances include receiving permission to die from another person," said Callahan and Kelley. "Permission may be given indirectly—'Everything will be fine'—or more specifically—'Just let go. I'll miss you, but I know you need to go now.'"[4] Once permission is given, a peaceful death quickly ensues.

In Lillian's case, a vivid encounter in the dreamscape made it possible for her to take the final step of releasing her mother without further delay.

Don't Feel Guilty

Often, we feel guilty over the death of a loved one, blaming ourselves for something we did or did not do, wondering if we contributed to the death. Stacy had the following vivid dream about her grandmother that helped to relieve her feelings of guilt. It also bears some resemblance to Lillian's dream, in that it portrays the deceased as potentially trapped in a failing body.

I am a thirty-one-year-old single mother. After my divorce two years ago, I began a spiritual quest. I began reading everything I could get my hands on about angels, near-death experiences, and religions of all kinds. In my studies, most of the concepts were extremely easy for me to grasp. It was as if I had awakened from a dream (my old consciousness) to a new reality. My soul embraced the concepts of angels, an afterlife, spirit guides, and being able to communicate with those who had gone on before, as if I had always known they were real and possible deep down inside but was just now remembering them. The more I embraced these things as truth, the more experiences I had with them. That is why when my grandmother visited me in my dreams two days after her death, I was not at all surprised and was wholly delighted.

My grandmother died under dire circumstances. She was eighty-six and well nearly all the time. My father, her only child, checked on her every day to bring her dinner and make sure she was okay. But on this particular Sunday, I had come down with a terrible case of influenza. I was so faint I couldn't get out of bed, but I still had to care for my daughter. So, I called my father and asked him to care for her. Since he had spent the entire day with us, he did not have time to check on my grandmother. She had a massive stroke. He did not find her until the following day. The coroner told us she had laid there on her kitchen floor several hours before dying.

I was devastated. I felt like it was all my fault and I couldn't stand the thought that she lay there suffering for hours with no one to help her. And I told myself, if we had just found her, she would still be alive today.

When she came to me in the dream, it was very vivid. We were in her home and she was trying to get out the front door. She was not in her right mind, she could not talk, but just make noises. I could not reason with her. I had to physically take her back into her home and make her stay there because she was trying to escape. I was very frustrated and so was she. She was not the grandmother I had always known and loved.

When this sequence of the dream ended, she came to me, beautiful, peaceful, and loving, and told me, "This is what I would have been like if I had lived. I would not have wanted that and neither would you." I now knew she was happy where she was. And, I now know she did not suffer. It was her way to tell me to leave the guilt behind because things had happened the way they were supposed to have happened.[5]

Here, the front door has a similar symbolism as the top of the cage door around the bed of Lillian's mother. It represents the exit place for the soul. Stacy's grandmother is unable to exit her house—her body—and is frustrated at her inability to communicate. By showing Stacy the dramatic contrast between what might have happened and what did happen, the grandmother was able to set her granddaughter's mind at rest.

Impending Death

In their years of working with the dying, nurses Callahan and Kelley have heard many dreams of people in the last stages of life. People develop what they call a nearing death awareness, which includes accepting death, coming to terms with their lives, dealing with anxieties and fears, and resolving unfinished issues and business. Dreams play an important role in the process, shedding light and revealing valuable information that can benefit all persons concerned.

People who care for the dying should be especially alert for dreams that are vivid, recurring, or in a series that seems to be progressive. The dreamer should be invited to discuss and interpret the dream. Often this can provide an opportunity for a dying person to discuss anxieties that he or she might otherwise be reluctant to broach.

For example, in *Final Gifts,* a woman named Isabelle had a repeating dream of being buried alive in a coffin. She knew exactly what it meant: She had a real fear of being pronounced dead while still alive. This fear is not uncommon. Isabelle was suffering from this fear but had not mentioned it prior to reporting the dream. Discussing the dream enabled others to explain precisely how death is determined and that there would be no doubt when the end came. After that, she was greatly relieved and the repeating dream ceased.

Dreams can foretell of impending death and help to prepare the individual for transition. Terminally ill patients often have transitional dreams close to the time of dying, usually within two weeks or so. Transition symbols include going through gateways, entering beautiful gardens, crossing bridges, climbing mountains, traversing the sea in a boat, or walking through doorways. These dreams often are vivid in colors and are permeated with an energy of love and tranquillity. They bring profound peace of mind.

I hasten to add that not all dreams with these images relate to death. Transition symbols occur frequently in dreams. They most often relate to major changes in life, such as jobs, homes, spiritual outlook, relationships, and so on.

Hello, I'm Fine

Dream encounters with the dead often have the characteristics of a lucid or OBE dream: brilliant light, a strange atmosphere or setting, vivid colors, and even smells associated with the deceased, such as a favorite perfume. (NDEs share these characteristics as well, for many NDErs are greeted by the deceased.) The dreams carry a strong emotional impact for the dreamer, who awakens certain that he or she has actually been with the one who is dead. "It wasn't a dream—it was real!" they will say. Such a dream occurred to Jerri B. after her grandfather passed away.

He had had one of his legs amputated due to complications of diabetes a couple of years before he died. In the dream he was jumping up and down, clicking his heels together, and looking so happy. He told me that he was very happy because he was with my grandmother and my mother, and he said to me, "See, I have my leg, back too!"[6]

Bill Guggenheim and Judy Guggenheim, authors of *Hello from Heaven!*, work with the terminally ill and the bereaved. They have collected many accounts of dream encounters with the dead, which they call "sleep-state After-Death Communications." Dreams are just one of the many ways we strive to maintain links with those who are close to us who have died. "A loved one who has died can contact you more easily if you are very relaxed, open, and receptive, such as when you are in the alpha state or asleep," say the Guggenheims. "This is the time you are most likely to set aside the distractions of the material world and attune your heart and mind to the spiritual dimension."[7]

There is a significant barrier between the worlds of the discarnate and the living. This barrier is quite purposeful and enables souls on both sides to go about their business. This is why it is not easy for the living and the dead to contact each other. At the very least, grief and emotional longings would hinder their respective evolutions of the soul. We can at times pierce this barrier, such as with the help of a medium, or, as the Guggenheims point out, when we are in altered states of consciousness.

Meaningful encounters with the dead are not limited to the immediate postdeath period. They can occur years later and continue to occur for years, even throughout a person's life. A dead loved one may appear at crucial times, such as when an important decision is being weighed, to offer advice and guidance.

Many appearances of the dead in dreams have the purpose of assuring loved ones that all is well. Ravindra Kumar (see chapter 20) had a significant dream encounter with his father three years after his father's death:

In the year 1995, I had a talk with my father who had expired in 1992, through the help of a medium in North Carolina. After a one-hour talk, my father offered to meet me after thirty days, if it was acceptable to me. Of course, I gave my consent to him.

Exactly on the thirtieth night, I dreamed of moving with my father, both of us in our light bodies, perhaps on some astral plane. The dream lasted about an hour in which we talked about many things of common interest. He told me many things that were to be conveyed to my mother in Delhi and other relatives. We embraced each other and parted happily.

In the dream he told me that he was taking a long rest after a long time. He said that he was going to get a new body very soon and then he will be transferred to a new "more lighted region."[8]

About two years after her father died, Shirley L. had this dream.

My identical twin and I were riding in an open motorized vehicle of some sort down a street in my hometown with my father's casket in the back, opened. We were conversing with him while riding around, and I asked him, "How can this be, Dad? You are dead." He answered, "I am always with you, Sissy, though my body is not."

We continued reminiscing as we drove around my hometown. The dream was in color, though I usually don't dream in color. I remember beginning to cry while still with him and crying and crying until I was crying aloud, which finally awakened me.

Six years later, Shirley still missed her father intensely. She tried to contact him through the ancient technique of scrying, or gazing into a darkened mirror. That was unsuccessful, but she had another dream encounter with her father:

I was in this house, something similar to my childhood home, talking with people when through the dining room window I saw him passing by, smiling. I ran to the front door. The rooms grew dark and no one seemed to notice my leaving.

I opened the door to let him in, and there he stood, a picture of health as he did when I was in high school. He had on a lightweight jacket, off-white, with pleated trousers, and was full of life! Smiling, he stepped in. We went into another room, and he sat on the couch while I sat by his feet, crying and telling him how much I missed him.

He patted my head telling me, "Sissy, I am so happy, do not grieve for me. I love you but would not want to come back. I am always with you." As he continued to stroke my hair, I wept until I thought my heart would break.

The crying eventually awakened me, leaving me with such a hole in my heart—a longing. I knew he had come trying to comfort me since I had been trying to contact him through mirror gazing.[9]

Shirley felt the visits were real. "These two visits stay with me to this day," she said. "I did not induce these dreams or do anything unusual. If I did, I would love to have him visit again. How to visit with him again and control it is a mystery I haven't been able to solve."

Dreams That Step into the Physical World

Sometimes in dreams involving the dead, evidence of the encounter is left behind in the physical world, showing that the two worlds truly are bridged in certain states of consciousness.

Richard L. has had numerous dreams of contact with relatives who have died. Two experiences involving his grandfather remain vivid to this day. The first was a psi experience that took place in 1947, when Richard was in the armed services.

I was lying in bed at a disembarking center in San Francisco, talking to a bunk mate about being shipped out to Japan for occupation duty the following day. Suddenly in midsentence, I said that my grandfather had just died. My bunk mate, Jerry E., said, "What?" I said, "My grandfather has just died." "You have got to be kidding me," Jerry said. The conversation continued while we wrote down the time and date. The next day, I received a telegram that my grandfather had died the night before a few minutes before the time we had written down.

In 1950, I was discharged and returned home to Michigan. The rooms at the old house were full of relatives, so I had to throw an old mattress down on the floor of my younger brother's bedroom to sleep. This room was my grandfather's bedroom before he died. My brother and I talked for awhile and I smoked two cigarettes, crushing the butts out in a coffee can that I placed on the table near my head. We turned out the lights and went to sleep.

Some time later, I was awakened by my grandfather sitting on the edge of the bed in which my younger brother slept. Grandfather talked to me and informed me that I had no future in the state of Michigan. He advised me to migrate to California where my future lay. During the conversation, I took the coffee can down from the table and smoked a cigarette. I don't remember all of the conversation. Then Grandpa said he had to leave. I said good-bye, and he walked out through the west wall. I put out the cigarette and lay back down.

The next morning I awoke, thinking, what a strange dream! Then I noticed that the coffee can with three *cigarette butts in it was sitting beside my pillow, not on the table where I had placed it the night before.*

At breakfast I told my folks about the dream. My mom asked me to describe what Grandfather had been wearing, which I did down to the silk stockings with the initial "R" in blue thread on them. My description of the clothing that Grandpa had was exactly what he had been buried in. The clothing had all been purchased new after he had died, because he didn't have anything but his overalls to wear when he lived.

I followed his instructions.[10]

Events worked out well for Richard in California, just as his grandfather had predicted. Richard's experiences have assured him of the continuity of existence on the other side. "I look forward to the next dimension," he said. "My wife and I are students of *A Course in Miracles*, hoping to find answers to help others to an understanding of what this life is all about."

Don't Worry

Richard L.'s wife, Shirley (not the same Shirley L. mentioned previously), had dream encounters with Richard's father, Harry, after his death.

Harry and I became very close. I didn't grow up around my father, so Harry (Dad) became more than a father-in-law. The years of 1960 through October 1981, Harry lived with us.

Dad passed away in October 1981. He was ninety years old. I knew he had had a good life. He told me that he was ready to go, because he couldn't walk without a cane and he had trouble doing things. Dad would read everything he could get his hands on. He was a genius. I have never been well read. So Dad helped me to start reading and enjoying different types of literature.

I'm not sure how long after we lost Dad that he came to me in a dream. He came to me at the old farmhouse that Richard was raised in. He told me he wanted something to eat and he couldn't walk into the kitchen, so would I get him some toast and peanut butter. When I returned with his snack, I found him to be about seventy-five years old and the cane was gone. He asked for something to drink, so I got him a cup of coffee. As I returned with the coffee, I found Dad looking like he was about fifty years old. He said, "Sit down with me for awhile and talk."

I don't remember what we talked about because I was still trying to figure out how he made himself younger. After he finished his snack and coffee, he said, "Well, I had better go now. You take care of Rick and all is going to be okay for him." (Rick is my son.) Dad knew how I worried about Rick and how he would make it in this world.

When I became aware of being awake, I remembered all of the dream. I had a feeling that maybe things would go okay for Rick. Dad came back to let me know that I didn't have to worry that Rick would be taken care of. Rick is now married, and they have a boy and are doing fine.[11]

When the Dead Need Our Help

The dead do not always appear in our dreams to help us. Sometimes they appear because they need *our* help.

Thirteen years after his dream with his grandfather, Richard L. had another unusual dream following the death of a sister.

In 1963, Susan, my oldest and closest sister, was on her way to visit us in California. She had gotten herself into a marriage that she wanted to get out of for many reasons. She and her husband and one boy about fourteen years old were on their way from the state of Washington to our home in Rancho Cordova. A station wagon crossed a double median and struck their car head-on, instantly killing my sister, who was driving. The next few days were hell for me and our family.

Approximately three months later, the following either occurred or I dreamed it:

I had gone to bed around 10:30 P.M. Some time during the night, I found myself lying on a brown couch. I sat up and looked around. There didn't seem to be any ground, just fluffy clouds. As I looked off into the distance, a figure seemed to be approaching. It was dressed in a brown burlap-type robe with a hood on it. No matter how close it came, I couldn't see a face inside the hood, just a black space.

The figure stopped a little distance from me and asked, "What are you doing here?" I answered, "I am here to help my sister across. She doesn't know she is dead." "What makes you think you can help her?" it asked. I answered, "My grandfather is waiting, and he will help me show her the way across." The figure turned and walked away.

Next I saw another figure approaching. It was my sister. She was mumbling, "It's so cold, where is everyone? Why won't somebody help me?" As she approached, she left footprints in the cloudlike stuff. I called to her, and she didn't seem to hear me, but continued toward me. When she came within reach, I took her hand. She looked at me but didn't seem to see me. All she said was, "I'm so cold and you're so warm." I started walking, holding her hand, as she kept mumbling the same words. In the distance ahead, I could see what seemed to be a bridge. I led her to the bridge. Standing on the other side were my grandfather and grandmother. They didn't seem to see me, but they stretched out their hands and called my sister to come to them. Susan recognized them, let go of my hand, and crossed to their arms.

I awoke the next morning feeling wonderful knowing that at last my sister had crossed to where our people were waiting and she could be at peace.[12]

Richard's experience indicates that Susan may have been confused by her sudden and unexpected death, and thus was unable to move on. Such circumstances can lead to a soul becoming earthbound.

Eddie Burks is an English medium and healer who is world-famous for his work in releasing earthbound souls. Eddie makes psychic contact with the souls and—just as Richard did for Susan—helps them find a way to fully enter the other side. His experiences and skills are described in my book, *Angels of Mercy,* and in Eddie's own book, *Ghosthunter.*

According to Eddie, immediately after death, consciousness moves up and into an etheric body. It stays in this body for a short period of time and then casts it off and enters the spirit world. A small number of souls—Eddie estimates that perhaps 1 in 500—remain stuck in their etheric bodies for various reasons: shock and nonacceptance of death, not knowing they are dead, unfinished business, unresolved emotions, and attachments to life. Sometimes a soul chooses to stay earthbound because of attachments or unfinished business. But when life ends abruptly, a person may simply not know he or she is dead. They "wake up" in a "body," but they wander in a gray area, frustrated that others are not responsive to them. The longer one stays in the etheric body, the more consciousness becomes clouded and the harder it becomes to move on, Eddie says.

Stuck souls often seem to need the help of someone who is living. Gifted and skilled mediums such as Eddie can tune in to them. For many others, the dreamscape, with its nonordinary reality, provides the setting that enables helpful contact to take place. Susan was able to reach Richard because they had been emotionally close during life and also because he was psychically gifted and thus was open. The living then can help the dead to find guide figures and a point of crossing so that the transition can be completed.

Transition involves such symbolic events as walking into a brilliant light, going through a doorway, or—as did Susan—going across a bridge. The transition point marks the barrier between the worlds. Sometimes the dreamer knows or is told that he or she cannot cross the barrier. These points of no return also are found in many near-death experiences.

I had a similar postdeath releasement dream after the death of my father in 1981. I had always been close to him, and was I devastated by his death due to a ruptured aneurysm. At the time of his passing, he was active in his passion, amateur astronomy. His calendar was filled with upcoming events.

Eighteen months prior to his death, Dad had suffered another aneurysm and been rushed to the hospital. Doctors said he would not survive the emergency surgery, but he did. He resumed much of his former life, although he was in chronic pain. When he died, I had the feeling that Dad felt somewhat cheated: He'd struggled through a painful recovery, only to have life snatched away.

About two weeks after his death, I had this dream.

I am at my parents' house, sitting in a chair in the living room. Mom is home, somewhere in the house. Across from me, sitting in his favorite easy chair, is Dad. I know he's dead, and he knows he's dead. I also know that I am the only one who can see him. The setting is lit with bright light, and there is a strange electricity in the air. I feel rather queer.

I say, "Dad, what are you doing here? You're dead! You can't stay here. You've got to move on."

Dad smiles and shakes his head. He explains to me that he has things he still has to do here. I argue with him: He's dead and he must not stay.

The scene suddenly shifts. I am no longer in my parents' house, but watching Dad disappear into the distance. He is walking into a large building. Somehow I know it is a factory. Dad is going to work.[13]

I had no doubt that I'd had a real encounter with my father, and that it concerned his need to leave the earth plane. In life, Dad could be stubborn. Now I could well imagine his irritation that death inconveniently interrupted his upcoming plans. The symbolism of being in the *living room* of the house was not lost on me.

Evidently, I prevailed upon Dad, since the next scene was one of transition. Dad going to work in a factory seemed apt symbolism. Throughout his life, Dad was a continual student, interested in learning about many things, especially the nature of the cosmos. Astronomy provided many hours of pleasure to him. He had projects going all the time: making things, building things, investigating things. He was recognized in amateur astronomy, with an observatory named after him: the Pettinger-Guiley Observatory in Puyallup, Washington, operated by the Tacoma Astronomical Society. I knew that in the afterlife, Dad would not be one to prop his feet up but would want to plunge into a new line of work.

I did not have the feeling that Dad was stuck and unable to move on, but perhaps the dream happened in order to prevent such a circumstance.

How to Evaluate and Work with Dreams of the Dead

Like any other dream, a dream involving an encounter with the dead should be examined for both psychological and spiritual contents. Some dreams are more of one than the other. Some are symbolic for resolving emotions. Others are real contact (which also resolves emotions). Contact dreams leave a strong impression. Look for these elements:

- Vivid imagery and bright light
- Sense of touch
- Intense emotions
- "Electrical" atmosphere
- Unusual settings
- Messages with an impact
- Lucidity

Let your heart be your guide.

How Should We Use Dreams of the Dead?

Encounters with the dead in dreams help us through our grief and unresolved issues. They open the door to another realm, perhaps convincing us or confirming for us survival after death and giving us a glimpse of eternity. They continue our bond with other souls on a new level of consciousness.

I do not believe it is wise, however, to try to summon the dead repeatedly in dreams, such as through incubation. It is fine to ask for assurances of their well-being. But once on the other side, the dead continue with their own existence and evolution, moving at times—as Ravindra Kumar's father described—into different regions. To constantly pull them back into our dreams serves neither us nor them. It prevents us from fully accepting their death and inhibits their own activity. It is much better to allow the dead to enter our dreamscape at the appropriate times for the appropriate reasons.

chapter twenty-four

DREAMS OF THE OTHER SIDE

ALL OF US WONDER WHAT WILL HAPPEN TO US WHEN WE DIE. WE TAKE A CERTAIN COMFORT, IF ANY, FROM OUR RELIGIOUS AND SPIRITUAL BELIEFS, AND PERHAPS FROM THE EXPERIENCES OF others who say they've seen the other side. For many of us, the Great Mystery remains the Great Fear.

Our questions about life after death are sometimes answered in dreams. We are shown places, usually of great beauty, and given stories about activities there. The Talmud holds that during sleep, one's soul rises into heaven and amuses itself with God. A powerful dream involving the other side can have a tremendous effect on releasing fear of death or satisfying our need for reassurance that something indeed awaits us when the final breath is drawn. Such dreams can occur any time in life but are especially likely to happen during times of stress or inner struggle or prior to our actual death. It should be noted that a dream of the hereafter does not necessarily presage one's death but may use the *symbolism* of the afterlife in order to address deep spiritual or philosophical matters.

Carl Jung relates the story of a sixty-year-old woman, a pupil of his, who had a dream of the hereafter about two months prior to her death.

She had entered the hereafter. There was a class going on, and various deceased women friends of hers sat at the front bench. An atmosphere of general expectation prevailed. She looked around for a teacher or lecturer, but could find none. Then it became plain that she herself was the lecturer, for immediately after death people had to give accounts of the total experience of their lives. The dead were extremely interested in the life experiences that the newly deceased brought with them, just as if the acts and experiences taking place in earthly life, in space and time, were the decisive ones.[1]

At the time of the dream, the woman was frightened of death. Jung does not comment on the effect of the dream upon her but notes that the dream provides a myth about death and the richness of the land of the dead, which can be reassuring.

Going to Heaven to Find God

Myrtle Fillmore, the cofounder of the Unity School of Nondenominational Christianity (see chapter 17), believed strongly in dreams for spiritual guidance, as did her husband, Charles. After her miraculous recovery from tuberculosis, Myrtle enjoyed a long life of robust energy. She did have bouts of sickness, however, as we all do. But she believed that if she maintained the right state of consciousness, the healing power of God would keep flowing through her. Once when Myrtle was not feeling well, she had a dream that reminded her where to find the true healing power of God.

For some days I had not been my usual self, and finally I had to go to bed. The world would say I was sick, dangerously ill, but I knew better. The trouble was that I had allowed some thought of negation to creep into my consciousness, and that thought was inhibiting the free flow of God's perfect health in my body. I knew that just as soon as I replaced that negative thought with the realization of "God is my health, I can't be sick," I should be well. With this thought on my lips I went to sleep.

Myrtle had a dream in which she went to a beautiful place and conversed with an angel.

The sky was so blue and the fields were so green, and the flowers everywhere—I can't tell you how beautiful it was—just like a dream! As I walked down the road, I met a beautiful woman dressed in a pure white robe with a gold girdle. She had wonderful golden hair and she smiled at me sweetly and said:

"How are you this fine day?"

"Very well," I faltered, "but can you tell me where I am?"

"Why, don't you know? You're in heaven."

I looked around in amazement. Then I looked at the woman, but I couldn't say a word. Then I thought of how as a little girl I had tried to imagine what heaven was like. I turned to the woman again and faltered, "Are you an angel?"

"Yes," she smiled, "I'm an angel. Wouldn't you like to be one too?"

"I suppose so," I replied, "but where's God? I'd like to see him."

"God! Why do you wish to see him?"

Her question puzzled me. Why wouldn't any one want to see God!

Still perplexed I replied, "That's one reason why I wanted to come to heaven—to see him."

"Did you think that you had to come to heaven to find him?"

"Well—I thought that I should find him here. I was looking for him when I met you, although I wasn't sure this was heaven."

"Where did you look?"

"Oh, I looked all about me! I thought that perhaps this road would take me to his palace."

"Dear one," the angel said in a tone full of assurance. "He has no palace. He is all about you. He is here. He is with you now as He was on earth. But you will not find him unless you look within yourself. At the center of your being He abides forever. Turn within and know that God is here."

Myrtle awakened abruptly, charged with emotion.

I looked about me. Where was I. Why—I was in my own bed; but something was changed. Through my mind rang the words, "God is here. God is here." I sat up exclaiming, "Yes, God is here, and in His presence I am well." I got up and dressed. When a friend came in a few moments later she found me as well and strong as ever.[2]

Going to "The Park"

My husband Tom was granted a glimpse of the other side after meditating for a prolonged period of time upon the question of life after death. In essence, this created an incubation that was answered in a dream. At the time, Tom had undergone an inner crisis about his spiritual and religious beliefs. He explains:

In the year prior to this dream, my worldview had radically changed. I had been a devoted Seventh Day Adventist Christian for about seven years. I had been a theology major with the SDAs for a year when I had a profound change of heart and left the faith. The change of heart concerned the issue of whether or not anyone—a person or a religion—could be the judge of the spiritual state of another human being. I was being taught how my religion was right and others were misguided. Suddenly, I could not see how an infinite God could require all people of the world to see one particular message as being the only right one and threaten to kill them later in a second resurrection if they did not accept this truth. Rather, most people were involved in a deep inner psychology of their own, which seemed rather real to me. What I was doing seemed unreal compared to the lives of others that I had either interacted with or read about.

However, instead of believing that a more rational, personal element to the universe existed, I immediately assumed that there was no God and that humanity existed as the result of a bunch of chemical reactions that would eventually fizzle out. This thought obsessed my mind for a full year. In all my spare moments of thought and all my quiet times I thought of this. I became angry and raged within myself on the absurdity of it all. I could not accept in my heart that when we die that was the end of existence, but I had no logical alternative. I had never been exposed to any other teaching. My life on the outside continued as normal, but my life on the inside was turmoil. I could not understand how I could have a mind to question but be given no answers; this enraged me. I desperately needed an answer from this mental trap, when I had a dream.

In the dream I find myself sitting naked in the "thinker's position" with my chin on my fist. I am thinking the same thought that had plagued me for the entire previous year: "What happens when you die?" Suddenly, I am addressed by a voice that seems to come from everywhere. The voice asks this question: "Do you want to know what it's like to die?" This is a crazy question, I think to myself. Every cell in every part of my body then reacts. I look up and state with incredulity, "What do you think I've been asking for the last year?" I do not expect the answer that I receive. The voice says, "Okay—you're dead!"

Anxiously, I think that I do not really *want to die just to find out what happens when you eventually die, but before I can finish thinking the thought, I hear a loud crack of thunder and find myself traveling through an upwardly sloped tunnel with great speed. I travel for what seems to me to be about fifteen seconds through more and more quickly passing arcs of light. I wonder if the light represents time. The tunnel then ends, and I find myself in a park, sitting on a bench. There is a lake in front of me with trees and walking paths. Birds are singing their songs and there are other people in the park, walking along enjoying the scene. I even see a woman walking her baby through the park in a baby carriage. As I survey the scene, I think to myself "Hey, this isn't too bad . . ." and then instantly open my eyes to find myself in my bedroom of my own apartment.*

I was so pleased with what I had experienced that I have never been seriously bothered by the thought of death since.[3]

The "thinker's position" is the chin-on-hand pose of the naked seated man sculpted by Rodin. This famous sculpture has come to represent an archetypal image of serious thought about weighty matters. Interestingly, nudity in dreams is often a symbol of the naked truth.

Later, Tom came across the writings of Robert A. Monroe in his now classic work about out-of-body travel, *Journeys Out of the Body.* Monroe describes a similar scene he calls "The Park." It is a post-death way station for incoming souls to relax, rest, and meet with deceased friends and relatives and with guides. On one of his out-of-body excursions, Monroe said:

I ended up in a park-like surrounding, with carefully tended flowers, trees, and grass, much like a large mall with paths crisscrossing the area. There were benches along the paths, and there were hundreds of men and women strolling by, or sitting on the benches. Some were quite calm, others a little apprehensive, and many had a dazed or shocked look of disorientation. They appeared uncertain, unknowing of what to do or what was to take place next.

Somehow I knew that this was a meeting place, where the newly arrived waited for friends or relatives. From this Place of Meeting, these friends would take each newcomer to the proper place where he or she "belonged."[4]

Many years later, Monroe returned to The Park in another excursion in his second body, which he describes in his last book prior to his death, *The Ultimate Journey*. While searching for a dead friend, Monroe is reminded by a guide figure about The Park, and so he goes there.

It was the same as when I had visited many years ago, with winding walks, benches, flowers and shrubbery, different-colored grass lawns, clusters of stately trees, small streams and fountains, and with a warm sun overhead among small cumulus clouds. The Park continued on a gently rolling terrain as far as I could see.[5]

Monroe realizes something he could not have perceived years earlier from his more limited perspective: The Park is a place of human creation, made by human thought. He is soon met by a woman from one of his past lives. She says:

"I am only the messenger. I am to tell you that you may by all means bring people to us, those who are newly physically dead. We will take care of them. That is why we are here. And you may teach others to do this. . . . It is a wholly objective way to remove the fear of physical death.[6]

The woman explains that The Park was created by "a human civilization many thousands of years ago," and it does not cease to exist if a person does not believe in it. Souls come here to make a transition, she said; they are shown their many options for the afterlife, which also are self-created. The only rule is that no one impose his or her will upon another.

This afterlife created by human thought intersects with ideas in Eastern mysticism. The *Bardo Thodol,* the Tibetan Book of the Dead, teaches that both life and death are dreamlike, illusory reproductions of one's own thoughts. A deceased person experiences thought-form visions that conform, positively or negatively, to his or her religion, background, consciousness, karma, etc. Thus, a Muslim would see the Muslim paradise; a Christian would see the throne of God in heaven—or perhaps the fires of hell; an atheist would find emptiness, and so on. The object of the *Bardo Thodol* is to awaken the dreamer to reality, to seek liberation of all states of phenomena (heaven and hell alike) by the attainment of nirvana, a supramundane, transcendent state of being that is beyond illusion.

According to Monroe, everyone, regardless of their beliefs, goes to The Park immediately after death, and from there to points beyond. In this scenario, the Tibetan Buddhist is still free to pursue nirvana, and others their own versions of the afterlife.

Swedenborg's Afterlife Dream-Visions

The mystical dreams and visions of Emanuel Swedenborg further support the idea of a self-created afterlife. Swedenborg was a scientist and scholar who gave little thought to spiritual matters until he experienced a breakthrough in 1743 at age fifty-six. For the remainder of his life (he died in 1772), he devoted himself nearly full-time to exploring his visions. As noted earlier, his lucid OBE journeys to heaven came during hypnagogic stages of sleep. Later, he learned how to self-induce trance states.

Swedenborg said that God created humans to exist simultaneously in the physical and spiritual worlds. The spiritual world is an inner domain that influences humankind, though most persons have lost their awareness of it. The inner world survives death with its own eternal memory of every thought, emotion, and action accumulated over a lifetime. The memory thus influences the soul's fate of heaven or hell.

After death, souls enter an earthlike transition plane called "The Spirit World" where they are met by dead relatives and friends. After a period of self-evaluation, they choose their heaven or hell. The afterworlds are products of the mind created during life on earth. (Swedenborg did not believe that Jesus's crucifixion automatically absolved the sins of humankind.) Hell is frightening and desolate, with souls with monstrous faces, but has no Satan by Christian definition. Heaven is a replication of earth; human souls become "angels." In both spheres, souls carry on life in physical-like bodies and pursue work, leisure, marriage, and, in hell, war and crime (excesses of vice and evil are met with punishment). Both spheres have societal structures and governments. According to Swedenborg, it is possible for souls to advance in the afterlife, but never to leave heaven or hell, which are permanent states. He did not believe in reincarnation.

But this heaven and hell are not all there is to the afterlife. Swedenborg said that beyond heaven is another heaven, made up of a brilliant streaming of light.

As one can imagine, Swedenborg was actively opposed by the Christian church. His ideas found favor in the nineteenth century among Transcendentalists, artists, and philosophers. Spiritualists adopted many of Swedenborg's views, and they refer to the after-death state as Summerland, which conjures a Park-like imagery. Today, the Swedenborg Society promotes his work. Of his various books, *Heaven and Hell* offers the most detail about the afterlife.

A Beautiful Field Where We Can Play

Susan is an experienced hospice nurse who works with terminally ill children. Some of her young charges have suffered from spinal muscle atrophy, a condition in which muscles gradually deteriorate until the child is paralyzed and suffocates. The last thing to go before death are the facial muscles, making these cases particularly tragic. The little bodies lie still and limp, but the minds are alert and the faces can smile.

In the past five years, Susan has experienced unusual dreams with several of her terminally ill children. The dreams are full of brilliant imagery and intense joy and happiness, and they occur just before—or just as—a child dies. At first she felt guilty about these dreams, which seemed so enjoyable—until she understood what was happening.

One of Susan's cases was a seven-month-old boy, A., who suffered from spinal muscle atrophy. The condition was discovered when he was about three or four months old, and he came down with pneumonia. Taken to the hospital, he did not get better. More tests were done, and the disease was discovered. His parents were devastated and wanted to do whatever they could to prolong, even try to save, his life. He was fitted with a respiratory device that went through the mouth and nose, and his parents took him home.

Little A. deteriorated as the disease took its toll. He had to be on constant life support. Heartbroken at watching the baby suffer, the parents at last made the agonizing decision to turn off his life support system. Susan was informed and arrived at their home. The life support was disconnected, but A. was able to breathe on his own through the night. By six A.M., he was still alive, and the mother told Susan to lie down and get some rest.

I had the most magnificent dream. It was a beautiful field with children all around. We were playing, riding horses and petting them, and roaming in the field. Animals were everywhere. It was incredibly beautiful. While I was dreaming, the mother came and woke me up. I was disoriented. She told me A. was gone. I had this tremendous guilt that here I was, having this dream while the baby was passing away, and I wasn't there for support like I should have been.

Susan remained disturbed by this experience. She was supposed to be one of the best in her field. How could she be having fun in a dream when she should have been alert?

About a year later, she was caring for another baby boy, B., who suffered from the same disease. She was also pregnant with her own baby. She constantly dreamed of B. walking and climbing around, even though he could not do those things in waking life. The parents tried many measures to help their child, including faith healing. Nothing worked.

One night, when Susan was five months along, she fell into an exhausted, deep sleep at home.

I had an incredible dream with B. flying around, playing, and running. He lasted two more months. The night he died, I had that same dream. The phone rang and woke me up. I just knew he was gone.

Another child, a girl suffering from spinal muscle atrophy, was under Susan's care on and off for more than seven years while the child lived in an iron lung. She had been in the iron lung since nine months of age. Up until the time when she was about two or three, she could be taken out for an hour or two at a time, but then the ravages of the disease required her to be in the lung around the clock.

When the little girl was seven years old, shortly before she died, Susan began having vivid dreams of her calling to Susan, asking her to play.

In these dreams the children are always playing with me. The disheartening thing is that the children I take care of can't play. They just lie flaccid. You might get a little arm movement. The only thing they can do is smile and laugh. In the dreams there are butterflies and horses, and always a field with flowers and trees. It's always the most beautiful, peaceful dream I've ever had. Each time there are different children there, and we play different games. We play ring around the rosie a lot, and I can feel the touching hands. I can feel the ponies when we pet them. The dreams feel very real to me. I wake up with my heart accelerating, and feel like I was actually running and playing and touching them.

When Susan saw a pattern to the dreams—preceding or accompanying the death of a child—she felt anxiety after awakening. Then she realized that perhaps this was the only way her paralyzed children could reach out to her and say good-bye—in the dreamscape where we are freed from the bonds of the body.

I now see the dreams as very liberating. You want the children to have joy and comfort. Their brains are working, but their bodies aren't. You try to think of ways to play with them. Playing in the dreams gave me a lot of joy. The children were always telling me not to be sad. I was always teary-eyed in the dreams, but it was a full-of-joy teary-eyed.

I'm not certain the field is heaven, but I do feel that heaven is a place of great joy and beauty. I've now been able to release the guilt I felt. These dreams have helped me to redefine my purpose through God or the universe, and not through my ego, wanting to be the best.[7]

The dream state provided a place where souls in their second bodies could meet and experience the gift of love and joy.

The Other Side of the River

As a child, dream researcher Val Bigelow had a recurring dream about the "other side" of a river, which she later saw as a glimpse of the other side or the afterlife:

In real life, our family lived in a nice apartment building in the very northernmost section of the Bronx. About two or three blocks to the west of where we lived was the Bronx River, a north-south–flowing river with a nice, well-used green park all along its banks. I only recently realized that on the other, or western bank, of the Bronx River was the huge Woodlawn Cemetery, well treed, fenced, and with many elaborate statues.

The dream always started with me on our side of the Bronx River somehow swimming, wading, or getting across it to the other side. The feeling of the other side was always happy, fun, joyful, even numinous. I would often seem to spend a lot of time over there with many friends (friends I didn't know in my six-, seven-, or eight-year-old life here). I got the impression that these friends were more adult than my chronological age, and maybe I was, too.

Toward the end of the dream, I had to make my way back across to my side of the river, and when I did this, I would wake up. I would be sorry to wake from that dream and hoped I would have it again.

It is only now, as an adult and dream researcher, that I believe that those dreams may have been real excursions to the "Other Side," and only today that I realize the added symbology of the cemetery being on the other side of the river, too (although in the dream state there wasn't a cemetery there, but a wonderful place with a feeling like a fair or happy amusement park). I wonder how many other children may have had similar dream experiences with the other side?[8]

An interesting touch of archetypal symbolism here is that the other side is across a *river* and is to the *west*. In many mythologies around the world, the dead must cross a river or other body of water in order to reach the land of the dead. In Greek mythology, the River Styx separates the world of the living from Hades, the underworld. The dead are ferried across in a boat by Charon. (It remained a custom throughout Europe well into later centuries to bury the dead with coins placed on the eyes to pay the ferryman.) The west, the direction of the setting sun, has long been associated with the underworld. The ancient Egyptians buried their kings, queens, and nobility on the western bank of the Nile at Thebes (now Luxor). West was the direction of the Hall of Amenti, the realm of the dead. According to *The Book of the Dead* (which the Egyptians called *The Book of Coming Forth by Day*), souls of the dead had to navigate treacherous swamplike areas and waters in their underworld journey.

Traditionally, the land of the dead cannot be accessed easily by the living. This is seen in modern accounts of near-death experiences in which people who clinically die have experiences of tunnels of light, beautiful places, visions of the dead and angels, a life review, and so on. As we saw in the previous chapter, many tell of reaching a point of no return, such as a bridge or an entrance to a garden. They know or are told that if they cross the threshold, they cannot go back to life; they will be irrevocably in the land of the dead. Some are told by their guides that they must go back; others are given a choice.

Mediums who contact the dead also speak of a barrier that is difficult to penetrate. It seems to be primarily one-way. The dead seem to be able to meet us under certain circumstances and for a limited time, such as through mediumship or dreams, but we cannot attempt to go to them in their realm without great peril.

The limited ability of the two worlds to meet is illustrated in the next dream.

Saint Bosco's Trip to Heaven

Saint John Bosco, the lucid-and OBE-dreaming saint of Italy in the nineteenth century (see chapter 6), had a long and vivid lucid dream involving his dead beloved pupil, Dominic Savio. Dominic was so pure that he died at age fifteen, ready for heaven. He was canonized in 1954. On December 6, 1876, twenty years after Dominic's death, Bosco met him in a dream. The dream is filled with the images seen in dreams of the other side: brilliant colors, flowers, beautiful landscapes, and happy, radiant children. This is not technically heaven, Bosco is told in the dream (perhaps because heaven lies across the point of no return), but is a place of great happiness—a between place perhaps like The Park.

It seemed to me that I was standing on a hill, looking down on an immense plain that stretched away into the invisible distance. It was as blue as the sea in perfect calm, but what I was looking at was not water; it seemed like crystal, unblemished and sparkling.

Long and broad avenues divided the plain up into large gardens of indescribable beauty, in which were lawns, groves of ornamental trees, flowering shrubs and flower-beds with an amazing variety of ornamental flowers. What you have seen in gardens can give you little idea of how wonderful all this was. There were trees whose leaves seemed to be of gold, the branches and trunks of precious stones.

Scattered here and there in the gardens were buildings whose appearance and magnificence rivaled the setting in which they stood. I could not estimate what immense sums of money even one of these would have cost to build. The thought ran through my head: "If I could have any one of these buildings for my boys, how happy they would be."

As I stood there rapt in wonder, the sound of sweet and entrancing music filled the air; all possible instruments seemed to be combining in wonderful harmony, and together with them choirs of singers.

I then saw great numbers of people in the garden, some walking, some sitting, all radiantly happy. Some were singing, some playing instruments, and it was obvious that they derived equal pleasure from hearing the others as they did from the music they were making themselves. They were singing in Latin these words: "All honor and glory to God the Almighty Father—Creator of the ages, who was, who is and who will come to judge the living and the dead through all ages."

There now suddenly appeared a great army of boys. Many of them I knew, boys who had been with me at the Oratory or in one of our schools; but the majority I did not know. This endless line began moving towards me; at its head was Dominic Savio; after him several priests and many other priests and brothers, each at the head of a group of boys.

I did not know whether I was awake or dreaming; I clapped my hands together and felt my arms and chest in the endeavor to see how real was what I was seeing.

An intense, brilliant light now shone all around. All the boys were radiant with happiness; it shone from their eyes, and their faces had a look of ineffable peace and contentment. They smiled at me, and they looked as though they were going to say something, but no word was uttered.

Dominic now walked forward on his own until he stood close beside me. He stood there silently for a moment, smiling and looking at me. How wonderful he looked, how exquisitely he was clothed! The white tunic which reached to his feet was interwoven with golden threads and sparkling jewels. Around his waist he had a broad red sash, also interwoven with precious stones of every color, which sparkled and glittered in a thousand lights. Around his neck there was a necklace of wild flowers, but the flowers were made of precious stones and the light they reflected lit up further still the beauty and dignity of Dominic's face. His hair, which was crowned with roses, hung down to his shoulders and completed the quite indescribable effect of his total appearance.

The others were dressed in varying degrees of splendor, all of which had their own symbolic meaning you would not understand. One thing they all had in common was the broad red sash round their waists.

I thought to myself: "What does all this mean?—Where on earth am I?" *And I stood there silently, not daring to say a word.*

Dominic then spoke:

"Why are you standing there as though you were dumb? Are you not the one I knew who was always so fearless, able to sustain persecutions, calumnies and dangers of every kind? Have you lost your courage? Why do you not speak?"

Half stammering, I replied:

"I don't know what to say. Are you really Dominic Savio?"

"Yes, indeed. Don't you recognize me?"

"How is it that you are here?"

"I have come to talk with you," Dominic replied affectionately. "We spoke together so often when I was alive; you were always so kind and generous to me, and I responded to your love with my complete confidence and affection. Ask me anything you wish."

"Where am I?" I asked.

"You are in a place of happiness," he replied, "where all that is beautiful can be enjoyed."

"Is this Heaven, then?"

"No, whatever is here is of the earth, although improved beyond conception by the power of God. No living person can ever see or imagine the wonders of eternity."

"Would it be possible to have natural light more brilliant than this?"

"Yes, quite possible . . . look there in the distance."

I looked, and a ray of light suddenly appeared, so penetrating and of such brilliance that I had to close my eyes, and I cried out in alarm so loudly that I woke the priest who was sleeping in the room nearby. I opened my eyes after a moment and said:

"But that is surely a ray of the divine light . . ."

"No, even that does not give you any idea. In Heaven we enjoy God, and that in everything."

I had by now recovered from my initial amazement and was looking at Dominic as he stood before me. I said:

"Why are you wearing that dazzling white tunic?"

Dominic did not answer, but the choirs of voices beautifully sustained by the many instruments sang in Latin:

"They had their lions girt and have washed their tunics in the blood of the Lamb."

I then realized that the blood-red sash was a symbol of the great efforts and sacrifices made, the quasi-martyrdom suffered, to live a completely pure life. It symbolized also the spirit of penance, which cleanses the soul of its faults. The dazzling white of the tunic represented a life from Baptism to death without any serious rejection of God.

My eyes were drawn to the serried ranks of boys behind Dominic and I asked him:

"Who are these boys, and why are they all so radiant and resplendent?"

The answer came from the boys themselves, who began to sing in wonderful harmony:

"These are like the angels of God in Heaven . . ."

Dominic, although the youngest, was obviously the leader, standing out well ahead of them. I therefore asked him:

"Why is that you take precedence over the others?"

"I am the oldest."

"I am God's ambassador."

The meaning of what it was all about suddenly dawned on me, and I hastened to say:

"Let us talk about what concerns me and my work. Perhaps you have

something important to tell me . . . Speak to me of the past, present, and future of our work and of my dear sons . . ."

Dominic tells Bosco that he has done well with the boys under his care at his Oratory, but that the Salesian order would be many more in number if he had greater faith and confidence in God. Dominic then hands Bosco a bouquet that includes flowers, sprigs of evergreen, and ears of corn. He says:

"These flowers represent the virtues and qualities which your boys need in order to be able to live for God instead of for themselves. The rose is the symbol of love, the violet of humility, the sunflower of obedience, the gentian of penance and self-discipline, the ears of corn of frequent Communion, the lily of purity, the sprigs of evergreen of constancy and perseverance."

"No one was adorned with these flowers better than yourself," I said to him. "Tell me what was your greatest consolation when you came to die."

"What do you think?" he answered.

I had several attempts at trying to say what I thought it might be, such as having lived such a pure life, having heaped up so much treasure in Heaven by all his good works, and so on, but to all he shook his head with a smile.

"Tell me, then," I said, quite crestfallen at my failure; "what was it?"

"What helped me most and gave me the greatest joy when I was dying," replied Dominic, "was the loving care and help of the great Mother of God. Tell your sons not to fail to keep close to her while they are alive. But hurry—the time is almost up."

Bosco asks about the future. Dominic discusses the upcoming deaths of eight boys in the congregation, the growth of the Salesians, and the future death of Pope Pius IX (who would die two years later in 1878). Bosco asks what is in store for himself.

"You have many sorrows and difficulties ahead of you yet . . . but hurry, as my time is almost up."

I stretched out my hands to detain him if I could, but they grasped only the air. Dominic smiled and said:

"What are you trying to do?"

"I don't want to let you go," I said, "but are you bodily here? Are you really my son Dominic?"

"This is how things are. If in God's providence someone who is dead has to appear to someone still alive, he is seen in his normal bodily appearance and distinguishing characteristics. He cannot, however, be bodily touched, since he is a pure spirit. He retains this bodily appearance until he is reunited with his body at the Resurrection."

Bosco has a final request: to know if all of his boys are "living with God." Dominic hands him three sheets of paper bearing lists of names. The first list is of boys who had never been overcome by evil. The second list is of boys who had "seriously offended God," but were trying to redeem themselves. The third piece of paper, bearing the name of boys who had been conquered by evil, was folded. Dominic warns Bosco:

"When you open this sheet, a terrible stench will be given off, which neither you nor I could possibly bear. It is likewise intolerable to the Angels of God, and God Himself."

"How can this be," I said, "the Angels and God being pure spirits?"

"It means this," he replied, "that just as you seek to put the greatest distance possible between yourself and what nauseates you, so those who reject God by serious sin are separated from Him more and more."

When Bosco opens the sheet, he sees no names, but rather sees in a flash the faces of all those who are listed. He is saddened that some of them are considered to be the best boys at the Oratory.

When the paper was unfolded, there arose from it such a horrible stench that I was completely overcome. My head throbbed agonizingly, and I began to vomit so violently that I thought I must die.

Everything became dark, and the vision was no more. A piercing flash of lightning tore across the sky, and as its frightening crash of thunder reverberated in my ear, I awoke trembling with fear.

The stench was still present in my room, clinging to the walls and furniture, and remained there for several days. Thus repugnant to God is the very name of those who reject Him and surrender themselves to the horrors of self-indulgence.

Whenever the memory of that stench comes back to me, I am seized anew with pain and nausea, and I can with difficulty prevent myself from vomiting.

I have spoken with some of the boys whose names I saw written on the lists, and I know for certain that what I saw in the dream is only too true.[9]

Note that Bosco was so swept up in the realism of the dream that he clapped his hands to try to determine if he was awake or asleep. This is a technique used by lucid dreamers today to verify their lucidity. NDErs also report touching themselves, clapping their hands, or pulling their hair to verify that their experience is real.

Twice Dominic tells Bosco to hurry because time is almost up. This corroborates the belief that the land of the dead is difficult to access. Even in a lucid, OBE dream, the bridge between the worlds of the living and the dead can last only so long.

As was the case with most of Bosco's dreams, they provided him information—which he could not have obtained otherwise without a great deal of time and difficulty—that helped him to take action for the interests of the Salesians and his young charges. The predictions that he was given in his dreams always came true.

Bosco's dream is a dramatic example of the contents of a dream—in this case, the stench—invading the physical world, similar to the black and blue marks that covered Jerome after he awoke from his flogging before God. This bleed-through between worlds is characteristic of shamanic journeys and belongs to Jung's psychoid unconscious, a level in the unconscious that is not accessible to consciousness but that has properties in common with the physical world. It seems that the dreaming mind can tap into this realm; sometimes it manifests in the physical.

In a more poetic vein, I am reminded of a poem by Samuel Taylor Coleridge.

What if you slept, and what if in your
sleep you dreamed, and what if in your
dream you went to heaven and there
plucked a strange and beautiful flower,
and what if when you awoke you had the
flower in your hand? Ah, what then?

chapter twenty-five

ENCOUNTERS WITH DEATH

MICHAEL TALBOT HAD A FINE TALENT AS A BEST-SELLING AUTHOR OF BOTH NONFICTION AND FICTION WORKS. HIS CAREER AND LIFE WERE CUT SHORT IN 1992, WHEN HE DIED at age thirty-eight of chronic lymphoscystic leukemia. Among his works are *Mysticism and the New Physics, Beyond the Quantum, The Reincarnation Handbook,* several novels, and *The Holographic Universe,* his last book.

In 1988, while I was researching my book *Tales of Reincarnation,* I spent an afternoon with Michael at his New York City apartment conducting a taped interview about his life, views and experiences. There was a mysterious quality about Michael, as though he perceived realms that few people ever glimpsed. I believe he was a bit of a psychic lightning rod himself. He'd had some experiences early in life that seemed to have opened his psychic channels.

Our conversation covered a range of topics beyond reincarnation, including some unusual dreams that he had experienced beginning at an early age. "My dreams are very important to me," said Michael, "and I am constantly watching them for their clues and guidance. Some dreams are just dreams, but others have a valance that you know they are something more."

One early experience in particular seemed to set the stage for the course his life would follow.

As a child I had a very moving experience. I don't know if it was a dream or a vision. It was in memory as an actual experience, but I could not remember where it began or where it ended. When I was about three or four, an entity came to me. I thought it was a woman, but in retrospect it could have been androgynous. It was a stereotypical guide figure with a long robe and white hair. It was taking me by the hand through the woods at night. At the time, we lived in Michigan, and the landscape seemed to be near where we lived.

I thought, "This has got to be my mother," although I knew deep in my heart it wasn't, but I would have been too panicked to think otherwise. The entity took me to the shore of a lake and said, "Are you afraid, Michael?" I said, "Yes." She said, "Hold your hand upward palm toward the moon." I did that. She said, "Now close your hand." As I did I could feel the air, like when you hold your hand out of a car window, but there was no wind, there was just a softness. The being said, "Do you feel that?" I said "Yes." It said, "There's something I want you always to remember, no matter what happens to you in your life: Don't ever be afraid. For you, the darkness is soft."

It was always a very comforting message to me. Later, I thanked my mother for the experience. She said, "You're welcome," but she had no memory of taking me through the woods—she just passed me off as a child.

A psychic friend of Michael's told him the woman in white was a guide from another level of reality who had come to give a sort of blessing. "Something happened to you that had to do with your bones at around age fourteen," he told Michael. "Had she not blessed you, you would have died, but as it was, it developed into the problem that it did." Michael had never shared with the psychic that he had scoliosis—a curvature of the spine—and was in a spine brace for about five years.

Michael had other exceptional experiences throughout life, including a poltergeist who tagged along with him wherever he lived. I was particularly interested in his dreams that involved death and the other side, including this OBE dream.

I had several vivid dreams encountering Death, including one where I was taken to the predeath state, I believe. I knew [in waking life] that I was having a struggle with my life. The dream started out with a woman saying to me, "Will you pray with me?" She had a live ferret on one arm and a white owl on the other. She said, "While we are praying, I want you to watch these animals, and if one of them turns into a human being, you must talk to it." I said, "Yes, I understand." So we were praying and I was keeping an eye on these animals, and the owl reached out to me. At first I was frightened because I thought it was going to nip my ears, and I pulled back. Then I thought it was asking me, "Lend me your ear," so I let it take hold of my ear, and it turned into a woman. She was short, a bit stocky. Her presence was very wise, loving, powerful, and positive.

She said, "I'm going to take you somewhere." I said, "Okay." We went through this instant transition where suddenly we were in a very large room full of people. They all seemed rather excited. She introduced me to them and said, "This is Michael and he's in college." I thought that was amusing because I had been out of college for some time. I said, "No, I'm not in college." She said, "Yes, you are, you don't understand. You're in college on terra firma." She pulled on my sport jacket and said, "Judging from the way you are dressed, I would say somewhere on the East Coast." Then I realized that she was talking about being in the earth life.

Two young boys came up to me—they must have been about fourteen or fifteen—and they said, "We're about to go. What is it like?" I couldn't really answer. I said, "It's what you make of it. It's wonderful or awful depending on what you make of it." They said, "We're really looking forward to it," and I realized they were waiting to be born. I think most of the people in the room were about to be born.

The woman said, "Now you've got to shake hands with someone." I turned around and there was a strange-looking man coming toward me. He was bald and heavyset, very pale. The first thing I noticed was that his wrists had double joints in them. They were like tree limbs, very creepy looking. She said, "You've got to shake his hand." I said, "I don't want to shake his hand." She said, "That's all right, he doesn't want to shake yours." So I shook his hand, and it was ice cold and clammy. I said, "Oh, it's like something out of a crypt!" She said, "You've got that exactly right."

At that point, I realized he was Death. He said, "Do you want to go with me?" I said, "No, I don't." He said, "Then you must consider something." "What's that?" I said. He said, "What are your resources?" After I heard that, I knew that I had the wherewithal within me to decide whether I was living or dying. The Death figure looked almost passive and weak, like he could not overpower me and make me go with him.

The woman then said to me—she seemed to be sort of a psychic guide, she had a very powerful, glistening presence—she said, "I'm going to send you back now, but there's something I want you to remember. From time to time, I'm going to send you beautiful books. You'll know they will have come from me because they will be so beautiful." I did not know what that prediction meant, but it was kind of magical.

The next thing I knew, I was sailing through levels of reality. It was like swiftly passing by rock strata—each one was there for just a moment. But I could see an incredible distance, far vaster than it seemed an earth horizon should be. At first, I thought I was looking at integrated circuitry, because there was something so geometric and beautiful and colorful about the vista. Then I realized that I was looking at cities, but not earth cities. They were celestial, beautiful, alien, exotic cities, in very deep, rich colors: indigoes, blues, reds, purples. There were a lot of purples, although each one was different. The lights were glistening yellow like streetlights. I could see a vast geometry of streets, but it was more complex than normal city streets. There were mountain ranges, sweeping, almost lunar-looking, not stark, but alien and very rich. I didn't see any foliage or plants, but everything had a sense of richness. I was mesmerized by what was happening to me. They came one right after another, bam bam bam bam, zooming past, and then bam, I hit my body with a jerk.[1]

The woman is a guide figure; her instruction to pray may have pointed to a need for Michael to address his interior life. The ferret represents discovery through investigation (ferreting out information) and the owl represents wisdom. The owl becomes a woman (feminine wisdom, or the voice of the anima) in order to speak.

The place that Michael called "predeath" resembles descriptions of the between-life or intermission state in the literature pertaining to reincarnational memories: rooms or buildings filled with souls awaiting their next incarnation on earth, or newly deceased souls awaiting integration into the afterlife.

Michael interpreted the books in the dream as new systems of knowledge that he would encounter. Indeed, until the end of his life, he absorbed himself in a study of the subjects he loved so much: mysticism, consciousness, the eternal.

The rushing through levels of reality and seeing cities of light has parallels to "The Park" dream of my husband Tom. Celestial cities of light appear in the literature of mystics, shamans, NDErs, OBErs, and lucid dreamers. Swedenborg described visiting brilliant cities of staggering architecture and beauty. The cities are vast in size, glowing with light that seems to emanate from within. They seem to be made literally from gold and silver that have an unearthly translucence or sheen. The cities are filled with enormous buildings, such as libraries that house all of the records of the universe (the Akashic Records). This description comes from an NDE reported to researcher Kenneth Ring.

Suddenly there was this tremendous burst of light and . . . I was turned . . . to the light. I saw in the distance a great city. . . . And then I began to realize that the light was coming from within this city and there just seemed to be a laser beam of light and in the midst of that, that was directed to me. And I just rode that laser beam of light through a vastness, being aware that there were other life forms going by . . . Oh, tremendous speed, tremendous speed . . . I just went right down into [the city] . . . Everything was very defined, on the one hand, but it also had a blending with everything else. The flowers and the flower buds by that street—the intensity, the vibrant colors, like pebbles that have been polished in a running stream, but they were all like precious stones: rubies and diamonds and sapphires . . .[2]

Michael's dream also foreshadowed an impending health crisis for him. Around Easter time in 1988, Michael, said, "I had my own little resurrection. I got very ill and was in the hospital for ten days. They didn't think I was going to survive, but I pulled through." Michael remained ill for several weeks. During that time:

I had three dreams in which Death came to me. The first dream was very simple. I was on a desolate, desertlike landscape at night, and a train came by. I knew immediately that it was a death train. The conductor looked spectral. He said, "This is the night train—would you like to get on?" I said, "No." I had a very clear understanding that were I to get on, I would have died—it was taking souls away.

The last dream took place a few days before my recovery. The scene looked like Mexico City at night, with a lot of wrought-iron gates. I knew I was being pursued by a psychopath. I'd had a glimpse of him. He was a young man, his hair was very disheveled, and he was glistening with sweat. He had glassy eyes and he was totally mad. I knew he meant my death, and that if I were to confront him, I would be dead instantly. I was trying to get away. I had a beautiful estate that I had to leave and go through these wrought-iron gates into the city, which was labyrinthine and like a surrealist painting. The whole thing was Kafkaesque, with this psychopath after me.

I managed to get back to my estate. I was coming down this street and I knew I had to shut the gate. I shut it, but it was making too much sound. I didn't want to attract his attention, so I left it without locking it, and I hid in a Rolls Royce that was in the courtyard. I heard him come in. I was crouched down below the window. I heard his feet crunching in the gravel all around the car. Then he went out. I heard the gate close. I got up.

Another man was there. I didn't sense any menace from him. He gave me a bone with Anubis's [Egyptian god of the dead] head carved on it. He said, "This one is for you—it's from that man who was just here." I realized that the psychopath had represented Death, which was Anubis, and I had been through the gates of the underworld, and that he had almost got me. When I had come back in to the estate, the game was over, and he was saying, "Here, you have your life back, I have gone back to my world."

That was the third encounter with Death, and shortly after that, I recovered.[3]

The setting of Mexico City has associations with the realm of the dead, with its famous annual festival, the Day of the Dead (comparable to All Hallow's Eve), in which the ancestral spirits are honored. In Egyptian mythology, Anubis is the jackal-headed god who leads the souls of the newly dead into the underworld. Gates, as Michael observed, represent points of transition, in this case, from earthly life to the after-death state. The estate represents Michael's earthly life.

The series of three dreams (note: Michael did not share the details of the second dream; he seemed to think the first and third were the most significant) points to another gateway, one through which Michael eventually would pass for the final time. Several years later, his illness got the upper hand, and Michael could no longer outrun and outsmart Death.

I have often wondered about his last dreams, and the mysteries of the eternal they must have shown him.

PART VII

Timescape Dreaming

c h a p t e r t w e n t y - s i x

PAST LIVES AND LOVES

HAVE WE LIVED BEFORE? THREE-QUARTERS OF THE WORLD'S POPULATION BELIEVES IN SOME FORM OF REINCARNATION OR REBIRTH. THE NUMBER OF WESTERNERS BELIEVING IN REINcarnation—or at least being open to the idea—is rising as more people explore consciousness and spiritual paths.

Reincarnation memories are recalled in a variety of ways. Spontaneous memories, those that seem to be part of an individual from an early age, are given the greatest credence by investigators. Thousands of cases of spontaneous recall among children and adults have been documented around the world.

Children are more likely than adults to have spontaneous memories, probably because they simply haven't accrued much life experience, and therefore new memories. Among adults, past-life memories surface most commonly through deja vu (feeling familiar about something that is new or unfamiliar, such as a place) and dreams. Some recover memories through induced recall, such as hypnosis. Dreams in which we are another person in a strange place in a distant time can leave such a strong impression that we awaken wondering who we really are.

Past-life dreams may occur once in a great while or with great frequency. Distinguishing past-life dreams from ordinary ones is not always easy. Individuals who have experienced many past-life dreams learn to recognize them by their characteristics and the impact they have, just like people learn how to recognize psi in their dreams. Such dreams usually are extremely vivid and clear and remain sharp in the memory for a long time. Many are lucid or OBE, in which the dreamer may be aware that the dream is a past life. Recurring dreams sometimes have past-life connections. Sometimes, the dreamer awakens just *knowing* that the dream was about a past life.

Carl Jung was skeptical about reincarnation until he had a series of dreams "which would seem to describe the process of reincarnation in a deceased person of my acquaintance," as he wrote in his autobiography *Memories, Dreams, Reflections.* "But I have never come across any such dreams in other persons, and therefore have no basis for comparison . . . I must confess, however, that after this experience I view the problem of reincarnation with somewhat different eyes . . ."[1] Jung did not elaborate on the content of his series of dreams.

Jung may have felt differently about the possibility of reincarnational dreams if he had the benefit of modern Western research and interest into the subject. While most dreams of past lives do not contain verifiable information about a previous personality, many documented cases of apparent reincarnation do involve dreams. Fragments of the past life surface in both dreams and waking visions.

Dr. Ian Stevenson, perhaps the best-known Western researcher of "cases of the reincarnational type," observes in his book *Children Who Remember Previous Lives* that vivid dreams may have paranormal content. He says that "some vivid and recurrent dreams may stem from actual memories of previous lives. . . . The quality of vividness in a dream may provide an indication of paranormality, but no proof of it: A vivid dream is more likely to have a paranormal component than a nonvivid one, but most vivid dreams do not have this component."[2] Stevenson cautions people not to automatically interpret vivid and recurring dreams as having paranormal—and possibly past-life—content.

Nonetheless, dreams do play a role in our ability to see past lives. They are reported in the academic literature of many convincing reincarnation cases that have been investigated, as well as in popular dreamwork literature.

One case cited by Stevenson is that of Arif Hamed (a pseudonym), a Lebanese child who said that in his previous life he was a man. He was sitting beneath a balcony when a large stone fell from above, hit him on the head, and killed him instantly. The last thing he saw was a group of goats in the area. As Arif, he had recurring dreams of goats climbing over piles of building stones and knocking some over. Stevenson verified many of the boy's spontaneous memories with the life of the dead man (whose identity was determined), although he could not ascertain whether goats actually were present on the day the man died. Since goats are common in the area, the detail probably was accurate, he said. The building stones may symbolize the stone that fell and killed him.

Why do past lives present themselves in dreams? The reasons may be many. If we believe that a thread links all of our lives together, and that we have a pattern of karma from one life to the next, then reincarnational dreams show us past lives involving pieces of that karma. These might include fears, phobias, prejudices, behavior patterns, and so on that are repeating in the present life.

Reincarnational dreams can become activated when we start new relationships—we may have past-life connections with certain people. They also may be stimulated by travel. Visiting a strange country, for example, can elicit feelings of deja vu—a feeling of having been there before—as well as dreams of a past life in that area. Intense interest in and study of certain cultures, time periods of history, and great events (such as wars) also may trigger the release of memories forgotten to waking consciousness but accessible by the dreaming consciousness.

Meditation can bring waking visions of past lives. Patanjali (c. 400 C.E.), the compiler of the Yoga sutras, or truths, stated that memories of past lives may be awakened by a special method of Yoga meditation. The memories, including all details of past lives and all impressions of karma, reside in the *chitta,* or subconscious mind. Meditational stimulation in turn can stimulate the dream life.

Hello, I'm on My Way!

In many cultures, announcing dreams are experienced during pregnancy. The soul that is about to be born announces itself as desiring another incarnation and its intent to be born to a particular person or family. Typically, these dreams occur to the pregnant woman before birth; sometimes they even occur prior to conception. To a lesser degree, they also occur to the father-to-be or other close relatives. In most cases, the dream reveals the identity of the reincarnating soul, who is likely to be known to the prospective parents, such as a deceased relative or friend. Sometimes the identity is not apparent from the dream. The previous personality is identified after birth by appearance, birthmarks, and such.

An announcing dream may be highly symbolic, such as a visitor with lots of baggage who comes to stay or even to occupy the parents' bedroom with them. It can also be quite direct, featuring a known deceased person who asks prospective parents for permission to be born to them.

The term *announcing dreams* was coined by Stevenson. These dreams occur in cultures around the world, but are most common among Indians in northwestern North America, the Burmese, and the Alevis of Turkey. They also surface in Western culture, though rarely. The low incidence of them is probably due to lack of cultural interest in and encouragement of such dreams.

One Western case investigated by Stevenson was that of Mr. and Mrs. E. of Idaho. Their six-year-old daughter, W., was struck by a car and killed in 1961. Mrs. E. especially suffered from grief and wanted W. to somehow come back. She knew little about reincarnation and belonged to a church that discouraged belief in it. About six months after W.'s death, her sister dreamed that W. was in fact returning to the family. Two years later, Mrs. E. became pregnant and dreamed of W. being with the family again. She had a girl, whom they named S.

When S. was about two years old—the age when reincarnational memories can begin surfacing spontaneously—she began making remarks that seemed to refer to W., especially herself as W. She told people she was six and said that photos of W. were of herself. She would make statements like, "When I went to school . . ." before she attended school. She made comments about relatives, former playmates, and household habits known to W. but not to her. While she never explicitly said, "I am W.," she seemed to possess fragments of memories that W. would have had.

Sometimes the incarnating soul is not known to the family. Another case investigated by Stevenson is that of Ma Tin Aung Myo, who was born in Burma in 1953. During pregnancy, her mother dreamed three times about a Japanese soldier who followed her and said he was coming to stay with her and her husband.

By age three, Ma Tin Aung Myo exhibited a great fear of airplanes. When she was older, she said she had previously been a Japanese soldier stationed in Burma during World War II. An Allied plane strafed the village she was in and killed her. She described what she was wearing and how the bullets had pierced her in the groin. However, she provided no names or concrete details that enabled a trace of her previous life.

Ma Tin Aung Myo thought of herself as a man and had great

difficulty coming to terms with herself in a female body. She dressed in masculine clothes and said she wanted a wife. She also said that others were welcome to kill her, if they could guarantee that she would come back a man.

In some announcing dreams, the discarnate personality correctly predicts birthmarks or unusual features that the infant will bear, which will help to validate the identity of the incoming personality. Birthmarks, abnormalities or even deformities may match characteristics of the deceased or may correspond to fatal wounds suffered by the deceased. A Chinese woman relates a dream about unusual skin color that occurred to her husband.

The time I was pregnant with my third daughter, I went into labor during my sleep. My husband woke up and told me he was dreaming that a woman floated in through the window. She was naked, and had long hair and very fair skin, even though she was Chinese. I gave birth to a girl with fair skin. I think it's reincarnation.[3]

Another Burmese case documented by Stevenson describes the announcing dream had by the aunt of a pregnant woman, U Po Min. The aunt dreamed that her dead sister, U Po Min's mother, announced she would be born into U Po Min's family (thus reincarnating as her own granddaughter). "If you don't believe me," the dead woman said in the dream, "the child will be born with the feet first. You will also see that the toes will be joined on its foot."[4] Sure enough, the baby girl was born feetfirst, and had the second and third toes of her right foot partially joined.

The cases of announcing dreams provide a fascinating glimpse into how dreams might be used as message boards among souls both incarnate and discarnate. Couples intending to conceive a child should pay greater attention to their dreams—and perhaps even ask the incoming soul to identify itself in a dream. The incidence of announcing dreams in Western culture would be much higher if we expected such information to be revealed in dreams.

Holocaust Dreams

No other event in modern times has caused the psychic scarring of the Holocaust, when millions of people lost their lives in war. Especially tragic were the millions, mostly Jews, who perished in Nazi torture and death camps. In the years following the close of the war, numerous cases of reincarnated Holocaust victims have come to light. The number of documented cases has risen steadily since the early 1980s, when Rabbi Yonassan Gershom began collecting them.

Rabbi Gershom didn't set out to look for reincarnated Holocaust victims; by some strange synchronicity, they found him. Perhaps it was because he was a rabbi, a person who could be trusted with deep confidences, and because as a Hasidic Jew, he believed in reincarnation.

At first, Rabbi Gershom kept the stories to himself, not wanting to appear to sensationalize the Holocaust. By the mid 1980s, however, he had collected much anecdotal material and saw a pattern to it. He felt compelled to speak out about it. Churches and metaphysical organizations not only were not interested, they wished to avoid the subject of the Holocaust altogether. It was too heavy, too depressing.

Rabbi Gershom continued to work on his own, and in 1987, succeeded in placing an article in *Venture Inward,* the magazine of the Association for Research and Enlightenment. The A.R.E., located in Virginia Beach, Virginia, was founded by the famous trance medium, Edgar Cayce, who had talked about reincarnation in many of his trance readings.

The article drew a tremendous response. Rabbi Gershom began receiving calls from others who wanted to talk about the certainty that they had died in the Holocaust. The response led to two books by Rabbi Gershom, *Beyond the Ashes* and *From Ashes to Healing,* both published by the A.R.E.

Most of the people who contacted Gershom were born between 1947 and 1953 in the United States to non-Jewish families. They felt an unexplained familiarity with Judaism and knowledge about some of its rituals and customs—some so much that they felt compelled to convert. Most experienced frightening past-life recalls in the form of dreams and waking visions; frequently, these experiences replayed their deaths.

Rabbi Gershom counseled many of these people. As the volume of respondents increased, he often felt emotionally drained by the stories of "nightmares, visions, and vivid memories of torture and betrayal." Many times, he said, he went to bed "asking my Creator why I had been given this overwhelming sad burden." He was answered in a dream.

One such night, I dreamed that I was a young Hasidic boy, about eight or nine years old, living in Eastern Europe. The Jews of the village had gathered together, and we could hear the sounds of battle in the distance. My father, who was the village rabbi, was trying to comfort the people. He explained that although they were about to die, they should not be afraid, because the body is only a garment. The soul, he said, lives forever, and will one day return to earth in a new garment.

But the rabbi explained sadly that there was a problem. For many, many incarnations, their souls had returned to this same village to be born as their children's children. This time, however, the village would be destroyed completely, and none would survive to provide new bodies for the souls. They could never again come back to this place and might, therefore, become separated from one another in the next life. How would they ever find each other again?

It was decided to draw straws. The person thus chosen would incarnate immediately and look for a new place for the villagers to return to. After preparing the way, he would serve as a psychic beacon for the other souls, who would seek him out. In this way, it was hoped, the villagers would not become lost to one another.

Solemnly the Jews said a prayer together, then each took a straw, while the sounds of battle drew closer and closer. Suddenly everyone gasped—I had drawn the short straw! Just as I was about to protest that I was too young and didn't know how, the Nazis entered the village and began shooting everyone. I woke up.[5]

Rabbi Gershom did not know if the dream was literally true, but it certainly was "more than symbolic. Like the boy in the dream, I have been entrusted with a responsibility that is not entirely of my own choosing." He has served as a door-opener for wounded souls to find each other and heal.

One woman ("Beverly") related to Rabbi Gershom how an unsettling, realistic dream led her to think she had died in another life during the war.

In the dream she was a little boy about seven or eight years old, standing in a line with his mother. Beverly described how they got to a table where a man was telling some people to go to the left and others to the right. He pointed and they went through a door.

The scene shifted, and they were suddenly in a horrible place, where there was a terrible smell. Some men were throwing people into a fire alive, and then the little boy was thrown in too. He kept patting himself trying to put out the flames, then he died.

The scene shifted again, with the little boy and his mother finding themselves standing once again in a long line of people. Up ahead were the most beautiful gates, and the little boy knew it was Heaven. Strangely, the men in the line were wearing hats, and Beverly remembered thinking it was odd that they didn't take off their hats to go into Heaven. Then the little boy grew tired of waiting and wandered off down to a lower level where he met a "male angel." The angel said, "Now that you have come down this far, you will have to go back to earth again." He didn't want to go and kept asking for his mother, but the angel said they would have to find him another mother. The boy was then shown a beam of light that he followed into the womb of a woman. And then "he" became Beverly.[6]

The Past Explains the Present

Past-life dreams can sometimes help us understand why we are the way we are, and what we are doing in life. Anne Beckley (see chapter 5) grew up with a scientific bent, and worked professionally as a systems engineer for a leading computer firm. In her thirties, she was drawn to a very different field, energy healing, and enrolled in a comprehensive program to train as a healer. During her study, she experienced a dream with a past-life theme. It explained some of her early interests and decisions as well as a present phobia and an issue of self-confidence.

I am a point of consciousness flying into this home. It is a green, upscale house dating to about the 1870s or 1880s. It has a mansard-style roof and green clapboard siding with scalloped shingles on the third floor. There is an exposed stairwell lighted with gas lamps.

I go into the top floor and see what I realize is myself sitting in a room. I am a male physician. In this room there is a library. I look at the titles. A lot of them have to do with what we now call alternative medicine. There is a lot of occult literature as well: alchemy, astrology, astronomy. Lots of botanical literature. I go inside this man, and see that he is very arrogant and superior, but all of it masks feelings of inferiority. All he really wants to do is help his patients. He has a good heart, but he has a hard time showing it. He's also received a lot of criticism and is having a hard time dealing with it. He is an intellectual and has a lot of knowledge, which he is trying to synthesize.

The next thing that happens is a fire in the stairwell. I don't know if he sets it or if there is a problem with one of the gas lamps. He is dying in the fire. I wake up.[7]

Anne felt certain she had witnessed a scene from one of her past lives—a life that had bearing on her present life. "The dream was so real, I was scared out of my wits when I woke up," she said. "It explains some of the same issues that I'm wrestling with in my life. It brought to the forefront my issues with inferiority and superiority. I've always had to be number one. I think I was trying to live up to my mother's expectations to achieve well academically. I put down things that required physical skill because I was never that good at them.

"The lesson for me is that everyone has something they're good at. Failure at some things is okay. I need to be more confident without being arrogant.

"As a small child, I wanted to be a physician. When I was four, I went around telling everyone I wanted to be a doctor. When I entered college, I intended to apply for premed. Then I had a dream in which an inner voice said, no, you're going to be an engineer. I changed my major the next day. My mother was appalled. She couldn't understand it. I went to engineering school and took industrial engineering. Now I've come back to medicine, but to the other, alternative side. I think if I'd gone to med school, I would have become that arrogant doctor I saw in the dream."

The dream also pointed to a strong phobia that had no apparent explanation. "Whenever I go anywhere, I always sit where I can get out quickly in case there's a fire," said Anne. "If I have to go into a basement, I always sit by the stairwell."

New Light on Relationships

Even if we feel or assume that we have lived before with the people in our lives now, a past-life dream can add new information about relationships. My husband, Tom, had this dream when his father was still living.

I find myself in a building with a lot of people dressed in heavy clothing made for winter. The clothing is not modern, and everyone appears to be wearing at least some animal skin covers. We are in very mountainous country. As I scan the surroundings, I am aware that a lot of these people are known to me either as family or community family. I am male and there seems to be equal numbers of males and females around. I like the living environment. The building that I am in seems to be a community house where all of us lived. The house is much longer than it is wide. A large group of people are gathered around the fireplace, which is on my left, and are involved in some sort of game or entertainment. There is lots of jostling and laughing going on.

I am a big guy and I meander over to another male off to himself at one of the eating tables on the right side of the room. He is huddled, keeping away from the frivolity going on near the fireplace. I go over to him and mockingly challenge him by giving him a shove on his shoulder. He just grunts a mock growl back, so I push at him a little harder. I am not worried since I am his brother and I just want him to know that I care. The second shove gets his attention so he turns to look at me and our eyes lock. When they do, I know the individual as my father in this life. The me in the dream stares at him. My father does not physically look in the dream as he looks in this life, but the energy in his eyes leaves no doubt as to who he is. In an instant, my point of view changes from being in the dream to watching the dream. As I watch, I repeat over and over to myself, "Dad? . . . Dad? . . . Dad?"

I fade off, watching the two individuals in the dream interacting with each other. In the morning I awaken, totally surprised by the dream.[8]

"It was very eerie to see my father's eyes in another individual," said Tom. "He had always considered himself a loner in this life, which was very consistent with the personality of the dream figure. I told my dad of the dream. He listened and appeared thoughtful and seemed to think the dream was as eerie as I did."

No location was readily apparent in the dream, but Tom said that it felt Nordic or Scandinavian. Although Tom has long had a curiosity about those cultures, he has never visited that part of the world and knows little about its history. Several years after this dream, Tom learned that in the Middle Ages, people lived in long houses such as he saw in his dream. The medieval period may also match the clothing and animal skins that the dream people were dressed in.

For Tom, the dream illuminated the relationship with his father, fostering a sense of kinship that transcended time. "The dream did help me to understand his personality," he said. "There were a lot of characteristics in him that seemed to also be in the dream figure. Overall, the dream helped me understand my father a little better."

Love from Life to Life

When my husband and I met, we felt a strong past-life connection between us. Shortly after our engagement, I had a series of lucid dreams that were glimpses of past lives. One of the strongest was this.

I am a Polynesian woman, brown, with long, dark hair. I am very pregnant—close to delivery. I want to do something to honor the impending birth. I go down to the seashore at night under a full moon. Naked and alone, I wade into the warm water. It buoys me. I ride the incoming tide to shore. I do this over and over. The waves are big enough to carry me, but are not threatening to me; I know the water will support me, not overwhelm me. I hear and feel the water. Everything is very vivid, and I am filled with joy. An intoxicated or opiated feeling permeates the dream. I switch between being the woman and watching the woman but knowing that it is me.[9]

The Polynesian woman reminded me of a Gauguin painting of the women of Tahiti. I had never before recalled a dream in which I was someone of another race. Nor had I ever had a dream in which I was pregnant. The usual symbolic associations with emotions, creativity, and birthing something new in life did not fit, despite the fact of our impending marriage. I felt strongly that this was a past-life scene and that Tom had been my husband in that life, too.

I shared the dream with Tom. He told me that about a year prior to our meeting, he had a lucid dream in which a blonde woman (I am blonde) to whom he is very attracted changes into a Polynesian woman before his eyes.

We honeymooned in Hawaii, and before going, I wondered if I would have any past-life resonances there. Though we enjoyed our stay immensely, neither of us felt any clicks.

A few months later, an unexpected opportunity arose to visit New Zealand, a country neither of us had been to before. Immediately upon arrival, we felt very much at home there, as though we had returned to familiar territory. We were quickly drawn to the Maori culture. I thought about the dream. Had Tom and I shared a happy life along the shores of this spectacular land in the distant past?

Both of us feel that we had more than one life together in a variety of Pacific Islands. Tom continues to envision a much smaller island than New Zealand. Perhaps we will find it someday in our travels.

After the island-pregnancy dream, I had another dream that pointed to sharing numerous past lives with Tom.

Tom is bringing some boxes up from storage for me. They have been downstairs somewhere, like the downstairs of the house or a basement. The boxes are like my brown cardboard file boxes with lids, only they are all white. They do not contain any material things, but nonmaterial things. One contains love. Another contains emotions that are all pleasant: joy, happiness, etc. Now I can have easy access to them.

The dream has a specific tone, a feeling that is heavy and opiated. It hangs in the air like sweet and heavy perfume. The sensation is very pleasant, and I am briefly lucid in the dream, thinking that I must be sleeping very heavily, because the dream is so "dreamlike."

Finally, there is one box left to bring up but no apparent room to put it out. I am upset because I want access to this box, too. Tom assures me not to worry, there is room; he will arrange the other boxes so it will fit.

The label on the box is "Memories of the Past."[10]

The opiated tone of the dream was similar to the tone of the Polynesian dream. Tom, who is an astrologer, made the observation that his sun is in my twelfth house. The sun represents the self, the ego. The twelfth house is the house of the subconscious and unconscious. This configuration means that Tom naturally would illumine the unconscious for me, hence his bringing of the boxes up out of storage.

I also felt that now I could remove barriers to past-life recall. Bits and pieces began surfacing in more dreams as well as in spontaneous waking visions. The process continues, like fitting together pieces of a jigsaw puzzle.

Most dreams of past lives are not as dramatic as announcing dreams or as the traumatic dreams of victims of violence, such as the Holocaust. Most are fragments, little glimpses through a window of time, like Anne's scene of the doctor, or my dream of the pregnant Polynesian woman. But even these fragments help to fill our picture of the story of our soul. They help to show us that we are more than a single life, a single personality. They reveal the threads that weave the tapestry of the cosmos—a tapestry that is eternal and infinite.

chapter twenty-seven

FAR FUTURE DREAMING

OUR DREAMS ARE PLAYING AN IMPORTANT ROLE IN THE EVOLUTION OF BOTH OUR INDIVIDUAL AND COLLECTIVE CONSCIOUSNESSES. WE'VE OBSERVED IN THE WORLD OF NATURE THAT evolution does not follow an even track but makes large and sudden leaps. Numerous scenarios of the evolution of humanity have been put forward. Futurists such as Peter Russell, Kenneth Ring, Michael Grosso, and others generally agree with the theory that the pace of our evolution is increasing, driven by our own consciousness. Evolution is not something that happens to us; we create it. We are now poised on the edge of a major leap forward in the evolution of our consciousness.

Major leaps open the way for evolutionary transcendence, a new order of existence. The emergence of life from inorganic matter was one such transcendent leap, and the development of consciousness another. Future transcendent leaps will depend on the collective consciousness, as we learn that our beliefs, thoughts, and projection of will create and shape our reality, and as we also learn that we are inseparably part of a whole pattern. Our own self-reflective consciousness is leading an accelerating evolution: an inner evolution as well as an external one.

Where are we headed? The answer, according to all the mystical traditions, is back to God, or back to the Source. To this end, we are experiencing increased multidimensional awareness in the exceptional human experiences documented in the parapsychology, psychology, and medical literature. These come in the form of psi, out-of-body experiences, near-death experiences, UFO encounters, apparitions of the Virgin Mary, encounters with angels and other-worldly beings, and transcendent dreams. In fact, all of those can and do take place in the medium of dreams.

Dreaming for Survival of the Human Species

We think of our dreams as personal, relating just to us, but actually, they have a much larger role. Clinical psychologist and dream researcher Montague Ullman has advanced the hypothesis that our dreams are not concerned primarily with us as individuals but rather with the survival of the human species. Granted, we are the stars of our nightly shows, but if we look beyond the personal meanings of dreams, we see that they do address a larger social arena. Our dreams are brutally honest, telling us how we truly feel about ourselves and about life. They often concern our "disconnects," not only about our personal life but about societal issues, and how we as individuals are affected by those issues. Dreams reveal to us our state of connectedness to the whole of humanity and how we feel about it.

The human species has been so fragmented into different cultures and geographies that the survival of the whole is at risk, says Ullman.

[D]reams move us toward a more realistic assessment of the nature and depth of social disconnects that perpetuate the historically determined fragmentation that the human species has been subjected to down through the years. We've grown up differently in different cultures and different geographies evolved different races and so on. The species has been fragmented to the point where its survival as a species is at risk. I believe there is built into each of us, probably genetically, a concern with something larger than the self, namely, the preservation of the unity of the species.

. . . Dreams and dreamwork help us to realize we are more than we think we are. . . . [T]hey are all experiences of connections, which is the essence, in my opinion, of dream work. They rise out of this incorruptible core of our being that is sensitive to the needs of repairing and maintaining connections.[1]

Dreamwork, especially in groups, can bring fresh perspectives to how we should deal with collective concerns.

The model of David Bohm's implicate order supports this hypothesis of dreams as necessary for survival of the species. If the universe is indivisible and dreams emanate from a collective source, then the primary purpose of a dream does concern survival—and evolution—of the whole. Ullman has posited that the wisdom that flows into our dreams may come from the implicate order—the infinite source. Perhaps dreams then are a bridge, a natural transformation of the implicate order into the explicate: the invisible and spiritual moving into the visible and material.

Michael Talbot commented in *The Holographic Universe*:

If Ullman is correct in this supposition it stands the traditional psychoanalytic view of dreams on its ear, for instead of dream content being something that ascends into consciousness from a primitive substratum of the personality, quite the opposite would be true.[2]

Precisely. However, it is neither one nor the other, but both. As we have seen, dreams are both upwellings of contents from the personal and archetypal realms and expansions into the realm of the spiritual. Dreams are both ordinary, revolving around personal matters and the physical plane, and nonordinary, dealing with expansion of consciousness into otherworldly realms. I believe that the nonordinary content of dreams is increasing as part of the evolution of human consciousness. As more of us experience this kind of dreaming and acknowledge and work with it, we add to the acceleration of the evolution.

We find the same idea in Aboriginal Dreamtime: We must dream in order to know our connection to a greater whole and to realize our role and responsibility in it.

Full and Conscious Living

One of the purposes of dreaming is to help us live more consciously, and that is part of our overall evolution. Physicist Fred Alan Wolf observes that our dreams influence us whether we remember them or not. Unremembered, they enter life as patterns, and we live unconsciously. Ironically, we sleep through life. If we remember dreams—if we dream consciously—then we live consciously, too. The energy flows between the implicate order and the explicate order.

What does it mean to live consciously? It means acquiring self-knowledge and a sense of one's place in the larger scheme of things. It means realizing one's potential. It means allowing the flower of life to open to its fullest. Perhaps the simplest answer is this: to live consciously is to enjoy the journey.

Willis Harman, metaphysician and author, was known to thousands for his work as president of the Institute of Noetic Sciences (IONS) in Sausalito, California. IONS was founded as a research and educational organization by astronaut Edgar Mitchell, who had a peak experience of transcendence while on the moon in 1972. For Harman, a spontaneous out-of-body experience as a young man changed his metaphysical worldview and influenced him to devote a lifetime to investigate the frontiers of inner space.

Prior to his death in 1996, Harman recorded a series of three dreams that laid groundwork for the transition from physical life but also spoke volumes about conscious living.

In the first dream I am walking along over rough terrain, on the way to climb a high and rather forbidding mountain, the top of which is concealed by mist and clouds. It is clear that the ascent of this mountain symbolizes my whole life. Clambering over the rubble in front of me is not too daunting, but as I look ahead I see that my way is blocked by several cliffs that appear to be around ten feet high. Beyond those are some still higher cliffs, the farthest being perhaps hundreds of feet high. I have no idea how I will deal with those when I get to them, but meanwhile there seems nothing to do but forge ahead. However, although I didn't know notice it at first, I am growing in stature as I go along, so that by the time I finally reach the ten-foot cliffs I am tall enough that I can simply step up over them. The same with the hundred-foot cliffs.

In the second dream I am in a cafeteria. I take a tray, place it on the rails, and proceed to move down the food line. At the end of the line is a door. Somehow I realize that this also symbolizes my life, and the door at the end is what we call death. Behind the food line is a gigantic figure who is ladling out the food; I can't see his head, he towers so far above me. I notice that the persons in the line on either side of me have trays with large round holes in the middle, so that the food simply falls through the holes onto the floor. This seems to me a strange way to run a cafeteria, and I ask the food ladler about it. He replies that the food is available to everyone, and the choice of tray is optional; some people just choose the trays with holes.

In the third dream I am in a solo spaceship which has somehow become a derelict, destined to travel around the Earth for centuries. There is no way to deflect its orbit and manage a return to Earth. It is clear that I have only two choices. I can stay alive as long as possible, eventually run out of air, food, and water, and die a slow death. Or I can open the hatch and let the remaining air rush out, the cold come in, and have it all over within seconds. It is an agonizing decision, but I finally decide on the latter. I open the hatch and feel the air rushing past, and immediately find myself in a space which is not cold and black, but wonderfully illuminated and somehow "loving." I seem to be everywhere in this space, and nowhere in particular. I had never given the idea of heaven much thought, but this seems to fit. I feel intensely alive, supported in every sense, and totally content to stay here forever.[3]

Evolution of Archetypes

Although archetypes exist apart from our individual experiences, our experiences influence archetypes. As we transform and grow, we help the archetypes to grow as well. Dreamwork offers one of the best avenues for access to the archetypal realm. As dream researcher Jeremy Taylor states, so-called ordinary people do the psychospiritual work of evolution on themselves and on archetypes on a daily basis.

This "individual influence on the archetypes" may not be overwhelming or decisive in any single instance, but I believe that in encounters of this kind the whole species, and by implication the entire cosmos (since everything is alive and profoundly interconnected), is brought to fuller development and self-awareness.[4]

Taylor says that an archetype of crucial importance in the evolution of both individual and collective consciousness is that of the "Willing Sacrifice." The Willing Sacrifice is the Divine. It often begins in animal form and develops into human form. It is characterized by conscious self-awareness, intelligence, curiosity, courage, creativity, and compassion—all hallmarks of the paradigm shift of consciousness.

Apocalyptic Dreaming

David (pseudonym) had a vivid, recurring dream that greatly disturbed him every time upon awakening.

A huge tidal wave engulfs our city and many people die. I am caught up in flood waters and struggle to stay afloat. Somehow I know it is the end of the world. The ground is shaking and is going to tear apart. I'm going to die . . . everyone is going to die. I think, "So this is it—this is how it ends."[5]

The dream seemed incredibly real. Finally, David shared his dream with his wife, who told him she had had a similar dream of the city being swept over in a tidal wave, with mass destruction. Their dreams made them more aware of end-of-the-world scenarios popularized in the media. They heard of people having prophetic dreams forecasting great cataclysms. They read about dreams predicting earthquakes that had come true. What was more worrisome, others they knew in their city also were having various dreams of disasters. What if it were true that the coastal city in which they were living would be drowned in the not-too-distant future?

David and his wife decided to move inland to another city in one of the "safe zones" they'd read about in end-of-the-world popular literature. However, people there were also having disaster dreams. Was no place safe?

As I mentioned earlier, dreams of great disasters often mirror inner psychic upheavals related to events in our own lives. In dreams, death is a metaphor for change and renewal. Such personal circumstances do account for some doomsday dreams, in which the dreamer perceives their entire world threatened by catastrophe. But other doomsday dreams address a collective process.

In the waning years of the twentieth century, apocalyptic dreaming has increased, fueled in part by media attention on the alleged end of the world some time between 2000 and 2025, depending on the prophecy, and also by collected reports of NDEs, in which experiencers were shown visions of a coming end to the world. Perhaps the biggest boost came from the collective unconscious, wherein resides an archetype of death and resurrection that is triggered by cycles of time.

Within the last 2,000 years, nearly every decade has had dates that have been prophesied for the imminent end of the world.

Some predictions have aroused sufficient panic to cause people to abandon their homes and possessions and even to commit suicide—all for naught, since the dates keep coming and going without cataclysmic end. In recent decades, a proliferation of NDE and UFO contact literature filled with predictions of the world's end, which experiencers were shown or told, called for cataclysms or nuclear holocaust by the end of the 1980s, by the late 1990s, or into the early years of the twenty-first century.

Historically, there has always been little agreement as to just when the world will come to an end, assuming that it will end. Of course, our little planet will come to its demise when our sun dies, but that astronomical event is millions of years away.

Many Christians put stock in Christ's second coming for 2000, based on biblical interpretations that each of the seven days God spent making the world equals 1000 years, and the year 2000 marks the sixth millennium since the time of Adam. After rains of plague, vermin, destruction, and a great heavenly war between the forces of light and dark, Satan would be bound and the martyrs would rule with Christ untroubled. After another 1000 years, Satan would make a brief reappearance before being dispatched by God, and a new heaven and a new earth would emerge.

The Mayans predicted 2012 for the end of the world. The Hopi added another twenty-five years beyond that, give or take a little, before a world war ushered in the Great Day of Purification, and the earth would be purged by fire. The famed Nostradamus, sixteenth-century French clairvoyant and physician, gave us at least until 3797, the final year of his prophecies. But the last years of the 1990s would be ruined by nuclear war and great natural disasters such as earthquakes, droughts, famine, and volcanic eruptions, according to Nostradamus.

Other doomsday scenarios exist in which the present world collapses and a new world is born, usually with the help of a hero or savior figure.

Many dreams of these apocalyptic events are terrifyingly real and filled with urgency. How much attention should we pay to them? Are they truly prophetic, or are they metaphors for something more personal?

The Messiah and the Beast

The apocalyptic dream resides as a powerful psychic force in the collective unconscious. In *Dreaming the End of the World: Apocalypse as a Rite of Passage,* author Michael Ortiz Hill characterizes these dreams as a Messiah/Beast complex, arising from the biblical image of Christ as savior subduing the Satanic Beast so that a new world of the resurrected can be born. The images have shifted on down through the centuries, but the core essence remains the same. In modern terms, the Beast has become the nuclear bomb. The existence of the Bomb, a threat that can annihilate us all, has scarred us deeply with fears that bubble up through dreams.

Adding to this (but not included in Hill's study) are the New Age fears of cataclysmic earth changes and end-of-the-world prophecies, which, we are told, are the products of our own selfish abuse and pollution of the earth.

Although nuclear terrorism is still a threat, and our pollution of the planet continues to take a serious toll, I believe that apocalyptic dreams point to the emergence of a new paradigm of consciousness rather than to a literal end of the world. This emergence is akin to a rebirth (the Messiah), and thus requires a death—the death of the old consciousness (the Beast).

These dreams point to a healing process taking place within the collective psyche of humanity. The collective is breaking through to us on an individual level to call us to the need to heal inner wounds and our disconnection from each other. The Beast cannot be healed by demonization or vilification, but by love. As Hill observes, ". . . it is abundantly clear that healing the dream of the apocalypse depends on descending into the Beast's lair with tenderness of heart, surrendering our inflated conceptions of ourselves and learning how to live peaceably with the wildness of nature—and even of human nature."[6]

Apocalypse As Initiation

Going within to confront the Beast is akin to the mythological descent into the underworld as a rite of initiation. Indeed, says Hill, our dreams of apocalypse fall into the three stages of initiation. First is the death of the old, which in apocalyptic dreams appears as chaos, disaster, upheaval, poisoned surroundings, mutant beings and creatures, looking for but not finding refuge, and children (the emerging new) needing safety. Second is the initiation itself, which appears in dreams as saving others, defeating those who would wreak havoc, a marriage of opposites (from which the sacred is born), and the dawning of new light. Third is the return to the world in rebirth, in which the initiate brings gifts to the world. This stage appears in dreams as compassionate helping of others, restoration of the environment, rebuilding, feasts of plenty, and so on. Here we find the archetype of the "Willing Sacrifice" described by Taylor.

Any one person may not have all three stages of apocalyptic dreams, but perhaps experience one stage. In the face of collective fears of doomsday, stage-one dreams are prevalent in a population. The following are some examples of the different stages.

Stage 1: A desolate world. Russell dreamed of moving through time, first backward to view a more verdant earth, and then forward to view a more desolate world populated with mutant creatures.

I dreamed that I could go backward and forward in time. This concept was shown to me by guide(s) unknown who stayed in the background but whose presence I knew but did not see.

1. I saw a scale, something like a ruler with markings. I then saw a scene I knew to be in the past somewhere in the period 1200–1500 and perhaps in England. I saw verdant hills and fields and yeoman and peasants working the land. I saw this all from above looking down over the land. The scale appears in the present, in Washington, D.C. From this point on, I see devastation and complete ruin: no buildings, no green, total upheaval such as at a construction site. Years, tens of thousands of years pass, and I see the land erode and change as nearby hilly areas are eroded nearly level. Maybe 70,000 years have passed into the future. There are no people about. Then, gradually, vegetation appears. I see buildings, barns, etc., in rural areas, green land, verdant as before. At first there are no people about, and I look for them. At this thought, people appear. They see me but do not acknowledge me. They have odd, golden to golden green–colored eyes.

2. The scene changes and I see holes being drilled and undrilled in rock. There is no drill present. A silvery, metallic creature comes out of the drill hole. It appears mercurial, like a rising column. I grab it and it writhes in my hands. I am not afraid, but I've had enough, and I pass the creature on to a coworker from my workplace.

Interpretation:

I really thought this was an instruction from the unseen guide(s) who seemed to be telling me that I (we?) are multidimensional and that time is a two-way movement as easily manipulated as walking back and forth on the ground. This is not my personal philosophy, but I consider the "demonstration" interesting. The future people may be a different race of man. I suspect they are telepathic, perhaps a humbled race much more in touch with themselves.

As regards to the destruction, I've heard that a lot in discussion groups, but I have no personal fears. I've felt for some time that something was up, and destruction is one possibility that I've considered. But, frankly, I haven't felt this peaceful internally for years as I've been lately. Perhaps it's acceptance of whatever is unavoidable. Interesting about the mass suicide of thirty-nine people in California [the Heaven's Gate cult, which believed in a coming doom and interpreted the appearance of the Hale-Bopp Comet in 1997 as a heavenly sign that it was time for them to shed their bodies]. The cult suicides spoke of the earth being "spaded under." That's pretty much what I envisioned.

I have no explanation for the silver creature. In reviewing my notes, I note a copper-based creature, again in the future, in a dream [ten days later].

Russell's second dream was:

There were these copper-based entities that didn't like people. They looked sort of like short lengths of fat noodles, perhaps three to four feet long. (Note: This is about the size of the silvery creature I mentioned; however, these were more rubbery sort of like semi-Gumbys if you can envision them, while the silvery creature was like a living column of mercury.) They evolved from acid-based (sulfuric acid came to mind in this dream—this acid is common in some polluted waters and of course there is the ever-present acid rains) environments of the future. People watched carefully where they went in the wilds because they seemed to be in pockets or groupings and not found throughout (origins: toxic waste dump areas?). I saw one entity throw a portrait (painting) into the rapids of a river. A person rose out of the water to grab the painting. The person was then hauled out of the water and tortured by the entity(s). I also saw a child being bothered by of these creatures. However, by sprinkling the kid's head with baking powder the entity(s) could be repelled.

My overall reaction to this dream is that this is payback for polluting the earth. These entities arose out of environmental pollution and the results are in the future.

I am not an environmentalist (although I am a gardener) and have no real ax to grind. The fishing-for-humans scene with a painting (vanity for bait?) tossed into the water is perhaps nature's reversal of mankind's torture of the environment.[7]

Russell wondered if his dreams might be in part a product of the periodic doomsday stirrings in the mass consciousness. "I can't believe that something like these thoughts of apprehension didn't occur around 999 A.D. as well," he said.

Russell is right in his observation that these images arise periodically in the collective. Nonetheless, they do bring great potential for change and healing. In Russell's dreams, the destruction has already taken place. The creatures of the earth are mutated. People are significantly changed: They are humble and telepathic, implying that their spiritual/psychic faculties have opened. The child being bothered by the entity is symbolic of the new struggling to gain dominance.

Stage 2: Initiation. Hill gives this dream from one of his interview subjects.

I am the General, a gentleman/saint who presides over the apocalypse—calm and benevolent; everyone wants to negotiate with me. In each of my hands, I hold a sheaf of wheat.[8]

Here the dreamer is both destroyer and savior, the General, who presides over the apocalypse, with the power to go either way. The dream augurs healing and opens the way for stage 3 in the image of the General as benevolent gentleman/saint, and in the wheat he holds in both hands. The hands symbolize opposites: one represents salvation and one represents destruction. Either way brings healing, represented by the wheat, a symbol of resurrection and rebirth. The wheat also makes a direct connection to the earth and to the descent into the underworld. It is associated with Ceres/Demeter, the goddess of the grain, whose daughter Kore/Persephone is kidnaped and raped by Hades/Pluto. The goddess in her despair brings winter to the earth and descends into the underworld to try to rescue her daughter. Mother and daughter are tricked by Hades/Pluto. The fate of Kore/Persephone is to spend six months with her mother and six months in the underworld, thus establishing the seasons. The descent is the confrontation with the Beast. The Beast cannot be made to disappear—it must be integrated.

Stage 3: Bringing the Gifts. Roxanne Bonnette is among many who feel their dreams are helping to prepare them for life in the new world. She learned how to lucid dream following a car accident that left her in great pain. The accident was a turning point in her life. For relief from the pain, she turned to craniosacral work, a type of body work that involves releasing blockages to the flow of cerebral spinal fluid. Roxanne now is a craniosacral therapist. Her lucid dreams began when she was a patient herself. Some of the dreams happened while she was "out" on the body work table.

I started having dreams about healing myself. One of the first was a golden pyramid coming up out of sand saying, "Keep a journal, keep a journal." It kept at me until I said, "Okay." As soon as I agreed, I flew past the pyramid to the Sphinx. It was completely surrounded by lush green countryside. There was an arena with a stone table. The Sphinx spoke to me and said, "Welcome back, my daughter." Then it told me telepathically that I knew all the herbs I needed to have and that I had the healing touch. I could heal with my intention and love. The Sphinx talked to me about releasing my fears. I did, and my body became more relaxed. I saw myself with three other priestesses and a high priest. Each of us had our role—mine was herbs and healing.

In another dream, the Sphinx came to me while I was on the body work table and told me that the doors of the great mystery school were going to be opened to me soon, and to others that I will be with. He told me about the Seven Sisters. He said I would know each one of them when they would come into my life. We would all recognize each other. There was going to be some sort of need for each one of our individual skills. Each one of the Seven Sisters would in turn have seven sisters, and we would become a giant web. I also saw times of great distress on the earth. I had just read The Celestine Prophecy. *I thought I was going to transmute. The Sphinx said, "No, some people have to stay behind and help the others. You'll all be okay. Your responsibility is to dispel fears."*

At that point, I had never heard of the Pleiaides, or the Seven Sisters. Later, I had a vision of three blue beings, very bright, with big eyes, no nose, and no mouth. They were talking with me on the table, laughing and giggling. They said, "We think you're ready now." They took me to a past life when I was an old woman living in a manor house, somewhere in Europe. I was happy and content and had had a full life. I was ready to go. I had my loved ones around me. I died. Suddenly I saw myself floating in a dark void, not scary. Gradually, I could see things. I was traveling in space with beings. They said, "Go ahead, think of someplace you want to be or something you want to know about." I thought about the Anasazi; I always wondered what happened to them. Then I was in the Southwest. I was a man warrior, and I was with another man, and we were hunting. Then I thought of Cleopatra and suddenly I was on the Nile. The beings were laughing. I asked if I could see where they lived. Then I was in a crystal chamber like a giant stadium, with a large crystal pyramid and some smaller ones around. The big pyramid gave off a pure white light and the others were different colors. The pyramids would change into beings with robes. I wanted to go inside the pyramid, but they said no, I had seen enough for one day. They told me to be patient.

When I have these lucid dreams, I think I'm tapping into something on a higher consciousness level, that I've always known but have forgotten. The message I keep getting is that I have my own power. I don't have to keep looking outside of myself for it. I don't need to seek, I just need to remember. For the first time in my life, I believe in myself. I am centered and balanced and focused in the moment. This is what all of us have to do. We've been living too long in our insecurities and fears. Life as we know it is coming to an end, but real life is eternal.[9]

When the consciousness paradigm shifts, the world will not be the same. Some people will adjust easily, others will not.

Soul of the World

The consciousness that emerges from passage through apocalyptic dreaming is reconnection to the *anima mundi,* or world soul, the animating force that unites the world and forms the web of unified consciousness. This is what the Messiah represents, says Hill.

The Messiah strikes me as a truly transpersonal presence that gathers the plurality of self and world into a field of peaceable relatedness. Not "of this world" in a personalized sense, the Messiah embodies the soul of the world that lends everything its coherence. In that respect the Messiah seems to come from "elsewhere" the moment we perceive that the world has a soul.[10]

This perception of the world soul will enable us to transform the earth, which is our true purpose, according to Rudolph Steiner.

[W]e must transform the earth by implanting in it what we discover of the spiritual realm. Our task is the transformation of the earth. Therein lies the only reason for seeking higher knowledge. The earth as we know it with our senses depends on the spiritual world, and this means that we can truly work on the earth only if we share in those worlds where creative forces are concealed. This realization should be our only motivation for wanting to ascend to higher worlds.[11]

A Global NDE

Apocalyptic dreaming is part of a larger picture of collective transformation that is under way. Philosopher Michael Grosso likens the transformation to a global NDE that incorporates individual NDEs; encounters with UFOs, alien beings, and angels; and visions of the Virgin Mary. Many of the exceptional experiences are apocalyptic in nature, containing messages of dire warnings to humanity to change its ways or else suffer dreadful consequences. We are sensing a probable future and are evolving accordingly. Grosso observes:

[W]e are all summoned to be magi, to form a network of magi, to hazard the desert and follow where strange stars lead. These lights that flash from the heaven of Mind At Large inspire us to say farewell to the old, the life-denying self. They give us glimpses of where we could go and charge us with the energy to go there. The function of the visions is pretty much the same: to grant courage to change in the heart and soul, to sacrifice the gift of ourselves to the infant god or our own higher future. They help us to make the final choice, to take the leap beyond death to new life.[12]

The apocalypse associates the serpent with the Beast, which Grosso says "puts us at odds with the best part of ourselves."[13] The serpent, as we saw earlier, is a universal symbol of wisdom, regeneration, creativity, and the life force. Here is another reason why we cannot simply vanquish the Beast; to do so would be to cut ourselves off from this vital essence. The only way to free ourselves from the Beast (and what Jung would call the shadow) is to integrate this side of our being.

Our dreams are playing a valuable role in this evolution of transformation by showing us the need for change and healing and how to accomplish it.

The Dream of Humanity

The evolution of our consciousness is pulling us more and more into the realization and experience of our interconnectedness. This is the "noogenesis," or growth of the collective human mind within the biosphere of Earth, envisioned by Pierre Teilhard de Chardin (1881–1955); the "supramental mind" envisioned by Sri Aurobindo (1872–1950); and other similar states of group integrated consciousness described by other mystics, futurists, and philosophers.

In these scenarios, all living organisms evolve toward their highest expression. In the human being, evolution becomes conscious of itself, which speeds the very process of evolution. Teilhard saw human consciousness becoming increasingly collective, fusing with the consciousness of other living things and the very planet itself. The ultimate goal, he said, is the "Omega point" at which human consciousness finds the ultimate cosmic integrity and unity. (In theological terms, the Omega point is the Christ consciousness.)

Aurobindo saw humanity at a crossroads in its evolution, and at a crisis of transformation as well. The supramental mind is an expanded consciousness, a Truth-Consciousness that embraces the Divine in the All. Our evolution calls us to bring the Divine into the realm of matter. This process eventually will change not only our consciousness, but our bodies as well—we will become more etherealized, more like energy. But we are likely not to achieve that, he said, if we do not consciously participate in the spiritual process.

Precisely what will happen to us as we evolve is still an open question. It is clear, however, that our exceptional human experiences and awareness of nonordinary realities are changing us in profound ways. In the not-too-distant future, we are likely to be more psychic, more mystical, more creative, more compassionate and loving, and more filled with vitality—if we become conscious co-creators in our evolution.

Dreams are one of our most important tools for facilitating this evolution. The inner world of the dream can help us experience the renewal and creative power to transform the outer world. Dreams are a true direct experience of God—a nightly call of the divine. Dreams are accessible to all persons, regardless of station in life.

The dream is not just an encounter with the divine but also a metaphor for our ability to be visionaries—to dream the big dreams that advance civilization. We must honor our dreams. We must see them not from just a self-serving standpoint but from a transpersonal standpoint as well. Every dream contains elements of the voice of God, some more so than others. When we attune our inner ear more to that voice, we realize ourselves on a higher level and move closer to merge with the One.

As H. G. Wells said in *The Dream*, "It was a life . . . and it was a dream, a dream within this life; and this life too is a dream. Dreams within dreams, dreams containing dreams, until we come at last, maybe, to the Dreamer of all dreams, the Being who is all beings."[14]

NOTES

1. The Divine Gift of Dreams

1. Morton Kelsey, *God, Dreams and Revelation: A Christian Interpretation of Dreams* (Minneapolis: Augsburg Publishing House, 1991), p. 33.
2. Joel Covitz, *Visions of the Night: A Study of Jewish Dream Interpretation* (Boston: Shambhala, 1990), p. 10.
3. Kelsey, op.cit, pp. 136–137.
4. *Ibid.*, p. 156.

2. The Renaissance of the Dream

1. Carl Jung, *Memories, Dreams, Reflections* (New York: Vintage Books, 1965), p. 12.
2. *Ibid.*, p. 15.
3. *Ibid.*, p. 160.
4. *Ibid.*
5. *Ibid.*, p. 306.
6. *Ibid.*, p. 5.
7. For a detailed account of how White's accident was transformed from an exceptional experience to an EHE, see the *Journal of Near-Death Studies*, Vol. 16, No. 3.

8. Rhea A. White, "The Influence of Four Dreams over a Period of 35 Years," submitted for publication.
9. Pioneer dream researcher Montague Ullman points out the psychodynamic features that are found in both EHES and dreams in general in an article in the *ASPR Newsletter,* Vol. 18, No. 4.

3. *Inner Alchemy*

1. Jung, *op. cit.*, p. 204.
2. *Ibid.*, p. 203.
3. Private communication to author.
4. Tony Crisp, *Do You Dream?* (New York: E. P. Dutton, 1972), p. 150.

4. *Psi in Dreams*

1. Private communication to author.
2. *Ibid.*
3. *Ibid.*
4. *Ibid.*
5. *Ibid.*

5. *Out-of-Body Dream Travel*

1. Michael Talbot, *The Holographic Universe* (New York: HarperCollins, 1991), pp. 272–273*n*.
2. Private communication to author.
3. *Ibid.*
4. *Ibid.*

6. *Lucid Dreams*

1. Stephen LaBerge, *Lucid Dreaming* (New York: Ballantine Books, 1985), pp. 21–22.
2. Private communication to author.
3. Author's dream journal.
4. Private communication to author.
5. *Forty Dreams of St. John Bosco* (Rockford, Ill.: TAN Books and Publishers, 1996), pp. xi–xii.
6. *Ibid.*, pp. 2–5.

7. Stephen LaBerge and Howard Rheingold, *Exploring the World of Lucid Dreaming* (New York: Ballantine Books, 1990), p. 121.
8. Author's dream journal.
9. G. Scott Sparrow, *Lucid Dreaming: Dawning of the Clear Light* (Virginia Beach, Va.: private press, 1997), p. 7.
10. Private communication to author.

7. Sharing the Dreamscape with Others

1. Monford Harris, *Studies in Jewish Dream Interpretation* (Northvale, N.J.: Jason Aronson, Inc., 1994), p. 26.
2. Private communication to author.
3. Linda Lane Magallón, *Mutual Dreaming* (New York: Pocket Books, 1997), p. 50.
4. *Ibid.*, pp. 88–89.
5. Harold Sherman, *Thoughts through Space* (Amherst, Wis.: Amherst Press, 1983), p. 160.

8. The Language of Symbols

1. Author's dream journal.
2. Private communication to author.
3. *Ibid.*
4. Author's dream journal.
5. Private communication to author.
6. Author's dream journal.
7. Morton Kelsey, *op. cit.*, pp. 116–117.
8. Author's dream journal.

9. Interpreting Dreams

1. Jung, *op. cit.*, pp. 161–162.
2. Private communication to author.
3. *Ibid.*
4. Morton Kelsey, *Dreams: A Way to Listen to God* (New York: Paulist Press, 1978), p. 37.
5. Edward B. Bynum, *Families and the Interpretation of Dreams* (New York: Harrington Park Press, 1993), p. 192.

10. The Ancient Art of Dream Incubation

1. Gayle Delaney, *Living Your Dreams,* rev. ed. (San Francisco: Harper & Row, 1988), p. 26.
2. Private communication to author.
3. Geraldine Pinch, *Magic in Ancient Egypt* (London: British Museum Press, 1994), p. 68.
4. Wallis Budge, *Egyptian Magic* (New Hyde Park, N.Y.: University Books, n.d. First published 1899), pp. 216–217.
5. Private communication to author.

11. The Meaning of Colors

1. The significance of the number three is explained in chapter 12.

12. The Power of Numbers

1. Paul Meier and Robert Wise, *Windows of the Soul* (Nashville: Thomas Nelson, 1995), pp. 166–167.
2. Author's dream journal.
3. Private communication to author.

13. Messages from Animals

1. Private communication to author.
2. Paul Meier and Robert Wise, *op. cit.*, pp.104–105.
3. Private communication to author.
4. Author's dream journal.
5. Roger Jahnke, "The Six Pillars of Healing," *Venture Inward,* March–April 1996, p. 18.
6. Private communication to author.
7. *Ibid.*

15. Dreams That Heal

1. Carl Jung, *op. cit.*, p. 68.
2. Patricia Garfield, *The Healing Power of Dreams* (New York: Simon & Schuster, 1991), p. 17.
3. Stephen LaBerge and Howard Rheingold, *op. cit.*, p. 226.
4. Private communication to author.
5. *Ibid.*

6. *Ibid.*
7. *Ibid.*
8. *Ibid.*

16. Enhancing Creativity

1. Heyoka Merrifield, *Sacred Art Sacred Earth* (Inchelium, Wash.: Rain Bird Publishers, 1993), p. 50.
2. *Ibid.*, p. 31.
3. *Ibid.*, pp. 31–32.
4. *Ibid.*, p. 88.
5. Private communication to author.
6. *Ibid.*

17. Getting Guidance

1. Carol W. Parrish-Harra, *Messengers of Hope* (Sparrow Hawk Village, Okla.: Sparrow Hawk Press, 1983), pp. 126–127.
2. Private communication to author.
3. Author's dream journal.
4. Private communication to author.
5. *Ibid.*
6. Neal Vahle, *Torch-Bearer to Light the Way: The Life of Myrtle Fillmore* (Mill Valley, Calif.: Open View Press, 1996), pp. 64–65.
7. Private communication to author.
8. *Ibid.*
9. *Ibid.*

18. Voices of Authority

1. Evelyn Underhill, *Mysticism* (New York: New American Library, 1974), p. 276.
2. Susan E. Mehrtens, "Exceptional Human Experience 15: Guidance Dreams, A Life Reoriented by 'Voice Over Dreams,'" *Exceptional Human Experience*, Vol. 11, No. 1, June 1993, pp. 33–37.
3. Private communication to author.

19. Turning Points

1. Private communication to author.
2. *Ibid.*
3. Private communication to author, excerpts of a paper by Beverly Rubik presented to the "International Conference on the Study of Shamanism and Alternate Modes of Healing" in Phoenix in 1996.

20. Spiritual Awakenings

1. Rudolph Steiner, *How to Know Higher Worlds* (Hudson, N.Y.: Anthroposophic Press, 1994), p. 163.
2. Private communication to author.
3. *Ibid.*
4. *Ibid.*

21. Working with Masters and Guides

1. Private communication to author.
2. *The Nag Hammadi Library,* James Robinson, general editor (San Francisco: Harper & Row, 1988), p. 46.
3. Tony Crisp, *op. cit.*, pp. 153–154.
4. Author's dream journal.
5. *Ibid.*
6. Private communication to author.
7. Rudolph Steiner, *op. cit.*, p. 72.
8. Author's dream journal.
9. Private communication to author.
10. *Ibid.*

22. Encounters with Angels

1. Private communication to author.
2. *Ibid.*
3. *Ibid.*
4. Private communication to author.

23. Contact with the Dead

1. Private communication to author.
2. *Ibid.*

3. *Ibid.*
4. Maggie Callahan and Patricia Kelley, *Final Gifts* (New York: Bantam Books, 1993), p. 233.
5. Private communication to author.
6. *Ibid.*
7. Bill Guggenheim and Judy Guggenheim, *Hellow from Heaven!* (New York: Bantam Books, 1996), p. 126.
8. Private communication to author.
9. *Ibid.*
10. *Ibid.*
11. *Ibid.*
12. *Ibid.*
13. Author's dream journal.

24. Dreams of the Other Side

1. Carl Jung, *op. cit.*, p. 305.
2. Neal Vahle, *op. cit.*, pp. 64–65.
3. Private communication to author.
4. Robert A. Monroe, *Journeys out of the Body* (Garden City, N.Y.: Anchor Books, 1973), pp. 80–81.
5. Robert A. Monroe, *The Ultimate Journey* (New York: Doubleday, 1994), p. 239.
6. *Ibid.*, p. 239.
7. Private communication to author.
8. *Ibid.*
9. *Forty Dreams of St. John Bosco, op. cit.*, pp. 60–69.

25. Encounters with Death

1. Private communication to author.
2. Kenneth Ring, *Heading Toward Omega: In Search of the Meaning of the Near-Death Experience* (New York: William Morrow, 1984), pp. 72–73.
3. Private communication with author.

26. Past Lives and Loves

1. Carl Jung, *op. cit.*, p. 319.
2. Ian Stevenson, *Children Who Remember Previous Lives* (Charlottesville, Va.: University Press of Virginia, 1987), p. 51.

3. Charles F. Emmons, *Chinese Ghosts and ESP* (Metuchen, N.J.: The Scarecrow Press, 1982), p. 9.
4. Ian Stevenson, *Reincarnation and Biology: A Contribution to the Etiology of Birthmarks and Birth Defects* (Westport, Conn.: Praeger, 1997), p. 727.
5. Rabbi Yonan Gershom, *Beyond the Ashes: Cases of Reincarnation from the Holocaust* (Virginia Beach, Va.: A.R.E. Press, 1992), pp. 18–19.
6. *Ibid.*, pp. 20–23.
7. Private communication to author.
8. *Ibid.*
9. Author's dream journal.
10. *Ibid.*

27. Far Future Dreaming

1. Montague Ullman, "Dreams as Exceptional Human Experiences" (*ASPR Newsletter*, Vol. XVIII, No. 4, 1995) p. 6.
2. Michael Talbot, *op. cit.*, p. 63.
3. Obtained from the Institute of Noetic Sciences, Sausalito, California.
4. Jeremy Taylor, *Where People Fly and Water Runs Uphill* (New York: Warner Books, 1992), p. 242.
5. Private communication to author.
6. Michael Ortiz Hill, *Dreaming the End of the World: Apocalypse as a Rite of Passage* (Dallas: Spring Publications, 1994), p. 44.
7. Private communication to author.
8. Michael Ortiz Hill, *op. cit.*, p. 103.
9. Private communication to author.
10. Michael Ortiz Hill, *op. cit.*, p. 140.
11. Rudolph Steiner, *op. cit.*, pp. 175–176.
12. Michael Grosso, *The Final Choice* (Walpole, N.H.: Stillpoint Publishing, 1985), p. 314.
13. Michael Grosso, *The Millennium Myth: Love and Death at the End of Time* (Wheaton, Ill.: Quest Books, 1995), p. 357.
14. Joseph Head and S. L. Cranston, *Reincarnation in World Thought* (New York: The Julian Press, 1967), p. 354.

BIBLIOGRAPHY AND RECOMMENDED BOOKS ABOUT DREAMS

Azam, Umar. *Dreams in Islam.* Pittsburgh, Pa.: Dorrance Publishing Co., 1992.

Baylis, Janice Hinshaw. *Sex, Symbols & Dreams.* Seal Beach, Calif.: Sun, Man, Moon, Inc., 1997.

———. *Christophers' Dreams: Dreaming and Living with AIDS.* New York: Delta, 1997.

Bosnak, Robert. *Tracks in the Wilderness of Dreaming.* New York: Delacorte Press, 1996.

———. ed. *Among All These Dreamers: Essays on Dreaming and Modern Society.* Albany, N.Y.: State University of New York, 1996.

Bulkeley, Kelly. *Spiritual Dreaming: A Cross-Cultural and Historical Journey.* New York/Mahwah, N.J.: Paulist Press, 1995.

———. *The Wilderness of Dream: Exploring the Religious Meanings of Dreams in Modern Western Culture.* Albany, N.Y.: State University of New York Press, 1994.

Bynum, Edward B. *Families and the Interpretation of Dreams.* New York: Harrington Park Press, 1993.

Carrington, Hereward. *The Nature of Dreams.* Girard, Kan.: Haldeman-Julius Co., 1923.

Clift, Jean Dalby, and Wallace B. Clift. *The Hero Journey in Dreams.* New York: Crossroad, 1988.

———. *Symbols of Transformation in Dreams.* New York: Crossroad, 1989.

Covitz, Joel. *Visions of the Night: A Study of Jewish Dream Interpretation.* Boston: Shambhala, 1990.

Crisp, Tony. *Do You Dream?* New York: E. P. Dutton, 1972.

Delaney, Gayle. *Living Your Dreams,* rev. ed. San Francisco: Harper & Row, 1988.

Edgar, Iain R. *Dreamwork, Anthropology and the Caring Professions.* Aldershot, U.K.: Avebury, 1995.

Engle, David. *Divine Dreams.* Holmes Beach., Fla.: Christopher Books, 1994.

Forty Dreams of St. John Bosco. Rockford, Ill.: TAN Books and Publishers, 1996.

Gackenbush, Jayne, and Jane Bosveld. *Control Your Dreams.* New York: Harper & Row, 1989.

Garfield, Patricia. *Creative Dreaming.* New York: Ballantine, 1974.

———. *The Healing Power of Dreams.* New York: Simon & Schuster, 1991.

Gillespie, George, "Light in Lucid Dreams: A Review," *Dreaming,* Vol. 2, No. 3, Sept. 1992, pp. 167–179.

Gouda, Yehia. *Dreams and Their Meaning in the Old Arab Tradition.* New York: Vantage Press, 1991.

Green, Celia, and Charles McCreery. *Lucid Dreaming: The Paradox of Consciousness During Sleep.* London: Routledge, 1994.

Guiley, Rosemary Ellen. *The Encyclopedia of Dreams: Symbols and Interpretations.* New York: Crossroad, 1992; Berkley, 1995.

———, "The Return of the Dream as a Direct Experience of God," The Academy of Religion and Psychical Research *Proceedings* 1997, pp. 30–40.

Harris, Monford. *Studies in Jewish Dream Interpretation.* Northvale, N.J.: Jason Aronson, Inc., 1994.

Hill, Michael Ortiz. *Dreaming the End of the World: Apocalypse as a Rite of Passage.* Dallas: Spring Publications, 1994.

Hoss, Bob. *Dream Mapping: A Guide to Working with Imagery and Color in Dreams.* Brewster, N.Y.: Private press, 1996.

Hughes, Scott. *Inner Light: Your Fantasies and Dreams.* Littleton, Colo.: Sanbro Press, 1993.

Hunt, Harry. *The Multiplicity of Dreams.* New Haven, Conn.: Yale University Press, 1989.

Johnson, Robert A. *Inner Work.* San Francisco: Harper & Row, 1986.

Jung, C. G. *The Archetypes and the Collective Unconscious.* Princeton: Princeton University Press, 1968.

———. "Dreams," *The Collected Works of C. G. Jung*, Vols. 4, 8, 12, and 16. Princeton: Princeton University Press, 1974.

———. *Man and His Symbols*. New York: Anchor Press/Doubleday, 1988.

———. *Memories, Dreams, Reflections*. New York: Vintage Books, 1965.

Kaplan-Williams, Strephon. *The Jungian-Senoi Dreamwork Manual*. Berkeley, Ca.: Journey Press, 1980.

Kelsey, Morton. *Dreams: A Way to Listen to God*. New York: Paulist Press, 1978.

———. *God, Dreams and Revelation: A Christian Interpretation of Dreams*. Minneapolis: Augsburg Publishing House, 1968, 1974, 1991.

Klemp, Harold. *The Dream Master: Dream Your Way Home to God*. Minneapolis: Eckankar, 1997.

Krippner, Stanley, ed. *Dreamtime and Dreamwork*. Los Angeles: Jeremy P. Tarcher, 1990.

Krippner, Stanley, and Joseph Dillard. *Dreamworking: How to Use Your Dreams for Creative Problem-Solving*. Buffalo, N.Y.: Bearly Limited, 1988.

LaBerge, Stephen. *Lucid Dreaming*. New York: Ballantine Books, 1985.

LaBerge, Stephen, and Howard Rheingold. *Exploring the World of Lucid Dreaming*. New York: Ballantine Books, 1990.

Linn, Denise. *The Hidden Power of Dreams*. New York: Ballantine Books, 1988.

Magallón, Linda Lane. *Mutual Dreaming*. New York: Pocket Books, 1997.

McPhee, Charles. *Stop Sleeping through Your Dreams*. New York: Henry Holt, 1995.

Meier, C. A. *Healing Dream and Ritual: Ancient Incubation and Modern Psychotherapy*. Einsiedeln, Switzerland: Daimon Verlag, 1989.

Meier, Paul, and Robert Wise. *Windows of the Soul*. Nashville: Thomas Nelson, 1995.

Mehrtens, Susan E. "Exceptional Human Experience 15: Guidance Dreams, A Life Reoriented by 'Voice Over Dreams,'" *Exceptional Human Experience*, Vol. 11, No. 1, June 1993, pp. 33–37.

Michaels, Stase. *The Bedside Guide to Dreams*. New York: Fawcett Books, 1995.

Moss, Robert. *Conscious Dreaming*. New York: Crown, 1996.

Radha, Swami Sivananda. *Realities of the Dreaming Mind.* Boston: Shambhala, 1996.

Raffa, Jean Benedict. *Dream Theatres of the Soul: Empowering the Feminine through Jungian Dreamwork.* San Diego: LuraMedia, 1994.

Reed, Henry. *Caring for the Creative Spirit.* Virginia Beach, Va.: Hermes Home Press, 1996.

Rogers, L. W. *Dreams and Premonitions.* Los Angeles: Theosophical Book Co., 1916.

Sanford, John A. *Dreams and Healing.* New York: Paulist Press, 1978.

———. *Dreams: God's Forgotten Language.* San Francisco: Harper & Row, 1968, 1989.

Savary, L. M., P. H. Berne, and S. K. Williams. *Dreams and Spiritual Growth: A Christian Approach to Dreamwork.* Ramsey, N.J.: Paulist Press, 1984.

Schmitt, Abraham. *Before I Wake . . . :Listening to God in Your Dreams.* Nashville: Abingdon Press, 1984.

Siegel, Alan B. *Dreams That Can Change Your Life.* Los Angeles: Jeremy P. Tarcher, 1990.

Sparrow, G. Scott. *Lucid Dreaming: Dawning of the Clear Light.* Virginia Beach, Va.: private press, 1997.

Stuart, Rosa. *Dreams and Visions of the War.* London: C. Arthur Pearson Ltd., 1917.

Taylor, Jeremy. *Dream Work.* New York: Paulist Press, 1983.

———. *Where People Fly and Water Runs Uphill.* New York: Warner Books, 1992.

Tedlock, Barbara, ed. *Dreaming: Anthropological and Psychological Interpretations.* Santa Fe: School of American Research Press, 1992.

Teillard, Ania. *Spiritual Dimensions.* London: Routledge and Kegan Paul, 1961.

Ullman, Montague. "Dreams as Exceptional Human Experiences," *ASPR Newsletter,* Vol. XVIII, No. 4, 1995, pp. 1–6.

Ullman, Montague, and Claire Limmer, eds. *The Variety of Dream Experience.* New York: Continuum, 1987.

Ullman, Montague, and Nan Zimmerman, *Working with Dreams.* Los Angeles: Jeremy P. Tarcher, 1979.

Van de Castle, Robert L. *Our Dreaming Mind.* New York: Ballantine Books, 1994.

Vaughan-Lee, Llewellyn. *In the Company of Friends: Dreamwork within a Sufi Group*. Inverness, Calif.: The Golden Sufi Center, 1994.

von Franz, Marie-Louise. *Dreams*. Boston & London: Shambhala, 1991.

Watt, Henry J. *The Common Sense of Dreams*. Worcester, Mass.: Clark University Press, 1929.

White, Rhea A., "The Influence of Four Dreams over a Period of 35 Years," submitted for publication.

Whitmont, Edward C., Sylvia Brinton Perera. *Dreams, a Portal to the Source*. London: Routledge, 1990.

Wilde, Lyn Webster. *Working with Your Dreams*. London: Blandford, 1995.

Wolf, Fred Alan. *The Dreaming Universe*. New York: Simon & Schuster, 1994.

Zadra, Antonio L., D. C. Donderi, and Robert O. Phil. "Efficacy of Lucid Dream Induction for Lucid and Non-Lucid Dreamers," *Dreaming*, Vol. 2, No. 2, June 1992, pp. 85–97.

BIBLIOGRAPHY OF RELATED SUBJECTS PRESENTED

Brier, Bob. *Ancient Egyptian Magic.* New York: Quill, 1981.

Bucke, Richard Maurice. *Cosmic Consciousness.* New York: E. P. Dutton, 1928. First published 1901.

Budge, Wallis. *Egyptian Magic.* New Hyde Park, N.Y.: University Books. First published 1899.

Burks, Eddie, and Gillian Cribbs. *Ghosthunter.* London: Headline Book Publishing, 1995.

Callahan, Maggie, and Patricia Kelley. *Final Gifts.* New York: Bantam Books, 1993.

Cott, Jonathan. *The Search for Omm Sety.* Garden City, N.Y.: Doubleday & Co., 1987.

Cranston, Sylvia, and Carey Williams. *Reincarnation: A New Horizon in Science, Religion and Society.* New York: Julian Press, 1984.

Emmons, Charles F. *Chinese Ghosts and ESP.* Metuchen, N.J.: The Scarecrow Press, 1982.

Evans, Hilary. *Visions, Apparitions, Alien Visitors.* Wellingborough, England: The Aquarian Press, 1984.

Evans-Wentz, W. Y. *The Tibetan Book of the Dead.* London: Oxford University Press, 1960.

———, ed. *Tibetan Yoga and Secret Doctrines,* 2nd ed. London: Oxford University Press, 1958.

Finucane, R. C. *Appearances of the Dead: A Cultural History of Ghosts.* Buffalo, N.Y.: Prometheus Books, 1984.

Fox, Oliver. *Astral Projection: A Record of Out-of-the-Body Experiences.* Secaucus, N.J.: The Citadel Press, 1962.

Gershom, Rabbi Yonan. *Beyond the Ashes: Cases of Reincarnation from the Holocaust.* Virginia Beach, Va.: A.R.E. Press, 1992.

———. *From Ashes to Healing: Mystical Encounters with the Holocaust.* Virginia Beach, Va.: A.R.E. Press, 1996.

Greenwell, Bonnie. *Energies of Transformation: A Guide to the Kundalini Process.* Cupertino, Calif.: Shakti River Press, 1990.

Grosso, Michael. *The Final Choice.* Walpole, N.H.: Stillpoint Publishing, 1985.

———. *The Millennium Myth: Love and Death at the End of Time.* Wheaton, Ill.: Quest Books, 1995.

Guggenheim, Bill, and Judy Guggenheim. *Hellow from Heaven!* New York: Bantam Books, 1996.

Guiley, Rosemary Ellen. *The Encyclopedia of Angels.* New York: Facts On File, 1996.

———. *The Encyclopedia of Ghosts and Spirits.* New York: Facts On File, 1992.

———. *Harper's Encyclopedia of Mystical and Paranormal Experience.* San Francisco: HarperSanFrancisco, 1991.

———. *The Mystical Tarot.* New York: New American Library, 1991.

———. *Tales of Reincarnation.* New York: Pocket Books, 1991.

Heline, Corinne. *Sacred Science of Numbers.* Marina del Rey, Calif.: DeVorss & Co., 1991.

Jahnke, Roger, "The Six Pillars of Healing," *Venture Inward,* March–April 1996, pp. 17–19ff.

Jayne, Julian. *The Origin of Consciousness in the Breakdown of the Bicameral Mind.* Boston: Houghton Mifflin, 1976.

Kumar, Ravindra. *Secrets of Numerology.* New Delhi: Sterling Paperbacks, 1992.

Luck, Georg. *Arcana Mundi: Magic and the Occult in the Greek and Roman Worlds.* Baltimore: The Johns Hopkins University Press, 1985.

Lundahl, Craig R., and Harold A. Widdison. *The Eternal Journey: How Near-Death Experiences Illuminate Our Earthly Lives.* New York: Warner Books, 1997.

Merrifield, Heyoka. *Sacred Art Sacred Earth.* Inchelium, Wash.: Rain Bird Publishers, 1993.

Mishlove, Jeffrey. *The Roots of Consciousness,* rev. ed. Tulsa: Council Oak Books, 1993.

Monroe, Robert A. *Far Journeys.* Garden City, N.Y.: Dolphin/Doubleday, 1985.

———. *Journeys out of the Body.* Garden City, N.Y.: Anchor Books, 1973.

———. *The Ultimate Journey.* New York: Doubleday, 1994.

Nadler, Jeremy. *The Temple of the Cosmos.* Rochester, Vt.: Inner Traditions, 1996.

Parrish-Harra, Carol W. *Messengers of Hope.* Sparrow Hawk Village, Okla.: Sparrow Hawk Press, 1983.

Pinch, Geraldine. *Magic in Ancient Egypt.* London: British Museum Press, 1994.

Quirke, Stephen. *Ancient Egyptian Religion.* London: British Museum Press, 1992.

Ring, Kenneth. *Heading toward Omega: In Search of the Meaning of the Near-Death Experience.* New York: William Morrow, 1984.

Robinson, James, ed. *The Nag Hammadi Library.* San Francisco: Harper & Row, 1988.

Sannella, Lee. *The Kundalini Experience.* Lower Lake, Calif.: Integral Publishing, 1987.

Sherman, Harold. *Thoughts through Space.* Amherst, Wis.: Amherst Press, 1983.

Siegel, Bernie S. *Love, Medicine & Miracles.* New York: Harper & Row, 1986.

Steiner, Rudolph. *How to Know Higher Worlds.* Hudson, N.Y.: Anthroposophic Press, 1994.

Stevenson, Ian. *Children Who Remember Previous Lives.* Charlottesville, Va.: University Press of Virginia, 1987.

———. *Reincarnation and Biology: A Contribution to the Etiology of Birthmarks and Birth Defects.* Westport, Conn.: Praeger, 1997.

———. *Twenty Cases Suggestive of Reincarnation,* 2nd ed. Charlottesville, Va.: University Press of Virginia, 1974.

Swedenborg, Emanuel. *Heaven and Hell.* New York: Swedenborg Foundation, 1984.

Swift, W. Bradford. "Connecting the Cosmos: Rhea White and the Exceptional Human Experience Network," *Intuition,* Issue 18, October 1997, pp. 23–25ff.

Talbot, Michael. *The Holographic Universe.* New York: HarperCollins, 1991.

Underhill, Evelyn. *Mysticism.* New York: New American Library, 1974.

Vahle, Neal. *Torch-Bearer to Light the Way: The Life of Myrtle Fillmore.* Mill Valley, Calif.: Open View Press, 1996.

von Franz, Marie-Louise. *Number and Time.* Evanston, Ill.: Northwestern University Press, 1974.

PERMISSIONS AND ACKNOWLEDGMENTS

In addition to the individuals cited in the text who granted permission to use their dreams, the author gratefully acknowledges permissions from the following authors, publishers and organizations:

Carol W. Parrish-Harra, *Messengers of Hope,* copyright © 1983 by Sparrow Hawk Press.

Neal Vahle, *Torch-Bearer to Light the Way: The Life of Myrtle Fillmore,* copyright © 1996 by Open View Press.

Susan E. Mehrtens, "Exceptional Human Experience 15: Guidance Dreams, A Life Reoriented by 'Voice Over Dreams,'" *Exceptional Human Experience,* Vol. 11, No. 1, June 1993.

Rabbi Yonan Gershom, *Beyond the Ashes: Cases of Reincarnation from the Holocaust,* copyright © 1992 by A.R.E. Press.

Paul Meier and Robert Wise, *Windows of the Soul,* copyright © 1995 by Thomas Nelson.

Morton Kelsey, *Dreams: A Way to Listen to God,* copyright © 1978 by Paulist Press.

Forty Dreams of St. John Bosco, copyright © 1996 by TAN Books and Publishers.

Jeffrey Mishlove, *The Roots of Consciousness* (rev.), copyright © 1993 by Council Oak Books.

For Beverly Rubik's dreams, permission from the "International Conference on the Study of Shamanism and Alternate Modes of Healing," Phoenix, 1996.

For Willis Harman's dreams, permission from the Institute of Noetic Sciences, Sausalito, California.

INDEX